Hitler's Europe Ablaze

Hitler's Europe Ablaze

Occupation, Resistance, and Rebellion during World War II

Edited by Philip Cook and
Ben H. Shepherd

Skyhorse Publishing

Contents

List of Plates

1. An RAF Westland Lysander evacuating wounded Italian partisans.
2. *Maquisards* gathering supply canisters dropped by an Allied aircraft, 1944.
3. Officers of SOE and the French FTPF resistance group in Sussac, Limoges, August 1944.
4. Partisan sabotage in the Louvain region.
5. *La Libre Belgique*, printed in a clandestine press in Liège in 1944.
6. German troops enter Brno, Moravia, March 1939.
7. Corpses of two of Reinhard Heydrich's assassins in Prague, May 1942.
8. General de Gaulle speaking on the BBC French Service.
9. A French resistance member setting an explosive charge on a railway line.
10. EDES guerrillas in Epirus.
11. General Napoleon Zervas, leader of EDES.
12. A body found in the river, Po di Ficarolo (Rovigo), April 1945.
13. Italian partisans killed in reprisal.
14. A variety of Dutch resistance newspapers.
15. A Dutch resistance wireless operator.
16. Jubilant Polish Home Army members conversing after the outbreak of the Warsaw Uprising, August 1944.
17. The Warsaw Rising monument.
18. Jewish refugees are ferried out of Denmark aboard Danish fishing boats bound for Sweden.
19. Squadron Leader J. Macadam meets three Norwegian resistance fighters in Oslo following the arrival of British forces in Norway.
20. Soviet partisans attack a village.
21. Two members of the Kovpak partisan group.
22. Soviet partisans young and old.
23. German troops search suspected Yugoslav Partisans.
24. Marshal Tito with Cabinet ministers and staff in his mountain headquarters, May 1944.

Note: the maps in this book are intended to give the reader a general idea of the scale and location of events, and therefore omit a certain level of geographical detail.

List of Contributors

Philip Cooke is Professor of Italian History and Culture at Strathclyde University. He is a specialist in twentieth-century Italian history and culture and the author of numerous books and articles on the Italian Resistance movement and its long-term impact, including *The Legacy of the Italian Resistance* (New York, Palgrave, 2011). He is co-editor of the journal *Modern Italy*.

Ben H. Shepherd is Reader in History at Glasgow Caledonian University. He specializes in the military history of Germany and Austria during the first half of the twentieth century, with particular focus on the origins and conduct of counter-insurgency warfare. His two monographs, *War in the Wild East: The German Army and Soviet Partisans* (2004) and *Terror in the Balkans: German Armies and Partisan Warfare* (2012), were both published by Harvard University Press, Cambridge, Mass. *Terror in the Balkans* will also be published in Serbo-Croat by Magellan Press, Belgrade, in late 2013. Shepherd was also co-editor, with Juliette Pattinson, of *War in a Twilight World: Partisan and Anti-Partisan Warfare in Eastern Europe, 1939–45* (Basingstoke, Palgrave Macmillan, 2010). He is currently working on a general history of the German army under the Third Reich, to be published by Yale University Press in 2015.

Evan Mawdsley is Honorary Professorial Research Fellow at the University of Glasgow. Author of *The Russian Civil War* (Edinburgh, Birlinn, 2008), *Thunder in the East: The Nazi-Soviet War* (London, Hodder Arnold, 2007), *World War II: A New History* (Cambridge, Cambridge University Press, 2009) and *December 1941* (New Haven, Conn. and London, Yale University Press, 2011), he is also general editor of the forthcoming *Cambridge History of the Second World War*.

Fabrice Maerten studied history at the UCL (Catholic University of Louvain-la-Neuve). In 1996, he defended his doctoral thesis on political and ideological resistance in the province of the Hainaut (Belgium) during the Second World War. He has worked at the Centre for Historical Research and Documentation on War and Contemporary Society (CEGESOMA) in Brussels since 1995. Since 2011, he has been Head of the Documentation sector. His main research interests are the resistance and Catholicism in Belgium during the Second World War and he has published widely in these areas. He is the author of many entries in the *Dictionnaire de la Seconde Guerre mondiale en Belgique* (Bruxelles, André Versaille, 2008). His most recent book (co-authored with Alain Colignon) is *La Wallonie sous l'Occupation, 1940–1945* (Bruxelles and Waterloo, SOMA-CEGES/Renaissance du livre, 2012).

Christina Vella is a consultant for the United States State Department and teaches history at Tulane University in New Orleans. She holds a PhD in modern European and US history, lectures widely on a range of historical topics, and is a frequent consultant to National Public Radio, PBS, and the History Channel. She is the author of several book chapters and five books, including, with Radomir Luža, *The Hitler Kiss: A Memoir of the Czech Resistance* (Baton Rouge, Lou., 2002).

Juliette Pattinson is Reader in History in the School of History at the University of Kent. She has published widely on the history of the Second World War. Her books include: *Behind Enemy Lines: Gender, Passing and the SOE in the Second World War* (Manchester, Manchester University Press, 2007; paperback 2011); with Ben Shepherd, *War in a Twilight World: Partisan and Anti-Partisan Warfare in Eastern Europe* (Basingstoke, Palgrave Macmillan, 2010); and with Lucy Noakes, *The Cultural Memory of the Second World War in Britain* (London, Bloomsbury, 2013). She also contributed the chapter '"You didn't think about being a woman at that time": British secret agents during the Second World War', to Celia Lee and Paul Martin (eds), *Women and War* (London, Pen & Sword, 2011).

Vangelis Tzoukas studied Sociology in Panteion University of Social and Political Studies (Athens). His dissertation thesis (2003) is titled 'The Warlords of EDES in Epirus. Locality and Political Integration'. A revised edition of his PhD will soon be available from Hestia Publications (in Greek). He has written many articles on the period of Resistance and Civil War in Greece (1941–9). Some of his writings include: 'The origins of Civil War in Epirus: the case-study of Koliodimitraioi in Lakka-Souli', in Kl. Koutsoukis-J. Sakkas (ed.), *Aspects of the Greek Civil War 1946–49* (Athens, Filistor, 2000), pp. 343–57); 'Warlords and Chieftains in the decade 1940–50: the case of Epirus', in N. Marantzidis (ed.), *The other Kapetanioi-anticommunists armed in the period of Occupation and the Civil War* (Athens, Hestia Publications, 2005), pp. 375–430; 'Treason and Resistance in the political writings of EDES', in I. Mihailidis, I. Nikolakopoulos and H. Fleischer (eds), *Enemy Inside. Aspects of collaboration in occupied Greece* (Athens, Ellinika Grammata, 2006), pp. 197–207. He is currently Teaching Fellow in the Department of Philosophy and Social Studies (University of Crete).

Massimo Storchi is Director of Historical Archives for Reggio Emilia. He studied contemporary history at Bologna University. His research has focused on the Italian Resistance and political and social conflicts in northern Italy in the first half of twentieth century, with particular attention to issues of violence. He is the author of *Uscire dalla guerra. Ordine pubblico e forze politiche. Modena 1945– 1946* (Milan, FrancoAngeli, 1995); *Combattere si può vincere bisogna. La scelta della violenza fra Resistenza e dopoguerra. Reggio Emilia 1943–1946* (Venice, Marsilio Editori, 1998); *Sangue al bosco del Lupo. Partigiani che uccidono partigiani. La storia di 'Azor'* (Reggio Emilia, Aliberti, 2005); *Il sangue dei vincitori. Saggio sui crimini* *fascisti e i processi del dopoguerra (1945–1946)* (Reggio Emilia, Aliberti, 2008); with Italo Rovali, *Il primo giorno d'inverno. Cervarolo 20 marzo 1944. Una strage nazifascista dimenticata* (Reggio Emilia, Aliberti, 2010) and *Question Time. Cos'è l'Italia. Cento domande (e risposte) sulla storia del Belpaese* (Reggio Emilia, Aliberti, 2011).

Marjan Schwegman is director of NIOD, Institute for War, Holocaust and Genocide Studies in Amsterdam (NL), a research institute of the Royal Dutch Academy of Arts and Sciences. She is also professor (chair of 'Political and Cultural History in the Long 20th Century') in the Faculty of Humanities of Utrecht University. From 2003 until 2007 she was director of the Royal Dutch Institute in Rome. Her research is characterized by a biographical approach and focuses on Italian history of the nineteenth and twentieth centuries. The books she has authored include *Maria Montessori* (Bologna, il Mulino, 1999) (Dutch version *Maria Montessori: 1870–1952: kind van haar tijd vrouw van de wereld* (Amsterdam, Amsterdam University Press, 1999)); *Gualberta Alaide Beccari: emancipazionista e scrittrice* (Pisa, Domus Mazziniana, 1996) (Dutch version *Feminisme als boetedoening : biografie van de Italiaanse schrijfster en feministe Gualberta Alaide Beccari (1842–1906)* ('s-Gravenhage, Nijgh & Van Ditmar, 1989)). Schwegman's current research concentrates on the impact of gender and war-related heroism on processes of nation-building.

Paul Latawski is a senior lecturer in the Department of War Studies, Royal Military Academy Sandhurst. He completed his PhD at Indiana University, USA, specializing in Central and Eastern European history with particular emphasis on modern Poland. He has written on British policy towards the Polish question during the First World War, nationalism in East-Central Europe, Balkan conflict, Polish defence transformation and the Battle of the Falaise pocket. He is currently writing a history of the 1st Polish Armoured Division in Normandy.

Christopher Mann is a senior lecturer in the Department of War Studies of the Royal Military Academy Sandhurst. He holds a PhD from the Department of War of King's College London and is an Honorary Research Fellow in the Scandinavian Studies Department of University College London. He is the author of *British Policy and Strategy towards Norway, 1941–1945* (Basingstoke, Palgrave Macmillan, 2012).

Alexander Statiev teaches Russian and Eastern European history at the University of Waterloo, Canada. He is the author of *The Soviet Counterinsurgency in the Western Borderlands* (Cambridge, Cambridge University Press, 2010), and various articles on pro- and anti-Soviet resistance during the Second World War, Soviet counterinsurgency, blocking and penal units in the Red Army, Soviet deportations, Russian war memory and Romanian military history.

Vjeran Pavlaković is an assistant professor in the Department of Cultural Studies at the University of Rijeka, Croatia. He received his PhD in history in

2005 from the University of Washington. He has published articles on the politics of memory, Second World War commemorations, war criminals and war crime tribunals, and democratization in Croatia, and co-edited, with Sabrina P. Ramet, *Serbia since 1989: Politics and Society under Milošević and After* (Seattle, University of Washington Press, 2005). Recent publications include 'Contested Pasts, Contested Red-Letter Days: Antifascist Commemorations and Ethnic Identities in Post-Communist Croatia', in Ljiljana Šarić, Karen Gammelgaard and Kjetil Ra Hauge (eds), *Transforming National Holidays: Identity Discourse in the West and South Slavic Countries, 1985–2010* (London, John Benjamins Publishing, 2012), 'Collaboration and Resistance: The Comparative Culture of Memory and Yugoslavia's Contested World War Two Past', in Darko Gavrilović (ed.), *Facing the Past, Searching for the Future: The History of Yugoslavia in the 20th Century* (Sremska Kamenica, CHDR, 2010) and 'Flirting with Fascism: The Ustaša Legacy and Croatian Politics in the 1990s', in Lorenzo Bertucelli and Mila Orlić, *Una storia balcanica: Fascismo, comunismo e nazionalismo nella Jugoslavia del Novecento* (Verona, Ombre Corte, 2008).

Acknowledgements

The editors would like to express their thanks to a number of individuals and organizations that have assisted in the preparation of the book. We are particularly grateful to Rupert Harding at Pen & Sword for realizing that it was time for a new book on the European Resistance, and for his input and patience throughout. Alison Miles did a first-class job in turning around the copy editing so quickly yet meticulously. We would also like to thank our own version of the 'shadow army' – our anonymous reviewers – who read each chapter with great care and provided helpful and critical feedback to our authors. Many thanks are also due to a further valuable member of our shadow army, our highly industrious clandestine map maker.

The book is, in a real sense, a product of the unique atmosphere provided by the city of Glasgow. We would like to thank our respective institutions, the University of Strathclyde and Glasgow Caledonian University, for their support. The two universities' proximity, as well as the special meeting facilities in and around George Square, has been invaluable. We would also like to thank the staff of the two university libraries who have helped us; of the National Library of Scotland; and of the photographic archives of the German Federal Archive, the Imperial War Museum, the United States Holocaust Memorial Museum and the Museum of Yugoslav History, all four of which provided images for use in the book.

Assembling a team of experts who shared our vision and ambitions for the book looked, initially, to be a daunting task. Given the pressures facing academics, we are extremely grateful to all of our contributors for their endeavours and for meeting our many deadlines and requests for information with patience and good humour.

Philip Cooke would like to thank Caroline Verdier and Alan Morris for assistance with the translation of Fabrice Maerten's chapter.

Finally, we are saddened that M.R.D. Foot passed away shortly before the book was submitted to Pen & Sword. We would like to dedicate our own Resistance book to his work and his memory.

Introduction

Philip Cooke and Ben H. Shepherd

Between 1939 and 1945, following the spectacular military successes that Hitler's Germany achieved during the first two years of the Second World War, much of mainland Europe fell under occupation by Germany, and – albeit to a much lesser extent – by Germany's European allies and satellites. The occupation regimes of the Axis Powers subjected the peoples of Europe to an ordeal that, tolerable or indeed benign as it may have been for some, spelt fear, indignity and hardship for many, and outright terror and rapacity for many others. Some Axis officials and departments, both civilian and military, did seek to cultivate a spirit of partnership with selected parts of occupied Europe. Increasingly, however, the exigencies of ideology – above all Nazi ideology, of short-term political calculation and of wartime economic pressures all generated an array of harsh, exploitative and often murderous occupation polices which together inflicted ever greater misery upon the Continent's peoples. The germ of resistance that had been engendered from the start of occupation, even in those countries that the Axis occupiers had earmarked for relatively lenient treatment, began to burgeon ever more noticeably. The resistance movements that developed varied immensely in the forms that they took, how they conducted themselves and how their impact was felt among the wider occupied population.

One thing that did unite these different resistance movements was their profound, often controversial and sometimes embittering legacy within the societies of post-war Europe. In the immediate post-war period there was an entirely understandable desire on the part of those men and women who had participated in the resistance to see their efforts carried forward into the new post-war societies for whose freedom they had fought. But various factors would hold the resistance spirit in check, and make it difficult for the European movements to become part of a shared national (let alone European) memory, to be celebrated by all at appropriate moments of commemoration. The bloody settling of accounts in some countries, such as France and Italy, and the transition from partisan war to civil war in Greece, meant that the fratricidal nature of the conflict would always be a problematic issue, resurfacing periodically, particularly at times of political crisis.

Furthermore, the advent of the Cold War and the fierce ideological struggle that characterized it turned the resistance movement into what one historian has vividly described as a 'blunt instrument to be waved around in political debate'.[1] For these reasons, and others, the way that the resistance was portrayed in

KEY

Greater Germany
Allied to Germany
Germany/Axis
Occupation
Allies
Neutral

1. German Reich

**Allied to Germany/
German satellites**
2. Bulgaria
3. Finland
4. France (Free Zone)
5. Hungary
6. Italy
7. Romania
8. Slovakia

German/Axis occupied
9. Albania
10. Belgium
11. Croatia
12. Denmark
13. Egypt
14. France
15. French North Africa
    (administered by
    Vichy France)
16. German/Axis Zone of
    Military Occupation
17. Greece
18. Libya
19. Montenegro
20. Norway
21. Reichskommissariat
    Ostland
22. Reichskommissariat
    Ukraine
23. Serbia
24. Netherlands

**Allied states or under
Allied control**
25. Egypt
26. United Kingdom
27. Soviet Union
28. Cyprus

Neutral states
29. Portugal
30. Republic of Ireland
31. Spain
32. Sweden
33. Switzerland
34. Turkey

Axis-occupied Europe, early 1942.

individual memoirs, works of history, documentaries, feature films, television programmes and other forms of media was inevitably coloured by the context in which these works were produced. These factors help to explain the formation of the various post-war 'heroic narratives', as well as opposing counter-narratives, which tended to gloss over, or alternatively emphasize, difficult aspects of the resistance struggle, particularly the violence of it. They also helped to underpin (or undermine) the foundation myths of the countries concerned, as well as those political parties who could trace their origins to the resistance. Nowhere would this be more the case than in those countries where resistance leaders became senior post-war political leaders, as happened in Yugoslavia and France with Tito and de Gaulle respectively. In both countries the contribution of other internal resistance forces would inevitably be downgraded or indeed airbrushed out.

In each country where there was a resistance movement there are different patterns, with the resistance tradition going through a complex series of highs and lows. In Italy a resistance leader in the shape of Ferruccio Parri became prime minister for a short period in 1945, only to be ousted by political parties – Christian Democrats and Liberals – who had made a less significant contribution to the resistance than his own Action Party. As a consequence of Parri's removal and the rapid collapse of his party, as well as the exclusion of the Italian Communist Party from government for decades, each political party and its supporters engaged in a battle to claim that their resistance efforts had been more significant than those of their opponents.[2]

With the collapse of the Berlin Wall in 1989, battle commenced once more. Indeed, there is much evidence to suggest that the resistance debate is even fiercer today than it was during the Cold War. The quality of debate has, however, been mixed. Although it is right to question and challenge received interpretations, there was certainly a danger, now perhaps passed, that the contribution of the European resistance movements to the war effort was going to be 'thrown away'.[3]

Italy continues to be a rich source of resistance polemics, with the figure of Silvio Berlusconi usually at the centre of things. From his appointment as prime minister in 1994, the national day of 25 April (the official date of the liberation of Milan) became a focus for anti-Berlusconi feelings. Needless to say, he has sought on various occasions while prime minister to remove 25 April from the Italian calendar of celebrations.

The situation is a little different in France, but no less intriguing. When Nicolas Sarkozy first came to power he made a conscious attempt to recall the resistance spirit when, at his inauguration ceremony in May 2007, the French Republican Guard sang the moving partisan song, the 'Chant des Partisans'. In one of the first acts of his presidency he appeared to decree that the last letter of Guy Moquet, a 17-year-old partisan executed by the Nazis in 1941, be read out in every school in France on the anniversary of his death on 22 October. Various objections were raised, above all by the Communist Party, for whom Moquet, author also of an anti-capitalist poem, was not only *their* hero, but the anathema of all that Sarkozy represented. Things worsened for Sarkozy when the letter was read out to the French rugby team before their encounter with Argentina in the

2007 World Cup. The decision to read the letter was taken by the French coach Bernard Laporte, who went on to become a junior sports minister. The French team lost to Argentina, on home soil. Clement Poitrenaud, the full-back who read the letter, later claimed that the television footage made his team mates look like 'cretins', as they listened on in silence to what is an extraordinarily sobering text. Indeed, *Le Parisien* newspaper asked whether the words 'I'm going to die' could have affected the team's morale. The resistance made another appearance during the 2012 presidential elections, initially at Limoges, when François Hollande's supporters sang the 'Chant des Partisans' before his speech, and then at the May Day celebrations in Paris. On that occasion the song had even more redolence, in view of Sarkozy's reference to 'real work' – an expression first used during the Vichy period.

In Belgium, too, the issue of wartime collaboration can provoke heated debate, as happened in 2010 when Bart De Wever, leader of the nationalist New Flemish Alliance, questioned the idea that the French-speaking Belgians had *not* collaborated during the Nazi occupation. De Wever's pretensions to being an historian (he has a degree in history, but never finished his doctorate) were questioned, particularly and most effectively by a real historian, Jean-Pierre Nandrin, who convincingly demonstrated that the politician wilfully ignored the results of years of research into this issue, and was driven by political motives.

The 'public use of history', as well as the deep resentments caused by collaboration, can also help to explain the case of Vasily Kononov, whose last years were characterized by judicial hearings, and in 2010 by a deliberation of the European Court of Human Rights, which found against him. Kononov had been the leader of a partisan outfit which executed a group of Latvian villagers for collaborating with the Nazis. One of the villagers was a pregnant woman who was burned alive. With the collapse of the Soviet Union the Latvians decided to pursue Kononov over the killings. Few sympathized with this decision, and even *Time Magazine* and the *Daily Telegraph*, hardly known for their communist sympathies, published articles in defence of Kononov.

The alleged crimes of communist partisans were also at the centre of the polemic sparked by the publication of Louis de Bernières' novel, *Captain Corelli's Mandolin*, later made into a feature film. While de Bernières depicted the Italian occupying soldiers as benign and irenic, the communist partisans of the ELAS organization were portrayed as a murderous rabble. Interviewed by journalist Seumas Milne, one Greek veteran described de Bernières' book as 'an insult to the whole Greek people' and denounced it as 'part of a global drive to rewrite history, to reverse historical facts, to convince people that political and social change is a dead end and that if you struggle for a better world, it only leads to bloodshed, suffering and failure'.[4] De Bernières robustly defended himself and his book. Seventy years after the Second World War, the effects of the resistance therefore continue to resonate today.

*   *   *

This new work collects eleven chapters, all by internationally recognized scholars, and together these survey resistance in all the major countries of Axis-occupied Europe. Not since the 1970s has a single work attempted such an extensive survey. As such, the chapters presented here benefit greatly from three important developments that have been in train in recent decades. The first is the opening up of archives in Eastern Europe and the former Soviet Union, with the veritable treasure trove of new historical sources they have proffered, following the fall of European communism during the years 1989–91. The second is the amount of time that has elapsed since the end of the Second World War. This has seen the emergence of a new generation of historians ready to examine the past with an altogether fresher eye, one less influenced by the mythologies about the resistance that were established during earlier post-war decades. The third development, a direct result of the first two, is the vast body of new scholarship that has emerged. As has already been made clear, the scholarship is not always good – much of it, as already demonstrated, has pandered to divisive and sometimes unsavoury political agendas in various European countries. But a great deal of the scholarship, there can be no doubt, has greatly advanced our understanding of the resistance and its impact.[5]

If resistance across Axis-occupied Europe was an immensely diverse phenomenon, no less varied were the national and regional settings in which its effects were felt. All this ensures that the historians who investigate it will continue to enjoy a rich field for their endeavours. So too do the heated controversies, both public and scholarly, which remain such a marked legacy of the resistance in many of the countries in which it operated. But a quarter of a century after the opening up of vast new reservoirs of historical source material in Eastern Europe, and with the seventieth anniversary of the end of the Second World War rapidly approaching, the appearance of a new, fully updated survey of the European resistance is timely.

The book's geographical scope encompasses the Axis-occupied territories of – in the order in which they were conquered – the Czech lands of Bohemia and Moravia, Poland, Denmark and Norway, the Low Countries, France, Yugoslavia, Greece, the Soviet Union and Italy. A preliminary chapter examines the role that the European resistance played in the wider strategies of the three main Allied powers. For necessary reasons of space, the book does not cover resistance within the small occupied territories of the Channel Islands, Luxembourg, Monaco, San Marino and Albania. Nor has it been possible to include an examination of anti-Axis resistance within Finland, temporarily if somewhat ambiguously allied to Germany between 1941 and 1944, or within the Axis satellites of Slovakia, Hungary, Romania and Bulgaria. That said, it should be acknowledged that one such satellite, Hungary, was itself briefly occupied by the Germans during 1944–5, and that another, Slovakia, saw one of the largest and most bloodily suppressed anti-German revolts of the war, in the latter months of 1944. Finally, the book of necessity excludes resistance within the German Reich itself – though it is possible at least in this case to direct readers to the particularly copious volume of English-language scholarship that has been generated on the German anti-Nazi resistance, and in particular on its attempt to assassinate Hitler in July 1944.[6] Even with these caveats, however, the book's geographical scope is vast.

The development, conduct and effectiveness of the resistance movements that this book examines were shaped by manifold forces: the form that the Axis occupation took and the impact it went on to have upon the occupied populations; the social and economic character and the physical environment of the occupied territories; relations between the resistance and its sponsors abroad, be they the main Allied powers or the various governments-in-exile, and the practical and organizational support those parties proffered to the resistance; the response to resistance, often brutal though sometimes relatively restrained, of the Axis occupiers; relations between resistance and population, as well as between occupiers and population, on the ground; and relations – whether constructive or hostile – between the resistance groups themselves. This introduction sets the scene by briefly surveying all six of these forces.

* * *

The impact of occupation upon European populations ranged, generally speaking, from the rather bleak to the truly devastating. Much of the cause of this was ideological. Most far-reaching in their ideological effects were the National Socialist principles which underpinned so much of German occupation policy. Nazi ideology ordered the populations of occupied Europe in accordance with what the Nazis perceived to be their racial 'superiority' and 'inferiority'. Bottom of the pile in Nazi eyes, and earmarked within a remarkably short space of time for outright extermination, were the Jews of occupied Europe. One level up from the Jews in the Nazis' warped scheme of things was the Slavic peoples of Eastern Europe and the Soviet Union, albeit with certain gradations. The occupation policies that were inflicted upon many of the Slavic regions of occupied Europe, and above all upon Poland, invoked ideological justification for the brutal terror, economic rapacity and cultural destruction that they meted out. Yet it was not only German occupation that was shaped by ideology. Both Germany's main European ally Italy, and the various countries among the European Axis satellites, also maintained an ideologically influenced conception of how they should rule the territories allocated to them following the initial wave of Axis victories. Italy, to take just one example, sought to impose a soon to be bitterly resented policy of cultural assimilation upon much of the Balkan territory which it was allotted following the Axis conquest of Greece and Yugoslavia in spring 1941. Thus did ideology play a significant part in determining both the conditions that provoked the growth of resistance in the first place, and the levels of anti-Axis support that resistance movements eventually went on to accrue.

So too did the economic pressures to which the increasingly rapacious Axis occupation regime subjected Europe as the war went on. Economic demands upon occupied Europe grew especially acute as the might of the new Allied coalition of Great Britain and her empire, the Soviet Union and the United States increasingly tilted the balance against the Axis from 1942 onward. The pressures placed upon occupied civilians to provide food and other economic resources for an ever more desperate war effort eventually alienated them so extensively as to stymie any attempts at conciliatory occupation policy which the Axis continued to make. The starkest effect, set increasingly in train from 1942 onward, was a swelling of support for and indeed active participation in the resistance, caused by the thousands of men and women seeking to evade the ever more voracious German labour draft. The economic pressures, and the concomitant swelling of resistance support, were felt not just among those Eastern European populations that Nazi racial thinking already deemed worthy of slavery. They were felt also among Western European populations, most prominently that of France, whose treatment at the hands of the occupiers had on the whole been hitherto comparatively mild.

From 1942 in particular, then, resistance across occupied Europe was an active and burgeoning phenomenon. The historian Henri Michel identified no fewer than ten forms that resistance across Axis-occupied Europe assumed during the Second World War: passive resistance; go-slow by workers; strikes; secret tracts and newspapers; escape lines for Allied airmen; information-gathering; sabotage; assassination; *maquis*[7] and guerrilla warfare; and particularly towards the war's end, the emergence, successful or otherwise, of full-scale liberation movements.[8] Yet, as the chapters in this book demonstrate, different resistance movements were compelled by their various strengths and weaknesses to employ different combinations of these tactics.

* * *

In much of Europe it was not just the increasing harshness of Axis rule that encouraged resistance; the fact that numerous countries retained age-old traditions of resistance to foreign invaders helped lay the groundwork also. Poland, Yugoslavia, Greece and the Soviet Union in particular had all been the scene of such struggles in centuries past. Within two additional occupied countries, France and Belgium, such traditions had not taken root quite so deeply. But more recent decades had seen these two countries also take up resistance against foreign occupiers. The historical resonance of those particular struggles was intensified by the fact that on both occasions – the Franco-Prussian War of 1870–1, and the First World War – the occupiers in question had been German.

Beyond that, the form that resistance took in different parts of Europe was greatly influenced by the social, economic and geographical character of the areas in which it operated. In relatively advanced, urbanized Western Europe, and in the Czech lands and Poland also, such was the level of economic, technological and communicational infrastructure that resistance movements were able to engage relatively easily in covert types of activity, such as publishing secret newspapers, running escape lines for Allied airmen, information-gathering and sabotage. But if their regions' relatively developed infrastructure facilitated such tactics, the topographical character of those same regions *compelled* such tactics. For the numerous urban centres that dotted these countries, the superior transport infrastructure that connected them, the often flat and open terrain within which they were situated, and the often limited geographical space in which resistance groups could operate, all meant that visibly larger and more spectacular shows of resistance were much easier for the occupier to crush.

But in the Soviet Union, Greece, Yugoslavia, Italy and, albeit less widely, France and Belgium, the topography lent itself to a very different kind of resistance. Such was the extent of forest, swamp and mountain range in these countries that many resistance movements there rapidly assumed the specific character of *guerrilla* movements. Such terrain was often both remote and impenetrable; it was therefore ideal ground for mobile irregular units, comprising not just armed civilians but also groups of fugitive soldiers, which operated across country to sabotage the occupier's communication and supply lines, terrorize its troops with hit-and-run tactics and generally harass all its efforts to administer and exploit its territory effectively. The guerrillas operating in occupied Europe during the Second World War are referred to more specifically as *partisans*.

*   *   *

Many of the partisan movements operating in occupied Europe during the Second World War were affiliated to regular armed forces seeking to re-establish democratic government. The regular forces in question were those of the Western Allies, the Soviet Union and, albeit much less extensively, the various governments-in-exile of the occupied European countries. The significance of each party's contribution to the resistance – be it partisan-type movements or other types of resistance – varied across countries. The Soviet Union, for instance, was swifter to provide meaningful practical and organizational support to the partisan movement on its own occupied soil than were the Western Allies to provide such support to resistance elsewhere in occupied Europe. This was partly because, by late 1942, the Soviet High Command regarded the partisan campaign as an important, if relatively small, complement to its conventional war effort. It also regarded it as an important means by which it could retain some degree of practical and political control over that part of the Soviet population that was penned in behind Axis lines.

Whatever kinds of action the different resistance movements engaged in, however, one thing they did have in common – save in the final months of occupation, and on isolated occasions before that – was that they soon abandoned any pretension of liberating themselves by means of a national popular uprising. British hopes for such uprisings, and their potential for fatally undermining the German war effort more generally, were loudly expressed by Churchill in the dog days after the Fall of France in June 1940. The means by which he sought to transform hope into reality was by utilizing the organization of the newly formed Special Operations Executive (SOE) to support the development of indigenous 'secret armies' which would covertly build their strength and then rise up to overthrow the German occupiers with limited British support. Yet such were the material shortcomings of both the British and the European resistance, and the practical impossibility of secretly organizing the latter on the necessary scale, that the idea of defeating Germany in this way was not even remotely feasible. An early occasion on which a large popular uprising was attempted, by the Serbs of Yugoslavia in summer 1941, merely had the effect of sparking a ferocious German reprisal campaign which was instrumental in crushing the revolt by the end of the year.

*   *   *

How the Axis responded to the threat of resistance was, of course, a further crucial factor in its development. And though the Axis response was not always brutal, it more often than not *was* brutal.[9] Hostage-taking and reprisals in response to guerrilla-style action have been a commonplace aspect of counter-insurgency campaigns.[10] Such campaigns operate on the principle that a population whose loyalties are torn, for whatever reasons of pragmatism or inclination, between insurgents and occupiers is even more likely to plump for the latter if threatened with sanctions for *not* doing so, as well as enticed with rewards *for* doing so. Even so, the Axis campaign against the European resistance, particularly albeit not exclusively the *German* campaign, very often displayed an especially marked proclivity for terror. In their Eastern European territories in particular, the Germans' profoundly coercive approach corresponded with the racially based contempt with which the Nazis regarded the populations of those regions, and with the Reich's aim of subjecting them to ruthless economic exploitation and cultural subjugation. Indeed, the German occupiers employed selective terror in such territories from the outset, irrespective of whether the population showed signs of actual resistance. For instance, leadership groups such as clerics and army officers in Poland, communist functionaries in the Soviet Union, or the intelligentsia in both, were identified as ideological enemies and potential nuclei of future resistance, and singled out for liquidation even before the Germans invaded. But as resistance grew across occupied Europe, German terror tactics became more commonplace throughout the Continent.

The composition of the personnel whom the Axis deployed against the resistance differed from country to country. The Germans utilized varying numbers of their own army, SS and police personnel. However, such was the size of German-occupied Europe, and such also was the German military's particular preoccupation with the 'cutting edge' operational aspects of warfare at the expense of more humdrum concerns such as military occupation, that German forces were often deployed in insufficient numbers against the resistance. And frequently, the *quality* of the army personnel, at any rate, whom the Germans earmarked for the task left much to be desired also. The deficiencies among the personnel whom the Germans' Axis allies committed to the anti-resistance effort were usually even greater. One outcome of this state of affairs was that by far the greatest contingent of manpower whom the Axis eventually deployed against resistance was home-grown – be it pro-Axis collaborationist militia, or indigenous police personnel of collaborationist or merely apolitical bent. Among collaborationist elements the Axis also sought to establish extensive informer networks.

The active measures that the Axis employed to deter or quell resistance included mass shootings of civilians and destruction of purportedly 'pro-bandit' villages, particularly in Eastern and Southern Europe. Against partisan movements, the Axis – especially the Germans – also employed aggressive mobile patrols, static security measures and, where necessary, major sweeps involving large numbers of troops and sometimes armour and air power also. All too often, however, such sweeps employed troops that were too low in quality and quantity actually to locate and destroy significant partisan concentrations. Instead, they terrorized and killed tens of thousands of civilians who purportedly were aiding the 'bandits'. And across occupied Europe, ever greater numbers of Jews, viewed in Nazi thinking not only as racially inferior but also as a security threat, fell victim to the security campaign too. In this way, the security campaign became intertwined with the vast programme of persecution and killing which eventually mushroomed into the 'Final Solution' of the 'problem' of European Jewry.

In much of Europe, the Axis practice of terror clearly had a quietening effect upon the propensity of occupied populations to resist. The fact that the resistance across much of occupied Europe failed to develop into truly mass movements until the final months of the war, if at all, testifies to the effectiveness of brutal Axis measures. However, because the Axis often lacked suitable manpower on the ground, such terror was not always effective in cowing civilians into submission. Indeed, in regions such as the Soviet Union and Yugoslavia, where particularly numerous partisan groups were often a much more frequent everyday presence among the population, indiscriminate Axis terror simply alienated the population and drove it still more surely into the arms of the partisans. And public indignation at the persecution of the Jews, whether or not such persecution was intertwined with the Axis security campaign, could sometimes fuel resistance also. Nowhere was this more so than in Denmark, the country that enjoys the best record of all occupied Europe for helping Jews evade capture during the Holocaust.

Nevertheless, particularly but not exclusively in Western Europe, the Germans and their Axis allies often employed conciliatory measures also in their security campaign. Sometimes the measures were specific, such as pledges to treat captured partisans as prisoners of war instead of shooting them. Sometimes they were more all-encompassing, such as the various social, political and economic initiatives that were part and parcel of hearts and minds campaigns. Many of these measures were born of grander ideas, harboured by some Nazi officials, for a programme of partnership, albeit unequal partnership, between the Reich and the countries of occupied Western Europe.

Yet such constructive initiatives were debilitated by the increasingly rapacious economic needs of the Axis, and by the ongoing tendency of many German officials to view much of the occupied population through racial blinkers and rely excessively on terror. And none of this is to mention the massively destabilizing effects of the actions of some of Germany's allies. This is exemplified most harrowingly by the barbarism that the fascist Ustaša regime of the so-called Independent State of Croatia inflicted upon its country's Serbian population during 1941–2.

* * *

All this, of course, reflects the importance to both resisters and occupiers of the fifth factor that was in play: the co-operation, whether willing or not, of the population caught in the middle of the conflict. Civilian populations, after all, constitute a vital source of food, shelter, intelligence, recruits and other practical help for insurgents. Securing that source, or – in the case of the occupiers – depriving insurgents of it, is therefore essential to the success of either side. And given that the Axis itself could be capable of more conciliatory conduct, the resistance could ill-afford to assume that it enjoyed the population's automatic support. Indeed, Mao Tse-tung himself – a man particularly qualified to comment, given his leadership of the especially vast insurgency that eventually brought all China under communist control in 1949 – maintained that insurgents had to display orderly behaviour, and offer attractive social, economic and practical measures, if they were to enlist the population's co-operation effectively.

Most fundamentally, the essence of relations between resistance and population was such that the population's willing cooperation was not automatically assured. For a population caught between resistance forces and occupation forces needed to make calculations, on an often daily basis, as to which side to support actively, or at least placate, the better to ensure its own survival. Indeed, despite all the wartime hardships to which the Axis occupation subjected European civilians, the majority sought not so much to resist the occupation as to keep their heads down and survive from day to day. Over time, as the Axis occupation grew ever harsher and more exploitative, resistance movements better-resourced and more experienced, and eventual Allied victory ever more probable, the population's calculations did increasingly favour the resistance. But such calculations continued until late in the day nonetheless.

Consequently, some resistance movements sought to encourage the population into supporting them, rather than coerce it. This was a common characteristic among resistance movements in Western Europe, in the Czech lands and in Poland. A covert 'secret army' approach to resistance employed the kinds of actions that were less likely to provoke fearsome Axis retaliation. Such resistance movements favoured this approach partly because they feared that particularly ferocious retaliation from the occupiers might seriously disrupt the sabotage, intelligence-gathering and other important activities in which they were engaged. Yet it was also because they feared what such ferocity might do to the population in whose name they were ostensibly resisting.[11] This particular fear developed partly because such movements stood for constitutionalist forms of government, and contained few extremely ruthless elements among their number. Moreover, because the countries in which they were operating were relatively small, they were more likely to interact with civilian communities with whom they felt a measure of common local or regional identity.

Soviet partisans, in particular, very often presented a considerably different picture. As the instruments of a ruthless regime, they were far from averse to brutally coercing the population into aiding them. They operated in large areas often very far from their own regions of origin, amid communities with whom they felt no particular affinity. Their callous, sometimes murderous treatment of civilians also reflected the often chronic state of discipline within their own units.

*   *   *

The final factor that helped determine the form and effectiveness of the various resistance movements was their relations with one another. At national level, alliances could be formed between hitherto politically or ethnically antagonistic groupings, often harbouring very different visions for the post-war future of their country. Some such groupings could be backed at different times by the Western Allies, some by the Soviet Union, some by both, and some by neither. Some of the alliances that resulted endured for the duration of the war; such an alliance was laudably achieved by the French resistance. More often, however, such alliances were fractious at best and liable to collapse into brutal civil conflict. Resistance groups animated by intense mutual loathing generated a murderous state of affairs in Greece, Yugoslavia and the Ukraine. In situations such as these, the danger to civilians not just from their occupiers, but from their own country-men also, was clear.

*   *   *

In providing a new, updated synthesis of the resistance movements of occupied Europe, and by illuminating how the resistance was shaped by all these afore-mentioned forces, this book seeks to provide readers with an analysis that neither eulogises nor condemns the movements. Much of the anglophone scholarship of earlier post-war decades was concerned with the crucial but necessarily somewhat narrow question of how far partisan movements contributed to eventual Allied victory.[12] But since the 1980s in particular, the focus of many studies has shifted to the occupied countries themselves. Many such studies have concerned them-selves with explaining how and why the population as a whole responded to occupation – whether that response was to resist, collaborate or seek simply to reach some sort of tolerable accommodation with the new regime. Such studies, particularly those emanating from the countries that were once occupied, have often been affected by the fierce emotion and the social, cultural and political controversies that debates on resistance often still generate.[13] Indeed, some of the historians whose work is presented in this book themselves hold different positions, albeit positions based firmly upon scholarly expertise, on some of the controversies that this topic encompasses.

Such was the complexity and diversity of the forces that shaped the European resistance during the Second World War, the multiplicity of the national, regional and local settings in which its effects were played out, and the on-going controversies that surround it, that the need for further in-depth study of it is clear. It is hoped, however, that this book will provide the reader with a useful and engaging overview of European resistance during the Second World War as scholars understand it at this point in time, nearly seventy years after the conflict's end.

Notes

1. Santo Peli, *La Resistenza in Italia* (Turin, 2004), p. 13.
2. On the Italian case see Philip Cooke, *The Legacy of the Italian Resistance* (New York, 2011); John Foot, *Italy's divided memory* (New York, 2010). For broader-based studies see M. Evans and K. Lunn, *War and memory in the 20th Century* (Oxford, 1997); M. Macmillan, *The uses and abuses of history* (London, 2009); P. Lagrou, *The Legacy of Nazi Occupation: Patriotic Memory and National Recovery in Western Europe, 1945–1965* (Cambridge, 2000).
3. Simone Neri Serneri, 'A Past to be Thrown Away? Politics and History in the Italian Resistance', *Contemporary European History*, 4/3 (November 1995), 367–81.
4. Seumas Milne, 'Greek Myth', *Guardian*, Saturday, 29 July 2000, available online: http://www.guardian.co.uk/books/2000/jul/29/fiction.features.
5. Prominent English-language overviews of resistance and occupation include Matthew Cooper, *The Phantom War: The German Struggle against Soviet Partisans 1941–1944* (London, 1979); M.R.D. Foot, *Resistance: An Analysis of European Resistance to Nazism, 1940–1945* (London, 1976); Jørgen Hæstrup, *Europe Ablaze: An Analysis of the History of the European Resistance Movements, 1939–45* (Odense, 1978); Tony Judt (ed.), *Resistance and Revolution in Mediterranean Europe 1939–1948* (London, 1989); Mark Mazower, *Hitler's Empire: Nazi Rule in Occupied Europe* (London, 2008); Henry Michel, *The Shadow War: European Resistance, 1939–1945* (New York, 1972); Bob Moore (ed.), *Resistance in Western Europe* (Oxford, 2000); Ben Shepherd and Juliette Pattinson (eds), *War in a Twilight World: Partisan and Anti-partisan Warfare in Eastern Europe, 1939–45* (London, 2010).
6. See for instance Hermann Graml, Hans Mommsen, Hans-Joachim Reichardt and Ernst Wolf, *The German Resistance to Hitler* (London, 1966); Theodore S. Hamerow, *On the Road to the Wolf's Lair: German Resistance to Hitler* (London, 1997); Hans Mommsen, *Germans Against Hitler* (London, 2008); Ian Kershaw, *Luck of the Devil: the Story of Operation Valkyrie* (London, 2009).
7. See Chapter 4 on France in this volume. The *maquis* (directly translated as scrubland) were French guerrilla bands, initially composed of men who had escaped into remote hilly and mountainous areas to escape the labour draft to Germany.
8. H. Michel, *Les Mouvements Clandestins en Europe* (Vendôme, 1961), pp. 11–16.
9. For a comprehensive overview of German-occupied Europe and accompanying bibliography, see Mazower, *Hitler's Empire*.
10. See for instance G.H. Lovett, *Napoleon and the Birth of Modern Spain* (New York, 1965), p. 693; C.J. Esdaile, *Fighting Napoleon* (New Haven, Conn., 2004).
11. Mazower, *Hitler's Empire*, p. 473.
12. See especially Foot, *Resistance*; David Stafford, *Britain and the European Resistance, 1940–1945* (London, 1980).
13. For relevant historiography concerning occupation and partisan warfare within the individual countries, see relevant individual chapters in this volume.

Chapter 1

Fifth Column, Fourth Service, Third Task, Second Conflict?

The Major Allied Powers and European Resistance

Evan Mawdsley

The most obvious way to think about the European resistance[1] is as a movement 'from below'. Across the Continent, in countries or regions overrun by the Axis powers (mainly, of course, by the Germans), individuals and groups undertook opposition activities. The resistance developed within the particular countries and regions – in France, in the Low Countries, in Scandinavia, in Italy, in east-central Europe, in the Balkans, in the western Soviet Union – in quite different ways. There is, however, another way of looking at the resistance, one that also takes into account the entire range of European experience. That way is to examine the movement 'from above', through the role that the major Allied governments (Britain, the USSR, and the United States) and their military establishments played in sustaining and exploiting it. The emphasis here is on the resistance and military operations, rather than use of the resistance to collect intelligence or to gain political influence. This chapter will discuss, in particular, how resistance featured in wartime grand strategy.

* * *

From the perspective of the Allied triumph in 1945 it is difficult to grasp how desperate the situation had seemed in London five years earlier, during the summer of 1940. France had collapsed; Italy had entered the war and now threatened the British position in the Mediterranean. Air bombardment of Britain seemed imminent, and even invasion. There was certainly little sense of how the war could ever be taken back to the Continent. Neither of the great neutrals – the United States and the Soviet Union – showed any enthusiasm for involvement on Britain's side. Meanwhile, those Europeans who had been brought under the control of the Third Reich could see no external force that might bring about their liberation. Many thought that Britain would soon go the same way as France, either invaded by the Wehrmacht or forced to make a humiliating peace, one that accepted Axis domination of Continental Europe. The 'realists' on the

Continent often came to the conclusion that collaboration with the occupiers was the only rational policy.

And yet as the British government saw it, one way forward to victory was to nurture the tender shoots of resistance. This ambition actually dated back before the May 1940 catastrophe, and even before the outbreak of war; it had been assumed that the Germans would overrun at least parts of Eastern Europe and that guerrilla warfare might be organized there. A small mission had been rushed to Poland, but it achieved nothing before the quick German victory.[2] As early as 19 May 1940, the Chiefs of Staff (COS) put forward a famous paper entitled 'British Strategy in a Certain Eventuality' – the 'eventuality' being the fall of France. In this paper they outlined three ways of continuing the war, including economic pressure through blockade, air bombing and 'the creation of wide-spread revolt in [German-]conquered territories'. Economic warfare was the essence of the strategy, but it was believed that internal revolt would become more likely as living conditions in the occupied territories deteriorated. In any event, the task of organizing a revolt was described as being 'of the very highest importance', requiring a special body.[3]

In July 1940 the Special Operations Executive (SOE) was set up under the dynamic Minister of Economic Warfare, the Labour MP Hugh Dalton. Churchill – famously – instructed Dalton to 'set Europe ablaze'.[4] Dalton, for his part, had great aspirations for SOE, and saw it as a force comparable to the conventional services, the army, navy and air force. 'Subversion,' Dalton declared, 'should be clearly recognized by all three Fighting Services as another and independent Service.'[5] Among the professional military planners those of the British army, at least, attached high importance to the resistance, for eighteen months or so – until the end of 1941.

One of the more detailed outlines of this strategy was laid out by the British Joint Planning Staff (JPS) in a strategic review of June 1941, just before the German invasion of the Soviet Union. The extraordinary section on the role of the resistance and subversion was evidently prepared by SOE. As the official historian J.M.A. Gwyer pointed out, in the relevant *Grand Strategy* volume, what was intended was the '*antithesis*' of a protracted guerrilla war, fought out in remote mountainous areas (i.e. along the lines of what would actually develop later in Yugoslavia and Greece). The model was not such a guerrilla war, but rather the German invasions of Norway, the Low Countries and France in 1940. Much of the success of those operations had been due – it was believed in London – to support for the Panzer spearheads by 'fifth columnists'. The JPS expected that the balance would be reversed for future British operations; rather than a handful of fifth columnists there would be a large number of enthusiastic and well-prepared 'patriots', who would support a relatively small attacking British force. These patriots would be able 'overnight' to reduce key occupied areas to anarchy. This 'Allied' version of May 1940 would involve a fairly small number of British divisions ('ten or more' divisions, mostly armoured), which would seize the ports and forward airfields and isolate the area in revolt from German intervention. Meanwhile, after the operation began '"free" allied contingents now in our territories' would be sent back to their home countries to work directly with the patriots and provide them with specialist capabilities – radios, engineers, anti-tank and air defence weapons.[6] This concept, in which a British landing would be used to set off a prepared uprising on the Continent in the occupied territories, was known as the 'detonator strategy'.[7]

As late as December 1941, immediately after the entry of the United States into the war, Churchill at least still conceived of the 'detonator strategy' playing a central part in future campaigns. He submitted to the first Washington Conference in December 1941 a memorandum in which he envisaged multiple British-American landings taking place in 1943, 'strong enough to enable the conquered populations to revolt'. 'If the incursion of the armoured formations is successful,' the Prime Minister predicted, 'the uprising of the local population, for whom weapons must be brought, will supply the corpus of the liberating offensive.'[8]

The 'detonator strategy' was in reality military nonsense, and this should have been obvious to the British planners in mid-1941. It was impossible secretly to construct, under the noses of the German garrisons, a well-equipped and unified 'patriot' force or 'secret army'. Even the task of dropping by parachute the required amount of small arms would have taken up, it was later estimated, the total resources of RAF Bomber Command for six months. The 'one-off' nature of the scheme meant that there could be no chance for practice or for assessing in advance how far the organization and training of the 'secret army' had progressed. The British official history later emphasized the paradox: 'Since it [the resistance uprising] could only take place once, it was necessary to ensure its success; but the only conditions which would make success certain [i.e. strong invading regular forces] were also those that would make the rising strategically unnecessary.'[9]

William Deakin, the Oxford don who became famous for his work with Tito's Partisans, argued after the war that the British – supposedly in contrast to the Russians– had given no thought before 1939 to organizing irregular warfare on the Continent.[10] That claim was not altogether true, in a literal sense, but in any event the 'detonator strategy' was quite in line with the 'British way of war' – employed over centuries – of enlisting armies on the Continent to fight for British interests. The 'secret armies' were simply an unusual variation on a theme.

In any event Britain had – and would have – few resources to commit to the detonator strategy. After Dunkirk, Britain had no capability even for raids on the Continent; as for an invasion, an operation in any strength – even ten divisions – was years away. In particular, long-range aircraft were in short supply and the Royal Air Force was reluctant to divert them from the bombing campaign. Mark Mazower is correct to state that Dalton had underestimated the possibilities for repression available to the authorities of the Third Reich in the occupied regions: 'Fortunately for all concerned, SOE's rhetoric was not matched by its funding, nor by its access to military resources.'[11]

During the twelve months after the formation of SOE the position of Britain improved somewhat, thanks to the unflinching policy of the Churchill government and the morale-raising success of the Battle of Britain. Invasion of Britain by the Germans, or an unfavourable peace forced on Britain, now seemed less likely. The United States provided military and economic aid in increasing quantities. Even the success of Germany in the Balkans in the spring of 1941 could be interpreted in a positive sense, as it spread Axis resources more thinly. It was also at this time that the broadcasting of propaganda through the BBC and the covert transmitters of the Political Warfare Executive became a major, if intangible, element in influencing public opinion in occupied Europe. The Russians used Radio Moscow, and the United States was also involved from 1942, but their impact was probably less than that of the British.[12]

And yet there was still little sign of effective resistance from below. The collaborationist government of Pétain in France still seemed in a strong position. De Gaulle's Free French were a very small force, even in French possessions overseas. The Danes, Norwegians and Dutch lived under collaborator regimes of a sort. There was a greater sense of resistance in parts of Eastern Europe – the former territory of Poland, Czechoslovakia and Yugoslavia – where German treatment was more brutal and traditions of revolt existed. But here there was no way of Britain providing support. The first parachute drop into Poland was made in February 1941, and it would be a year before there would be a second one. In the summer of 1941 SOE cut back aid to Czechoslovakia and Poland, as there was no prospect of British forces acting as 'detonators' for the resistance there.[13] The military coup in Belgrade in March 1941 involved SOE, but it was 'political warfare' in a neutral country rather than support for 'resistance' in territory occupied by the forces of the Third Reich. In any event, the new Yugoslav government was swept away by the ensuing German invasion.[14] The emphasis shifted, for a period, to France and Norway, where geography made delivery of weapons more straightforward.[15] But overall the situation was disappointing. As the historian of SOE put it, describing the first eighteen months of the organization's activities, 'the twigs of early resistance were still too damp . . . to do more than smoulder'.[16]

*   *   *

When Germany invaded the Soviet Union in June 1941 – a year after the fall of France – a new stage began. Deakin, in his survey of the resistance, argued that 'the appearance of the Soviet Union as a major belligerent inevitably transformed the whole picture [of the European resistance]'.[17] This was true in the broadest sense – from hindsight – because it meant that there was now a powerful conventional ground force on the mainland which would first preoccupy the German army and then destroy it. The 'patriots' of the occupied European countries would not have to liberate themselves – even with some help from the British army. But this potential for liberation was far from evident at the time. In London there was real doubt as to whether Stalin and the Russians would survive the onslaught. And the war with the communist Soviet Union also allowed the Germans to pose in the occupied regions as the defenders of Christian Europe against Bolshevism.

There were two ways in which the invasion of the Soviet Union did change the situation in the Allies' favour. First of all, the Soviet Union became the site of the largest resistance movement in Europe. The zone occupied by the Germans was inhabited by 60 million people (although certainly not all of them were enthusiastic about Soviet power). Secondly, in occupied western and southern Europe the local communists, hitherto restrained by the dictates of the August 1939 Nazi-Soviet Pact, now threw themselves into the resistance movement.

And yet there was little the Soviet government could do to develop the movement either on its own soil or abroad.[18] The government in Moscow in the months after 22 June 1941 was in much the same position as that of the British in May/June 1940; they were confronted by an unexpected (and even worse) military defeat, and they had little immediate prospect of being able to right the situation by conventional military means. Neither Britain nor the Soviet Union had done much to prepare for the eventuality in which they found themselves. The difference was that, unlike the British, the Soviet government was for the most part attempting to build resistance in what could be called its 'own' territory (once the German army had passed through the belt of territory that until 1939–40 had been part of eastern Poland or the independent Baltic states).

Deakin argued that for the Russians (unlike the British), guerrilla warfare played a central part in policy.[19] Like his claim about British pre-war policy (or non-policy), this is hard to sustain. Even during the Civil War of 1917–20 the advocates of *partizanshchina* ('guerrilla-ism') in the Soviet Union had been defeated by the advocates of a regular Red Army. The stress in Soviet interwar strategy had been placed on offensive warfare fought on enemy territory, using conventional forces. Any military theorist in the Soviet Union who before 1941 had advocated a defensive guerrilla strategy on Soviet territory would have been accused of treasonous defeatism. In addition, the Soviet retreat in 1941 was so quick and so deep that little had been done to prepare a resistance force. By the time the front stabilized at the beginning of December much of occupied Soviet territory (the Baltic republics, Belorussia, central and western Ukraine and Moldavia) were out of range of help from the 'mainland' (as the unoccupied territory was sometimes termed). Many of the 'partisans' were the stunned and starving survivors of conventional Soviet armies that had been destroyed during the battles of the summer and autumn. Meanwhile, the Red Army, in the desperate military situation of 1941–2, had very few personnel, and very little equipment and supplies, to send to the resistance fighters.

As for the *organization* of the resistance within the Soviet Union, the task was complicated by the fact that the Soviet Union was a 'dictatorship of the proletariat', a totalitarian state dominated by the Communist Party. Despite its revolutionary pedigree, the Party was not enthusiastic about simply encouraging a mass uprising from below, based on popular initiative. Moscow very much wanted to keep control of 'its' resistance; it had an image of the resistance, like the rest of the Soviet system, being run 'from above' by communist cadres. So the orientation (like that in the revolutionary Leninist Bolshevik Party before 1917) was 'top down', a mass movement guided by an elite. And the problem was complicated – as in Britain – by a failure to agree about who would organize the resistance. The Communist Party (central and regional), the Red Army and the secret police (NKVD/NKGB) argued about who would be in charge. It was not until eleven months after the beginning of the war, in May 1942, that Moscow created a central headquarters – the Central Staff of the Partisan Movement (TsShPD) – under the *Stavka* (Stalin's 'general headquarters'), and headed by the Belorussian partisan leader P.K. Ponomarenko.

Unlike London (and later Washington), Moscow was involved with resistance both on its own territory and in foreign occupied countries. Stalin, in his famous 'brothers and sisters' radio speech of 3 July 1941, stressed that what was going on was not just a 'fatherland war' of the Soviet Union, but also a war of 'help to all the peoples of Europe who were suffering under the yoke of German fascism'.[20] Soviet propaganda, and some of Stalin's speeches, stressed the volatility of German-occupied territory, and indeed the volatility of the Reich itself. In his Revolution Day speech of November 1941 the Soviet leader remarked on the 'instability of the European rear of imperial Germany'. The 'new order', he declared (in a rather awkward extended metaphor), was 'a volcano which is ready to explode at any time and to bury the German imperialist house of cards'. In his memorable Red Army Day speech of February 1942, in which he brought out 'stability of the rear' as one of the 'permanently operating factors' in modern war, he noted that this stability was something that the Soviet Union possessed and Nazi Germany did not.[21] (This was not so different from British thinking, although the planners in London argued that volatility would be increased by blockade and growing economic hardship.)

William Mackenzie, in his secret in-house history of SOE, laid emphasis on the value the communists in the major European countries obtained from having had a pre-war organization: '[t]heir cadres existed and were well drilled long before German occupation'. They had made political mistakes in the past 'but at least they were a force in being'. He also expressed some envy at the way the Russians had organized their links with the resistance abroad. He described an all-powerful NKVD (the Soviet secret police) as 'the only [organization] ... which approached the theoretical conception of an all-embracing service dealing with all subversion and also with all "black" activities of whatever kind'.[22] In reality, the NKVD was one of several stakeholders, and it was more involved in the resistance movement on *Soviet* territory (and its role there involved an element of *counter*-insurgency against non-communist resistance groups).

As in Britain, conflicting bureaucratic interests in the Soviet Union complicated the task of encouraging resistance abroad. The Soviet Union had for twenty years possessed a body essentially devoted to organizing the resistance of the 'oppressed' population of foreign territories, in the form of the Communist International or Comintern, which had been founded in 1919. The Red Army (notably its intelligence section, the 5th Directorate of the General Staff, later the GRU) naturally also claimed a role in the question of dispatching arms and military advisors. Georgi Dimitrov, the head of the Comintern, recorded in his diary in August 1941 a conversation with Stalin about the coordination of 'the partisan movement and sabotage' abroad, and about the rival demands of the Executive Committee of the Comintern (IKKI), the NKVD and the Red Army. According to Dimitrov, Stalin doubted the suitability of the military authorities. 'The comrades from the 5th Directorate [of the General Staff] want to lead the movement,' he supposedly said. 'That will get us nowhere.'[23] Although Dimitrov did not mention this, another interested party was the People's Commissariat for Foreign Affairs (NKID), which for two decades had been in conflict with the Comintern.

The main problem, however, was not organization or ideology, but distance. Of the major Allied states, the Soviet Union was in the worst position to offer direct practical support to the European resistance. Soviet-controlled territory, already remote from western and central Europe, had been pushed back as much as 600 miles from the 1941 western frontier. Even in eastern Europe there was no way of sending advisors or equipment. Practically, all links by land and sea had been blocked by the Wehrmacht, and effective air supply was ruled out by the great distances involved and the lack of effective long-range aircraft in the Red Army Air Force. Britain was in a much better geographical position than the Soviet Union for 'setting Europe ablaze'. Some help was offered to the Soviets in western Europe. The most notable joint enterprise was Operation Pickaxe, in which transport from Britain was provided by the RAF. Pickaxe, however, involved only a few dozen agents over two years. It also provoked serious disquiet in the British Foreign Office.[24]

What the Russians *could* do – and it was not insignificant – was to lead the resistance in other parts of Europe by example. First of all they survived the initial German onslaught, and then, in the winter of 1941–2, they demonstrated an ability actually to mount a large and successful counter-offensive against the Germans, notably in the Battle of Moscow. The partisan movement in the Soviet Union, whatever its actual shortcomings, could also be held up as a model for other countries.

*   *   *

Like the entry of the Soviet Union into the war, the entry of the third major Allied power, the United States, had, in hindsight, a deep effect on the European resistance. The very entry of the United States into the war encouraged the resistance; it made it seem in the occupied territories that the long-term success of Nazi Germany had become more difficult. On the other hand, the Americans could not have any immediate effect on the situation, and their approach to the resistance was also conditioned by a fundamentally different view of grand strategy from that of the British. For the British the resistance was a plausible, if long-term, alternative. For the Americans – at least for their military high command – the way to defeat Germany was always to smash her by conventional and direct means, mounting a cross-Channel invasion with mass armies as soon as possible; in this scenario the resistance could make only a limited contribution. The American government had hoped that by cultivating the Vichy government it might encourage a turn against Germany. But this approach yielded few positive results, even when, twelve months after they entered the war, the Americans were actually able to deploy significant military forces in North Africa.

The Americans did create an organization roughly comparable to SOE, known from July 1942 as the Office of Strategic Services (OSS). The precursor of the Central Intelligence Agency, the OSS had a somewhat broader remit than that of the British organization, including espionage. As with other aspects of the American war effort, considerable time elapsed before real forces came into play. The British were at least eighteen months ahead, they already had some links with resistance organizations on the ground, they hosted the governments-in-exile in London and elsewhere, and they ran the supply bases in Britain and North Africa.[25] There would certainly be significant differences of opinion between SOE and OSS about the strategy of resistance in specific localities, just as there were planning conflicts among the conventional fighting services of Britain and the United States. In part these had to do with (imperial and anti-imperial) ideology and national 'interests'.[26] The relationship varied with time and place but the trend, as the war years passed, was for greater independence. But both organizations had one notable common motivation – to prove the value of subversive warfare. Bradley Smith has commented on the conflict between the 'political warfare mission' of the OSS and the 'big battalion mentality' of the (US) Joint Chiefs of Staff; the relationship between SOE and the British Chiefs of Staff involved the same conflict. In the end the two special warfare organizations worked together reasonably effectively.[27]

* * *

In 1942 the 'grand alliance' of Britain, the United States and the Soviet Union was functioning. In the early months of the year the Allied 'resistance' strategy did show more signs of effectiveness, even though, paradoxically, it was now less necessary. The spectacular killing of the senior Nazi official Reinhard Heydrich in Prague in May 1942 was organized by the Czechoslovak government-in-exile and SOE (with an assassination team dropped into the region in December 1941).[28] It was a hollow success and never repeated. This was partly because of the scale of German reprisals, which shocked the Czechoslovak government in exile in London, and partly because the general policy of the Western Allies toward the resistance had changed.

In Britain the removal of the propaganda function from SOE (it was given to the Political Warfare Executive) and the replacement of Dalton as the minister in charge, in February 1942, reduced the organization's influence and freedom of action. Dalton's replacement at the Ministry of Economic Warfare was Lord Selborne – a compliant Conservative politician. The regular military services now carried more weight. With their new American partners they were concerned with the resistance as an adjunct to conventional forces, gathering intelligence and preparing to interdict lines of communication rather than carrying out uprisings on a large scale or acts of terror. The general directive of the British high command (the Chiefs of Staff Committee) to SOE in May 1942 stressed the need to avoid 'premature large-scale rising of patriots'.[29] This approach, it must be said, echoed that of the governments-in-exile, which feared German reprisals and wished to keep their forces intact for the moment of liberation and its aftermath. The policy towards the resistance was dictated by the immediate demands of Allied strategy. In London by late 1942 the geographical focus had changed again, this time to the Mediterranean and southern Europe.

The British were especially interested in the situation in Yugoslavia and Greece, partly because of the location of German supply lines to North Africa and partly because of the existence, particularly in the former country, of traditions of armed resistance. The particular question that developed in Yugoslavia concerned which anti-German force to support. This was determined ultimately by the level of anti-German activity rather than by ideology; it led to an important shift of support by SOE to the communist 'Partisans' in 1943.[30] One might also mention here the attempts by the Americans and British, working independently, to convince the French forces in occupied North Africa to come over to the Allied cause. This was less engagement with resisters than an attempt to woo collaborators, and it probably did not have a decisive effect on the outcome of Operation Torch, the Anglo-American invasion of French North Africa in November 1942.

The attitude of the Soviet war leadership to the resistance, both in its own occupied territory and in other parts of Europe, developed significantly in 1942. Moscow had recovered from the initial shock of the surprise attack. The Red Army counterattack that began at Rostov and Moscow in November–December 1941, and which pushed forward in the early months of 1942, initially raised hopes that Soviet territory would be cleared of German occupiers in the near future. This success of conventional forces proved to be only temporary, and then more thought had to be devoted to the resistance movement. A consequence of the serious Soviet setback at the Battle of Kharkov in May 1942 was the aforementioned creation of the Central Partisan Staff. In late June the second great Wehrmacht offensive began, this time concentrated in the southern Soviet Union. The loss, in short order, of Sevastopol, Voronezh, and Rostov (the last on 28 July 1942), the headlong retreat of the southern Soviet armies towards Stalingrad, and a perceived threat to Moscow, provoked another basic change of policy. Stalin issued his famous 'Not one step backwards' decree after the fall of Rostov, and in the following month he attended a conference of the partisan movement in Moscow.

The result of this conference was Order No. 189 of 5 September, entitled 'On the Tasks of the Partisan Movement'. In this directive Stalin stressed the importance of the movement, and ordered that the organization of the struggle against the occupiers be fundamentally changed: 'It is necessary before anything else to achieve a situation where the partisan movement has become still wider and deeper, necessary that the partisan struggle takes in the very widest [*shirochaishie*] masses of the Soviet people [*narod*] in the occupied territory. The partisan movement must become an all-people's [*vsenarodnoe*] one.'[31] Soviet propaganda also now treated the Soviet resistance forces as comparable to the army and the navy – somewhat along Dalton's lines of the 'fourth service'. Stalin's November 1942

Revolution Day speech set the tone: 'Long live our Red Army! Long live our Navy! Long live our glorious men and women partisans! Death to the German-Fascist aggressors!'[32]

In early 1942 the Soviet leadership also devoted more attention to the resistance elsewhere in Europe. On the eve of the new year, Dimitrov, the head of the Comintern, had recorded in his diary the main tasks of his organization: 'Assist in preparing pop[ular] masses in the occupied countries for deci[sive] armed actions against the occupiers, simultaneously with the Red Army's gener[al] counter-offensive in the spring.'[33] A Comintern letter of February 1942 to Jacques Duclos, the head of the French Communist Party (PCF), noted that 1942 was to be 'the year of victory'. The letter instructed Duclos that the PCF was to create 'a broadly-based partisan movement in the villages and important centres' and it was to 'begin this very day' preparations for 'mass armed actions' so that 'the uprising of the French people ... and the military operations of the Red Army can be combined for the defeat of the common enemy'.[34] The Comintern May Day appeal of 1942 still urged mass armed actions; the workers of the occupied territories were to be made to see 'both the necessity and the real possibility for the popular masses to offer armed resistance'. The appeal noted that the resistance was 'assuming the character and scale of a genuine people's war' in Yugoslavia, and that there had been successes in Norway and France. 'Partisan war' was possible everywhere and depended not on *conditions* but rather on the *will* of the oppressed: '[R]eality visibly contradicts the false assertion that the partisan war demands specific geographical conditions – woods, swamps, inaccessible mountains, as though there can be no thought of it in densely populated European localities.' Everything depended on willpower: 'The tempo and the scope of armed resistance of the peoples ... will depend to a large extent on the working class in the occupied countries'.[35] Dimitrov himself was at this time an advocate of both immediate armed action and of crude uniformity, judging by his comments at a Comintern Executive Committee meeting in June 1942: 'The action of the insurgents [*bortsy*] must be simultaneous and co-ordinated so that the Germans cannot put down uprisings in the [various] countries one by one.' 'Slogans and methods', Dimitrov insisted, 'can and must be the same in different countries.'[36]

This simplistic Comintern approach to foreign resistance had much in common with the theoretical strategy circulating in the British leadership in 1940–1. Both assumed large-scale co-ordinated resistance action, to the level of insurgency, even in urban areas of north-western Europe. There were significant differences. The British project had stressed long-term preparation; the Russians were urging immediate action. In the British case the theory was that resistance action would – when it eventually came – be directly supported by British forces; for the Russians the non-Soviet resistance was predominantly on the far side of the Continent and would be part of a European effort to wear the Germans down gradually. But neither concept corresponded very closely to reality.

*　　*　　*

The strength and activity of the European resistance increased in late 1942 and early 1943, and by 1944 it had reached full development. The general situation had changed. The Allies, no longer fighting for survival and with their war economies more fully developed, had greater resources available with which to supply underground groups. They were now evidently winning the war, and it would be a very short-sighted opportunist in occupied Europe who gambled on a German victory; the formal collaborator regimes were mostly abolished by the Germans. Meanwhile, because the screws were indeed tightening elsewhere, the German occupation was becoming more arduous: large-scale labour conscription caused great discontent, and reprisals for resistance activity had a polarising effect. The governments in exile, notably that of de Gaulle and the Free French, had developed into a significant force.

What might be called a 'mature' resistance movement developed behind German lines. In occupied Soviet territory it was more closely organized from outside than anywhere else. The Battle of Stalingrad in the winter of 1942–3 finally ended the German advance even in the south, and the enemy now began to retreat. From the Battle of Kursk in the summer of 1943 the Red Army kept and held the initiative, and the pace of advance westwards now became rapid, especially in the Ukraine. Equipment – small arms, explosives, radios, light aircraft – and trained advisors were now available in larger quantities to support the partisans. The number of people in the movement grew, reaching a peak of about 250,000 by January 1944.[37]

The mission of Soviet resistance fighters was clearly defined: to provide tactical assistance to the conventional forces as they advanced westwards. Stalin's February 1943 Red Army Day 'Order of the Day' stressed three overall tasks for the Soviet armed forces: (1) military training and discipline, (2) strengthening blows against the enemy, with unceasing pursuit, and (3) use of partisans. Stalin's message gave the partisans the main task of disrupting the enemy's communications, but in a situation of German withdrawal they also had the mission of protecting the population and preventing demolition and looting by enemy troops.[38] (Similar missions were carried out by SOE and resistance forces in Italy during the period of German retreat in 1944–5, when they were known as 'anti-scorch' operations. These may not have hastened the German defeat, but they did save the post-occupation infrastructure.) Co-ordinated strikes against German lines of communications, especially the railways, now had considerable effect, beginning with Operation Lampa in November 1942, Operation Rail War at the time of Kursk and the seizure of the Dnepr River crossings in the autumn of 1943. Probably the largest coordinated strike preceded the Red Army's Belorussian offensive in June 1944, Operation Bagration. The resistance also provided long-range intelligence about German dispositions. Nevertheless, the partisans did not succeed in paralysing German communications, and many partisan bands were able to survive because they operated in areas of marginal importance to the occupiers. Nor did they succeed in tying down large numbers of first-line German troops.

In the early spring of 1944 the Red Army had re-captured the southern part of the European Soviet Union, and by the autumn of that year it had overrun Belorussia and most of the Baltic region. There was now virtually no more German occupation of the territory of the Soviet Union, and no more anti-German resistance. The Russians were the first of the Allies to have to deal with the redundant veterans of the resistance movement, and their policy was to use them to replenish regular Red Army formations, which were now running low on personnel. There was also a considerable resistance movement of a new type, resistance to the re-imposition of rule by Russians and communists in parts of the Ukraine, in the Baltic republics and in the Polish-inhabited borderlands.

However developed the resistance movement had become on occupied Soviet soil in 1943–4, there was still little Moscow would do physically to support the resistance elsewhere in Europe. Until late in the war even the western Balkans could only be reached from British and American air bases in Italy. Supply flights to Yugoslavia from Soviet territory began only in February 1944, and they were on a small scale until the end of the summer. The communist Partisans in Yugoslavia were armed by the British, not the Russians. There could be no question of direct Russian aid to comrades in France or Italy.

On the other hand the prestige of the Soviet Union had never been higher. As the French historian Henri Michel put it, the Soviet Union had become 'the land of the resistance, *par excellence*' thanks to the way it had, largely through its own efforts, successfully overthrown a most cruel occupation regime.[39] Moscow's policy also became more flexible, and in 1943 the local communists were ordered to join in coalitions of resistance fighters. The disbanding of the Comintern in the spring of 1943 was an important part of this process. Stalin publicly explained this development in the Western press, declaring that the end of the Communist International 'exposes the Hitlerite lie about the supposed intention of "Moscow" to interfere in the life of other states and to "Bolshevize" them.' Stalin related this directly to the resistance: '[the disbandment of the Comintern] makes easier the work of the patriots of the freedom-loving countries in the unification of pro-gressive forces of their countries . . . in a united national-liberation camp – for the development of the struggle against Fascism.'[40] This did not mean that Stalin had abandoned centralized control in practice: the apparatus of the Soviet Communist Party's Central Committee, especially the secret 'International Information Department' (OMI) took over many of the functions of the Comintern; Dimitrov headed the OMI.

Although historians still argue about it, the political-diplomatic strategy of the Soviet Union, as conceived by Stalin, was probably to divide Europe into Western and Soviet spheres of influences, while maintaining good working relations with Britain and the United States. The best-known expression of this – although it specifically related only to the Balkans – was Stalin's famous 'per-centages' agreement made with Churchill in Moscow in October 1944. The policy, however, had been taking shape for some time. Stalin reined in the more radical elements of the communist resistance, and this even led to disagreements with Dimitrov and the OMI – disagreements that naturally were resolved in

Stalin's favour. When Dimitrov and the Italian Communist leader Togliatti balked at his having to enter the new government created by the Western Allies in Italy, Togliatti was summoned to the Kremlin (in March 1944) and told to concentrate on fostering unity in the resistance (a successful strategy as it turned out). By the terms of this strategy, the PCI was to enter the new government and not demand the abdication of the King. At the same time, Thorez in France was ordered to move with caution; the Russians privately urged that the PCF (French Communist Party) not insist on separate communist armed detachments.[41]

The policy of the British developed in late 1942 and in 1943–4, both in terms of tactics and geographical emphasis. The stress was now very much on support operations rather than general 'detonation'. In an executive directive of March 1943, SOE specified that 'guerrilla activities' were not to interfere with gathering intelligence or acts of sabotage.[42] And from the point of view of geography, the interest of SOE had turned from Poland and Czechoslovakia, then to France and Norway, and now to southern Europe and the Mediterranean, where British military operations were concentrated. The Allies were also very keen to mislead the enemy as to their intentions regarding invasion operations on the north coast of the Mediterranean. SOE's first notable sabotage attack, in November 1942, was against the Gorgopotamos railway viaduct in Greece, which was regarded as an important link in Axis supply lines to North Africa.

A striking new front in the resistance appeared with the fall of Mussolini and the defection to the Allies of the successor regime. The collapse of Fascism had little to do with the resistance, although SOE did facilitate contacts with the Italian government that brought about the September 1943 armistice. The occupation of central and northern Italy by the Germans led to the creation of a powerful resistance movement, with which SOE and OSS, and latterly the successor to the Comintern, hastened to organize resistance among elements of both the (Royalist) right and the left.[43] The situation in the south developed very rapidly with the invasion of Sicily in the summer of 1943, followed by the overthrow of Mussolini and the attempted surrender of Italy, and by the Allied landing on the mainland of southern Italy. The first successful urban rebellion in Axis Europe was actually in Naples in September 1943, although this had little to do with external organizations.

An important indirect result of the invasion of Italy in the autumn of 1943 was that the Allies – including the Russians – gained much better access to the Balkans. The resistance there was encouraged by the disintegration of the Italian occupation forces. Once the British and Americans had established themselves in southern Italy they could provide much help to the resistance in Yugoslavia and Greece.

For the Western Allies the cross-Channel invasion of June 1944 was the ultimate test of the value of the resistance as a military force. The event took the strategy back to the heady days of 1940, although the 'patriot forces' were now very much the 'auxiliaries'. In some cases German counter-measures had paralyzed the local resistance, or at least confounded Allied attempts to support the movement from outside; the classic example was the complete failure of SOE in the Netherlands from 1942 to early 1944 after its communications system was compromised.[44] The British invasion planners did not attach much importance to the French resistance until the beginning of 1944. The underground there was, in the event, given little advance notice of the timing and location of the invasions (including those for the 6 June D-Day landings), in order to prevent loss of surprise by the Allied landing force. The resistance did interdict German railway lines and provide valuable intelligence on enemy deployments. It had limited impact in the first weeks of fighting in Normandy, but was important in Brittany, and also in the south of France in August; these successes resulted in a much more positive evaluation by General Eisenhower and other Allied military leaders.[45] The Germans abandoned most of France when the back of their armies was broken in the Normandy fighting, but the resistance played an important part in the transition of authority in those large parts of France where there were no invading troops.

The invading Western Allies did not count on urban insurrection or serious guerrilla warfare. The most famous guerrilla uprising organized by the French resistance – at Vercors – was an attempt immediately after D-Day to create a liberated base area on a high plateau in south-eastern France, but this was brutally crushed by the Germans. After the Normandy breakout the Allies were surprised when resistance forces staged an uprising in Paris on 19 August 1944, and they were actually forced to divert forces to 'relieve' the great city. The Paris uprising of the resistance was set off by the imminent abandonment of the city by the Germans, which was caused by the defeat of their army in the Battle of Normandy; it was not the uprising that brought about the German defeat. A potentially more important event in 'grand-strategic' terms was the capture intact of the huge port at Antwerp by the Belgian resistance; unfortunately, the advancing British army proved unable to secure the sea approaches to the port, and it took some months before it could be used.[46]

* * *

The final period of the war in Europe – from June 1944 – represented a separate stage in the history of Allied relations with the resistance. In this period the Western Allies established themselves firmly back on the Continent, and – almost simultaneously – the Russians, with very little of their own territory now occupied, began operating directly in Eastern Europe.

Some remarkable resistance operations took place. The Vercors uprising and Paris uprising have already been mentioned. The Slovak National Uprising, which began at the end of August, was another example, although its origins – in elements in the puppet Slovak army – were rather different. The uprising initially promised the Red Army a quick passage through the Carpathian Mountains, but unfortunately the base of the rising, at Banská Bystrica, was overrun by the Germans at the end of October 1944. The most significant example of successful co-operation between resistance forces and conventional armies was in Belgrade in Yugoslavia, which was captured in late October 1944 by the combined efforts of the Yugoslav Partisans and two armies of the Soviet Third Ukrainian Army Group.

It was, however, political complexities involving the great powers that were the special feature of this period. Paradoxically, as the German hold on Europe weakened (due to defeats at the hands of regular Allied forces) the resistance became, in some places, a danger to the long-term interests of one or other of the major Allied states. This was not so much the case in France, Belgium, the Netherlands or Norway, where there was a recognized government-in-exile and the resistance facilitated the creation of a new order 'on the ground'. Even in Yugoslavia, both East and West had come to recognize Tito's Partisans as the main force, even though there are interesting questions about the role of British communists in SOE in the decision to give whole-hearted support to the communist Partisans and Tito.[47] But where the political outcome was more uncertain, and where there was no generally recognized post-occupation authority, matters could become very strained.

One outstanding case of the military and political difficulties in this period was the Warsaw Uprising, which began on 1 August 1944. The uprising involved the classic example of a 'secret army' and the largest urban rebellion mounted by the resistance of any country. It also exemplified the 'detonator strategy' of 1940, as it was set off by the movement of an Allied army. The Red Army did attempt to bring about a popular uprising in Warsaw as their troops approached the city from the east. In operational terms any disruption of the German rear and any success in capturing intact communications links would have been extremely valuable. But the Warsaw Uprising was implemented by the Polish 'Home Army' (AK) under General Bór-Komarowski, a resistance organization which was nationalistic and anti-communist. The rising had two aims, to drive out the Germans and to secure Polish control of the national capital before the Red Army arrived.[48]

Even in purely operational terms, the Warsaw events illustrated the practical difficulty of co-ordinating conventional military forces and the large-scale action of 'patriot forces'. The British had been able to provide only minimal support to the Polish resistance, and there was no improvement during the time of the 1944 Uprising.[49] Marshal Rokossovskii, the local Soviet army-group commander, commented to a British journalist that it was the Red Army that would liberate Poland: 'Bór-Komarowski and the people around him have butted in ... like the clown in the circus who pops up at the wrong moment and gets rolled up in the carpet'.[50] The failure of the Red Army to support the rising that August was probably due to genuine operational factors; the Soviet troops had run out of supplies after a long advance, and – unlike Paris – the Germans had committed themselves to defend Warsaw. Nevertheless, the Warsaw Uprising also demonstrated the growing difficulty of *political* co-ordination. The Soviet government was certainly unwilling to see a Poland under the authority of the hostile Home Army. And after the rising was crushed by the Germans, NKVD forces were committed to liquidate what was left of the AK.

For the Western Allies, especially the British, the extreme case was Greece, after the Wehrmacht hastily abandoned the Balkans in late 1944. Power appeared likely to pass to the communist EAM-ELAS resistance, rather than to the British-sponsored Royalist government-in-exile. In the reverse of the early wartime detonator strategy, British troops were landed in December to *defuse* a resistance uprising, preventing the seizure of Athens by a 'secret army'. Churchill would declare in Parliament that democracy was 'no harlot to be picked up in the street by a man with a tommy gun'.[51] In northern Italy in November 1944 the local Allied commander-in-chief, Field Marshal Alexander, famously ordered a hibernation of the partisan movement, although this was probably more an attempt on his part to preserve partisan bands for future operations, rather than to take the wind out of their sails.[52]

* * *

Henri Michel argued that the resistance was more than a 'fourth service' (after the army, navy and air force) and that it developed into a 'second conflict parallel to, or rather underlying, that of the coalitions of states and the armies of the classic type'. The outstanding Danish historian of the resistance, Jørgen Hæstrup, contended that, side by side with conventional fighting, 'the decisive battle of undermining activities were stubbornly carried out behind the back of the Axis powers ... and influenced the course of the War decisively, both in [the] material, and perhaps even more in the psychological sector.[53] Both Michel and Hæstrup were almost certainly thinking in terms of *spontaneous* resistance from below, rather than resistance promoted from outside by the 'special' services of the major powers.

In reality the resistance did not do a great deal to achieve the *strategic* objectives of Britain, the Soviet Union or the United States. The movement did inevitably figure in the military plans of the major powers, and it would certainly be unsatisfactory to discuss 'grand strategy' without taking it into account. Its importance, however, changed over time. In 1940–2 exaggerated hopes were placed on the resistance, at least in London and Moscow, but they were soon abandoned. At no point – even in 1940) – were Allied military strategy and action driven, in *practical* terms, by the potential of resistance fighters or the need to support them. None of the resistance groups, not even the Yugoslav Partisans, could have ended the German occupation of their countries without the involvement of regular Allied armies. There were some successful urban uprisings, but they came either at the very end of the war, or at a time when German setbacks at the hands of regular Allied forces had created a power vacuum. The largest uprising, at Warsaw in July 1944, was a military and political disaster. The resistance was also unable to make occupied territories ungovernable, or to exact a very heavy price from the occupiers, or even tie down first-line enemy troops. In this strategic sense the 'secret armies' were phantom armies.

The attempt to use special forces, working with the local resistance, to achieve political goals had only limited success. Neville Wylie has perceptively argued that SOE, for example, became 'more than simply an adjunct to Britain's military operations' and its approach was distinctively 'modern' and one that remains central to 'a state's politico-military armoury today'. On the other hand, Wylie concedes that the practitioners of political warfare were unwelcome in Whitehall, at least in the immediate post-war years.[54] Going a few years forward, and turning to the American case, Bradley Smith has contended that over-reliance on 'shadow warfare' set a precedent for the post-war world for an over-reliance on covert operations that damaged American interests.[55]

The argument of this chapter is that the resistance was considerably *less* than a fourth service, and that in military terms its activities were not truly decisive. The war was certainly won by 'armies of the classic type'. The resistance did, however, play a significant auxiliary role in the area of sabotage and the gathering of intelligence. And it is certainly not the intention here to discount the great *political* and *moral* (and propaganda) importance of the resistance, and the role that it came to have in collective memory.

Notes

1. In this chapter I use the word 'resistance' – in lower case – in a general sense, although the term was not used everywhere; the Russians, at least, rarely employed it to describe the anti-occupation movement on Soviet territory. The term is taken to cover a spectrum of activities from urban armed uprising and large-scale guerrilla campaigns to individual acts of sabotage and anti-occupier propaganda. I do not use the word to describe the activities of Axis leaders and elites who changed sides, or attempted to do so.

2. Peter Wilkinson, *Foreign Fields: The Story of an SOE Operative* (London, 2002), pp. 62, 67–85; Peter Wilkinson and Joan Bright Astley, *Gubbins and SOE* (London, 1993), pp. 38–45. Wilkinson and Astley give a good account of the formation of SOE from the perspective of its most important leader, Colin Gubbins (pp. 75–96). For a useful recent introduction see Mark Seaman, '"A New Instrument of War". The Origins of the Special Operations Executive', in Mark Seaman (ed.), *Special Operations Executive: A New Instrument of War* (London, 2006), pp. 7–21.

3. J.R.M. Butler, *Grand Strategy* (London, 1957), Vol. II, pp. 209–15.

4. Hugh Dalton, *The Fateful Years: Memoirs 1931–1945* (London, 1957), p. 366.

5. Cited in David Stafford, *Britain and European Resistance, 1940–1945* (London, 1980), p. 29.

6. J.M.A. Gwyer, *Grand Strategy* (London, 1964), Vol. III, Part I, pp. 42–4.

7. David Stafford, 'The Detonator Concept: British Strategy, SOE and European Resistance after the Fall of France', *Journal of Contemporary History*, 10:2 (1975), 185–217.

8. The National Archives (TNA, formerly the Public Records Office, Kew), CAB 69/4, 'Memorandum on the Future Conduct of the War', pp. 2–3.

9. Gwyer, *Grand Strategy*, p. 46.

10. F.W. Deakin, 'Great Britain and European Resistance', in *European Resistance Movements 1939–1945: Proceedings of the Second International Conference on the History of the Resistance Movements held at Milan 26–29 March 1961* (Oxford, 1964), p. 98.

11. Mark Mazower, *Hitler's Empire: Nazi Rule in Occupied Europe* (London, 2008), p. 481.

12. On this important subject, see Jørgen Hæstrup, *Europe Ablaze: An Analysis of the History of the European Resistance Movements, 1939–45* (Odense, 1978), pp. 204–18. Hæstrup described the European resistance movements as fundamentally 'home-grown', but he admitted that they were 'strongly influenced from without, and ... their activities depended to a great extent upon connexions – particularly radio connexions – with the free world'. For the development of British radio propaganda in the first half of the war and its links with the resistance, especially in France, Denmark, Poland and Yugoslavia, see Michael Stenton, *Radio London and Resistance in Occupied Europe: British Political Warfare 1939–1943* (Oxford, 2000).

13. E.D.R. Harrison, 'The British Special Operations Executive and Poland', *Historical Journal*, 43:4 (2000), 1071–91; Terry Chapman, 'Hugh Dalton, Poland and SOE, 1940-42', in Seaman (ed.), *Special Operations Executive*, pp. 61–70.

14. On the Belgrade episode, see Neville Wylie, 'Ungentlemanly Warriors or Unreliable Diplomats? Special Operations Executive and "Irregular Political Activities" in Europe', in Neville Wylie (ed.), *The Politics and Strategy of Clandestine War: Special Operations Executive* (London, 2006), pp. 109, 114–15, 124–5. Wylie treats the 'political warfare' ('irregular diplomacy') of SOE as something distinct from its *military* contribution of arming and training the resistance.

15. M.R.D. Foot, *SOE in France: An Account of the Work of the British Special Operations Executive in France* (London, 2004); Ivar Kraglund, 'SOE and Milorg: "Thieves on the Same Market"', in Seaman (ed.), *Special Operations Executive*, pp. 71–82; Knud J.V. Jespersen, 'SOE and Denmark', in Seaman (ed.), *Special Operations Executive*, pp. 193–200; Charles Cruickshank, *SOE in Scandinavia* (Oxford, 1986).

16. M.R.D. Foot, *SOE: An Outline History of the Special Operations Executive 1940–1946* (London, 1999), p. 37

17. Deakin, 'Great Britain and European Resistance', p. 104.

18. For a recent summary see Kenneth Slepyan, 'The People's Avengers: The Partisan Movement', in *The Soviet Union at War, 1941–1945*, ed. David R. Stone (Barnsley, 2010), pp. 154–81; his fuller discussion is *Stalin's Guerrillas: Soviet Partisans in World War II* (Lawrence, Kan., 2006).

19. Deakin, 'Great Britain and European Resistance', p. 104.

20. I.V. Stalin, *O Velikoi Otechestvennoi voiny Sovetskogo Soiuza* (Moscow, 1951), p. 16 (3 July 1941) (hereafter cited as Stalin, *OVOVSS*).

21. *Ibid.*, pp. 31 (6 November 1941), 42 (23 February 1942)

22. William Mackenzie, *The Secret History of SOE* (London, 2000), pp. 30, 393–4.

23. N.S. Lebedev and M.M. Narinskii (eds), *Komintern i vtoraia mirovaia voina* (Moscow, 1998), Vol. 2, pp. 146–7 (hereafter cited as *Komintern*).

24. Mackenzie, *Secret History*, p. 399.

25. For a dismissive, but generally accurate, discussion of the role of the United States in working with the European resistance, based on American inexperience and reluctance to make long-term commitments abroad, see Norman Kogan, 'American Policies towards European Resistance Movements', in *European Resistance Movements 1939–1945*, pp. 72–97. For a fuller treatment of the OSS, albeit one that admits a degree of self-deception by its leaders on the actual and potential success of the 'shadow war', see Bradley F. Smith, *The Shadow Warriors: O.S.S. and the Origins of the C.I.A.* (London, 1983).

26. For relations between SOE and the OSS see especially Jay Jakub, *Spies and Saboteurs: Anglo-American Collaboration and Rivalry in Human Intelligence Collection and Special Operations, 1940–45* (Basingstoke, 1999). Jakub demonstrated that relations between the British and American organizations varied throughout the war period. There were also significant differences between SOE–OSS relations in north-western Europe and those in southern Europe, North Africa and Asia (pp. 196–7). Conflict between OSS and SOE in the Balkans is discussed in Matthew Jones, '"Kipling and All That": American Perceptions of SOE and British Imperial Intrigue in the Balkans, 1943–1945', in Wylie (ed.), *The Politics and Strategy of Clandestine War*, pp. 90–109. Co-operation between SOE/OSS and the Russians (in the form of the NKVD) was less important, but see Smith, *Shadow Warriors*, pp. 330–59, for some of the practical issues involved.

27. Smith, *Shadow Warriors*, pp. 330–3; Jakub, *Spies and Saboteurs*, p. 185.

28. Callum MacDonald, *The Killing of SS Obergruppenführer Reinhard Heydrich* (New York, 1989), includes the role of SOE.

29. TNA, CAB 80/68, COS(43)142(0) (20 March 1943).

30. For the Balkans see Mark Wheeler, 'Resistance from Abroad: Anglo-Soviet Efforts to Coordinate Yugoslav Resistance, 1941–42', in Seaman (ed.), *Special Operations Executive*, pp. 103–22. For divergence between OSS and SOE in this area, see Jakub, *Spies and Saboteurs*, pp. 110–45. Yugoslav Partisans are referred to with a capital 'P' rather than a small 'p', as is the usual practice, because this was the name of their organization as well as a descriptive term.

31. *Partizanskoe dvizhenie v gody Velikoi Otechestvennoi voiny: Dokumenty i materialy*, in series *Russkii arkhiv. Velikaia Otechestvennaia* (Moscow, 1999), Vol. 9, doc. 78 (5 September 1942), pp. 132–5.

32. Stalin, *OVOVSS*, p. 81 (7 November 1942).

33. Georgi Dimitrov, *The Diary of Georgi Dimitrov, 1933–1949*, ed. Ivo Banac (New Haven, 2003), p. 207 (30 December 1941).

34. *Komintern*, Vol. 2, pp. 41–2, 196–7.

35. 'K Pervomu maia 1942 goda', *Kommunisticheskii internatsional*, 1942, no. 3–4, pp. 6–7.

36. *Komintern*, Vol. 2, pp. 50–1, 228.

37. *Velikaia otechestvennaia voina, 1941–1945: Voenno-istoricheskie ocherki* (Moscow, 1989), Vol. 3, p. 139.

38. Stalin, *OVOVSS*, p. 95 (23 February 1943).

39. Henri Michel, *La Guerre de l'Ombre: La Résistance en Europe* (Paris, 1970), p. 60.

40. I.V. Stalin, *Sochinenie* (Stanford, Cal., 1967), Vol. 2/15, pp. 104–5.

41. *Komintern*, Vol. 2, pp. 82–7, 426–32; Dimitrov, *The Diary of Georgi Dimitrov*, pp. 303–4 (4–5 March 1944), 342–3 (19 November 1944).

42. TNA, CAB 80/68, COS(43)142(0), 20 March 1943.

43. On the Italian resistance and the British see Christopher Woods, 'SOE in Italy', in Seaman (ed.), *Special Operations Executive*, pp. 91–102, and David Stafford, *Mission Accomplished: SOE and Italy 1943–1945* (London, 2011).

44. Mackenzie, *Secret History*, pp. 302–8. Less well known was the 'control' of many supposed SOE agents in Italy by Italian military intelligence (SIM); see Stafford, *Mission Accomplished*, pp. 99–101, 335.

45. M.R.D. Foot, *SOE in France: An Account of the Work of the British Special Operations Executive in France* (London, 2004), pp. 339–67; Wilkinson and Astley, *Gubbins*, pp. 193–7. For a concise account of the contribution of SOE in France, see Mackenzie, *Secret History*, pp. 617–25. The inter-dependent relations of OSS and SOE in France are also dealt with in Jakub, *Spies and Saboteurs*, pp. 146–84

46. M.R.D. Foot, *SOE in the Low Countries* (London, 2001), pp. 379–82.

47. On this issue of subversion within the subversives see Roderick Bailey, 'Communist in SOE: Explaining James Klugmann's Recruitment and Retention', in Wylie (ed.), *The Politics and Strategy of Clandestine War*, pp. 66–89. Klugmann, a known member of the CPGB, was second-in-command of the Yugoslav Section of SOE from February 1942 to August 1944.

48. See Jan M. Ciechanowski, *The Warsaw Rising of 1944* (Cambridge, 1974).

49. Harrison, 'The British, SOE and Poland'. The British failed to make clear that they were interested in diversion and not an uprising. In this case, Harrison concludes, 'SOE did little good, and much harm' (p. 1091).

50. Alexander Werth, *Russia at War 1941–1945* (London, 1964), p. 878.

51. *Parliamentary Debates, House of Commons*, 6 December 1944, col. 929–930.

52. Stafford, *Mission Accomplished*, pp. 232–3; Woods, 'SOE in Italy', p. 99.

53. Michel, *La Guerre de l'Ombre*, pp. 378–9; Hæstrup, *Europe Ablaze*, p. 235.

54. Wylie (ed.), *The Politics and Strategy of Clandestine War*, p. 12. This argument about 'irregular political activities' is developed more fully in his article within this collection, 'Ungentlemanly Warriors', pp. 109–29. For an influential view of the general replacement of 'conventional war' by 'low-intensity operations' see Martin van Creveld, *On Future War* (London, 1991), pp. 192–223.

55. Smith, *Shadow Warriors*, pp. 418–19.

Guide to Further Reading

Jakub, Jay, *Spies and Saboteurs: Anglo-American Collaboration and Rivalry in Human Intelligence Collection and Special Operations, 1940–45* (Basingstoke, 1999).

Mackenzie, W.J.M., *The Secret History of SOE* (London, 2000).

Moore, Bob (ed.), *Resistance in Western Europe* (Oxford, 2000).

Seaman, Mark (ed.), *Special Operations Executive: A New Instrument of War* (London, 2006).

Smith, Bradley F., *The Shadow Warriors: O.S.S. and the Origins of the C.I.A.* (London, 1983).

Stafford, David, *Mission Accomplished: SOE and Italy 1943–1945* (London, 2011).

Wylie, Neville (ed.), *The Politics and Strategy of Clandestine War: Special Operations Executive* (London, 2006).

Chapter 2

Belgium

Fabrice Maerten

The Belgian resistance never developed into an open struggle against the invader.[1] It was, nevertheless, relatively well developed, particularly during the last two years of the occupation.[2] The long-term impact of the resistance on the nation was, however, very limited. This was linked to the lack of will, as well as the lack of means available to its leaders, who failed to use the forces gathered together during the resistance for any other purpose than assisting in the immediate struggle to rid the territory of the occupier.

Belgium was among the most densely populated countries of Europe. In 1938 there were more than 8,400,000 inhabitants over 30,528km². More than 90 per cent lived in the highly built up low-lying areas in the west and centre of the country. The hilly and heavily forested Ardennes region, which constitutes the eastern third of Belgium, was much less populated with only one sizeable city, Verviers. Because of this concentration of people and land, Belgium did not lend itself to the establishment of the *maquis*. On the other hand, her position between Germany, France and Great Britain as well as her extraordinarily dense network of communications made her a key strategic theatre. Belgium was also characterized by its heavy industry, particularly advanced in the areas of coal mining, steel production, metalworking, textiles and chemicals.

The importance of the secondary sector meant that more than half of the active population was employed in these activities, with the majority of them working as labourers. It is hardly surprising, then, that the socialists in the Belgian Workers' Party (POB) won more than 30 per cent of the votes in 1939. The POB was, however, beaten into second place by the Catholic Party, which received around 33 per cent of the votes in the same elections. The Catholic Party was particularly powerful in the Flemish part of the country where it was supported by a significant section of the working class, whereas in the Walloon industrial areas the working class tended to vote socialist.[3]

Moreover, the tensions between the Dutch-speaking majority and the francophone minority led, in the interwar period, to the increase of a nationalist current in Flanders which demanded the independence of that region. The political embodiment of that current, the Vlaamsch Nationaal Verbond (VNV), won more than 15 per cent of the votes in Flanders in 1939. Another party of the extreme right, on this occasion the Belgian nationalist Rex Party, appeared in francophone Belgium in 1936 before collapsing soon afterwards. The Liberal Party represented the third political force in the country with 17 per cent of the

Occupied Belgium and the
Netherlands, 1940–4.

vote in the 1939 election, while the Belgian Communist Party (PCB), though
only achieving 5.4 per cent of the vote nationally, had considerable support in
Brussels and around the Walloon industrial basins.

* * *

On 10 May 1940 Germany invaded Belgium for the second time in just over a
quarter of a century. Forced to retreat towards the west following the French
rout on the Meuse, the Belgian army had to lay down its weapons as early as
28 May. The campaign came to an end with the death of around 6,000 soldiers
and an equal number of civilians. But the political toll was just as heavy, as King
Leopold III decided to stay in the country, while his ministers fled to France to
continue the battle. The majority of them reached London in October 1940.
Little by little, this group, led by Hubert Pierlot, came to be seen in the eyes of
the Allies as well as in the eyes of the majority of the populace, as the embodiment
of official Belgium. All the movements and networks of Belgian resistance ended
up under their umbrella.

In the meantime, the occupier imposed his power on the country. On 1 June
1940 a military administration, led by General Alexander von Falkenhausen, was

installed to manage Belgium and the French departments of Nord and Pas-de-Calais. The *Militärverwaltung* was above all a surveillance organization. At the time the Nazi leaders did not have a precise idea as to the role of Belgium in the future Reich. Over the short to medium term, the German authorities wished to maintain order and security in order to facilitate the support of the German military effort. This largely involved employing a minimum of personnel and army equipment in the delivery of agricultural and industrial products. Approximately 12,000 soldiers and German civilians – not counting those soldiers who passed through at the beginning and the end of the occupation – administered and controlled the country. They were distributed fairly evenly among administrative personnel, members of the agencies of the Reich, the police and territorial guards.

From 1942 onwards, the army and the German administration that led the country saw their powers steadily undermined by more radical elements in the Nazi regime. But the actual removal from office of the military, which was replaced by a civilian administration in the hands of the SS, did not take place until 19 July 1944, only a few weeks before the rapid liberation (from 2 to 17 September) of most of Belgian territory by Allied troops. The turn of events allowed the country to get off relatively lightly, with fewer than 3,000 civilian victims over the duration of the occupation, but left few opportunities for the resistance to rise to the surface. It should be added that the terrible Battle of the Ardennes, which saw Germans and Americans in combat between 16 December 1944 and the end of January 1945, inflicted severe casualties upon the Belgian population of that region, encompassing widespread destruction and the deaths of at least 2,500 civilians.

The military administration was not hugely different from the Nazi bureaucracy. Indeed, as a partial reproduction of the German elites, the *Militärverwaltung* participated in the ideological transformation of society. Liberal democracy was rapidly abolished and replaced by a technocratic and corporatist system. The execution of hostages and the racial exclusion of Jews and Gypsies, among others, bear witness to the criminal nature of the *Militärverwaltung*'s policies.

In order to achieve their ends, the Germans relied on the co-operation of the already existing administration. At the beginning of the occupation, this did not create too many problems, as the administrative, judicial and economic elite that remained in Belgium hoped to manage affairs in such a way that, it was hoped, foreign interference in the country would be limited. From 1941 onwards, these same elites, realizing the possibility of a Nazi defeat, practised a policy of avoidance of German instructions. The occupying authorities made increasing use of those elements which collaborated, particularly the VNV in Flanders and Rex in Wallonia. This allowed the occupier to penetrate various levels of the Belgian state.

This tendency became particularly evident following the introduction of compulsory labour in Germany in October 1942. The threat, to all men between 18 and 50 years of age and all unmarried women from 21 to 35 years, of being sent to Germany to work there in the service of the occupier encouraged the great majority of the Belgian population to take a definitive stand against the invader. Faced with the clear reluctance of civil servants to enact this measure, the military administration decided to concentrate on matters at a local level. Essentially, from the beginning of 1943, the German authorities, assisted by politically radical elements in Belgian society, imposed a concept of total war, hunting out all those who avoided forced labour or who fought in the resistance, which by then they were no longer able to control.[4] By this time opposition to the occupier was no longer the preserve of a few relatively harmless groups.

* * *

Following the defeat of the spring of 1940 there were only very few individuals who dared to refuse to submit to the law of their conqueror. The first combatants in the shadow war, as with the thousands of others who joined them later, were inspired in the first place by two values: anti-fascism and, above all, patriotism. But in addition to these two fundamental concepts other elements were needed, such as pro-communism, Anglophilia, the love of liberty and of justice, the commitment to democracy, a sense of solidarity and above all hatred of the German. On the other hand, Anglophobia, anti-communism and Germanophilia constituted powerful obstacles to action against the occupier, and could even in some circumstances lead to collaboration.[5]

This interpretative framework allows a better understanding of why the resistance, from its very start, was particularly well developed in the middle and lower levels of the French-speaking middle classes, close to the environment of the First World War veterans, who espoused, from the beginning of the occupation, a patriotism that was characterized by a strong anti-German feeling. This sentiment, which was further encouraged by the fear that the middle classes might lose their relatively privileged situation within the Belgian state, explains why the mere appearance of the enemy, together with a sense that Great Britain was not on the point of collapse, encouraged a number of middle-class Belgians to initiate clandestine combat in the autumn of 1940. Some examples of the early activities of this initial nucleus of resistance are the aid given to British soldiers trying to return to their homeland, the establishment of nascent information services and the creation of large numbers of underground newspapers. But the most tangible sign of its development was the success, particularly in Brussels, of the campaign to commemorate 11 November 1918.

What could have constituted a second nucleus of resistance, that is to say those members of the anti-fascist struggle from the second half of the 1930s, collapsed in the wake of events. Its leaders, who were positioned on the moderate left (some Christian Democrats, but above all liberals and socialists), were profoundly shaken by the collapse of Western democracies and began asking themselves questions about the value of parliamentary regimes. The Pierlot government of the time hardly represented a suitable model for them. Only a few were willing to collaborate openly with the occupier, but there was a temptation to accommodate the Germans, in the absence of anything better. This was strengthened by the fact that the military administration showed a certain moderation and willingness to compromise. Only a few small groups made an effort to shake the general apathy, but they were too isolated to constitute a real force.

The communists of the extreme left felt that they must adopt a wait and see policy following the German-Soviet non-aggression pact of August 1939.[6] The gradual decay of the socialist organizations, however, provided the communists with the opportunity to occupy the social terrain where, little by little, discontent grew as a result of the degradation of daily living conditions. This restlessness surfaced as early as September 1940 in the shape of sporadic wildcat strikes in the great Walloon industrial basins. These actions were very quickly controlled by the PCB which, little by little, mixed social and national claims with the hope of wresting domination of the working classes from the socialists. Confronted by ever harsher repression, the workers engaged in these movements realized that the occupier was an even more redoubtable adversary than the bosses. It is hardly surprising, then, that this campaign came to a head in a large-scale strike which began on 10 May 1941. This action, which lasted more than a week, involved many thousands of workers, particularly in the town of Liège, where tensions with the occupier, but also between socialists and communists, ran high.[7]

The invasion of the Soviet Union by Germany on 22 June 1941 completely changed the outlook of the PCB. There were no longer any ambiguities. With the party pursued by the occupier, and spurred on by the Kremlin to attack the enemy from behind, the PCB now made the struggle for the liberation of Belgium its absolute priority. The PCB was, however, aware of its marginal position in the Belgian political landscape. This prevented it from gathering under its own flag the ever increasing number of opponents to the occupation regime. As a result, in autumn 1941 the party launched the 'Independence Front' (FI).[8] The movement dressed itself in the cloak of patriotism in the hope of bringing together all resistance initiatives, but only partially succeeded in this. The various networks created before the war in the context of the struggle against fascism, coupled with the voluntarist state and populist characteristics of the organization, allowed it to attract many willing individuals from the moderate left. The organized socialists, however, like the patriotic right, kept their distance.

At the same time, a section of the patriotic right was wooed by a grouping that came, on this occasion, from certain military milieus. From its beginnings in the autumn of 1940, the Belgian Legion, which espoused an extreme nationalist 'belgicist' ideology, did not regard the fight against the occupier as an objective. Characterized by authoritarian ideals, the Belgian Legion considered itself an elite body which had the self-ordained task of protecting the King from attack by the communists, the Rexists and the Flemish nationalists in the event that the Reich gave Belgium a limited form of autonomy. The inanity of this position, and the growing popular irritation with a regime perceived as ever more oppressive, slowly transformed the Belgian Legion into an opposition movement which would provide support to the Allies as the liberation approached.[9]

* * *

By now the principal elements of the resistance were in place. But at the beginning of 1942 it comprised only a few hundred groups concentrated above all in the large cities of the country and the industrial regions of Wallonia. It slowly developed so that by the summer of 1944 it covered the entire territory of Belgium and numbered between 100,000 and 150,000 participants. Different elements contributed to this development.

First of all, in a state with democratic traditions like Belgium, people were generally speaking not prepared to embark on a 'shadow' war in the immediate aftermath of defeat. As a result, it took many months for resistance to develop into a clandestine organization capable of carrying out actions that could genuinely do damage to the invader. The huge numerical superiority of the enemy meant that, from the outset, all initiatives of this type were particularly difficult. It is easy to understand why, from the very start, the resisters relied on the logistical support of the Allies on the other side of the Channel.[10]

From the summer of 1940 the British, aware of the benefits of co-operation with the 'interior forces', sought to make alliances with the first opposition cells, who tried in vain to make contact with 'London'. In contrast, the Belgian State Security Service, which had been set up in the British capital in November 1940, only sent its first agent to Belgium in June 1941. The Belgian State Security Service did not, furthermore, establish permanent contact with the networks established on the ground until the end of 1941.[11] The inefficiency of the Belgian State Security Service at the beginning can in large part be explained by the lack of interest in the resistance shown by the Belgian government-in-exile. Matters began to change from the second half of 1941 with the development of closer contacts between the Belgian exiles in London and the British government, who were happy to rely on individuals with a perfect knowledge of the terrain. From that moment onwards the Allied missions, which became more and more frequent, gained in efficiency.

From the summer of 1942, however, the Belgian State Security Service and the second section of the National Defence Ministry, together with SOE, were in open opposition. The Belgian State Security Service was supported by the leading members of the Belgian government-in-exile, and linked to the SIS, while the Second Section was theoretically in charge of the collection of military information. The SIS and SOE clashed over issues of strategy, such as the question of whether information gathering should prevail over action. There were also issues over efficiency, with the failure of a large number of attempts carried out from the spring of 1941 onwards by SOE to set up sabotage cells in Belgium.[12] The conflict between the Belgian State Security Service and the second section, in other words between civilians and the military, was of a political nature. The Belgian State Security Service wished to exercise control over all the missions decreed by the military for fear that they might support a resistance of the extreme right, which would favour a system where strong powers would be invested in the King.

The consequences of these misunderstandings were catastrophic. From August to November 1942, the Belgian government broke all links with the SOE, leaving many agents on the ground without any contact with London. The Belgian

Legion was on the point of disappearing entirely. In the end the stand-off was won by the Belgian State Security Service which became from then on the obligatory point of contact between the British and the resistance networks and movements in the occupied country. The Second Section, renamed the Second Bureau, had to content itself with information supplied by the Belgian State Security Service and the business of planning missions relating to military action. In essence, it only had powers over the Belgian Legion.

In 1943 lines of escape were consolidated, and above all information services, thanks to the frequent deployment of operatives and radio officers equipped with transmitters. Furthermore, from 1943 onwards, a greater amount of experience, enhanced coordination between the Belgians and the British, an increased willingness to engage in armed actions and, above all, the priority given to supporting resistance organizations on the ground in accordance with the potential assistance they could provide to Allied landings, all considerably enhanced the efficiency of military style missions. Indeed, from the beginning of the summer of 1943, agents who had been parachuted into Belgium provided precise instructions for close-working relations, and money for the principal resistance movements. These same agents, or others, enabled dozens of weapons drops in the spring and summer of 1944. Some of them attempted to coordinate the actions of the largest organizations at the heart of a National Committee for the Coordination of the Resistance, but the split between the FI and the Secret Army – the new name for the Belgian Legion – caused the project to fail.

Generally speaking, the co-operation between Belgians based in London and the British, and in particular the nearly 300 agents sent to the occupied country, were from 1942 onwards a precious source of help to the resistance organizations. Nevertheless, the resistance fighters themselves frequently claimed that they were not listened to and above all not given sufficient materiel assistance by London.

While it was essential for the resistance, this exterior support was not enough to move these opposition groups out of their marginal position. A certain degree of agitation may be observed after the introduction of the Star of David for the Jews and their deportation in the summer of 1942. However, the Jews' concentration in four Belgian cities – Antwerp, Brussels, Charleroi and Liège – and above all their already marginalized position in Belgian society ensured that such measures only provoked a very minor reaction. The introduction from 1942 of compulsory labour in Germany elicited a response of an entirely different order.[13] Once the first period of shock was over, a vast movement of civil resistance was set in motion, organized by the large resistance movements, in particular the FI, but also by various traditional sections of society, such as the Young Christian Workers. Their aim was to encourage young males, the principal victims of the forced labour measures, to go into hiding and provide them with material assistance. From the summer of 1943, this activity was co-ordinated by the Socrates mission, which had been put in place by agents sent by the Belgian government-in-exile in London.[14] Assisted financially by Belgian industrialists and financiers, Socrates employed the services of the FI and other resistance organizations, but above all traditional Catholic and socialist networks, to distribute funds to the roughly 40,000 young people who avoided the call. At a general level, the inclusion of a certain number of these young people in clandestine organizations and above all the large amount of solidarity required to come to the aid of many thousands of people on the run contributed greatly to an enlargement of the resistance base, which from then on spread to the countryside and to the forest areas.

The increasing number of people who joined the active resistance owed a great deal to the growth in anti-German feeling and to popular hatred of the collaborators. As the occupation regime grew harsher there were mounting problems and privations, as well as ever more cases of repression organized by the occupation forces working together with Belgians on their payroll. These factors led to large numbers of patriots and/or anti-fascists joining the struggle. Finally, it goes without saying that the evolution of the international situation from the end of 1942 onwards, and in particular the events that heralded the eventual demise of the Third Reich – the Soviet victory in Stalingrad at the beginning of 1943, the Italian capitulation in the summer of 1943 and, above all, the landings on the Normandy beaches of June 1944 – further encouraged people to join the clandestine organizations.

The arrival of new blood did not, however, radically change the power struggles at the top of the resistance which were described above. At the end of the occupation there was still an array of organizations dominated by the lower and middle French-speaking bourgeoisie, the group of organizations gravitating around the FI, and the equally powerful Secret Army. Put simply, the significant expansion of the FI and AS meant that they represented the broad spectrum of public opinion, with the FI on the left and the AS on the right.

Indeed, the French-speaking bourgeoisie were over-represented in the roughly 20,000 Belgians who participated in information gathering. But for obvious reasons pertaining to the accessibility of information, numerous employees in the public administration, in the telephone and telegraph sector and above all in the railways were also involved. Information on the displacement of troops and weapons, the identification of potential bombing targets (aerodromes, factories, centres of communication) as well as the description of the results obtained by the bombing, were of precious importance to the British. The thirty-seven information networks that were officially recognized after the war were also useful to the Belgian government, which thus accrued many economic and political benefits in preparation for the post-war period. Of these networks, four – Luc-Marc, Zero, Clarence and Bayard – had more than 2,000 agents.[15]

The sociological profile of the thousands of Belgian resisters has not been studied in detail. It is known, however, that the most important escape line, Comet, which from August 1941 to spring 1944 came to the aid of around 700 aviators, had among its 2,000 members a relatively high number of nobles and young women. Generally speaking, the aristocracy had a noteworthy presence in the resistance, above all in the movement's more military style elements as well as in the information and escape networks.[16] Women were less involved except when, as was frequently the case among the bourgeoisie, they were relatively emancipated vis-à-vis their husbands or fathers, and to the extent that they stuck to the relatively traditional roles of assistance and liaison. One can perhaps better understand the role that they played in Comet for these reasons.[17]

Originating in the autumn of 1940 from within the lower and middle French-speaking bourgeoisie, the Belgian national movement (MNB) had, like the FI, the ambition to become a mass organization involved in all types of resistance activities. It was active above all, however, in the areas of the clandestine press, information gathering and providing assistance to people who were on the run. Impressed by the large numbers of recruits to the resistance (15,000 members were officially recognized) and by its professionalism and devotion to duty, the Belgian government-in-exile in the autumn of 1943 hoped to make it one of its principal points of reference for maintaining order at the time of the liberation. But a wave of arrests carried out in the upper echelons of the MNB in February 1944 deprived it of a large number of its key players, and prevented it from later playing the role that the government-in-exile had initially assigned to it.[18]

Conversely, the FI had by the liberation become the mass movement hoped for when it had been set up. That said, two factors mitigated the apparent success of the PCB. First, if the FI was relatively well established in Brussels and in the Walloon industrial basin, it was much less so in the rural regions to the south of the country and above all in Flanders.[19] Secondly, the renewal of the party leadership, which had been regularly decimated, was not fast enough to ensure sufficient control of the movement. This was particularly the case from the spring of 1943, a period when the FI attracted more and more women and men from different backgrounds and when the PCB was frequently ravaged by waves of arrests. Of the many different elements in the FI, two were particularly visible in September 1944, the Patriotic Militias and the Belgian Partisan Army (with respectively 22,000 and 13,000 recognized combatants).

Originating at the end of the summer of 1941, the partisans began with small sabotage attacks. From the spring of 1942, these actions developed further – including a campaign of strikes against collaborators which continued to grow until the moment of liberation. From the autumn of 1942 the partisans began to attack the members of the army of occupation, a development that the occupier could not tolerate. From then on, the number of hostages, chosen from arrested partisans suspected of communist sympathies, increased.[20] In order to avoid the loss of its best forces, the PCB decided to suspend attacks against the invader. In exchange, the Germans decreased the number of executions. But the relentless pursuit of the partisans continued. The aggressive enquiries of the SS-Police, between the spring and the summer of 1943, led to a vast raid, the effects of which were felt at the top of the partisan command and in the PCB.

The PCB and the partisans put in place new leaders at the end of the summer of 1943. From then on the partisans increased the number of sabotage acts and other attacks throughout the country. These were carried out despite the constant repression and the lack of equipment – only three weapons drops were made by the Allies in the period. Indeed, the majority of the 850 killings of collaborators were carried out by these forces.[21] Nevertheless, the partisans never constituted a mass movement: even close to the liberation, they were an elite group whose main function was to support the organization that was supposed to represent the armed population, the Patriotic Militias (MP). This body, which only really took on this guise in June 1944, recruited the majority of its members from the ample resources of the FI. The MP initially had a strong Walloon element,[22] which was quickly erased by a Belgian communist party keen to present a pro-Belgian image. The MP supported partisan-style operations from 1942 onwards, as well as non-violent forms of engagement, an example of which was the establishment of an organization that provided aid to the families of the victims of repression. This was called Solidarity and it officially affiliated itself to the FI in November 1942. From then on, thousands of men and, above all, women committed themselves selflessly to the collection and distribution of funds to the relatives of FI resisters captured by the enemy.

Propaganda was another activity widely carried out by the FI. Thousands of members mobilized to compose, print and/or distribute the roughly 150 newspapers that were either directly or indirectly linked to the FI. A further hundred or so newspapers were produced by the Committees for Trade Union Struggle (CLS), which were linked to the movement. As with the numerous papers claiming a direct link to the PCB, the FI clandestine press also encouraged direct action and ferocious attacks on the collaborators. In contrast, the other half of the 700 prohibited journals that were printed during the occupation, products of the moderate left or right, supported less violent forms of resistance (assistance to illegal operatives, collection of information); furthermore, they trusted the post-war justice system to carry out a firm, yet controlled, purge of collaborators.

While it did contain a number of discussions about the future organization of society, the clandestine press sought from the very start to boost the morale of the population and to counteract German propaganda. The press also helped recruitment to the nascent formations. Written mostly in French, these papers, which appeared above all in Brussels, only usually appeared once a month and rarely comprised more than a few pages. Moreover, they were rarely printed, so each issue did not often exceed 1,000 copies. Finally, the dangers linked to production and above all distribution frequently led to the dismantling of the production teams. Only twenty or so clandestine papers survived the entire course of the occupation.[23]

In addition to propaganda and assistance to families, the FI committed itself from the end of 1942 to the fight against deportation. From the spring of 1943, following the appeals to the young workers not to go to Germany, the FI set up assistance committees for those avoiding forced labour. From the summer of the same year, the Socrates mission was subsumed into the movement. But just as it was on the point of taking charge, the FI was obliged by the Belgian notables who financed Socrates to adopt a relatively minor role.

The MP attempted to maintain its own network for gathering and distributing funds for the draft evaders, with the clear aim of keeping them under their control until an insurrection could be launched. But this was not enough to turn the MP into the large-scale organization that its adherents hoped it would become. First, many draft-dodgers simply refused to get involved in the action; secondly, movements like the AS had superior leaders and were better equipped to attract those who wished to prepare for battle. Essentially, the majority of members of the MP were members of the FI who had previously been involved in non-violent forms of activity. The lack of means and of men, the instructions from London to remain cautious and the rapid liberation of the country all limited the involvement of MP members in the armed struggle and deprived the PCB of a decisive bargaining chip at the moment that the Belgian authorities regained control of the country.

The PCB also created other organizations under the control of the FI, such as the CLS. Launched at the beginning of 1942, the CLS encouraged workers and employees to claim better work conditions, but also to rail against the occupier. Their patriotic gestures and actions of protest (diffusion of slogans, production-line sabotage and strikes) attracted the sympathies of large numbers of workers who had been sorely tested by the occupation and deprived of any contact with an efficient socialist trade-union organization. In the Walloon industrial basins they even threatened the socialists' control.[24] Indeed, the socialists were not heavily involved in direct acts of resistance. They preferred to concentrate on drawing up a plan of future reforms, and negotiating a social security plan with State representatives, employers and Catholic trade unions. Concerned not to lose too many of their best people, they essentially fought the Nazi regime by producing and distributing clandestine newspapers, and by supporting the Socrates organisation.[25] This strategy was only likely to be politically profitable after the war was over, but the CLS disappeared in the storm that carried off the PCB once peace was established.[26]

Finally, after the large-scale Jewish round-ups of summer 1942 in Antwerp and Brussels, some communist Jews and some left-leaning Zionists decided to join forces to assist those who had avoided deportation and created the Committee for the Defence of the Jews (CDJ). People from all walks of life joined this organization which was, from the beginning, affiliated to the FI. This allowed for the development of a multitude of contacts which helped gather funds, make false documents and offer shelter to people on the run. The CDJ helped save several thousand Jews, including more than 2,000 children.[27]

The FI was thus the main creator of a humanitarian resistance which, in addition to the families of political prisoners and clandestine resisters, helped many French soldiers who had escaped from Germany, huge numbers of Russian and Polish prisoners, tens of thousands of draft-dodgers and around 30,000 Jews who, with its help, escaped certain death.

Before moving on to the military resistance, and in particular the Secret Army, it is useful to discuss an atypical movement, the G Group. With its origins in the anti-fascist milieus of the Free University of Brussels, and with the support of the Belgian authorities in London, this elite group, with 4,000 recognized members, was led by outstanding individuals. It began in the autumn of 1943 and developed methodically and efficiently, taking hold of some rail and waterways, as well as some power sources. Despite relatively little external support and, above all, the loss of 20 per cent of its members during the struggle, it carried out its mission until the arrival of the Allies, and even managed to increase its acts of sabotage on railway lines following the Normandy landings.[28]

G Group was joined in its activities by the Secret Army (AS), the most fully developed movement on the eve of the landings (54,000 recognized members). The AS, however, had a chequered history. The desire to contribute to the liberation of the country and the quality of the leadership established in the summer of 1941 allowed the group to grow until the spring of 1942. But wave after wave of arrests from the summer of 1942 to April 1943, linked to a lack of experience in clandestine combat, almost annihilated the organization. It was disavowed in autumn 1942 by the Belgian authorities in London, who suspected it was an instrument for reinforcing the power of the King.

Some leaders, however, did escape from the German police. Their efforts to rebuild the movement were henceforth encouraged by the government-in-exile in London which, in summer 1943, sent it both instructions and funds. Even greater sums were provided, beginning in March 1944. In the same month, the first drops of arms and explosives took place since the first wave in May 1943. In total, from the beginning of 1943 to the liberation, 1,789 containers full of military materiel were dropped.[29]

Now protected from financial problems and with a relatively rich arsenal at its disposal, the AS also enjoyed a permanent radio link with London from May 1944. The following month, on the instructions of the Belgian government, it began a series of actions against the road, rail and communications networks used by the German army. The AS thereby contributed to the increase in sabotage attacks throughout the country. The number went from 100 to 250 per month from September 1943 through to May 1944, when such attacks were primarily the work of the partisans and G Group, to between 400 and 600 per month from June to August 1944. These attacks went a long way to increasing the occupier's difficulties.[30]

As the liberation approached the AS harried the enemy with a series of guerrilla actions. During the first fortnight of September, the AS provided precious assistance to the advancing Allies by carrying out numerous liaison missions and flushing out small pockets of German resistance. The AS contributed, together with the FI and the National Royalist Movement (a group even further to the right than the AS),[31] to the rapid liberation of the town and above all the port of Antwerp, the only Atlantic port to be recaptured virtually intact from the Germans.[32]

With its military backbone, the AS recruited from all levels of society, even if the workers who joined it were less numerous than they were in the FI. Moreover, its development in Flanders was remarkable given that the struggle arrived there later and was fought with less intensity. Indeed, several reports drafted by the Belgian Secret Service in London during the course of the occupation lament the lack of resistance activity in Flanders. The statistics for armed actions by region back up these claims, since 72 per cent took place in Wallonia, 14 per cent in Brussels and only 14 per cent in Flanders. Finally, several analyses underline the under-representation of the Flemish in the resistance as compared to the Walloons or the Brusselians. While they constituted 54 per cent of the Belgian population, they only provided around a third of the resisters.[33]

The Flemish had little interest in anti-fascism before the war – indeed they were more taken in by authoritarian and corporatist ideas at the time. Above all, the Flemish seemed to have more difficulties than the people of Brussels and the Walloons in fighting for a Belgian nation for which they had suffered and made great sacrifices during the First World War, and which, as far as many of them were concerned, refused to give them what they felt was legitimately theirs, or else gave it grudgingly.[34]

That said, during 1943 and above all 1944, the resistance acquired considerable capital throughout the Belgian population, which was increasingly exasperated by the rigours of the occupation. Yet despite everything, the resistance was a minority phenomenon, encompassing no more than 2 to 3 per cent of the population of 'resistance age' (roughly 16 to 65 years). The truth is that the real risks involved required courage – or a spirit of adventure – which not everyone possessed; furthermore, the clandestine style of existence, which many of those who actively opposed the occupier were forced to adopt, had considerable consequences for working and family life. It is understandable why it was a phenomenon that affected above all men from 20 to 40 years of age, more desirous of distinguishing themselves, more invested with a strength of mind, more impulsive – perhaps more careless even – than their elders, and less restricted by domestic grind than women of the same age.

Among the resisters was a sizeable proportion of foreigners, particularly in the markedly anti-fascist organizations. Furthermore, the middle classes were over-represented. This can perhaps be explained by their high level of involvement in democratic life. By extension, state employees were more involved than other workers, perhaps because the workers themselves felt less directly threatened by the establishment of a new order. Furthermore, in the business world, the social struggle seemed, for evident reasons of survival, to be more significant than the patriotic struggle. The worsening of living conditions increasingly attributable to the occupier and the deportation measures brought in from October 1942 did, however, persuade more and more workers to get involved in the struggle. The agricultural workers, lastly, only started to intervene from 1943, the year in which more than 10,000 figures – Allied airmen, Russian prisoners, Jews, resistance fighters on the run and above all draft evaders – left the cities where informers were rife and difficult to pick out from the crowd. From the miserable conditions in the cities, they moved to the countryside, which was far more secure and better able to provide them with what they needed.

The case of the peasants underlines the fundamental importance of the concept of utility.[35] Since, essentially, involvement demanded great sacrifices, it had to be seen to be profitable for the common good. In particular, it had to meet the principal aspiration of the majority, which was to see the country liberated. And in the first years of the occupation at least, the majority of Belgians did not see the point of gathering information for some hypothetical liberators, nor could they conceive how distributing the clandestine press might contribute in a tangible way to a favourable outcome for the conflict.

Nevertheless, several thousand people judged the 'civil action' of the movements sufficiently useful to be worth the risk of participation. Utility does not therefore constitute an absolute value, it has a subjective quality also, which reflects a political culture. Thus, the communists acquired a wide experience in the interwar period in different activities that were relevant to resistance (propaganda, solidarity and even certain forms of violence such as street confrontations) which were aimed at contesting the powers that be. It was therefore entirely natural that they used these methods to attempt to unite the population against the occupation and destabilize it. Conversely, it was much more difficult for those who were generally associated with running the country to go against the automatic response of submitting to the established order. In order to do this, it was necessary for the planned act of resistance to have a legitimacy which could make it appear almost legal in their eyes. The support for the draft avoiders developed by the socialists and the Catholics clearly fell into this category. Furthermore, the experience gained during the First World War by some members of the francophone bourgeoisie in terms of the clandestine press, escape lines and information gathering eased the path to illegality among those who belonged to this section of society. As far as the military were concerned, when they were not disconcerted by the passivity of their supreme commander, the King, they were only capable of preparing large-scale battle plans. This was a dangerous tactic in the context of the shadow war, and one which would go on to cost them dearly.

These interpretative schemes were equally valid for those individuals who, in their own way, got involved in a form of resistance that they considered to be useful. If many Belgians helped the Jews, Allied airmen or draft evaders, it is undoubtedly because such actions required simple skills, involving familiar values (charity or fraternity) and leading to a result that was immediately understood. That said, the will to act is frequently thwarted by circumstances. Thus, after the Normandy landings, there were many people who felt it was useful to take up arms to help the Allies drive out the occupier. But the Germans' strike power, the density of the population and the lack of available weapons meant that the majority of the leaders of the movements urged these resistance novices to play the waiting game.

Essentially, how does one become a resistance fighter in such a basically urban, complex and densely populated society?[36] Commitment went from individual to individual, on the basis of mutual trust: either the person concerned asked his acquaintance to join the organization, or vice versa. The links that, initially, brought together the two protagonists could be family related or professional, associational, political, religious or trade union-related ones, or simply a matter of being neighbours. Most frequently there was a trial period during which, by means of minor tasks, the 'resistance capacities' of the new member were tested. If the results were convincing – the key criteria were organizational skills and resourcefulness, courage, sangfroid, discretion and prudence – and if the person accepted taking greater risks, then more significant activities were given to him or her, such as active participation in a sabotage attempt or escorting an Allied airman.

A relatively large number of resisters managed to maintain a fairly normal life, either because they simply restricted their activities or because they acted within their own work environment. This was the case, for example, with railway workers, postal employees, people who worked in administration or policemen. These were professionals who were regularly asked, because they were very useful in terms of assistance to those who were on the run, to gather information and/or get involved in armed actions. For other resisters, the days were frequently exhausting: either they combined their professional and their resistance activities, or, once they had gone underground for fear of being captured, they gave themselves entirely over to resistance. The clandestine fighters did not, generally speaking, have an exciting life. They were almost always required, for reasons of security, to spend most of the day and night alone. Furthermore, most of their time was taken up by difficult transfers from one place to another, either on foot or using other means of transportation such as bicycles, trams or trains, or else they were engaged in paperwork. All these tasks were necessary because of the danger the enemy, potentially lying in wait at every rendezvous, represented.

It is worthwhile recalling that everyone, from the individual who gave shelter to an airman to the head of a network, lived in justifiable fear of being arrested, tortured and killed by the occupiers, or by those who collaborated with them. In fact, around one in four resisters ended up in captivity, and one in eight died. Either they were executed or, more frequently, they perished from exhaustion or illness in a concentration camp. In absolute figures, that means that more than 30,000 combatants fell into the hands of the enemy and more than 15,000 of them did not have the chance to enjoy peace and liberty when they were re-established.

The evolution of the pattern of arrests confirms the initial slow development of clandestine combat (less than 5 per cent of the resisters who were arrested were captured before the end of 1941), and its increasing intensity from 1942 onwards (the number of resisters apprehended in this period is five times that of 1941). By 1944 the struggle was very harsh, and more than half of the cases of imprisonment took place during the course of the last eight months of the occupation. This explosion in incarcerations was not only due to intensifying levels of confrontation, but also to the way that the struggle evolved. Indeed, if the forms of non-violent resistance – propaganda, assistance to those on the run and information gathering – continued to develop, this growth was nothing compared to the increase in armed actions – sabotage, attacks on individuals and requisitions – which, granted, had started from a relatively low base in 1942. The German authorities estimated that there was one act of sabotage every three days at the beginning of 1942. This figure rose to three a day at the end of 1942, ten a day from the autumn of 1943 and peaked at twenty-five a day in the summer of 1944. Involving greater risks, this type of activity was also subject to more severe repression by an enemy that increasingly had its back against the wall.

It is therefore not surprising that if the workers seemed to commit themselves less and later to the resistance than the middle classes, their tendency to choose outright struggle means that they were subject to greater repression. In contrast, women (around 15 per cent of the participants), who were for most of the time restricted to courier work or to dealing with supplies, were less frequently apprehended than the men (one in five rather than one in four). Above all, the death rate was much lower for them (between 2 and 3 per cent as compared to 10 per cent for their male comrades).[37]

*   *   *

Despite its many forms, the resistance did not leave behind anything more than a very modest legacy. Its reputation was tarnished by violent excesses – unjustifiable attacks and thefts with personal motives – which were often committed by peripheral groups. Furthermore, its image suffered from the artificial inflation of its numbers at the moment of liberation, as well as from some miscalculations and blunders committed at that time.[38] Lastly, the activities of the resistance during the occupation were, in September 1944, largely unknown to the majority of the population who recognized the role of the Allied troops in liberating their country.[39]

More importantly, the resistance was foreign to the majority of the population for whom that sense of symbiotic co-operation, which was evident at the end of the occupation, was only short-lived and transient because it was solely linked to the struggle against the invader. The weakness of the political legacy of the resistance can also be explained by the insignificant position it occupied in the strategy of the three pillars of Belgian society, namely the Catholic, Socialist and Liberal parties.[40] Without any political conduit – after a brief electoral success in 1946, the PCB collapsed in 1949 – and also frequently divided, the resistance movement had many difficulties in getting its voice heard in the immediate post-war period.[41]

The defeat is, in fact, abundantly clear to those elements that had hoped to profit from their investment in the resistance so as to participate in a radical transformation of society. This is clearly the case for the communists, particularly those in the FI. Encouraged from Moscow, they committed themselves whole-heartedly to the struggle against the occupier, to the extent that they were the principal organizers of clandestine combat from the summer of 1941 to the D-Day landings. But they also lost a large number of their best people along the way. At the most, given its brief popularity, the PCB was able to function as a stimulus to those sections of society who in a way saw themselves obliged by the communists to proceed with important social reforms following the liberation.

The partisans of the extreme right, those who had been behind the creation of the Belgian Legion and later the National Royalist Movement, found themselves, in the face of impending Allied victory and the population's distaste for authoritarian regimes, having to moderate their political programme. They also were forced to ally with the conservative right, notably the Secret Army, in order to counteract the rise of the left. This belgicist extreme right managed, despite everything, to preserve some precious assets in time for the liberation. Its 'wait and see' style of participation in the resistance had cost comparatively few lives, and left it relatively intact while at the same time acquiring a certain aura of respectability.

That said, among the pioneering currents of the Belgian resistance, there was at the end of the conflict one clear winner, the French-speaking middle-class patriots. Despite the concessions granted in social and, undoubtedly, linguistic terms, they managed to obtain what they had fought for, the re-establishment of an independent and united Belgium, built on liberal principles, and in which the francophone elite maintained an important place.

Translated by Philip Cooke.

Notes

1. For an excellent discussion of the precise meaning of resistance, see Pierre Laborie, 'L'idée de Résistance, entre définition et sens: retour sur un questionnement', in *La Résistance et les Français: Nouvelles approches* (*Cahiers de l'IHTP*, no. 37) (Paris, 1997), 15–27.

2. There is only a limited historiography on the Belgian resistance. See Fabrice Maerten, 'L'histori-ographie de la Résistance belge. A la recherche de la patrie perdue', in Laurent Douzou (ed.), *Faire l'histoire de la Résistance* (Rennes, 2010), pp. 257–76. For general studies, which although a little dated are still useful, see above all Henri Bernard, *La résistance 1940–1945* (Brussels, 1969); George K. Tanham, *Contribution à l'histoire de la résistance belge 1940–1944* (Brussels, 1971); the section dedicated to the resistance in Etienne Verhoeyen, *La Belgique occupée. De l'an 40 à la Libération* (Brussels, 1994), pp. 331–511; Peter Lagrou, 'Belgium', in Bob Moore (ed.), *Resistance in Western Europe* (Oxford, 2000), pp. 27–63; Fabrice Maerten, 'La Résistance en Belgique, 1940–1944', in *Le fort de Breendonk. Le camp de la terreur nazie en Belgique pendant la Seconde Guerre mondiale* (Brussels, 2006), pp. 33–59; Herman Van De Vijver, Rudi Van Doorslaer and Etienne Verhoeyen, *Het Verzet (2)* (Antwerp/Amsterdam/Kappellen, 1988).

3. For a perceptive account of the demographic geography of Belgium between the two wars see C. Mertens, *La répartition de la population sur le territoire belge. Etude de démographie sociale* (Louvain-Brussels, 1946). For the socio-political aspects see Emmanuel Gerard, *La Démocratie rêvée, bridée et bafouée* (Brussels, 2010).

4. On occupied Belgium see Jules Gérard-Libois and José Gotovitch, *L'An 40. La Belgique occupée* (Brussels, 1971); Verhoeyen, *La Belgique occupée*; and, above all, the two recent edited collections: Mark Van den Wijngaert (ed.), *België tijdens de Tweede Wereldoorlog* (Antwerp, 2004); Paul Aron and José Gotovitch (eds), *Dictionnaire de la Seconde Guerre mondiale en Belgique* (Brussels, 2008).

5. On the question of values see the analyses in Jean-Marie Guillon and Pierre Laborie (eds), *Mémoire et histoire. La Résistance* (Toulouse, 1995), and also in *La Résistance et les Français. Nouvelles approches*. Their ideas have been applied to the Belgian case in Fabrice Maerten, 'Le poids du souvenir de 14–18 dans l'engagement résistant durant la Seconde Guerre mondiale. Le cas du Hainaut', in Fabrice Maerten, Jean-Pierre Nandrin and Laurence van Ypersele (eds), *Politique, imaginaire et éducation. Mélanges en l'honneur de Jacques Lory* (Brussels, 2000), pp. 89–125.

6. On the PCB during the occupation, see José Gotovitch, *Du rouge au tricolore. Les communistes belges de 1939 à 1944. Un aspect de l'histoire de la Résistance en Belgique* (Brussels, 1992); idem, *Du communisme et des communistes. Approches critiques* (Brussels, 2012), in particular part 3, 'Guerre, clandestinité, résistance', pp. 201–316.

7. On the strike of May 1941, see José Gotovitch, 'La grève des 100.000', in *Jours de lutte* (*Jours de guerre*, 7), (Brussels, 1992), pp. 91–100; Dirk Luyten, 'Stakingen in België en Nederland, 1940–1941', *Cahiers d'histoire du temps présent*, no. 15 (2005), 149–76.

8. On the composition of the FI, see also José Gotovitch, *Du rouge au tricolore*.

9. On the Belgian Legion and the Secret Army see Victor Marquet, *Contribution à l'histoire de l'Armée secrète* (6 issues) (Brussels, 1991–5).

10. On this support see Emmanuel Debruyne, *La guerre secrète des espions belges, 1940–1944* (Brussels, 2008), in particular the chapter 'Les rapports avec Londres', pp. 107–224; M.R.D. Foot, *SOE in the Low Countries* (London, 2001); Verhoeyen, *La Belgique occupée*, in particular the chapter 'Les liaisons secrètes avec Londres', pp. 425–511.

11. For an encyclopaedic overview of the various Belgian networks see Fernand Strubbe, *Services secrets belges, 1940–1944. Allemagne, Belgique, Espagne, France, Luxembourg, Pays-Bas* (Brussels, 1997).

12. See Etienne Verhoeyen, 'L'heure des saboteurs', in *Jours de lutte (Jours de guerre,* 7) (Brussels, 1992), pp. 72–89.

13. On this policy and its consequences for the resistance see *Le travail obligatoire en Allemagne 1942–1945* (Brussels, 1993).

14. See Etienne Verhoeyen, 'Le gouvernement en exil et le soutien clandestin aux réfractaires', in *Le travail obligatoire en Allemagne,* pp. 133–64.

15. See Debruyne, *La guerre secrète.*

16. See Marie-Pierre d'Udekem d'Acoz, *Pour le Roi et la Patrie. La noblesse belge dans la Résistance* (Brussels, 2002).

17. See Etienne Verhoeyen, 'La ligne d'évasion Comète (août 1941–février 1943)', *Jours mêlés (Jours de guerre,* 11-12-13) (Brussels, 1997), pp. 161–80.

18. On the MNB, see above all George K. Tanham, *Contribution à l'histoire,* pp. 51–9.

19. For an example of FI operations in industrial Wallonia see Fabrice Maerten, 'Le Front de l'indépendance comme instrument du Parti communiste dans le Hainaut en 1940–1944. Entre réalité belge et rêve soviétique', *Annales du Cercle d'histoire et d'archéologie de Saint-Ghislain et de la région,* Vol. 11 (2008), 437–518.

20. On this issue see, for example, Maxime Steinberg and José Gotovitch, *Otages de la terreur nazie. Le Bulgare Angheloff et son groupe de partisans juifs, Bruxelles, 1940–1943* (Malines, 2007).

21. On the attacks see José Gotovitch, 'Quelques réflexions historiques à propos du terrorisme', in *Réflexions sur la définition et la répression du terrorisme* (Brussels, 1974), pp. 15–24; Jan Laplasse and Karolien Steen, 'Het verzet gewogen. Een kwantitatieve analyse van politieke anslagen en sabotages in België, 1940–1944', *Cahiers d'histoire du temps présent,* no. 15 (2005), 227–62; Antoon Vrints, 'Patronen van polarisatie. Homicide in België tijdens de Tweede Wereldoorlog', *Cahiers d'histoire du temps présent,* no. 15 (2005), 177–204.

22. The Walloons who were most critical of the Belgian nation state identified with the 'Free Wallonia' movement, whose power bases were above all in Brussels and Liège. The principal activity of this organization was the publication of clandestine press hostile to Flanders, accused of monopolizing the levers of the State. On the resistance groupings in Wallonia see Marie-Françoise Gihousse, *Mouvements wallons de résistance, mai 1940–septembre 1944* (Charleroi, 1984) and Chantal Kesteloot, 'Belgique, Wallonie, Flandres: les identités déchirées du Mouvement wallon', in Christian Bougeard (ed.), *Bretagne et identités régionales pendant la Seconde Guerre mondiale* (Brest, 2002), pp. 353–68.

23. On the clandestine press see José Gotovitch, 'Presse clandestine en Belgique, une production culturelle?', in Bruno Curatolo and François Marcot (eds), *Ecrire sous l'Occupation. Du non-consentement à la Résistance France-Belgique-Pologne 1940–1945* (Rennes, 2011), pp. 97–114; *idem,* 'Photographie de la presse clandestine de 1940', in *Cahiers d'histoire de la Seconde Guerre mondiale,* no. 2 (1972), 113–56 José Gotovitch (ed.), *Guide de la presse clandestine de Belgique* (Brussels, 1991); Fabrice Maerten, 'De sluikpers in bezet België', in *Tegendruk. Geheime pers tijdens de Tweede Wereldoorlog* (Gand/Brussels/Antwerp, 2004), pp. 72–87.

24. See José Gotovitch, 'Les relations socialistes-communistes en Belgique sous l'occupation', in Etienne Dejonghe (ed.), *L'occupation en France et en Belgique 1940–1944* (Villeneuve d'Ascq, Vol. 2, 1988), pp. 809–32.

25. On the socialists during the occupation see Chantal Kesteloot, 'Du désarroi à l'engagement. Les socialistes et la clandestinité', in *Jours gris (Jours de guerre,* 9) (Brussels, 1993), pp. 35–47; and José Gotovitch, 'Ruptures et continuités: personnel dirigeant et choix stratégiques socialistes de la clandestinité à la Libération', *Socialisme,* juillet–août (1984), 305–20.

26. On this trade-union rivalry and its outcome see Rik Hemmerijckx, *Van Verzet tot Koude Oorlog, 1940–1949. Machtsstrijd om het ABVV* (Brussels/Gand, 2003); idem, *Le mouvement syndical unifié et la naissance du renardisme* (Brussels, 1986).

27. On the CDJ see Maxime Steinberg, *L'étoile et le fusil. La traque des Juifs 1942–1944* (Brussels, 1986), Vol. 1.

28. See William Ugeux, *Le Groupe G (1942–1944). Deux héros de la Résistance: Jean Burgers et Robert Leclercq* (Paris/Brussels, 1978).

29. Verhoeyen, *La Belgique occupée*, p. 423.

30. On the development of sabotage during the occupation see Laplasse and Steen, 'Het verzet gewogen'.

31. See Francis Balace, 'Le thème autoritaire dans la résistance belge – de l'"ordre national" au "retour à la démocratie"', in *Les courants politiques et la Résistance: continuités ou ruptures?* (Luxembourg, 2003), pp. 335–64.

32. See Victor Marquet, 'La sauvegarde du port d'Anvers', in *Cahiers du Centre de recherches et d'études historiques de la Seconde Guerre mondiale*, no. 13 (1990), 149–218.

33. Jan Laplasse and Karolien Steen, 'Het verzet gewogen', p. 255; Fabrice Maerten, 'Les courants idéologiques et la Résistance belge – Une adhésion limitée', in *Les courants politiques et la Résistance*, pp. 319–21; Fabrice Maerten, 'La Résistance en Belgique, 1940–1944', p. 36.

34. On these differences in the levels of commitment to the resistance between the Flemish and French-speaking Belgians see, above all, Emmanuel Debruyne, *La guerre secrète*, in particular pp. 269–82; Laplasse and Steen, 'Het verzet gewogen'; Fabrice Maerten, 'L'impact du souvenir de la Grande Guerre sur la résistance en Belgique durant le second conflit mondial', in Laurence van Ypersele (ed.), *Imaginaires de guerre. L'histoire entre mythe et réalité* (Louvain-la-Neuve), pp. 303–38; Patrick Temmerman and Bert Boeckx, *Deportatie en verzet, een eerste globale statistische analyse op basis van de erkenningsdossiers Politieke Gevangenen* (Brussels, 1995).

35. The reflections that follow are based on Fabrice Maerten, 'Les courants idéologiques et la Résistance belge – Une adhésion limitée', in *Les courants politiques et la Résistance*, pp. 302–34 ; and on Olivier Wieviorka, 'A la recherche de l'engagement (1940–1944)', *Vingtième Siècle*, no. 60 (1998), pp. 58–70.

36. See above all José Gotovitch, 'Quelques aspects de la vie quotidienne d'un clandestin', in *1940–1945. La vie quotidienne en Belgique* (Brussels, 1984), pp. 228–35.

37. The information on the sociological aspects of the resistance and on its repression are mostly drawn from Emmanuel Debruyne, *La guerre secrète*; Fabrice Maerten, *La Résistance politique et idéologique dans la province de Hainaut pendant la Seconde Guerre mondiale (mai 1940–septembre 1944)*, 3 vols (Mons, 1999); Fabrice Maerten, 'La Résistance, une école d'émancipation pour les femmes? La réalité nuancée du Hainaut belge', in Robert Vandenbussche (ed.), *Femmes et résistance en Belgique et en zone interdite (1940–1944)* (Villeneuve d'Ascq, 2008), pp. 165–98; Temmerman and Boeckx, *Deportatie en verzet*.

38. See Francis Balace, 'Les hoquets de la liberté', in *Jours libérés II* (*Jours de guerre*, 20), (Brussels, 1995), pp. 75–132.

39. See José Gotovitch, 'Communistes et résistants: les (en)jeux de dupes d'une libération', in *Jours de paix* (*Jours de guerre*, 22-23-24) (Brussels, 2001), pp. 49–100; and Geoffrey Warner, 'Allies, Government and resistance: the Belgian Political Crisis of November 1944', in *Transactions of the Royal Historical Society*, 5th series, no. 28 (1978), 45–60.

40. See Fabrice Maerten, 'Les courants idéologiques et la Résistance belge – Une adhésion limitée', in *Les courants politiques et la Résistance*, pp. 302–34.

41. On this period see Martin Conway's excellent recent study, *The Sorrows of Belgium. Liberation and Political Reconstruction, 1944–1947* (Oxford/New York, 2012).

Guide to Further Reading

Conway, Martin, *The Sorrows of Belgium. Liberation and Political Reconstruction, 1944–1947* (Oxford/New York, 2012).

Lagrou, Peter, 'Belgium', in Bob Moore (ed.), *Resistance in Western Europe* (Oxford, 2000), pp. 27–63.

Chapter 3

The Czech Lands

Christina Vella

When Hitler invaded Czechoslovakia, there were already local officials in place at every level of administration who could be charged with enforcing the dictates of the new government. The intricate administrative system of the Czech lands was thus taken over completely. The Germans did not have to spread their men across every farm and factory in the country to see that requisitions were met. The Czech officials, schooled in following orders, did it for them, unhappily but diligently. As a result, a relatively small number of German officials and soldiers were able to impose a harsh regime on a civilized and democratic country, putting out Czech resistance almost as soon as it appeared. Even as they lost the war, the Germans tyrannized the Czech population by using the well-organized bureaucracy already in place before the occupation.

These Czech bureaucrats were not collaborators, except in the sense that, after the occupation, everyone who worked, worked for the Germans and was therefore helping them. There were more Germans than ever in the country by the end of the war, as the Czech *Festung* became the last refuge of German soldiers and settlers retreating into the region. The overwhelming majority of Czech officials, from the district inspector checking identity cards to the Czech jailers, were hostile to the Nazis. But the Czechs took their occupational duties seriously. The men at the highest levels in particular were dedicated to fulfilling their public service obligations, above the political fray. To the Czech bureaucrat, service to the state was a duty, irrespective of any political regime, a duty to be performed sometimes reluctantly, but always reliably.

Resistance existed, nonetheless, in scattered pockets throughout the long years of occupation. The pattern for resistance movements in Bohemia, France and elsewhere was to begin with civil disobedience – demonstrations, protests, strikes, boycotts and other forms of passive resistance – then to focus on gathering intelligence, abetted by the governments-in-exile. Only toward the war's end did these resisters move to paramilitary action and partisan warfare.[1] Except for one dramatic act of resistance directed and executed from abroad, Czech resistance until 1944 consisted mainly of gathering intelligence. When the end was finally in sight, when the Germans were in retreat, the notion of an organized uprising again took shape among the resisters; but before the underground leaders could carry it out, the rage of the population all over the country broke out in fierce, futile, unarmed attacks against the departing occupiers. The Germans, their weapons still intact, were able to crush the climactic popular revolts just as they had stamped out the brush fires of resistance throughout the occupation. From the beginning to the end of the war, active resistance in Czechoslovakia was thus sporadic and largely ineffectual. But covert hostility toward the occupiers was consistently intense.

* * *

Czechs did not need Hitler's invasion to make them dislike Germans; Czech-German enmity was centuries old. As an unwilling part of the Austrian Empire, the Czechs were a subject people held in contempt by the German-speaking ruling class. During the First World War, many conscripted Czechs deserted the Austro-Hungarian Army and formed their own army. The Czechoslovak Legion developed into a huge volunteer force of perhaps 100,000 that fought with the Entente in the hope that Austria's defeat would bring about national independence for Czechs. Their wish was granted by the peacemakers in 1918 when the independent Czechoslovak Republic was carved out of the defeated and dismembered Austrian Empire. Many of the legionnaires joined the new Czechoslovak army, and virtually all maintained an old-boy network that would become a resistance nexus when Hitler came to power.

Czechoslovakia emerged from the First World War a first-class economic power, having inherited 70 per cent of the industrial production of the vast Austro-Hungarian Empire. The country retained its historic natural barrier against Germany, the Sudeten Mountains, and with it the Sudeten Germans – some 3 million Bohemians and Moravians scattered on the country's border rim. These descendants of Germans were traditionally pro-Austrian. But with the rise of Hitler, the great majority identified with the newly powerful Reich. They were German in their hearts and tongues, though their eyes may never have seen the Fatherland. Their relationship with the Czechs had until this point been that of master and servant. They generally considered all Slavs inferior to all Germans, and hated living under a new government of their former servants.

The Great Depression of the 1930s was harder on the German-speaking minority in the country than on the Czechs, and caused a huge surge of resentment against the Republic.[2] By the time Hitler occupied the Rhineland in 1936, it was obvious that he intended to shatter the Treaty of Versailles. The Sudeten Germans, as well as German speakers outside the mountain area, were not entirely homogeneous, being somewhat diverse in religion and comprising, moreover, a handful of Social Democrats, Communists and anti-fascists. But the vast majority of German-speakers supported Hitler and willingly absorbed his propaganda. They were pleased to hear that they were part of a closed community of Germans who did not need to recognize national frontiers or citizenship. With Hitler's invasion of Austria in 1938, Germany completely surrounded the historic provinces of Bohemia, Moravia and Silesia and controlled Czechoslovakia's north–south trade lines. Hitler was by then as popular in the German-speaking areas of Bohemia and Moravia as he was in Germany. He was sending regular financial subsidies to the Sudeten proto-Nazis and fomented demonstrations in which thousands of them demanded incorporation into the Reich. In

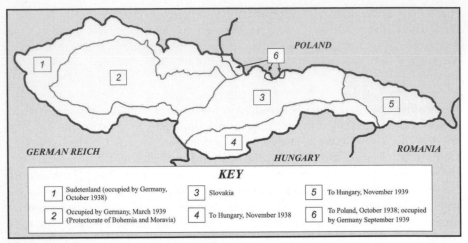

The dismemberment of Czechoslovakia, 1938–9.

vitriolic speeches Hitler screamed that he would no longer tolerate Czecho-slovakia's 'oppression' of its German-speaking minority. In the wake of one such violent speech on 12 September 1938, the followers of Konrad Henlein, the leader of the Sudeten German Party, staged demonstrations in which his fol-lowers poured into Bohemian towns, shooting policemen, breaking up Jewish shops and trying to seize public buildings. Britain and France, frantic to prevent a situation that would draw them into war with Hitler, urged the Czechoslovaks to accede to every German demand.

This was the famous Munich crisis, in which Hitler threatened to attack Czechoslovakia unless it surrendered the Sudeten territories to Germany, a demand that Britain and France pressured President Edvard Beneš to accept, finally presenting it to him as an ultimatum on 21 September 1938. The Germans had five armies massed on the frontier, prepared to attack Czechoslovakia. On 23 September, the Prague government decreed general mobilization and the sleeping streets throughout the country were suddenly alive with thousands of conscripts hurrying to their regiments. The entire army, 40 divisions and 1 million men, was moved into place, ready if necessary to face Hitler alone, without allies. The senior military staff was passionately opposed to giving in. The chief officers of the army went to Prague and demanded that Beneš reject capitulation. 'They entreated, threatened, begged, some wept,' according to Beneš' own account.[3] If ever there was a country angry enough for war, it was Czechoslovakia in September 1938. As soon as people heard about the Western ultimatum, they gathered in the squares, and the numbers swelled into massive demonstrations of tens of thousands demanding war. 'Give us weapons! Give us weapons,' they shouted.[4] The government left Prague on 27 September, expecting the city to be bombarded that very night.

There was to be no fight, of course. Beneš was called back to Prague a few days later to receive an ultimatum not from Germany alone, but from four powers together, France, Britain, Italy *and* Germany. They had met in Munich without him and decided that if Czechoslovakia refused to surrender the Sudeten territories, thus 'provoking' a war with Hitler, France and Britain would consider themselves absolved from their treaty commitments. The Czechoslovak army could have held out against Hitler for three months, according to the calculations of its generals, or six weeks according to cooler estimates.[5] Beneš reasoned that war would come anyway, with or without the sacrifice of millions of Czechoslovak lives. He made the agonizing decision to give in, a capitulation that haunted him for the rest of his life. He and his cabinet went into exile in Western Europe, eventually establishing a government-in-exile in London.

Germany moved unopposed into the fringe of the Bohemian lands containing mountain approaches and fortifications. The Germans came into possession of a huge endowment of war materiel and a strategic geographic advantage on both their western and eastern fronts. The eight territories in Bohemia and Moravia in which the ethnic Germans were settled were separated from each other by broad belts of land peopled by non-German speakers, so that the Sudeten areas did not form one administrative or economic pocket. The Czechs, Slovaks, Jews and anti-Nazi Germans in the region – perhaps a million people – fled at once to what was now called the 'rump' republic, leaving their property to be confiscated by the Germans. The countries around Czechoslovakia, observing its vulnerable situation, took the opportunity to seize territory with German approval. The Poles took the Teschen district; the Hungarians took 5,000 square miles of Slovakia.

The Munich Pact that permitted this German invasion was broken in just six months when, in March 1939, Hitler marched into Bohemia and Moravia and declared the country a protectorate of the Reich, an occupation that the rump republic, deprived of its fortifications, was powerless to resist. Slovakia, with less materiel to provide to the Germans, was not occupied. It was declared independent – independent, that is, of the Czechs – and became a German satellite.[6] Czechoslovakia disappeared from the map of Europe. Emil Hácha, the elderly and fragile judge who replaced Beneš, was retained as state president in Bohemia and Moravia, the hesitant and unwilling instrument of Hitler's Reich Protector, Konstantin von Neurath.[7] Karl Hermann Frank, a leader of the Sudeten German Party, exercised disproportionate control over security matters. Frank, altogether fiercer than Neurath, was his rival for the post of Reich Protector.

The Czechs in this new Protectorate government were not ministers in the usual sense. They exercised almost no authority in political affairs, yet were constrained to carry out German orders: expropriating Czech property, harassing the Czech intelligentsia and Germanizing the rest of the population. Whether or not an official was a true collaborator, willingly executing the Nazi directives, was a question that was still open after the war, when many people, including the hapless President Hácha, were carelessly accused of collaboration. Hácha appointed General Alois Eliáš prime minister of the non-ministers. Respected in diplomatic circles, Eliáš was personally acquainted with Reich Protector Neurath, whom he had met abroad. They communicated with each other in French, which perhaps kept Neurath in mind of the world beyond the aberrant Reich. Eliáš was a former French legionnaire, warm, urbane, 5 feet 8 inches of cosmopolitan civility, devoted to his wife and their pet monkey. He was the highest ranking of the Czech officials carrying out German orders. He was also one of the most prominent members of the secret resistance that had already begun to take shape among former legionnaires and former officers of the now dissolved Czechoslovak army.

* * *

In those early days, no obvious division separated the Czech nominal government – those Czechs whose every move was watched by the Nazis – from the resistance. At that time, the lines between collaboration and resistance were blurred, since the same people sometimes participated in both. The officials considered themselves a government temporarily in captivity. There was no body of active collaborators in Czechoslovakia as there was in France or Norway, no significant pro-German group except among the Sudetens. But neither was there widespread determination to oppose the regime among the general population. Certain individuals who became highly placed in the new government were indeed out-and-out collaborators, such as Emanuel Moravec, the Czech 'quisling'; but they did not represent the harassed majority of Czech officials.

In the view of Eliáš and the wiser heads among the former military officers, there could be no question now of taking on the occupiers with the remnants of a disbanded and crippled army, nor of planning futile uprisings. The role of the resisters was to gather intelligence and smuggle it abroad, and to wait for a war that would at first be fought by others. The Germans could not permanently occupy Czechoslovakia; war would eventually come. Unlike many of his fellow resisters, Eliáš foresaw that it would be a long war, requiring the military forces of both the Soviet Union and the United States to defeat Hitler.

The Nazi-Soviet Pact, announced in August 1939, put Eliáš and all Czechs into collective shock. It seemed that Czechoslovakia's only remaining friend had struck a deal with its killer. Dismay would change to relief later on, in June 1941, when Hitler discarded the neutrality pact and attacked the Soviet Union.

When the German occupation began in 1939, the anger of the Czechs was directed almost as much against the appeasers as against the Germans – an impotent rage against supposed allies who had left Czechoslovakia to its fate. But as the shock of invasion wore off, the Czech public began to react. Several mass resistance organizations formed. Foremost among them was ON (Obrana Národa), Defence of the Nation, which had at its core a group of former army officers. Though they probably should have known better, these military men believed that Germany would be defeated as soon as France and Great Britain decided to take up arms; therefore, they did not set up their group on the basis of having to exist in secret for a prolonged period. They kept files, met almost publicly in such places as coffeehouses, made up lists of their members and hatched far-fetched plans for igniting a mass revolt against the occupiers.

One of the main leaders of ON, General Sergej Ingr, was himself prudent and might have disciplined his cohorts; but he was in exile after June 1939.[8] Ingr was part of a generation of intense and dedicated army officers who found themselves thrust into the middle of political crises. Ingr escaped just before the Gestapo uncovered ON. Practically all of its members were arrested and eventually executed. ON had been the largest resistance group in Europe, yet in a matter of months in 1939 it was shattered by the Germans. As one member was arrested and tortured, he implicated another, until nearly all of the members of the organization had been tracked down. General Zdeněk Novák remained above ground, working as a brewing executive, and secretly tried to rebuild ON. The organization was never entirely wiped out, but kept reappearing as the few individuals left after each Nazi strike regrouped. Despite the German efforts to be thorough, every series of arrests left at least one former member free; that individual in time recruited others.

* * *

The war that the Czechoslovaks were praying for finally broke out in September 1939, when the Allies responded to Hitler's invasion of Poland. The Czech public now gathered in large demonstrations that were ostensibly patriotic or religious commemorations. Some of these rallies were spontaneous, others were planned by newly forming resistance organizations. Often the crowds numbered 100,000.[9] Besides boycotting the propagandist Protectorate press, Czechs succeeded in acquiring smuggled transmitters. The underground sent thousands of cables to London, providing the Allies with information about troop and supply movements, war production and all sorts of vital intelligence that could only be uncovered by people inside the country.

There was no single centre of the resistance, then or later. Underground groups sprang up here and there through the cracks in the Nazi system. Like ON, some were large organizations loosely connected to each other through individuals who were active in several groups. Some examples of these organizations were PÚ, Political Centre, a centrist group; PVVZ, and their coordinating committee, ÚVOD.[10] The Communist Party, KSČ, stood a little apart from the others, taking its orders from Moscow and changing its strategy in accordance with Stalin's shifting attitude toward the Allies. All of the resistance organizations, eventually even the communists, recognized President Beneš as the country's leader and the voice of free Czechoslovakia, a voice the Czech public heard regularly and riskily over the BBC. Even the communists accepted Beneš, who was still the most respected Czech statesman in Europe. He remained, for lack of a better alternative, the best representative of the national will among those who had some rapport with Stalin. For the most part, military people continued to nurse their plans for a popular insurrection that would overthrow the Nazis, while ordinary people, if they did anything at all, attended huge, apparently submissive, gatherings. Except for these patriotic displays, the Czechs adopted an attitude of 'Get along, don't provoke repression'.

With the outbreak of fighting, the Nazis ended even mild challenges to their authority. On 1 September 1939, simultaneously with the declaration of war by the Allies, the Germans arrested no fewer than 2,000 Czech public figures – a drastic and sobering crackdown.[11] People huddled around their radios each night as if gathering for prayer. They reinserted the device in their radios that the occupiers had required them to remove, the 'Churchill' that enabled them to hear short-wave broadcasts. For fifteen cherished and illegal minutes they listened to the BBC, which in June 1940 carried the astonishing news that France, too, had collapsed – France, which they had counted on to make all the difference.[12]

For all their plaintive brevity, these broadcasts were the breath of life to the Czechs, whether they were in hiding, listening in barns and cellars or living normally. People took frightful risks to listen to the BBC in Czech, though what they heard were the impersonal voices of men in comfortable studios, men who had only a vague notion of the sufferings of their audience. Prokop Drtina, secretary to President Beneš and one of the leaders of the Political Centre when he left for London in 1939, became one of the most popular of all Czech commentators on the BBC, using the name Pavel Svatý.[13]

While Hitler sought a reckoning, or at least an advantageous peace, with Britain, the Gestapo was sweeping through various organizations in the Protectorate. It attacked Sokol, a gymnastic organization with overtones of patriotism, something like the Boy Scouts but more nationalistic, which had been a natural centre of underground activity. Nearly 1,000 Sokol members were arrested; within 8 months, only a few were still alive. By the second year of the war, thousands of Czech breadwinners were in Gestapo prisons and thousands of others had fled the country to avoid arrest, leaving their families without any income.

The Nazis had created something called National Solidarity, an official political movement that was to replace the old party system. It was the only legal outlet for political expression. A huge majority of the male voters joined it as a way of showing more solidarity than the Nazis had bargained for. Prime Minister Eliáš saw to it that Jaromír Appel, a Sokol member, was on the central committee. Together with a few confidants, Appel funnelled relief to the families of prisoners, either through private donations or public funds that could be secretly diverted. Appel avoided arrest until 1941 and even then survived three interrogations by the Gestapo.

Another helpful official was Jaroslav Mezník, appointed the provincial president of Moravia in 1940, with access to certain moneys.[14] Alois Šilinger, a communications expert and former Czech legionnaire, helped the resistance acquire and set up transmitters. At first there was the Sparta network of eleven transmitters which sent some 20,000 intelligence messages until it was destroyed in 1941.[15] Šilinger became the head of telephone service maintenance on the Slovakian border, where he could move freely all over the district. Being able to talk to many people without arousing the suspicions of the Germans was important; hence, the resistance tried to recruit postmen, bartenders, salesmen, butchers, bus drivers and bus mechanics, dentists, doctors – especially doctors inside the prisons – and clergymen.[16] But even as various resistance groups were forming, they were being devastated by arrests. No large body could remain secret for more than a year before its members were rounded up, one by one. Time and again, fragments of shattered organizations would regroup and attempt to rebuild, only to be smashed in a new round of repression.

On the anniversary of Czech independence on 28 October 1939, the Czech underground organized a massive anti-German demonstration. It resulted in a confrontation with the police and the death of a student, Jan Opletal. That student's funeral the following month became the occasion for more rallies in Prague. Hitler decided he had had enough of demonstrations. He closed all Czech universities, and nine student leaders, picked at random, were shot without trial. During the temporary absence of Neurath from the country, Frank ordered the arrest of all students living in dormitories; 1,200 were deported to concentration camps.[17] Having concluded that Neurath was protecting the Czechs too much, Hitler removed him. But instead of replacing him with Frank, Hitler appointed as Acting Reich Protector the feared chief of Germany's Security Police, Reinhard Heydrich.

* * *

With Heydrich's arrival in Prague on 27 September 1941, the occupation moved into a new, ruthless phase.[18] Heydrich declared martial law and placed the entire country under a curfew that was to last four months. Summary courts were the main instruments of the terror he now imposed. A trial in a summary court had only three possible outcomes: the defendant was either acquitted, sentenced to death or sent to a concentration camp. Between the summer of 1941 and the end of the year, 10,000 people were arrested including thousands of Czech Communists. Every resister in prison, subject to interrogation, meant much greater danger for those still free. People who found out they were wanted for questioning immediately went into hiding.[19]

Over 100 crimes now qualified as capital offences – listening to foreign broadcasts, consorting with Jews, possessing guns of any type, failing to turn in an unregistered person, speaking against the occupation. Under such tight restrictions, anyone could be found guilty of so-called resistance. Every day in the yards of dormitories that were being used as jails, Czechs with bloody faces were shot and hanged. Boxes appeared on the front pages of the newspapers giving the names of people who had been sentenced to death, some twenty a day – peasants, journalists, captains and colonels. Among them – one of the first announced by Heydrich the day after his arrival – was Prime Minister Aloys Eliáš, charged with high treason, though his death sentence was not carried out immediately.

One of the most effective controls the Germans employed was requiring everyone to register his address. To live anywhere in the Protectorate without registering at a district office or gendarmerie station was to be an enemy of the Reich. Anyone who was not wanted by the police thus had an identity card, though sometimes a way was found to get a false one for a resister. A district office distributed the identity cards. A worker might manage to smuggle out a blank one, though the officials counted the cards as they were printed and counted them again as they were handed out to the applicants. Discovering that a resister had a false card meant exposing the worker in the office who had provided it.

Living without an identity card meant being without a ration card as well, so that the family sheltering the resister had to share their meagre rations or engage in illicit black-market trading. People who harboured a fugitive were shot, together with their families. Moreover, anyone who failed to turn in an unregistered person might also be executed. It was impossible simply to live outdoors: villagers were assigned to patrol the woods. In the towns and villages, the cottages were thin-walled and close together, so that it was not easy to keep someone hidden in a bedroom or attic. Anyone who gave the smallest help to a resister became a resister, too. He would be just as dead after his captivity as if he had plotted to kill Hitler. Once someone aided a resister – allowing him to sleep for one night in his barn, for example – he could never again feel safe. If the resister were caught, he might be tortured to reveal every link in his underground survival, every bit of assistance no matter how trivial, going back months and months. One arrest generally meant death for dozens of people.

Nevertheless, after the war it turned out that some well-known individuals had helped the underground, such as Cyril Musil, a famous Czech ski racer, who hid several unregistered fugitives. Funds had been donated to the resistance by several quite prominent men.[20] Families that considered themselves somewhat above the general community around them were sometimes the most willing to give shelter – men such as Jaroslav Kobylka, mayor of the town of Kadolec. They considered it fitting that they should do what average people would not.

Whenever the Germans encountered reverses in the war, instead of concentrating solely on the main battle, they reacted by tightening the occupation. This seemed ironic to many observers. The military front was the theatre where the German system would either live or die; the resistance could only harass the German government. Yet at crucial moments during the war, the Germans squandered their men and resources in keeping stricter control of the subject populations. Czechs could be arrested for not covering their windows sufficiently during a blackout; concealing a few scraps of leather or cloth; holding back a little something that was requisitioned. Because of Heydrich's controls, life was fraught with terror, not only for genuine resisters, but also for average Czechs who were simply trying to get along. In order to eat, many people traded on the black market – exchanging a dress for a little meat, swapping a child's toy for a few eggs. Since everybody was doing it, it seemed that one could get by with it; but it was impossible to be sure. There were continual executions of so-called black marketeers. Country people had to register their livestock and were required to deliver a certain quantity of meat, eggs and dairy products at certain times. Every farmer and villager kept some animals illegally, despite knowing that the authorities would show up now and then with the official goose or pig list and compare it to the tails they counted in the yard. If a family ate something at home that was severely rationed, they had to worry about the children making a comment at school that would arouse suspicion. Every life was scored with constant small lies, compromises and anxiety.[21]

Martial law was lifted in January 1942. From the German perspective, Heydrich's policy of controlled severity – harsh punishment for resistance, but not pushing the Czech population to the point of rebellion – was working; the country appeared to be pacified. Heydrich reorganized the administration so that German agents transferred a great deal of routine business to their Czech counterparts. The Germans acted merely as inspectors and supervisors of the Czechs. By the end of 1942, over 350,000 Czech administrators worked under the control of a mere 738 Germans in the Office of the Protector and another 1,146 who sat in various Czech agencies.[22] Heydrich's mission was complete; he apparently was ready to move on to another occupied country, possibly France. However, on 27 May 1942, exactly eight months after his arrival in Prague, a bomb was thrown into his car and Reich Protector SS-Obergruppenführer Reinhard Heydrich was killed.

Heydrich's assassination was Czechoslovakia's most sensational act of rebellion, but it was not carried out by the home resistance. The murder was planned and implemented by Czechs abroad, an assassination ordered by Beneš because the President wanted some dramatic demonstration of the strength of the Czech resistance. The British, acting on the advice of František Moravec, trained, equipped and transported two Czech agents who were dropped into the Protectorate in December 1941.[23] The assassins delayed their mission for five months, during which time their supporters in the Czech underground figured out what they were up to. The home resisters then urgently cabled Beneš, pleading and demanding that the assassination plan be cancelled because of the 'immeasurable' German retaliation it would provoke – but they were ignored.[24]

Beneš sometimes made controversial decisions; this one, to kill Heydrich, aroused criticism as well because of the violent retribution that was bound to follow. Just as the home resisters predicted, the Germans went into a frenzy of revenge, placing the whole country again under martial law. Before Heydrich had quite expired, Hitler ordered that 10,000 Czechs, primarily intellectuals, be taken hostage and 100 shot immediately. One by one, in 5,000 villages and towns, German police went from house to house searching for suspects. Though the bomb had been the work of only a handful, thousands of Czechs were arrested during the next 6 weeks, and over 1,000 executed, including the imprisoned General Eliáš.[25] The searches flushed out hundreds of men in hiding, but the slaughter was particularly directed against intellectuals and former army officers who were still free.[26] All of the security apparatus was brought to bear, both the Czech gendarmes stationed in the countryside, and the regular police in the cities – all under strict Nazi supervision.

At the height of the terror, the Germans burned down two villages, Lidice, not far from Prague, and Ležáky.[27] By that time seven paratroopers, including the two Czechs who were ordered by the London government to kill Heydrich, had died in a Prague church where they were cornered. In the face of the brutal retaliation, the British tardily renounced their participation in the Munich Pact – a classic example of 'too little and too late.'

*   *   *

After Heydrich's assassination, all hope – what there was of it – for rising up against the German occupiers lay with Slovakia. Its fascist government was closely monitored by the Germans; however, because Slovakia was not occupied, the resistance had more freedom to operate there than in the Czech lands. As in the Protectorate, one centre of the resistance was the army. It had not been disbanded in Slovakia, and still contained possible confederates who could smuggle heavy weapons to the Czechs. With these, the Czechs hoped to harass the rear of the German army as the Russians approached the Protectorate from the east. A former legionnaire and artillery major in the defunct Czechoslovak army, Jan Moravanský, was by then head of ON, living legally near Prague. His group was at first called Slezák, then later the Tau. It was eventually subsumed into the Council of Three. In 1942, Moravanský had a list of 1,400 former soldiers still living legally, 600 of whom he thought, optimistically, would respond if called to an uprising.

But who was there to lead such a revolt? By 1943 the underground was almost barren. Nothing remained of the large resistance organizations except a few scattered and frightened followers without leaders. Josef Grňa, a former professor of finance, was surviving underground and made contact with some of the military resisters also in hiding. These connections – between Grňa and a general, for example – were arduous undertakings involving a dangerous 15- or 20-mile walk, each man following a map so that the two could intersect at some ditch or tree in the middle of nowhere. People in hiding were totally dependent on those living legally to bring them news, communications and reading material, and to make contact with others in the underground. Grňa was no politician and hardly a leader of revolutionaries, but he was almost the last man standing after the retaliation against Heydrich's assassination. Another who survived the 1941–2 devastation of the resistance was Ambassador Arnošt Heidrich. He had been a frequent Czechoslovak representative at the Geneva disarmament conferences in the 1920s and a confidant of President Beneš. He avoided arrest until 1944.[28] Leopold Chmela was a chief member of the Heidrich group. He survived the war to write a book about Czech losses during the occupation. But none of these Czechs could lead an uprising.

The Germans had meanwhile destroyed all the transmitters used by the resistance. Karel Staller, a technical whiz, was the director of the Brno Small Arms Factory in 1943, and one of the few Czechs still allowed to travel to Slovakia.[29] Hiding microfilm in his shaving kit and in coins, he set up a courier route from Bratislava to Switzerland to London.[30] For over a year, the courier network organized by Staller was practically the only means of contact between the home resistance and President Beneš or between the Czech and Slovak resisters. Some of the information so perilously communicated was essential; some of it not, such as the intelligence that a new resistance group was forming around Grňa and

Vojtěch Luža, a former army division general. The London government would acknowledge the arrival of microfilm by giving a particular password or phrase in one of the BBC broadcasts. At the start of each Czech broadcast there was a string of such coded announcements: 'Erica watch. Spring is coming. Memory is watchful. The corn is growing.' The Germans, of course, heard the communications, too, but it was hoped that they could not decode them.

Radio Moscow, apparently oblivious to geography, was exhorting the home resistance to help the Russians by starting guerrilla warfare. Of all the occupied countries, Czechoslovakia was farthest from any front, too distant for either the Western Allies or the Russians to assist any partisan fighting. Broadcasts from Moscow even urged the home resistance to establish national committees, local bodies of a few cities which would represent the larger population – this at a time when any sort of meeting was a certain way to become a target for arrest. Moreover, the Czechs had no weapons with which to confront the German tanks. General Luža, for one, wanted to make contact with Colonel Theodor Lang of the Protectorate troops. Though these troops carried only light weapons, they were 10,000 strong. He had to argue down the communists in his group who scorned such 'bourgeois collaborators'.

By autumn 1943, Roosevelt, Churchill and Stalin had met in Tehran to plan the next offensives of the war. From Sicily, the Allies were progressing northward, while the Red Army had pushed the Germans back to the Dneister River, about 600 miles from the Protectorate. One would suppose that Hitler would be too busy preventing the collapse of his armies to continue the zealous tracking of unregistered Czechs, but in fact his reverses at the front were followed as usual by increased severity in the occupied land. The terror in the Protectorate was never as barbaric as in Poland, but it remained far worse than in Holland, Belgium or France. In 1944, the Germans were executing over 100 people a month in the Protectorate. Hitler continued to eliminate intellectuals and internal enemies just as if he were winning the war, even when Allied troops were at the border of the Reich and German cities were being bombed to rubble. Close observers of those years marvelled at the Nazis' security apparatus. In the stark face of annihilation, the Germans might have thrown every effort into the critical military struggle. Instead, they continued rooting out Jews, resisters and communists all over occupied Europe, probing into every classroom where contraband words might be lying about and every cellar where shortwave radio signals might penetrate.

By this time, there were finally too few Nazis to police whole populations. The Germans were turning their captured Czech victims into informers, people who purchased the lives of their loved ones with information they provided, however unwillingly. Though they might have had no heart for it, these informers were productive detectives for the Gestapo, and established entire bogus resistance organizations to attract good-faith resisters.[31] The informant system was especially effective against the communists.

Communists had been distinguished resisters in 1940 and 1941, either cooperating with the democratic resistance or vilifying it, according to their directions from Moscow. But they were largely wiped out in the two periods of martial law connected with Heydrich. The Germans were fierce toward anyone associated with communism. Their special attention to Communists thinned out the leftist population, so that it was not until late in 1944 that communist groups emerged. The attitude of the Czechs toward communism was not necessarily friendly, but it was not overwhelmingly hostile. The Communist Party had long been a part of the country's political life, just like other parties. For Czechs, there was no question that the fascists were the enemy and the Russians the probable deliverers. At the same time, the Czech attitude toward the West was deeply ambivalent, even during the war. After Munich, it was the French and British whom Czechs mistrusted, not the Russians – that is, until the communists imposed monopolistic control in 1948.

At the other end of the resistance's political spectrum was the right-of-centre PRNC, the Preparatory Revolutionary Nation Committee, preparing for the revolution that would burst forth as the Germans were retreating and the Russians were coming in. PRNC claimed to be the successor to the great resistance networks destroyed by the Gestapo in 1941. It was not a body of active resisters but rather a ramulose organization that served to put several groups in loose association. People around General Novák were among its leaders: Jaroslav Kvapil, a famous playwright; František Richter, the director of a printing enterprise and a former member of the Czech Legion, a volunteer army that fought in Russia against Austria-Hungary in the First World War – the Legion formed a kind of old-boy network that would later assist the resisters who had been part of it; Judge Emil Lány, former president for the land court for Bohemia; the poet Josef Palivec; literary critic Václav Čzerny; and the writer Jaroslav Kratochvil, who was also a member of the communist underground and used his influence to get the Party to cooperate more closely with the democratic resistance. Some of PRNC's other members were Jaromír Dvořak and Josef Mainer from Pilsen and Kamil Krofta, a former minister of foreign affairs. One component of PRNC was a group led by Professors Josef Drachovký, Josef Hutter and Růžena Vacek. Another component included representatives of the Czech Protectorate police, such as Bohdan Šefčik. Rudolf Fraštacký served, like Staller, as a courier. Jaroslav Krátký (Zdena), a major of the former Czechoslovak army, was sent by Beneš and Ingr to Slovakia to run secret transmitters connecting London with the main resistance groups there, and also to get information about resistance in the Protectorate. His contact in Bratislava was Rudolf Fraštacký. Zdena was eventually caught by the Gestapo and murdered in prison by the SS.[32]

The Russian parachutists who began coming into the Protectorate in 1944 taught the Czechs about *zemljankas*, a camouflaged hiding place that helped countless resisters survive that last terrible year of the war. First a hole was dug deep enough for a man to stand in and wide enough to hold a bench that could serve as a bed. Then it was walled inside with wooden planks, and a covering of earth and grass was placed over the top. The entrance was concealed in a nearby bush, some feet away.

*   *   *

It was in the dark of *zemljankas* and attics that many resisters learned of the Normandy invasion. Clearly, the Germans seemed to be losing the war.[33] The resisters had only to hold out and the nightmare would be over. Even then, the Germans squandered their resources hunting down internal resisters. While the Czechs were rejoicing over D-Day, they learned that almost the entire PRNC organization had been wiped out by the Gestapo. General Novák, who had been living legally, decided to await capture rather than flee and abandon his family to the Gestapo's revenge. Arrested during the night of 22 June 1944, he was tortured but not executed, and managed to stay alive in the Gestapo prison until the end of the war. Along with Novák, Moravanský, Colonel Lang and many others were taken. Leopold Chmela was arrested on 6 June, followed soon afterward by the capture of Heidrich himself.[34] General Novák's successor as head of PRNC was General František Bláha, who was then arrested in the autumn of 1944. Bláha's successor was General František Slunečko, who had been living underground since 1940 in Bohemia. As the Allies were closing in on the Germans, the Germans were closing in on the resistance, or so it seemed to the isolated souls trying desperately to hang on until the end. This was an illusion because resistance was actually resurging. Networks were popping up toward the end of the war almost faster than the Nazis could smother them.

The resistance could claim no authority without contact with the exiled government, and the London government could not claim to be the voice of Czechoslovakia unless it could maintain a minimum of contact. Secret transmitters were essential so that the home resistance and the exiles could communicate. The Germans, realizing this, dedicated great effort to locating and smashing transmitters. First there had been the Sparta network with eleven transmitters, which provided the Allies with some 20,000 intelligence messages until it was destroyed in 1941. Then the Czechoslovak army abroad trained special volunteers whom the British dropped into the Protectorate. These paratroopers restored communication, along with assassinating Heydrich; but by the beginning of 1943 they, too, had been hunted down. Throughout that year, the Czechs used only couriers, people smuggling messages in their clothing. However, the slow courier system was more and more impractical as the tempo of the war intensified. In April 1944, therefore, Beneš, Ingr and František Moravec, the head of military intelligence abroad, began dispatching new teams of paratroopers, fourteen in all, charged with gathering intelligence on their own and communicating information from the home resistance. Each team included at least one wireless operator with a transmitter.[35] It was difficult enough for paratroopers to land in the Protectorate and find groups to help them – the resisters were, after all, in hiding – but the transmitting itself was dangerous. The bulky transmitters had to be moved frequently lest the Germans follow the radio waves and track them down; yet the only vehicles the Czechs possessed were bicycles. Despite every precaution, the Gestapo usually located the transmitters within a few months.

With the transmitters, several important resistance groups learned of each other's existence and were able to discuss plans for an uprising. A former lieutenant colonel, Josef Svatoň, headed an organization that spread from western Bohemia into Moravia and included the remnants of ON. Another man, Josef Císař, led a very important group called Avala. Císař was living legally in Prague and had a regular job. His secret organization included the association of Czech volunteer firemen, men who could mobilize at a moment's notice and who were connected to all the other fire departments across the country. They were the only people in the Protectorate who had at their disposal both gasoline and vehicles – fire engines. The Gestapo could not quash their resistance group because firemen were too badly needed. Císař had also organized the Czech hunting societies. Hunters were spread over the whole country and, moreover, they possessed guns, which they had been allowed to keep. These two groups now joined with General Luža in what was called the Council of Three, or R3, *Rada tří* in Czech. Another supporter was Josef Ouředník, the leader of an organization south of Prague called Sázava. Luža, having been accepted by both London and the home resistance as supreme leader of the projected uprising, did his best to subsume all the diffuse groups, including a Prague association called Revolutionary Trade Unions. Luža's group was no longer a Moravian organization of a few hundred but a federation of scattered thousands.

The London government expected to direct the proposed insurrection from abroad, by use of transmitters, a method that would have been awkward and unreliable considering the tenuous position of all the various underground groups. Luža insisted that the home resistance must control the uprising, get credit for its success and organize the provisional government that would follow.[36] An insurrection was necessary even if the home resistance was not needed to defeat the Germans militarily. Without a revolt, the post-war political field would be dominated by party hacks returning from abroad. What changes were going to be made in the political system had to be made during the brief revolutionary beginning, he warned, or not at all. All the resisters except the communists assumed that at the end of the war these revolutionaries, that is, the resistance leaders who carried out the projected uprising, would take over from the defeated Germans and run the country until President Beneš returned and elections were held. It was expected that the major resistance figures would be offered ministerial positions in any post-war government. The arms for this revolution were to be seized from a storage repository and from an ammunition factory – enough weapons to arm 10,000 men.[37] The British were expected to drop weapons, and a shipment from the Red Army was also expected.

It appeared, however, that the British looked to the Russians to supply anti-German insurgencies. Perhaps the British feared that any weapons they dropped might fall into the hands of the communist allies with whom they were increasingly disillusioned. As for the Russians, having marched over 1,000 miles, they did not want to set things up so as to congratulate the Czechs on liberating themselves. Nor were they eager to take over a country with an independent army that looked to its own leaders for direction. They chose to ignore whatever expectations the resisters had in the way of arms.

In August 1944, Slovakia erupted in a protracted revolution, led by former military men and supported by both democrats and local communists. It was directed by Lieutenant Colonel Ján Golian, the head of a Slovak underground organization; he had been chosen by Beneš and the government-in-exile, in disregard of Luža's recommendation. The Czech resistance was then bombarded with broadcasts from Moscow exhorting it to follow the Slovak example and take up arms. But in September, before the Czechs could react to the Slovak situation, the Gestapo killed Ouředník and captured Luža's closest aides, shattering the entire Prague section of the organization. In October, Luža, making his difficult way toward Prague with an assistant and false identity cards, was killed by officious Czech gendarmes who, in an excess of punctiliousness, decided to double-check the identities of the two strangers passing through.[38]

* * *

That last autumn of the war marked the time when, by heart-sinking degrees, the resistance leaders realized that they could not carry out a national insurrection. Impulsive, disjointed revolts might break out – suicidal rebellions of poorly equipped and scattered groups. But the organized, massive death blow to a weakened German occupation army was a chimera. Not only did it seem to the resisters that the Allies were withholding heavy weapons, but by November the resistance had lost the only military leaders who could have used them effectively – Svatoň, Moravanský, Novák, Luža, the other generals. The Czechs watched the Warsaw Revolt that began on 1 August, just as the Red Army approached the Polish capital, and followed it to its frightful conclusion two months later – an insurrection waged in much the same way as the one various Czech underground groups were planning. They were not encouraged.

They watched the Slovakian insurrection right next to the Protectorate with the same sense of despair. The Slovak revolt had begun three weeks ahead of Golian's schedule, when the Germans ended the Slovaks' puppet rule and moved to occupy the country directly.[39] Because the uprising did not take place within their zone of operation, the British and Americans refused to provide arms to the insurgents except, towards the end, in sporadic and sparing quantities.[40] It was believed that the Russians were indifferent to the fate of resisters who owed obedience not to the Red Army, but to independent leaders. After two months the insurrection collapsed and Golian was captured and executed by the Germans. Czechs in the Protectorate knew nothing of the policies of the Allies that doomed the uprising, nor did they even know that 10,000 Slovaks had been sacrificed in that blood-drenched struggle.[41] But they did see that the uprising had not destroyed the Germans' power over the country, and that such revolts dwindled in the end into guerrilla skirmishes that had little military effect.

That autumn four main Soviet parachute groups floated down to the Protectorate – some sixty people in all – in advance of the Red Army. Though the parachute groups took the names of Czech heroes, such as Jan Hus or Miroslave Tyrš, they took their orders from the Red Army. Their task was to harass the retreating

Nazis who, followed by veritable brigades of civilian German sympathizers, were trying to get to some part of the Protectorate still occupied by Germans. German sympathizers would be ejected from Czechoslovakia after the war, in one of the transfers of populations that took place in several countries.

Partisan attacks, gnawing at the enemy at the margins of the front, became the main form of the Czech resistance from November 1944 until the war's end the following May. In the area around Brno, these attacks were carried out by various bands; there were no groups that were distinctly communist. After the war, the communists claimed to have been the backbone of the resistance; however, in the central Protectorate, it was non-communist resisters who were active.[42] This scattered partisan activity was no substitute for an armed insurrection, a fact that was proved by the failed insurrections of the Poles, Slovaks, Tito's Partisans in Yugoslavia in 1941, and even the *maquis* in France, who were fighting under more favourable conditions than the Czechs. One thing the paratroopers did accomplish was to organize escaped prisoners of war. At first these ex-prisoners were armed only with their hatred of the Germans. Some 50,000 Germans were in the Protectorate in 1944, retreating from the Allies. The partisans, now including the ex-prisoners, attacked their transports on the highways and stole their weapons; they also raided gendarme stations for their guns. The partisans would lay steel nails or a stolen steel cable across the highways (practically the only motor vehicles on the roads were German – everybody else rode bicycles). A truck would have to stop, whereupon the attackers would kill the occupants and take their weapons. They also raided gendarme stations where they typically took the small arms but did not hurt the Czech gendarmes. The Germans finally had to take away all the carbines from the gendarme stations so that they would not lose them to the resistance.

Having no consistent communication, a resistance group was never sure what other groups were doing. The partisans learned only after the war how many disparate and largely independent resistance clusters there were: 7,500 active resistance fighters, distributed in 120 groups, engaged in military or quasi-military activities, each one using or having at his or her disposal a personal weapon. In addition to these fighters, there were thousands of supporters who were outside of any structure and were not referred to as 'resisters'. The General Luža group (R3), made up of the son and followers of the murdered leader, had 856 active members centred near Brno, not counting the people who assisted them with supplies, shelter and silence. It was the most important organization within R3, which was in turn the largest organization in the Czech resistance by 1945, consisting of ten groups.

*   *   *

By late spring 1945, the guerrillas in the central Protectorate controlled the countryside, but not the towns, so that the Germans could not travel except in large groups. Still, villagers sheltering resisters and bringing them food in their *zemljankas* were putting themselves in danger. The latest Gestapo tactic was not to arrest those sheltering a resister, but to lock the whole family in the house and then set fire to it, a task they attended to conscientiously even while retreating.

The German response to the increased guerrilla activity was two-fold and effective. Karl Hermann Frank reorganized the German police force, detaching special units and placing them in every district to keep the roads safe for the German retreat. The *Jagdkommandos*, as they were called, shot and hanged partisans on the spot, including people who had only been marginally helpful to the resisters. An even greater nuisance to the partisans were the Vlasov troops – anti-Bolsheviks released from German prisoner-of-war camps.[43] By 1944 these formed an army of some 100,000, fighting at the side of Germans for the liberation of Russia from Stalin. They combed the villages looking for partisans, or helped the *Jagdkommandos* by posing as escaped Soviet prisoners and infiltrating the partisans.

The Americans were by now regularly dropping Czech parachute groups into the Protectorate, exiles who were returning to join in the final fight and bringing weapons with them. These were not the massive arms infusions the resisters wanted, but rather arms to aid the guerrilla activity – Sten guns, one or two machine guns, revolvers, plastic explosives and so on. The quantity of arms contained in the twelve drops was negligible. The deliveries were carried out, after a long bureaucratic process, by a US Army Air Force Special Group stationed in Livorno. Several delivery planes to the Protectorate were shot down, despite precise planning. The timing of a drop was signalled by code over a BBC broadcast. The weapons were packed in 300lb containers which were attached to parachutes. When they floated down, they had to be opened and divided among the partisans then and there. The partisans had to plan some means of taking the weapons away, as they still did not have cars or trucks. Though in headlong retreat, the Germans did not stand aside deferentially during these operations. Two of the paratrooper teams were struck by the Gestapo in May 1944, even as the home resisters were scrambling from one shelter to another, having to move constantly.

The Germans were being harried by free-for-all outbursts against them as they withdrew. It was not always clear whether Germans or Czechs were in control of a particular town. Once the Germans left and Czechs took over, the Germans might briefly come back to secure their line of communications, execute the new local officials who had begun setting up a post-war administration of the town and then retreat again. The front was not an obvious line with opposing armies on one side and the other, but a ragged no-man's-land where any soldiers one encountered might belong to either the Allied armies or the German army.

Throughout the war, the Czechs had heard from both London and Moscow that the home resistance, the people who were sacrificing and suffering, would form the post-war government. Long before the liberation, Beneš had decided that the survival of Czechoslovakia depended on the country's accommodation with both the Western powers and the Soviet Union.[44] But by the winter of 1944/5, as the Red Army covered more and more of Czechoslovakia, the balance between the Czech democratic parties represented by Beneš in London and the communists led by Klement Gottwald in Moscow had shifted in favour of the communists. According to the communists, they had been the predominant element in the resistance; they rewrote wartime history to exclude the activity of non-communists. By the end of the war, it was a foregone conclusion that the communists would predominate in any post-war government; but the majority of Czechs believed, along with the London government-in-exile, that the communists would follow a democratic system in Czechoslovakia.[45]

*   *   *

As often happens in the last spasms of war, the country suddenly exploded in revolt – not the organized national rebellion that the resistance had planned at the beginning of the occupation, but a spate of uprisings that erupted unpredictably in towns where the Germans were still on the way out. The uprisings were random, unconnected and ferocious. They started on 1 May in central Moravia just as the Russians were about to move in. Without waiting for the Germans to leave, people began seizing the government offices and appointing themselves the local representatives of the Czechoslovak Republic. These revolts swept the country. In some places, the rebels tried to disarm the Germans; in others, they let the Germans continue with the business of leaving. Sometimes the German commander in the region, not wanting to delay his withdrawal, ignored what was happening so long as his own forces were not molested. In others, each uprising was answered with a furious reprisal. In the middle of it all, on 30 April 1945, every radio in Europe broadcast the news that Hitler had committed suicide.

Several factors contributed to these revolts. As the Germans retreated westward, they emptied their concentration camps and transported the inmates, especially Jews, ahead of the front. Until then, the Czechs were still largely unaware of what became known as the Holocaust. Suddenly, one community after another in the Protectorate saw tens of thousands of naked, starving people packed into cattle trucks or stumbling over the hills in forced marches. They saw Germans mistreating these dying victims, who had once been Jewish teachers, housewives and schoolchildren, saw the Germans brutalizing them or shooting them without remorse. It shocked people who were past shocking, Czechs whose own relatives had suffered at the hands of the Nazis.[46]

The Moravian uprisings of late April and early May 1945 were futile – crushed in every place where the Germans responded to the provocations. Nevertheless, the fever of revolt spread to Prague on 5 May 1945. The Czech National Council, a colourless organization, had for several weeks been preparing an insurrection in the capital with the remnants of ON and other former military people. However, the mass uprising took the Council by surprise and prematurely forced the leaders into the open. Before the Council could mobilize, ordinary citizens and Protectorate policemen seized the Prague radio station and were broadcasting frantic calls to the Allies for help. The former generals František Slunečko and Karel Kutlvašr – the men who had put ON back together after General Novák's arrest – were at first the de facto military leaders calling for arms. The citizenry threw up 1,600 street barricades to paralyse German movement, barriers manned by 30,000 Czech civilians with no effective weapons. As the Germans got out of their vehicles to remove the obstacles, they were picked off by snipers. They soon learned to use Czech women and children as shields while they grappled with the barricades. The Vlasov troops that had been German collaborators now changed sides and fought alongside the Czechs. It was not manpower, however, that the Czechs lacked, but weapons. Men and women with rakes and pistols faced 30,000 to 40,000 trained fighters armed with tanks and artillery. Their battle raged for three days, broadcast all over Europe hour by desperate hour as they pleaded with the Allies to send arms.

All their appeals were ignored by the Americans, though General Patton and the Third Army were less than 50 miles from Prague. General Eisenhower steadfastly refused to allow American troops to move because Prague fell within the Soviet zone of proposed occupation. Even Beneš and the government in exile that had returned to the country and were waiting in Košice – even they were silent. As many as 2,000 Czechs were slaughtered by the Germans. The Germans, fearful of the approaching Red Army, were then induced to abandon the struggle. Anxious to evade the Russians and surrender instead to the Americans, they capitulated to the Czech National Council on 8 May and marched off to the American lines, carrying only their small arms. When the Red Army entered Prague on 9 May, they found it in the hands of the Czech National Council, a situation not at all to Stalin's liking, judging from his reaction. He refused to recognize the Council or have any dealings with it and, following Beneš' orders, the Council resigned.[47]

The war did not end sharply on 9 May in Czechoslovakia, but rather died by imperceptible degrees. The Germans moved out in orderly columns, sometimes accompanied by a tank; the Russians moved in, met by clumsy welcoming speeches and a party atmosphere in every community.[48] The next wave of the Red Army swept over the country, and the next and the next – young, child-like peasant draftees, goodhearted but uncontrollable. Their worst transgressions seemed minor compared with the brutality of the Nazis they had chased out.

The war was over. The cities were full of demolished buildings and damaged psyches. Behind each face were experiences that could never be erased. This girl had been raped. That man had been tortured. Another had lost a child in a bomb attack. It was a country of victims, one in which nobody looked forward to a new beginning. The Red Army, not local communists, had liberated the country. Except in a few places, Czech communists had not been leaders in the resistance, yet after the war they emerged as the prominent element in every administrative and political unit. The resisters allowed themselves to be outshouted by others clamouring for recognition. Soon everyone was hearing that the democratic resistance had not been important in the war, only the communists in the underground – propaganda generated from Moscow and repeated so incessantly that perhaps most people started to believe it.

* * *

The post-war government that emerged in Czechoslovakia was an appalling assemblage of old politicos, culled from the numerous and ineffectual pre-war parties, and communists. Since everything was done under the aegis of the Soviet liberators, Beneš was obliged to install communists in the crucial ministries. They ran most of the cities, appointed themselves to posts of authority at every level, and had a great deal of backstage power. The new prime minister was Zdeněk Fierlinger, formerly ambassador to the Soviet Union, a social democrat from the old pool who collaborated so closely with the communists that he earned the sobriquet 'Quislinger'. Gottwald was deputy prime minister. Thus, communist party members and spineless democrats back from exile held all the major posts.

As a sop to Beneš, the Communists agreed to the appointment of Jan Masaryk as minister of foreign affairs, the post he had held in the London government.[49] General Novák became military commander of Moravia at the end of the war. He joined the Communist Party, but fell foul of it. In 1950 he was arrested and tortured by the communists, just as he had been by the Nazis. He went to prison for six years, was rehabilitated in 1965 and died poor in 1988. As for the other resisters who were supposed to lead the new order, they were all waved aside. Non-communist resisters were characterized as anti-Soviet, and the resistance movement was described as having been split between rightists and communists. This was far from the truth. Everyone in the Czech resistance had been oriented toward the left, and those who were not communists were often Russophile. By 1947, Czechoslovakia was the last country in the Soviet sphere with a functioning parliamentary democracy; but not for long. In September, three non-communist ministers received parcels containing bombs, though all three, Jan Masaryk, Petr Zenkl and Prokop Drtina, survived the assassination attempts. In February 1948, the communists carried out a nearly bloodless coup that left them the sole masters of the country for the next forty years.

General Ingr, who had been appointed ambassador to the Netherlands, again went into exile and worked against the communists from Washington DC. Prokop Drtina, having been forced out as Minister of Justice, attempted suicide by jumping from of a window. He broke his legs and shattered the bones in his feet; after an excruciatingly painful period in the hospital he was imprisoned for many years. Jan Masaryk, whose very name was synonymous with Czechoslovak independence, astonished everyone by remaining in the Gottwald government. However, on 10 March 1948 his body was found in a courtyard of the Czernin Palace. He had either jumped or been pushed out of a third-floor window. Purges began – of the press, universities, civil service, sports clubs – in which people who were not overt communist sympathizers were expelled from their offices and consigned to disagreeable jobs. In particular, arrest warrants were issued for people who had been prominent in the resistance, that is, the people who had demonstrated a capacity for leadership that would make them magnets for anti-communist activity.

This time there could be no question of going underground and trying to survive until the end of the war, for there was to be no war. All of the resisters who could not transform themselves into obsequious communists tried to become invisible. Many went into hiding and were captured. Others managed to flee to the West, where they passed their lives in exile. The post-war years turned into the Cold War years. Their dreams of returning to their country gradually faded.

* * *

Many of those who sacrificed their lives in the resistance, especially intellectuals and military men, had no real choice as to whether to fight the occupation. They were persecuted whether or not they participated in anti-German activity. Others were sucked into the resistance when they could not turn away a hunted friend. Still others were drawn into the resistance by their very upbringing and the humanitarian ideals instilled in them. Separately and collectively, the resisters were inconvenient pests that the occupiers dispersed or destroyed in deadly waves, again and again. Despite their immense sacrifices, the resisters did not defeat the Germans in Czechoslovakia, nor hasten the end of the war, nor prevent the communist takeover of their country. To the dictators, they were a persistent nuisance – no more. It is only in the long view that the resisters can be seen as victors.

Nazism, which held Europe in terror, is nowhere a dominant force. Communism, which misshaped millions of lives and controlled whole continents, has collapsed in Europe. But liberal democracy, what most of the resisters fought for in the Czech lands, has finally, manifestly, won. On the palimpsest of history, where all stories eventually fade and are replaced by newer tragedies, the resisters, along with all those who fought the dictators – they alone – are remembered with respect.

Notes

1. See Jørgen Hæstrup, *European Resistance Movements, 1939–1945* (Westport, Conn., 1981).
2. The factories for consumer and export products – chinaware, textiles, goods that no one at home or abroad could afford any longer – were located in the German territories, whereas the Czechs were occupied in heavy industries that were not so hard hit.
3. Edvard Beneš, *Mnichovske dny (Days of Munich)* (London, 1955).
4. For an account of one such demonstration in Brno, see Radomir Luža and Christina Vella, *The Hitler Kiss: A Memoir of the Czech Resistance* (Baton Rouge, Lou., 2002), p. 20.
5. Of the extensive literature on appeasement, two readable studies are Martin Gilbert and Richard Gott, *The Appeasers* (London, 1963); John W. Wheeler-Bennett, *Munich: Prologue to Tragedy* (New York, 1964). A standard work is Boris Celovsky, *Das Münchener Abkommen 1938* (Stuttgart, 1958).
6. For Germany's subsequent policy toward Slovakia, see Jörg K. Hoensch, *Die Slowakei und Hitlers Ostpolitik* (Cologne, 1966).
7. See papers of Radomir Luža, Hoover Institute Archives, Stanford University.
8. Beneš in London had secretly dispatched him to Paris to act as ON's representative abroad.
9. Luža and Vella, *The Hitler Kiss*, p. 27.
10. PVVZ was literally the Committee of the Petition 'We Remain Faithful', named after a manifesto published before the Munich Conference.
11. To alleviate the manpower shortage, Czechoslovak students were required to work as labourers for six weeks during the summer.

12. The fall of France in June 1940 meant that all the representatives of the Czechoslovak liberation movement abroad became centred in London. Beneš was prominent among the many exiled chiefs of state who gathered there. The British allowed him to establish a government-in-exile.
13. He became Minister of Justice in the post-war Czechoslovak government and was arrested by the communists in 1948.
14. He was arrested in autumn 1941 and brought to the Kounic Student Home, which the Gestapo was using as a jail. Afraid of the torture that was in store for him, he committed suicide by leaning out of his cell between the bars and shouting so that a sentry shot him.
15. Consistent transmitter contact was not re-established until 1944; Luža and Vella, *The Hitler Kiss*, pp. 139ff.
16. *Ibid.*, pp. 54–7, 108ff.
17. The universities did not reopen until after the liberation of the country. The repression in the Protectorate coincided with a much larger terror campaign in Poland, in which the intelligentsia was again a particular target.
18. President Beneš ceased communicating with the home government, though not with the resistance. The Czech cabinet in the Protectorate was no longer any help to the resistance. President Hácha had become so ill that, by the winter of 1942–3, he would not even be able to sign his name; see Robert Gerwarth, *Hitler's Hangman: The Life of Reinhard Heydrich* (New Haven, Conn., 2011).
19. Luža and Vella, *The Hitler Kiss*, pp. 56ff; David Kahn, *Hitler's Spies* (New York, 1978), pp. 112ff.
20. Count Alois Lichtenstein-Podstatzky, an anti-Nazi German, gave between 2 and 3 million crowns to the Czech resistance. Eduard Hašek donated 300,000 Protectorate crowns. See Luža and Vella, *The Hitler Kiss*, pp. 63 n., 272, 277, 279.
21. See Peter Demetz, *Prague in Danger* (New York, 2008), pp. 102–71.
22. Vojtech Mastny, *The Czechs Under Nazi Rule* (New York, 1971), p. 201.
23. František Moravec was chief of the intelligence service of the Czechoslovak government in exile. His major contact was with the Three Kings Group until 1942. The resistance people communicating with London were remnants of UOVD and ON.
24. Such an act would 'cost thousands of additional lives and expose the nation to unprecedented suppression', quoted by Mastny, *The Czechs Under Nazi Rule*, p. 209.
25. Report by the Reich Security Main Office, 5 August 1942, YIVO Institute for Jewish Research, New York.
26. All of the resistance organizations – perhaps thirty, counting among them several hundred men – were smashed.
27. At Lidice, all the men were shot and the women were put in concentration camps. About 100 of the children were gassed. A few children who qualified on the basis of their Aryan looks were put out for adoption by German families. At Ležáky eleven of the inhabitants were shot; see Jan G. Wiener, *The Assassination of Heydrich* (New York, 1969).
28. In the post-war government he served as secretary general in the ministry of foreign affairs. He escaped to the West in 1948 and died in Washington in 1968.
29. Staller developed a new type of machine gun – the Bren – which he sold to the British before the war. Staller was willing to do anything against the Nazis, even though he worked under their noses as one of their essential technical experts. Aside from donating his own money to the resistance, he siphoned funds from the Small Arms Factory and smuggled it to the Allies. Luža and Vella, *The Hitler Kiss*, p. 85.
30. Staller brought the microfilm to his son in Bratislava. The Slovak resistance then smuggled the film to Switzerland through an exporter who was allowed to travel. From Switzerland, another courier took the film to the Czech exiled government in London. That courier was Rudolf Fraštacký, a Slovak sugar exporter, who carried the film in the heel of his shoes. His business transactions were ostensibly helping the Germans evade the Allied blockade. As part of his work, he regularly travelled from Bratislava to Switzerland. There he would meet the former Czechoslovak envoy to Swtizerland, Jaromir Kopecký, who then sent to London, through transmitters or couriers, the information Fraštacký brought him. Sometimes Fraštacký took the microfilm to

Istanbul, where the Czechoslovak government-in-exile had representatives. Fraštacký escaped Czechoslovakia in 1948 and became a banker in Toronto; *ibid.*

31. In 1941, the Gestapo established the Third Section, Nachrichten-Referate, at its two head-quarters in Brno and Prague, for the purpose of boring into underground organizations. The head of N. Referate picked his collection of informers, 'V-persons' (*Vertrauensmänner* (confidants)), from the Gestapo's supply of trapped resisters. These spies extracted information from 'A-persons' (*Auskunftpersonen* (informants)), usually genuine resisters. Each headquarters had a catalogue of all informers. To accommodate its increasing number of Czech agents in Brno by 1942 and 1943, the Gestapo set up the import firm Erlan with a liquor company as its official owner. Informers came there with their reports. By then the Germans had decided that it was a mistake to arrest every resister, since these would merely be replaced by others. Instead, they began trying to infiltrate the organizations and get as much information as possible before liquidating them; *ibid.*, pp. 125–6.

32. For information on how contacts were made between the scattered resistance groups, see the Ambassador Heidrich Papers, Hoover Institution Archives, Stanford University. No reliable statistics are available regarding the number and kinds of informants. For a general discussion of the Nazi coercion of informers, see Luža and Vella, *The Hitler Kiss*, pp. 185ff.

33. See Demetz, *Prague in Danger*, p. 183, for a summing up of the military situation.

34. For a fuller narrative of these events, see Heidrich papers, Hoover Institute Archives, Stanford University.

35. It was Czechoslovak paratroopers from the army abroad who first reported that the Germans were producing the V2 rockets with which they bombed Great Britain in 1944; Luža and Vella, *The Hitler Kiss*, p. 139 n.

36. It was this system of central control that prevailed in Slovakia, Poland, France and elsewhere.

37. The repository was in an SS training camp south of Prague. The insurgency would next move to an ammunitions factory in Vlaším; Luža and Vella, *The Hitler Kiss*, p. 149.

38. Luža and his aide had stopped at a tavern in Přbyslav when three Czech gendarmes burst into the tavern and killed Luža. The aide got as far as a nearby field and shot himself. Luža's son Radomír led an expedition a few weeks later in which the executioners were in turn executed. As news spread of the revenge assassinations of the three gendarmes, other gendarmes began actively protecting the resisters. The Přbyslav strike marked the beginning of the Czech guerrilla war that lasted until the German surrender to the Allies; *ibid.*, pp. 158–71.

39. Golian had planned to start the uprising when the Soviets reached eastern Slovakia, where he would have two divisions at hand to open up the Carpathian passes for them. However, weeks ahead of Golian's schedule for military action, the Germans reacted to a premature partisan strike – the Russians had been calling urgently for guerilla actions – by occupying the country. Golian was never able to coordinate his plans with the Red Army, which changed its timetable and its point of entry into Slovakia without his knowledge; Martin D. Brown, 'The SOE and the Failure of the Slovak National Uprising', *History Today*, December 2004.

40. See Luža and Vella, *The Hitler Kiss*, pp. 194ff.

41. Author's conversation with Radomir Luža, 20 July 1999, Princeton, New Jersey. Radomir Luža took over direction of the largest group in the Council of Three after his father's death and the death of Josef Svatoň.

42. Luža and Vella, *The Hitler Kiss*, p. 211.

43. They were under the leadership of a former Soviet general, Vlasov. When taken prisoner by the Germans, a Soviet could earn his release by volunteering to work as an anti-Bolshevik activist; see Frank Ellis, 'Georgli Vladimov's The General and His Army: The Ghost of Andrei Vlasov', *The Modern Language Review*, 96:2 (2001), 437.

44. Beneš' signing of the Soviet-Czechoslovak alliance treaty in Moscow in 1943 showed that he had made up his mind to come to terms with Stalin and with the Czechoslovak communists who spent the war in Moscow – men such as Gottwald, Rudolf Slánský, Jan Šverma and Václav Kopecký; see Josef Korbel, *The Communist Subversion of Czechoslovakia, 1938–1948* (Princeton, New Jer., 1959).

45. *Ibid.*

46. See Demetz, *Prague in Danger*. Of the 250,000 persons in the Czechoslovak Republic killed by the Germans during the occupation, 154,000 were Jews; Luža and Vella, *The Hitler Kiss*, p. 227.

47. The Council had accepted the help of the Vlasovs, who were Soviet traitors. This served as the Soviet pretext for rejecting the Czech National Council. Pressured by the Soviets, the Czech authorities demanded that the Council resign, thus ending the possibility that its resistance members would play any part in the new government.

48. Luža and Vella, *The Hitler Kiss*, p. 232.

49. Masaryk was the son of the first president of the Republic. The communists created a new post, state secretary of foreign affairs, so that the Slovak communist Vlado Clematis could act as Masaryk's watchdog; *ibid.*, p. 238.

Guide to Further Reading

Bryant, Chad, *Prague in Black: Nazi Rule and Czech Nationalism* (Cambridge, Mass., 2009).

Demetz, Peter, *Prague in Danger* (New York, 2008).

Dowling, Maria, *Czechoslovakia* (New York, 2002).

Duff, Sheila Grant, *A German Protectorate: The Czechs Under Nazi Rule* (London, 1942).

Kennan, George F., *From Prague After Munich: Diplomatic Papers 1938–1940* (Princeton, New Jer., 1968).

Luža, Radomir and Christina Vella, *The Hitler Kiss: A Memoir of the Czech Resistance* (Baton Rouge, Lou., 2002).

Mayer, Milton, *The Art of the Impossible: A Study of the Czech Resistance* (Santa Barbara, Cal., 1969).

Mastny, Vojtech, *The Czechs Under Nazi Rule* (New York, 1971).

Staar, Richard F., *Communist Regimes in Eastern Europe* (Stanford, Cal., 1977).

Wiener, Jan G., *The Assassination of Heydrich* (New York, 1969).

Chapter 4

France

Juliette Pattinson

To many British people, fed on a staple of *'Allo 'Allo* and *Wish Me Luck*, resistance during the Second World War was predominantly a French phenomenon. More books have been written in English about resistance movements in France than any other nation's partisan war effort. And yet unlike Greece, Yugoslavia and the Soviet Union, the French resistance never became a mass popular movement. There were 300,000 resistance veterans plus a further 100,000 who died during the war, either killed in action, executed in French prisons or who died in concentration camps, who were officially recognized by the State after the war. From a wartime population of 40 million, these 400,000 amounted to about 1 per cent.

Yet the actual figure of how many resisted is undoubtedly higher. Definitions of 'resistance' and what counts as 'resistance' are highly contested. There is a temptation to adopt a narrow military meaning but this greatly distorts the nature and diversity of resistance and omits the large number of men and especially women who participated in myriad ways that have not generally been labelled as such. Implicit in the words 'The resistance' is the notion that there was one singular, unified opposition. Rather, there were hundreds of groups and multiple ways of resisting and while de Gaulle might be considered to be the symbol of the resistance, he was profoundly distrusted by many, including the Parti communiste français (French Communist Party) and even his own representative, Jean Moulin.

Despite the common objectives to rid France of its German occupiers and overthrow Vichy, the collaborating French government, the resistance was riven by division. But out of a multitude of isolated, small and poorly organized groups emerged an umbrella organization under which many of the larger groups united and to which formal allegiance to de Gaulle was accepted. While tensions between different political factions remained and groups continued to operate independently, this movement towards unity increased efficiency. Nevertheless, the issue of effectiveness remains hotly contested. While militarily, the French resistance was generally of marginal significance, rarely posing a real threat to the occupiers and only making a minor contribution to the liberation of France, it was vital psychologically in terms of morale through the salvaging of national honour, and crucial politically in facilitating a relatively smooth transition of power at the liberation.

As we shall see, the resistance developed in various phases: the Armistice in June 1940 prompted a few individuals to resist and over the next few months small groups formed and distributed newspapers. The German invasion of the Soviet Union in June 1941 resulted in communists becoming far more involved in resisting and more violent strategies were practised. In 1942, supplies to resistance groups increased as links with London were established. There were moves towards greater unity with the establishment of a resistance council in 1943 and by 1944 groups had increased in size as the Allied invasion became imminent. Just as the resistance changed in form during the occupation, so too did the behaviour of German soldiers. Despite fears of rape, prompted in part by the alleged or actual atrocities committed by Germans in 1914, and actual incidents of looting and massacres in the 1940 campaign, including the killing of 124 civilians in the northern town of Oignies in May 1940, soldiers generally behaved in a disciplined manner. The relatively restrained nature of the occupation by the army contrasted starkly with the far more ruthless non-army administrations in Poland and the western Soviet Union. Yet as the resistance became more active the occupiers met violence with violence. Hostages were shot in reprisal from 1941 onwards and as soldiers with Eastern Front experience were posted to France in 1943 and 1944, several massacres occurred.[1]

And in addition to the occupiers, resistance forces had to contend with their fellow countrymen who served in the *milice*, a Vichy uniformed paramilitary organization that hunted Jews and resisters but which never numbered more than 30,000, with disparate groups of collaborationists, which totalled about 200,000 for the entire occupation period who saw Hitler as the saviour of Europe, as well as with individuals who collaborated for personal gain.[2] In spite of these impediments, ordinary men and women risked their lives to resist.

This chapter, which takes a broad definition of resisting, covering anti-German as well as anti-Vichy non-compliance, uses official records and personal testimonies to examine the fall of France, the emergence of both external and internal resistance, the different forms the underground war assumed, the social composition of the resistance, the attempt to unify the larger clandestine groups, the overall impact it had and the post-war myths that arose.

* * *

France was at war with Germany from 3 September 1939 and after a period of little military confrontation known as *la drôle de guerre* (the Phoney War), it was attacked on 10 May 1940. The Maginot Line, the 400km-long system of fortifications built along the eastern frontier with Germany was circumvented when the Germans crossed the border at Sedan in the heavily wooded Ardennes region and proceeded towards Paris.[3] The successful coordination of German land and air operations and the superiority of the armoured divisions that raced across northern France with remarkable speed rendered French counterattacks ineffective. Nearly 100,000 Frenchmen lost their lives in the battle for France.[4] In total, 1.8 million French combatants were captured and became prisoners of war, many of whom for the duration of the conflict.[5] As German soldiers swept through northern France, hundreds of thousands of French civilians fled their homes.

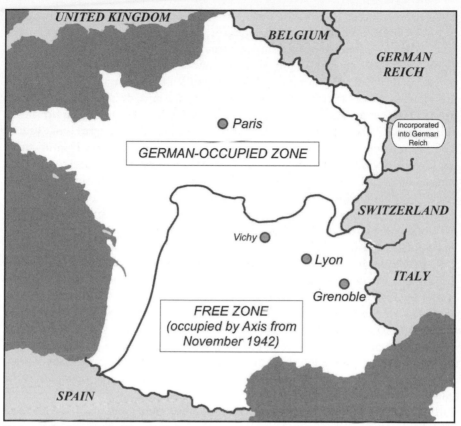

France under Axis domination, 1940–4.

This *exode* (exodus) saw northern towns shrink in size, while those in the south swelled to accommodate the refugees.[6] Paris became an open city as the government fled, surrendering on 14 June 1940 without a single shot being fired.[7]

Following the resignation of Prime Minister Paul Reynaud on 16 June, the deputy leader, Marshal Philippe Pétain, an 84-year-old First World War veteran, assumed power and without delay made enquiries about the terms of an armistice.[8] This was signed on 22 June in the same railway carriage in the forest of Compiègne that had been used to accept the German surrender in 1918. The terms of the armistice were particularly stringent. Unlike other defeated countries, France was divided into two: three-fifths of the country, essentially the northern half and the south-west corner, were occupied by the German army and the Alsace and Moselle regions were annexed by Germany; the southern zone remained nominally free, at least until November 1942 when it too was occupied in the wake of the Allied landings in North Africa.

Pétain established his government in the spa town of Vichy and pursued a policy of official collaboration, which included the passing of anti-Semitic laws and, from 1941, the round-up and deportation of over 75,000 Jews.[9] Thus, unlike several other occupied countries that established governments-in-exile in London, France retained some sovereignty. While Pétain sought accommodation with the occupiers, another man, a determined advocate of continuing the fight, set himself up in London as an alternative representative of France. The Undersecretary of State for War, Charles de Gaulle, who was invited to fly to London and promote resistance, arrived on 17 June and, despite attempts by the British Cabinet to block him, broadcast his *appel* or 'call to honour' radio speech on the evening of 18 June on the BBC French Service.[10] He asserted that France had lost a battle, not the war, that France could continue the fight from its overseas territories with Allied help and that 'the flame of French resistance must not and shall not die'.[11] De Gaulle was not urging French civilians to resist, however; he was calling on his compatriots, in particular soldiers and sailors, who were already on British soil to rally to him and mount an armed military response. As no senior politicians left France for Britain to establish an alternative government, de Gaulle went unchallenged and his role expanded from military to political leadership. This was the first of sixty-seven radio speeches he made during the occupation, each 5-minute slot on the 30-minute daily BBC programme *Les Français parlent aux Français* (*The French speak to the French*) prefaced with, 'This is the XXX day of resistance by the French people against oppression.' The *appel* was repeated the following day and recorded for posterity and the text was reproduced in various French newspapers. While de Gaulle's 18 June speech has retrospectively assumed great importance and has been a central part of postwar Gaullist mythology, it was not perceived as a momentous occasion at the time: very few people heard this original short broadcast by a comparatively junior officer who had little influence and whose name was unknown to most people. As Henri Frenay, leader of Combat, one of the largest networks in the southern zone, later recalled, 'It was not at the call of the General that we rose up.'[12] It is therefore important not to equate the resistance with de Gaulle, who was only ever an external symbol.

Indeed, the resistance began inside France as an individual response to the occupation borne out of frustration with Vichy's *attentisme* (wait-and-see policy), the inactivity of the Church, trade unions and political parties, and the prevalence of the defeatist 'hangover'[13] among the population. Isolated acts of individual defiance included Edmond Michelet, who in June 1940 typed out and distributed a protest against the armistice in Brive-la-Gaillarde; a Parisian photographer who displayed in his shop window a large portrait of Pétain with the sign 'sold' emblazoned across it, implying that he had 'sold out'; and a jockey racing at Longchamps in autumn 1940 who decorated his silk shirt with a large cross of Lorraine, the double-barred cross that was adopted by the Free French. Some scrawled anti-German slogans or daubed 'V' signs on public walls. Brigitte Friang, a university student in Paris, recollected struggling to find expression for her opposition: '[we] began to slash German propaganda posters, which were all over the city. It was stupid because the result was not worth the risk we took. We were just trying to find some way of contributing to the resistance.'[14]

While these small-scale impulsive acts of resisting were insignificant in the broader context, they were a visible sign that not everyone was passively accepting the German occupation. Gradually, small groups of people from similar backgrounds with shared political views met to discuss what they could do to undermine Vichy and the occupiers and, consequently, several distinct organizations formed. In the occupied zone, the first groups to be established produced clandestine leaflets. The earliest group is generally acknowledged as Musée de l'homme, named (somewhat spontaneously in 1945 when it was being dismantled) after the Parisian museum at which many of its members worked and which provided a duplicating machine to make copies of their pamphlets. Another group, dating from summer 1941, was Défense de la France (France's Defence), founded in Paris by students of the Sorbonne. Principal movements in the occupied north, which had a broader remit than the groups above which focused solely on producing pamphlets, included Ceux de la Résistance (The Men of the Resistance) and Ceux de la Libération (The Men of the Liberation), both of which were paramilitary groups providing intelligence to MI6, and which by the end of the occupation had up to 25,000 and 35,000 members respectively, drawn from all classes; Organization civile et militaire (Civil and Military Organization), a highly organized, very secure group which supplied MI6 with information and counted among its 40,000 members mainly right-wing, anti-communist Pétainists such as military officers, businessmen and public administrators; Libération-Nord (Liberation-North), which was more moderate politically and had a large number of trade unionists among its members; and Front national (National Front), an umbrella organization established by the PCF but which encompassed all political views and had up to 30,000 members, only 25 per cent of whom were committed communists, the rest having joined because they were impatient for action.[15]

Movements in the south were much larger than those in the occupied zone. Initially, this was because there were no German soldiers present in the south but it was following the German invasion of the unoccupied zone in November 1942 that the southern groups really grew. The three key southern movements were Combat (Fight), formed by Henri Frenay, a right-wing nationalist, in Lyon, which by the liberation had about 65,000 members; Libération-Sud (Liberation-South), established by Emmanuel d'Astier de la Vigerie in Clermont-Ferrand in December 1940 and which had about 19,000 members; and France Liberté (France Freedom), later renamed Franc-Tireur (Free Shooters), a radical left-wing group formed in Lyon in November 1940 by Jean-Pierre Lévy. This group organized a series of highly successful demonstrations, provided intelligence to the Allies and had a paramilitary wing which conducted sabotage operations and minor attacks on collaborators. All of these large groups, none of which were followers of de Gaulle, produced pamphlets and newspapers putting across an alternative message to that propounded by Vichy and the occupiers. There were also several groups in the unoccupied zone that solely produced newspapers, including *Le Coq Enchaîné* (*The Chained Cockerel*), *Les Cahiers du Témoignage Chrétien* (*Christian Witness Notebooks*) and *L'Insurgé* (*The Insurrectionist*). At this early stage of the occupation, the resistance was in an embryonic form: the groups were small, lacked coordination, had generally poor security and achieved very little.

These groups lacked the organization and activist experience of the communists. As a consequence of the Nazi-Soviet Pact of August 1939, the PCF were divided in their response to the occupation: some, who maintained allegiance to Moscow and adhered to its demands to abandon their anti-fascist tactics, advocated fraternization and sought accommodation with the occupiers, petitioning unsuccessfully in June 1940 for the right to publish their newspaper *L'Humanité*, while others, such as Georges Guingouin and Charles Tillon, rejected party directives and, acting independently, immediately began resisting.[16] Communists were not uniformly operational until the invasion of the Soviet Union in June 1941 when the PCF was released from the constraints imposed on it by Moscow. Over the next six months communist groups undertook over 100 acts of sabotage and carried out the first assassination of a German soldier on 22 August 1941 when Pierre Georges, who used the pseudonym 'Colonel Fabien', shot an officer at Barbès Rochechouart metro station. In keeping with this turn towards armed struggle, the PCF established in February 1942 a military branch under Tillon called Franc-Tireurs et partisans (Free Shooters and Partisans – not to be confused with Levy's Franc-Tireur). Not all resisters, however, supported the communist 'pinprick' tactic of attacking German soldiers for fear of reprisals, preferring instead restraint and preparation for a future Allied landing. Despite the brutal repression such as mass executions of hostages and the use of torture that communist tactics undoubtedly unleashed, the communists' involvement nevertheless strengthened the resistance in terms of organization, numbers and strategy.

Another way in which the clandestine war against the occupiers was made more potent was through the forging of links between indigenous underground movements within metropolitan France and external groups providing moral, material and financial support, such as the London-based Free French and the Special Operations Executive (SOE), both of which sent operatives to France to make contact with those who were resisting in whatever form. It took time for these connections to be made but by autumn 1941, messages to the resistance began to be broadcast on the BBC, which played a crucial role throughout the war in stimulating and sustaining opposition, and the first supplies were parachuted into the unoccupied zone a few weeks later. The number of trained agents infiltrated by the Free French and SOE, as well as the weapons and funds they provided increased dramatically from 1942 onwards. In total, SOE infiltrated over 600 male agents and 50 female operatives. During 1943 and 1944, 24,155 sorties (flights) were dispatched to France and 26,555 tons of supplies were delivered.[17] That the French resistance was regarded as especially significant is evidenced by the fact that only 484 tons were delivered to Belgium, 554 to Holland and just 1 to Germany.[18] Supplies included small arms such as pistols and Sten guns, as well as ammunition, high explosives, food, clothing, radio equipment, petrol, oil and specialized requests such as itching powder and poison capsules. After D-Day, the volume of supplies delivered to the resistance increased considerably and on 14 July 1944 the first daylight operation, codenamed Cadillac, in which 417 tons of supplies were dropped, was conducted by the Eighth USAAF (United States Army Air Force).[19] Initially, there was reluctance to equip groups with communist sympathies, but this changed over the course of the war. This mirrored the situations in Yugoslavia, Albania and Greece wherein monarchist groups, which had received the bulk of the supplies to begin with, were superseded by the communists who appeared to be more active, directly engaging with the enemy.

Weapons and explosives were crucial in order to undertake sabotage operations which damaged the German war effort. An important item used in sabotage was the time pencil, which delayed the detonation of explosive charges from minutes to several hours; 12 million of these were manufactured. They were of particular use in destroying the Peugeot plant at Montbéliard which had been converted to making tank turrets for the Wehrmacht and Focke-Wulf engine parts for the Luftwaffe. An unsuccessful RAF raid in July 1943 not only missed the factory but resulted in 110 civilian dead and a further 154 seriously injured. To avert further casualties caused by aerial bombing, SOE agent Harry Reé, organizer of the STOCKBROKER circuit, approached Monsieur Peugeot and, promising that there would be no more aerial bombing, convinced him to permit his men to sabotage the plant. This 'blackmail' policy was later adopted by other resisters across France. On 5 November 1943, a small team of local saboteurs accessed the plant and, using British supplies parachuted into the region, destroyed 6,000 tyres and put out of action turbo compressors and boring machines. A report in Reé's personal file held at The National Archives states that '(t)he workmen who carried out this operation understood the machine and put the explosive where they knew it would do most damage.' As a result of this operation, the factory was 'completely unproductive for five months'.[20]

* * *

While the popular stereotype of the young beret-wearing saboteur wielding a Sten gun emphasizes and indeed glorifies military action, the majority of resisters did not participate in sabotage, assassination or guerrilla warfare. Resistance took many different forms. Escape lines were established throughout France to enable downed Allied airmen and soldiers to traverse the demarcation line dividing the occupied and free zones, cross the Pyrenees into neutral Spain and travel onwards to Britain. Over 33,000 Allied service personnel were returned to Britain with the aid of escape lines. Each return was of both military and economic significance given the difficulty of finding men with the requisite flying expertise and that training a single RAF pilot cost about £15,000,[21] far more than the cost of a single Spitfire, which came to £10,000 in 1940.

Resistance might also take the form of intelligence-gathering by monitoring troop movements and reporting on the production of machinery. The MI6-run Alliance network, for example, provided reports on the location of the Luftwaffe's decoy airfields, on the German navy's submarine bases and on the site of the V1 and V2 rockets at Peenemünde, as well as on the size and range of the weapons. Moreover, the clandestine press, which began at the very start of the occupation, developed into a potent weapon despite the problems of printing, paper supply and distribution and was until 1944 the most tangible sign of the resistance, with about 2 million copies distributed every month.[22] Unique to France was the sheer number of pamphlets produced which targeted women specifically. Of the 1,100 resistance newspapers in circulation during the occupation,[23] 76 were for women.[24] As rationing, price increases and food shortages brought about by German requisitioning took hold, women's private domestic task of feeding their families became increasingly difficult and took on political significance. The communist newspaper *La voix des femmes* (*Women's Voice*) mobilized 30,000 housewives in July 1944 who marched alongside men protesting against food requisitioning and demanding more bread.[25] Indeed, hundreds of thousands of French nationals, many of whom did not belong to a formal network, marched in demonstrations: on 14 July 1942, Bastille Day, for example, thousands participated in simultaneous protests in Lyon, Marseille, Nice, Montpellier, Limoges, Grenoble and Toulon singing the *Marseillaise* after being called to demonstrate by the Free French service on the BBC. There was, then, no single way of resisting.

There was also no archetypal resister. Although the vast majority were from the poorer sections of society, not least because there were more of them and because they were more susceptible to the anti-conservative message implied in the call to resistance, resisters came from varied backgrounds (immigrants, Jews, intelligentsia, military, rural peasantry, urban working class, professional classes, petite bourgeoisie and, to a lesser extent, the aristocracy), different political persuasions (left-wing, right-wing and apolitical), all ages and both men and women. Participation was often irregular and intermittent and few resisters lived a fully clandestine life; most continued with their ordinary lives as, for example, teachers and farmers. Initially, resistance was more likely to occur in towns as this was where journalists and intellectuals, as well as printing presses, were to be found. Urban dwellers, who bore the brunt of material hardships as they could not supplement their rations, were far more likely up to 1943 to join the resistance than rural workers who were valued by Vichy.

What transformed the resistance into a mass movement with the mobilization of thousands of rural peasant men was the Service de travail obligatoire (STO; compulsory work service). This was an enforced two-year labour draft instituted in February 1943 to supply Germany with French workers and resulted in just under 800,000 Frenchmen, mainly townsfolk who could not avoid it, being deported to Germany.[26] As it became increasingly more demanding, requiring more and more workers, rural peasant men took refuge in the hills and mountains. By early September 1943, over 13,000 men had formed into small groups collectively called the *maquis*, a Corsican word meaning scrubland. These groups developed into guerrilla bands offering an alternative lifestyle wherein class boundaries dissipated. This was very much a male preserve, a band of brothers.

While women played important roles as liaison agents, couriering messages by bike and, as *marraines* (godmothers), providing food and clothing, it was extremely rare for a woman to belong to a *maquis* unit; unlike women in Yugoslavia and the Soviet Union, French women were very seldom armed.

Some women were involved in establishing the first groups including Musée de l'homme, Défense de la France, Libération-Sud and Combat. However, they only accounted for between 7 and 12 per cent of resisters according to the dossiers of the Combattant volontaire de la Résistance (Voluntary Resistance Fighters), which listed those who were proposed for official recognition after the war and who had participated actively for at least three months.[27] Women were thus less likely to be in the resistance than men, possibly because of the constraints imposed by elderly parents, husbands, children and the home, because of the responsibilities of running a household in the absence of their husbands who were POWs, because they were less politically aware, or possibly because they were excluded by men who had reservations about women's involvement. However, the real figure was undoubtedly much higher, as women were less likely to belong to formal organizations and often undertook (invisible) roles that were an extension of their domestic lives: providing a room for a resistance meeting, supplying *maquisards* with food and clothing, acting as a 'letterbox' where messages could be left, and bestowing food and shelter to downed Allied airmen, STO evaders and Jews. Few women traversed gender barriers by undertaking sabotage, occupying positions of leadership or engaging in combat, and yet they were essential to the day-to-day running of the resistance, as SOE agent Francis Cammaerts, leader of the JOCKEY network in southern France, recognized:

> The women were more important than the men because the women looked after us, fed us, clothed us, kept our morale up by running a household where the atmosphere is right ... The whole resistance was based on that, couldn't have happened without it. And that's something which unfortunately is very rarely spoken about ... That is a fact: it was the housewife who made resistance possible.[28]

While there are a few celebrated heroines in France such as Lucie Aubrac, the nature of women's contributions, which were highly gendered, have rarely been defined as 'resistance' and have been overshadowed by the popular image of resisters as 'Soldiers of the Night'.

* * *

As a military man, de Gaulle was highly sceptical of armed civilians, male or female, and did not want the resistance to become a people's army. Rather, he wanted military action to be directed from London and saw the Free French forces as the French resistance. It was imperative, then, for de Gaulle to unify the various forces of the internal resistance in order to cement his position as the true representative of French interests with both Churchill and Roosevelt, who was especially reluctant to recognize de Gaulle, perceiving him to be a potential dictator.[29] The man credited with spearheading and unifying the disparate strands of the resistance is Jean Moulin, the prefect of Chartres (the State's representative), who, having been dismissed by Vichy, travelled to Britain in October 1941 and provided the first comprehensive account of the resistance, conveying to London the need for moral support, regular communications, funds and weapons.[30] Following meetings with de Gaulle, Moulin returned to France on 2 January 1942 as his personal representative, despite misgivings about de Gaulle's commitment to democracy, something which Roosevelt and Churchill also questioned. Moulin's objectives were to unite the main groups in the southern unoccupied zone under the Gaullist banner and to get them to separate their military and political branches in order that their military activity could be controlled.[31]

Moulin's first attempts at uniting the resistance involved the setting up of joint services. In April 1942, he established the Bureau d'information et de presse (Press and Information Service) which functioned as a central repository for articles about the resistance to be sent to the international press, as well as information to be circulated to resistance groups for publication in their newspapers. He also formed a Comité général d'études (General Study Committee) in July 1942, thereby laying the basis for the future Gaullist state. It comprised high-ranking civil servants from a wide range of fields who at the liberation would advise the government on political, economic and social issues so that, following the collapse of Vichy, a smooth transition would ensue.

It took Moulin fifteen months to surmount the internal squabbles engendered by distrust, fear and very real political differences between resistance leaders and to bring together the three main networks in the southern zone – Combat, Libération-Sud and Franc-Tireur. This was achieved on 26 January 1943 when an umbrella organization called Mouvements unis de la Résistance (United Resistance Movements, MUR) was created.[32] Each group's newspaper included as a sub-heading the names of the other two organizations 'in order to impress upon the public the extent to which unity had been reached'.[33] The military sections of these networks formed a nascent armed branch of the resistance called Armée Secrète (Secret Army) under the authority of General Delestraint. Moulin thus achieved his objectives, getting the main southern groups to work together, recognize de Gaulle as their leader and detach their military sections, and was instrumental in the consolidation of the resistance in the southern zone.

The largest northern groups came to a similar agreement, establishing a co-ordinating committee on 26 March 1943. They, as well as those in the MUR, were deeply hostile towards the inclusion in a resistance council of political parties that had deserted the country in 1940. Despite this bitter opposition, Moulin succeeded in establishing a Conseil national de la Résistance (National Resistance Council) which included the political parties and brought together communists and Gaullists. Initially, the PCF had ignored de Gaulle, but it became increasingly clear by late 1942 that he would be influential in post-war politics, and that the communists would therefore have to work with the Free

French if they wanted to be involved. Moreover, the PCF was under pressure from Moscow to help precipitate an Allied landing in Western Europe which would alleviate the situation on the Eastern Front. Thus, a rapprochement led gradually to increased collaboration between Free French and communist groups that culminated in the creation of the CNR, which to a certain extent unified internal resistance. It had its inaugural meeting on the Left Bank in Paris on 27 May 1943.[34] In addition to Moulin in the chair, sixteen men were present including two trade unionists, six representatives of political parties considered *résistante* in spirit, five spokesmen from the major resistance movements from what had previously been the northern zone (Front national, Organisation civile et militaire, Ceux de la Libération, Ceux de la Résistance and Libération-Nord) and three representatives from the largest southern movements which had formed Mouvements unis de la Résistance (Combat, Libération-Sud and Franc-Tireur). Communists were particularly well represented with delegates from their party (the PCF), their resistance organization (Front national), as well as their trade union (Confédération générale du travail). The CNR, which was essentially a resistance parliament comprising forty members, called for the establishment of a provisional government under de Gaulle, who was recognized as the leader and sole representative of French interests. By involving the communists, the illusion of unity was projected, thereby considerably strengthening de Gaulle's legitimacy and alleviating some of Roosevelt's reservations about his propensity for being undemocratic. It also neutralized the PCF threat to de Gaulle's post-war ambitions.

Moulin was betrayed, arrested at a resistance meeting in Caluire on 21 June 1943 and died under torture on about 8 July. De Gaulle did not replace him and without his guiding hand resistance movements began to reaffirm their autonomy. Those who had been bitterly opposed to Moulin's plans to establish a national resistance leadership that incorporated representatives of the political parties merged MUR and some of the smaller resistance groups to form a Central Committee on 23 July 1943 which deliberately excluded political parties. Meanwhile, a CNR Bureau was established in opposition, comprising Front national, Parti communiste français, Ceux de la Résistance, Organisation civile et militaire and Libération-Nord. Despite the undoing of some of Moulin's efforts, the resistance was stronger and more effective as a result of increased co-ordination.

*   *   *

On 1 June 1944, the BBC broadcast the warning signal informing the resistance that the invasion was imminent. On 5 June, in contrast to the usual 5 to 10 minutes of coded messages broadcast on the French service of the BBC, over 200 messages were read out in a 20-minute transmission galvanizing individual resistance groups. The cryptic statement '*la giraffe a un long cou*' ('the giraffe has a long neck'), for example, was meaningless to all those listening except for the one group for whom it was intended and who interpreted it as their call to action.[35]

SOE agent Roger Landes, head of the ACTOR circuit in the Bordeaux region, recalled:

> We had two messages you see coming through the BBC, Message A and B
> ... If you hear Message A coming through, you have to get ready to do your
> sabotage ... We heard on the 1 June Message A, and Message B on ... 5 June.
> When I heard Message A, that's when I got in touch with all my leaders you
> see, and told them what they had to do, and gave them Message B ... I said
> 'well when you hear that, you go into action.' When Message B ... was
> transmitted on the news, all the men heard it, and on the same night they
> started to sabotage.[36]

Over the next 24 hours, hundreds of sabotage operations were undertaken throughout France – railway lines were cut, bridges were blown up and communication lines were disabled – and this significantly delayed divisions moving north to reinforce German troops in Normandy. It also hindered the transport of essential military supplies. A two-day journey from the south of France could take as long as a fortnight, as German troops were forced to abandon trains and main roads and use minor country roads, where they were frequently ambushed. This necessitated Germans being deployed in security roles which further tied down personnel. This undoubtedly saved the lives of thousands of Allied troops who were gaining a foothold in northern France. A SHAEF (Supreme Headquarters, Allied Expeditionary Force) memorandum written in July 1945 reflecting on the military value of clandestine operations concluded: 'There can be no doubt that at a time when the Germans were exerting every effort to obtain more manpower, the dispersion of troops in protective and internal security duties had an effect on the land battle.'[37] Between 6 and 27 June, the railway network was brought to a standstill with over 3,000 separate attacks confirmed.[38] The actions of the resistance in the wake of 6 June led to brutal reprisals taken disproportionately against the local population. On 10 June, a battalion of the SS Panzer division Das Reich, comprising many soldiers who had served on the Eastern Front and who were experienced in a very different kind of warfare, massacred 642 inhabitants of Oradour-sur-Glane near Limoges. Just five men and one woman from the village survived. This was the single worst atrocity committed on the Western Front.

After the Allied landings, the ranks of the resistance swelled to incorporate latecomers: many who had sat on the fence or even been active collaborators throughout the occupation flocked to join the ranks of the resistance. These '*Septembrisards*', 'resisters of the thirteenth hour', of the '32nd of August', were joined by '*napthalinés*' (mothballers), soldiers who, having drawn half-pay for the duration of the occupation, removed their musty uniforms from cupboards. Consequently, *maquis* units expanded ten-fold. Roger Landes recalled: 'In March '44 we started with about 200 people. By D-Day we have 2,000 people and by September when the Germans left about 5,000 ... It just snowballed. It got bigger and bigger.'[39] American troops landing in the south of France in August 1944 during Operation Dragoon were aided by the *maquis* and the Free French of the Interior (FFI).[40] Yet despite their numbers, the *maquis* were no match for the

Germans in conventional open battles. This was evidenced by the annihilation of hundreds of *maquisards* at Glières in the Alps in March 1944, at Mont Mouchet in the Auvergne in June 1944 and at Vercors near Grenoble in July 1944. The Vercors plateau, for example, was strafed by the Luftwaffe and attacked by over 10,000 German soldiers, resulting in 326 resistance casualties and 130 civilian dead.[41] The brutality was something rarely seen outside the war in the East: eye-witness evidence, for example, provides shocking tales of a woman being dis-embowelled and gang rapes.[42] These skirmishes between inadequately trained, poorly equipped and significantly outnumbered *maquisards* and an army of battle-experienced soldiers were doomed to failure.

Though the resistance might not have liberated the country by itself or even played a crucial supporting military role, there were isolated examples where a town or village was liberated by resistance forces.[43] On 15 August, Brive-la-Gaillarde, which witnessed one of the first acts of defiance with the distribution of Edmond Michelet's June 1940 pamphlet decrying the armistice, became the first French town to be liberated by resisters (as opposed to Allied forces). There were twenty-eight major cities including Nice, Toulouse and Le Havre that witnessed partial insurrectionary events and Paris, Lille, Lyon, Marseille and Limoges staged uprisings and were liberated with the help of the resistance. Paris, which had fallen in 1940 without a shot being fired, witnessed an uprising that held out for a week against the occupiers, with over 2,000 Parisians, FFI and police losing their lives.[44] Paris was liberated on 25 August. The uprising was not condoned by de Gaulle and is further evidence that his authority was by no means mono-lithic. Nevertheless, he triumphantly entered Paris in a symbolic liberation which exaggerated the role of the French troops and enabled him to rewrite history: 'Paris! Paris humiliated! Paris broken! Paris martyrized! But now Paris liberated! Liberated by herself, by her own people, with the help of the armies of France, with the support and aid of France as a whole, of fighting France, of the only France, of the true France, of eternal France.'[45]

From September 1944 onwards, de Gaulle toured France in an attempt to establish his authority and quash the independence of the local resistance. He frequently appeared dismissive of the efforts of the resistance and displayed cool-ness when meeting regional leaders. SOE agent Roger Landes, for example, recalled being invited to a reception to meet de Gaulle when he visited Bordeaux on 17 September and being told by him: 'You are a British officer and you have been ordered to go back to England straight away.'[46] Landes was by no means an exceptional case.

If in military terms the resistance was not decisive, the social and political significance of the role it played at the liberation was unparalleled. In short, France would have been liberated without the resistance but the political con-sequences would have been huge. Unlike Greece or Yugoslavia, France did not descend into civil war. A post-war report records the 'orderly transfer of power' and the 'remarkable ease with which France passed from Vichy to Gaullist control' and concluded that 'the fact that no disturbance occurred in France behind the liberating armies was a most valuable contribution to the war effort'.[47]

Nevertheless, atrocities perpetrated by resisters against suspected collaborators did take place. The most iconic visual symbol of the purges is the photographic and filmic footage of the *femmes tondues* (shaved women) who were punished for allegedly 'sleeping with the enemy' by having their hair roughly shorn off with scissors and clippers, and being stripped of their outer clothing, daubed with swastikas and paraded around town squares. Huguette Robert recorded her observations of an incident in her diary:

> A cortège of four shaven women ... is moving towards the rue du Bac, more and more people are joining the crowd. One of the women tries to escape. She is caught, people hit her, hurl insults at her, the crowd is inhuman. The poor woman is stripped ... on her knees ... A member of the resistance points his machine gun at her, to kill her. People force her to say she is sorry, she is kneeling there, half-naked, on her knees ... Are they going to kill her? No – a French officer arrives and says that she must be taken to prison and tried.[48]

About 20,000 women experienced this humiliating form of summary justice, conducted by men who had been in the resistance as well as those who had done little during the occupation and were keen to prove their loyalty to France.[49] The first recorded instance pre-dated the liberation, taking place in May 1943; the last in March 1946. There were also other forms of unofficial retribution: about 9,000 collaborators were executed without trial, over half of which occurred before the liberation took place. Men who had joined the *milice* were especially targeted.

Atrocities perpetrated by resisters against suspected collaborators certainly took place. Yet the generally restrained nature of the *épuration* (purges) in comparison to the horrors of the occupation owed much to the resistance, given the total collapse of the judicial and police system which was virtually entirely corrupt and collaborationist. Order was soon restored through the resistance's armed police force, the *milices patriotiques*, and committees led by resisters organized food, water and electricity supplies. Furthermore, following the collapse of Vichy, the resistance stepped into the political vacuum. A government-in-waiting, called the Comité française de la Libération nationale (French Committee of National Liberation), had been established in Algiers in mid-1943, and in June 1944 it formed the Gouvernement provisoire de la République française (Provisional Government of the Republic of France). The Allies intended to impose Allied Military Government of Occupied Territory (AMGOT) so that France was not under the control of the French. However, it abolished these plans for an interim administration due to the Allies' recognition of de Gaulle's Provisional Government created on 9 September. Despite not being elected, there were no challenges to his audacious seizure of power by either the communists, who lacked support from Moscow for a coup, or by the public, who simply desired a rapid return to normality. Significantly, the vote was finally extended to French women in 1944 and they exercised their newly acquired political rights for the first time in a referendum in October 1945. The assemblies of the Fourth Republic thereby included a few women as well as some ordinary men who had served their apprenticeships in the resistance – their war records bestowing on them moral legitimacy.

*   *   *

Despite the war being over, the experiences of the occupation were all-pervading. Henry Rousso, a leading French historian writing in the late 1980s, noted the presence of a 'Vichy syndrome'; an omnipresent shadow cast over the French psyche.[50] In the decade after liberation when memories were still raw, few authors confronted the occupation. This time of 'unfinished mourning' however was, according to Rousso, followed by a period of 'repressions' in which 'the truth' was suppressed and a potent and all-embracing myth of *la France résistante* (Resister France) developed. This propounded that the resistance had erupted immediately after the Germans occupied France, that it had expanded both exponentially and smoothly, and not only that it had been supported by the wider population but also that France had in fact been a 'nation of resisters'. In his *War Memoirs* published in the 1950s, de Gaulle barely acknowledged the various networks, thereby succeeding in projecting the view that the 'real' resistance had been the Free French based in London and later in Algiers, and effectively wrote out of history the internal resistance and in particular the communists. According to the Gaullist myth, de Gaulle was resistance; resistance was de Gaulle. Following his election victory in 1958, the myth greatly intensified. But it was not only the Gaullists who projected a somewhat distorted view. The PCF also played a key, albeit independent, part in cultivating this myth of widespread opposition. It depicted itself as *'le partie des 75,000 fusillés'* (the party of the 75,000 martyrs who had been shot), exaggerating not only the number of communists executed but also the number of all French killed in that way. Thus, the resistance evolved in popular memory to become synonymous with, on the one hand, the Free French in London, and on the other the communists in France. The diversity, richness and complexity of the resistance were forgotten. This image was simplified even further when Jean Moulin's ashes were transferred to the Panthéon in December 1964 and subsequently his name, which had not been known to the French public, came to represent the resistance. As Julian Jackson notes, the resistance myth 'imposed a unitary vision on what had been a highly fragmented experience'.[51]

Thus, in the twenty-five years following liberation, the darker tales of both popular and official collaboration were downplayed and purged from the collective memory of the occupation by this unifying myth. This collective amnesia was bolstered by novels and films glorifying the heroic actions of the clandestine war. While not the first film depicting the resistance, René Clement's *La Bataille du rail* (*Battle of the Railways*), released in January 1946 and winner of the Palme d'Or at the 1946 Cannes Film Festival, was a classic example of the genre, in which railway workers' sabotage of the German war effort was celebrated. Memorials and commemorative plaques were erected, museums opened in numerous towns, metro stations, streets and squares were named after celebrated individuals and postage stamps depicting 'heroes of the resistance' were produced. Thus, both local and national narratives of the resistance were constructed which served to solidify a cult of the Resistance.

This unbalanced view was challenged in the early 1970s during a period known as the Mode Rétro. De Gaulle's resignation as President in April 1969 and his death in September 1970, coupled with the student demonstrations in May 1968, the decline of the PCF and wider European events such as the Prague Spring, opened up a space in which to begin to scratch away the patina. The release in April 1971 of Marcel Ophuls' 4-hour documentary *Le Chagrin et la Pitié* (*The Sorrow and the Pity*) which recorded daily life in Clermont-Ferrand 'cracked the mirror', according to Rousso, of resistance mythology. Using archive footage, newsreel clips and interviews with resistance veterans, SOE personnel, members of collaborationist groups, German officers and a Frenchman who had joined the Waffen-SS, the documentary destroyed some of the myths that had developed about the occupation, making evident that some civilians had actively chosen to collaborate. De Gaulle was barely mentioned. It was considered so controversial that only a few small art house cinemas in Paris' Latin Quarter showed it; French television did not broadcast it until 1981.

Ophuls' documentary was followed in 1972 by American historian Robert Paxton's study *Vichy France*, which refuted the widely-held claim that Vichy had sought to shield France from the worst excesses of the occupation, asserted that collaboration was a French initiative rather than a German one and estimated that possibly only 10 per cent of Frenchmen and women had actively resisted.[52] This book, which further dented the orthodox view of widespread opposition, was poorly received in France when it was published there a year later: Paxton was vilified in the newspaper *Le Monde*, which asserted that his age and nationality precluded him from casting judgement on France's past. Paxton's book and Ophuls' film helped to supplant the myth of a 'nation of resisters' with that of a 'nation of collaborators'. The reality of course was somewhere in between; a minority actively resisted or collaborated, a few even did both and the vast majority tried to get on with their lives, despite the strictures of occupation, waiting for the liberation. Recent publications provide a more measured analysis of the diverse responses to German occupation and Vichy rule.[53]

The collective memory of the occupation continued to resonate; Rousso terms the period 1974 until the late 1980s, when he published his study, an era of 'obsessions' during which time the spectre of the occupation was ever-present. This obsession, which continued into the 1990s, included the arrest in 1983 and the subsequent trial in 1987 of Klaus Barbie, the head of the Lyon Gestapo who was directly responsible for the torture and death of Jean Moulin and thousands of others; the 1998 trial of Maurice Papon, a senior police official in Bordeaux and supervisor of its Commissariat général aux questions juives (Service for Jewish Questions), in which capacity he was actively involved in the deportation of over 1,500 Jews; the accusation in 1994 levelled against René Bousquet, the General Secretary to the Police, of playing a key role in orchestrating the July 1942 Vel d'Hiv operation, which rounded up over 13,000 Jews into a Parisian velodrome before their deportation to Auschwitz; the 1994 trial of *milice* chief

Paul Touvier; the 1997 publication of Gérard Chauvy's book that alleged Raymond Aubrac, who was arrested along with Jean Moulin and later rescued by his wife Lucie in an audacious ruse, was working for Klaus Barbie; and the subsequent roundtable discussion involving the Aubracs and eight historians arranged by the newspaper *Libération*, which quickly descended into an interrogation and left lingering suspicions about the Aubracs despite the fact that the historians rejected the accusation.[54] The war thus lived long in the French memory.

* * *

It should be noted that while de Gaulle was crucial as a symbol, a spur to action and a link with the Allies, we should not overestimate his significance: the resistance was created inside France, not outside, and was undertaken by ordinary men and women who risked everything to help bring about the liberation of their country. Resisting was indeed a highly dangerous activity which could result in betrayal, arrest, torture, captivity and either execution or deportation to a concentration camp. In unpicking the myths that abound concerning a 'nation of resisters' and by emphasizing the occurrence of collaboration, the sacrifice made by those individuals who were resisting becomes ever more admirable. It should also be recorded that while the internal resistance was faction-ridden, it did achieve a measure of unity. And while in military terms the effectiveness of the resistance was marginal, it did play a role, not least in maintaining morale, in preparing the ground for the Allied invasion and crucially, at the liberation, in ensuring a degree of restraint and a relatively smooth transition of power.

Notes

1. Peter Lieb, 'Repercussions of Eastern Front Experiences on Anti-Partisan Warfare in France 1943/44', in *Journal of Strategic Studies*, 31:5 (2008).
2. Gerhard Hirschfeld and Patrick Marsh (eds), *Collaboration in France: Politics and Culture During the Nazi Occupation, 1940–1944* (Oxford, 1989).
3. Julian Jackson, *The Fall of France: The Nazi Invasion of 1940* (Oxford, 2003).
4. Raymond Aubrac, *The French Resistance, 1940–44* (Paris, 1997), p. 8.
5. Sarah Fishman, *We Will Wait: Wives of French Prisoners of War, 1940–1945* (New Haven, Conn., 1991).
6. Hanna Diamond, *Fleeing Hitler: France 1940* (Oxford, 2007).
7. Herbert Lottman, *The Fall of Paris: June 1940* (London, 1992).
8. Nicholas Atkin, *Pétain* (London, 1997).
9. Paul Webster, *Pétain's Crime: The Full Story of French Collaboration in the Holocaust* (London, 1990).
10. Julian Jackson, *Charles de Gaulle* (London, 2003).
11. François Kersaudy, *Churchill and De Gaulle* (London, 1990), p. 80.
12. Julian Jackson, *France: The Dark Years, 1940–1944* (Oxford, 2001), p. 386.
13. The National Archives (TNA, formerly the Public Record Office, Kew), HS 7/123.
14. Shelley Saywell, *Women in War: First-Hand Accounts from World War II to El Salvador* (Ontario, 1985), p. 48.
15. TNA, HS 7/123.
16. Lynne Taylor, 'The Parti Communiste Français and the French Resistance in the Second World War', in Tony Judt (ed.), *Resistance and Revolution in Mediterranean Europe 1939–1948* (London, 1989).

17. These figures have been compiled from TNA, HS 7/123 and HS 8/434.

18. TNA, HS 8/434.

19. Jacques Poirier, *The Giraffe Has a Long Neck* (London, 1995), p. 157.

20. TNA, HS 9/1240/3.

21. M.R.D. Foot, *Resistance: An Analysis of European Resistance to Nazism, 1940–1945* (London, 1976), p. 311.

22. Aubrac, *The French Resistance*, p. 32.

23. La Bibliothèque nationale de France in Paris holds 1,106 clandestine press titles.

24. Joan Tumblety, 'Obedient Daughters of Marianne: Discourses of Patriotism and Maternity in the French Women's Resistance Press during the Second World War', *Women's History Notebooks*, 4:2 (Summer 1997).

25. *Ibid.*, p. 3.

26. Ian Ousby, *Occupation: The Ordeal of France, 1940–1944* (London, 1999), p. 252.

27. Hannah Diamond, *Women and the Second World War in France, 1939–1948: Choices and Constraints* (London, 1999), p. 99.

28. Personal interview with Francis Cammaerts, 2 July 1999.

29. Robert Dallek, 'Roosevelt and de Gaulle', in Robert O. Paxton and Nicholas Wahl (eds), *De Gaulle and the United States: A Centennial Reappraisal* (Oxford, 1994).

30. TNA, HS 7/123.

31. Alan Clinton, *Jean Moulin, 1899–1943: The French Resistance and the Republic* (New York, 2002).

32. John F. Sweets, *The Politics of Resistance in France, 1940–1944: A History of the Mouvements unis de la Résistance* (DeKalb, 1976).

33. TNA, HS 7/124.

34. *Ibid.*

35. This was the message for Jacques Poirier's DIGGER circuit in the Corrèze; Poirier, *The Giraffe Has a Long Neck*, p. 137.

36. Personal interview with Roger Landes, 25 August 1999.

37. TNA, HS 8/434.

38. *Ibid.*

39. Personal interview with Roger Landes, 25 August 1999.

40. See A.L. Funk, *Hidden Ally: The French Resistance, Special Operations and the Landings in Southern France* (New York, 1992).

41. Matthew Cobb, *The Resistance: The French Fight Against the Nazis* (London, 2009), pp. 252–3.

42. Report by Andre Edward Pecquet, held by TNA, HS 9/1160/1 but closed because of its sensitive contents. Seen by M.R.D. Foot in preparation for his official history, *SOE in France: An Account of the Work of the British Special Operations Executive in France, 1940–1944* (London, 1966), p. 393.

43. Rod Kedward and Nancy Wood (eds), *The Liberation of France: Image and Event* (Oxford, 1995).

44. Cobb, *The Resistance*, pp. 270, 382 n. 97.

45. Jackson, *France*, p. 565.

46. Personal interview with Roger Landes, 25 August 1999.

47. TNA, HS 7/124.

48. Robert quoted in Emmanuel d'Astier de la Vigerie, *De la chute à la libération de Paris* (Paris, 1965).

49. Fabrice Virgili, *Shorn Women: Gender and Punishment in Liberation France* (Oxford, 2002), p. 1.

50. Henry Rousso, *The Vichy Syndrome: History and Memory in France Since 1944* (Cambridge, Mass., 1991).

51. Jackson, *France*, p. 605.

52. Robert Paxton, *Vichy France: Old Guard and New Order* (New York, 1972).

53. Philippe Burrin, *Living With Defeat: France under the German Occupation, 1940–1945* (London, 1996); Ousby, *Occupation*; Peter Davies, *France and the Second World War: Occupation, Collaboration and Resistance* (London, 2001); Robert Gildea, *Marianne in Chains: In Search of the German Occupation, 1940–1945* (London, 2002).

54. Hanna Diamond and Claire Gorrara, 'The Aubrac Controversy', *History Today*, 41:3 (2001).

Guide to Further Reading

Cobb, Matthew, *The Resistance: The French Fight Against the Nazis* (London, 2009).

Collins, Margaret Weitz, *Sisters in the Resistance: How Women Fought to Free France 1940–1945* (New York, 1995).

Davies, Peter, *France and the Second World War: Occupation, Collaboration and Resistance* (London, 2001).

Diamond, Hanna, *Women and the Second World War in France, 1939–1948: Choices and Constraints* (London, 1999).

Gildea, Robert, *Marianne in Chains: In Search of the German Occupation, 1940–1945* (London, 2002).

Jackson, Julian, *France: The Dark Years, 1940–1944* (Oxford, 2001).

Kedward, Rod, *In Search of the Maquis: Rural Resistance in Southern France* (Oxford, 1993).

Pattinson, Juliette, *Behind Enemy Lines: Gender, Passing and the Special Operations Executive in the Second World War* (Manchester, 2007).

Rossiter, Margaret, *Women in the Resistance* (New York, 1996).

Vinen, Richard, *The Unfree French: Life under the Occupation* (London, 2007).

Wieviorka, Olivier, 'France', in Bob Moore (ed.), *Resistance in Western Europe* (Oxford, 2000).

Chapter 5

Greece

Vangelis Tzoukas and Ben H. Shepherd

Greece, at the crossing between Asia and Europe, has always been vulnerable to foreign invasion. The 1821 Revolution against the Ottoman Empire led to the creation of a tiny Greek state which then expanded its territory over the course of the nineteenth century and even more so following the Balkan Wars of 1912–13. When the First World War broke out, King Constantine favoured a policy of neutrality while the prime minister, Venizelos, wanted the country to join the Entente. From 1916 the country split amid violent clashes between the Venizelists and Monarchists. Venizelos formed a government in Thessaloniki and the Allies, predominantly Britain and France, intervened in his favour decisively.

After the First World War, Greek irredentism reached its height with the Greek army's landing in Smyrna in May 1919 and the military conquest of Asia Minor, a region containing a strong Greek element within its population. But Greece's internal politics were still tense. In August 1922 the Asia Minor front collapsed and millions of refugees swarmed into Greece. The 1923 Lausanne Treaty and a population exchange between Greece and Turkey delineated Greece's present boundaries (excepting the Dodecanese, which was incorporated in 1948).

The foundation of the so-called Second Greek Republic of 1924–35, following the monarchy's temporary abolition, was characterized by political instability, military movements and short-lived dictatorships. At this time the Greek military was actively intervening in politics, and the officer corps split along political lines between royalists and venizelists. The schism between the two parties still dominated a country facing the challenge of developing a modern state.[1] Though industrialization and modernization were promoted, small-scale peasant agriculture still provided a very significant proportion of employment.[2] From 1929 onward the economic crisis blighted the Greek economy, and at the end of 1932 the country defaulted.

Amid all this, both venizelists and royalists sought to defend bourgeois democracy and its institutions against the tiny Communist Party (KKE) that had emerged after 1918. At the end of 1935, following a failed *coup d'état* of venizelist officers, a notoriously rigged referendum led to the monarchy being restored in the person of King George II. On 4 August 1936, the pro-British king allowed the prime minister (and former general) Ioannis Metaxas to establish a fascist-inspired right-wing dictatorship. It banned political parties, suppressed civil liberties and trade-union action, unleashed extreme violence upon the KKE and its members, and geared the state more generally towards anti-communism.[3] The KKE's political infrastucture was almost destroyed, and prominent liberal politicians went into exile on various islands. All this set the scene for the foreign invasion and occupation which, during the early to mid-1940s, would challenge Greece's political elites and transform its society in ways no one could have foreseen.

*   *   *

Italy's entry into the Second World War in June 1940, and her geographical ambitions in the Mediterranean, made it increasingly likely that Greece would be pulled into the conflict. Metaxas turned down an Italian ultimatum, and on 28 October 1940 Mussolini invaded Greece itself.[4] In a relatively short period, however, the Greek army repelled the Italian offensive into the mountains of Epirus and western Greek Macedonia and pushed the Italians back into Albania. Hitler was infuriated at the comprehensiveness of the Italians' failure.

The British had begun to fortify the strategically important island of Crete in November 1940. Otherwise, however, British assistance to the Greeks was long in coming. Negotiations between the two sides were still ongoing following Metaxas' death on 29 January 1941. King George appointed Alexandros Koryzis, governor of the Central Bank, as prime minister, and in early March the British finally decided to dispatch an expeditionary force and a small number of aircraft to Greece and continue the fortification of Crete. All sides knew, however, that if the Germans attacked then Greece's position would become untenable.

After the failure of the Italian 'spring offensive', directed personally by Mussolini, German forces launched Operation Marita against Yugoslavia and Greece on 6 April. Three days later the Germans entered Thessaloniki and cut the Greek forces in two. Local army commanders on the Albanian front took the initiative and, in order to prevent their army's complete destruction, capitulated to the Germans. Lieutenant General George Tsolakoglou signed an armistice with the Germans and – more reluctantly and to the Greeks' immense chagrin – with the Italians, whose forces the Greeks had so comprehensively repelled only months before. King George and his government fled to Crete, while the British Expeditionary Force similarly sought to escape from the mainland. The Germans' entry into Athens on 27 April heralded the occupation of mainland Greece.

That left Crete.[5] Capturing the island would complete the German conquest of south-eastern Europe and eliminate any risk to the valuable Romanian oilfields. Operation Mercury, launched on 20 May, pitted German paratroopers and the 5th Mountain Division against the remnants of the British Expeditionary Force that had made their way to Crete and the tiny Greek force on the island. Allied troops fought bravely, but inefficient strategy and errors made by the Allied commander, Major General Freyberg, led to German victory at the end of May. Yet the battle also saw thousands of armed citizens, organized according to local and family ties, trying to assist the regular troops defending the island. The German reaction was immediate. By the end of August 1941, several hundred

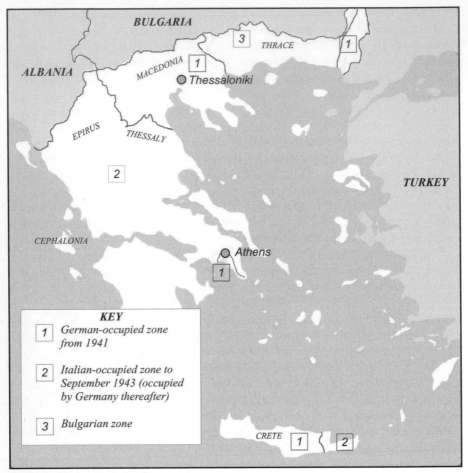

Occupied Greece, 1941–4.

civilians had been executed, mostly in the area of Khania in western Crete. Crete, then, was the first setting for that new kind of warfare that would make itself felt to such dramatic effect during the occupation of Greece over the next three-and-a-half years.

By June 1941 Greece had been divided among the Germans, the Italians and their Bulgarian allies. Hitler, eyes set firmly on the impending invasion of the Soviet Union and conscious of the already overstretched state of German occupation forces across Europe, sought to parcel off as much of Greece as possible to his Axis allies. The Italians occupied most of mainland Greece, including the areas of the Peloponnese, Epirus, Thessaly, Greek Macedonia and the islands of the Aegean and Ionian Seas; the latter were to be incorporated directly into the Italian state. At the Italian military administration's disposal were three armies, comprising between eleven and twelve divisions. Meanwhile, Bulgarian forces held eastern Greek Macedonia and Thrace, regions considered part of a 'Great

Bulgaria'. The Germans themselves held Athens, Thessaloniki, part of central Greek Macedonia, a buffer zone along the Turkish frontier, and a number of islands including much of the strategically important island of Crete. The various German-occupied areas were divided into two regional commands, Salonika-Aegean and Southern Greece, together with a fortress command on Crete, all of which were subordinate to Wehrmacht Command South-East. The Germans' military forces consisted primarily of the 6th Mountain Division and auxiliary and police units. Political administration was the preserve of the Reich Plenipotentiary for Greece, Dr Gunther Altenbourg, who was based in Athens.[6] Lieutenant General Tsolakoglou, meanwhile, was appointed by the Axis as head of a collaborationist government in Athens with an appearance of sovereign power.

Axis economic exploitation of Greek territory began almost immediately after the Greek collapse. Conditions were consequently very harsh for the civil population, and by winter 1941–2 thousands of people were suffering from malnutrition and famine.[7] These conditions were in part a legacy of Greece's pre-war dependence on food imports, but the effects of wartime made them incomparably worse. Not only Axis demands but also the British blockade contributed to a humanitarian crisis, one that could only be temporarily alleviated by intervention from the Red Cross. Problems in transportation between rural and urban areas, meanwhile, helped fuel the emergence of a flourishing black market. How many people perished as a result of famine conditions is in dispute.[8] What is clear, however, is that the suffering that hunger inflicted upon the general population throughout the occupation was superseded only by the suffering of the Greek Jews. This particular group was subjected to vicious and increasingly murderous persecution in those regions that the Germans occupied.[9]

* * *

Already, however, groups were forming that aimed to resist the occupying forces. Some were connected with British espionage networks and SOE agents. Others, particularly on the political left, sought the political and military mobilization of the entire population against the Axis and the puppet Greek government.[10] The main resistance organizations were the right-wing EDES (National Democratic Greek League) and the left-wing EAM (National Liberation Front) with its military branch ELAS (Greek People's Liberation Army). Both organizations, from 1942 onwards, began forming political committees and military units and eventually succeeded in controlling a large part of Greece. Their strongest centre, however, was in the mountainous region of Pindus, which stretches from near the Greek-Albanian borders in Northern Epirus, through Epirus and Macedonia in northern Greece and down to the north of the Peloponnese. EDES was a pro-British, conservative and nationalist organization, officially founded on 9 September 1941, and had its main base in Epirus in western Greece. EAM was officially founded eighteen days later as a political coalition of KKE and small left-wing parties. Its bases of support were spread all over Greece.

EDES started as an anti-monarchist organization favouring social reform measures, and was commanded by former colonel Napoleon Zervas. He was born in Arta, a town in Epirus, and he was considered a venizelist officer. He had participated in all the Greek army's major campaigns between 1910 and 1920, and had achieved fame by organizing a failed *coup d'état* in 1926 against the short-lived dictatorship of Theodoros Pangalos. Yet Zervas' opportunism, fondness for gambling and other bad habits had also earned him a reputation for unreliability. Nevertheless, the leader of EDES possessed a strong network of relatives and friends in Epirus, something that would prove crucial to his efforts at creating a guerrilla force there.

EAM, meanwhile, was commanded by members of KKE and by other left-wing sympathizers.[11] By winter 1941–2 EAM had established local committees in most parts of the country, organized the workers of the leftist organization EEAM (Worker's National Liberation Front), and was supporting Ethniki Allilleggii (National Solidarity) – a group seeking to help the most vulnerable in society. In May 1942 the communist Aris Veloukhiotis, whose real name was Athanasios Klaras, led a tiny group of guerrillas (*andartes*) in the mountains of Roumeli in central Greece. Before the war Veloukhiotis had been a KKE member, jailed by the Metaxas regime but released after signing a 'declaration of repentance'. He had served in the Greek army against the Italians, and after the front's collapse had rejoined KKE. Though he was considered unreliable by the party's leadership, his persistence and organizational skills led EAM to assign to him the task of developing a guerrilla force. These guerrillas depicted themselves as the vanguard of a new national revolution in the spirit of 1821. Thus was the nucleus of ELAS created in a region Veloukhiotis knew well.

Both organizations drew their forces mainly from the peasant population. The Pindus mountain region offered great advantages for guerrillas. State control there was a difficult task, with many communities responding negatively to modern institutions that tried to impose central authority. Despite significant political and economical developments in the interwar period, Pindus mostly remained isolated from the modernization processes that characterized urban Greece, its population's main economic activities being semi-nomadic stock-breeding and agriculture. During the Metaxas dictatorship the state's attempt to suppress banditry had been considered successful to a great extent, but the structure of society remained essentially unaltered. In particular, family and local ties remained dominant in the lives of the villagers, thus dictating the limits within which behaviours were judged permissible or not.[12]

The region's peculiarities, and its propensity for guerrilla warfare, were rein-forced by the slavophone Macedonians, a group that may have numbered any-thing between 100,000 and 200,000 persons. They were particularly suspicious of central government, still more so after the Venizelos government had transferred 600,000 Greeks from Asia Minor to Macedonia and Thrace following the Greco-Turkish War. The influx of so many new smallholders which this population transfer had created, and the claim upon territory that they made, had exacer-bated tensions between the 'old' and 'new' populations of these regions, and between the Macedonian Slavs and central government. By contrast, the communists, with their long-standing championing of ethnic minorities, held considerable attraction for the Macedonian Slavs. EAM built on this advantage by allowing the Macedonian Slavs to retain their own organization, the Slav-Macedonian Popular Liberation Front (SNOF), their own schools and armed detachments, and their communication links with fellow Slavs beyond Greece's borders. Faced with such enticements, the Macedonian Slavs aligned themselves predominantly with EAM in preference to the Bulgarian occupiers, who were also seeking to woo them. And they were certainly going to prefer EAM to non-EAM resistance organizations which advocated national expansion beyond Greece's borders *at the expense* of Greece's Slavic neighbours.[13] The formation of the People's Republic of Macedonia under Tito's regime in Yugoslavia would eventually prove a crucial factor in shaping the political and military involvement of the slavophone Macedonians in the Greek Civil War of 1946–9.[14]

The withdrawal of the state following the collapse of the front and the capitulation of April 1941 drove the need to organize everyday life from the bottom up. Local communities had to find their own solutions to the multiple problems posed by the new situation. The protection of individual property from the re-emerging danger of bandits, the safeguarding of civil rights and indeed the population's very survival were all at stake. An active mechanism 'from below' began to manage everyday life. One effect was the formation of militias in the villages in order to resist outlaws and bandits. Networks emerged covering a broad geographical scope, and a barter economy began gradually replacing cash transactions that had in fact become inactive.[15] But the different resistance organizations sought to renovate and expand quasi-state mechanisms. EAM was particularly active in this respect, seeking to establish its hegemony in the political arena and challenge the political elites of pre-war Greek society.[16]

In summer 1942, meanwhile, Napoleon Zervas made an appearance in the mountains of Valtos in western Greece. He was facing serious difficulties in his attempt to establish a guerrilla army, the main one being limited British support and the lack of a political infrastructure similar to that of EAM. In October, the first conflicts broke out between EDES guerrillas and Italian forces in the Radhovizi mountains. The Italian attack was conducted by the 37th Modena Division; Zervas' guerillas were mainly villagers from the region, mobilized on the basis of locality and kinship. Most of them were incorporated into EDES after Operation Harling, which took place in November of the same year and led to the destruction of the Gorgopotamos bridge.

The British wanted to destroy a railway bridge in central Greece, and a group of twelve saboteurs was formed in pursuit of this objective. Operation Harling would be one of the most impressive actions of sabotage in occupied Europe. Eddie Myers led the mission, with Christopher Woodhouse as his deputy.[17] Members of the group arrived by parachute in the mountains of central Greece in autumn 1942 with a mandate to come into contact with the Greek guerrillas. However, the British authorities in Cairo had no clear information as to the political and military goals of the resistance. Members of the mission finally managed to restore contact, following some fleeting British visits in late summer 1941, with Aris Veloukhiotis and Napoleon Zervas. Veloukhiotis had doubts about the mission, fuelled by negative instructions from EAM's political committee in Athens, but nevertheless agreed to help. Zervas, by contrast, was wholehearted about participating in a mission that would help restore contact with the British. Thus the two protagonists temporarily set aside their differences and cooperated, and the bridge was blown on 25 November 1942. This highly successful mission was the only major common enterprise between ELAS and EDES during the whole period of 1941–4.

During winter 1942–3 the armed groups active in the Pindus region began to proliferate and live up to their self-depiction as the warriors of 'the New 1821'.[18] By summer 1943 most of Greece's mountainous regions was held by the *andartes*. The main focus of guerrilla activity remained the mountains of Pindus, a fact that the occupying forces recognized. In western Macedonia, Evritania (and the wider area of central Greece) and Thessaly and Epirus, the two movements began properly implementing state-like structures. ELAS had its base in Evritania in central Greece, and EDES its base in Tzoumerka in Epirus. At this point a third resistance organization, the politically liberal EKKA (National and Social Liberation), formed a military unit, 5/42 Evzonoi Regiment, with British help. 5/42 Regiment had its main base in Roumeli and was headed by the venizelist colonel Dimitrios Psarros. The number of guerrillas at this time was estimated at approximately 20,000 for ELAS, between 4 and 5,000 for EDES and between 500 and 1,000 for EKKA.[19]

The crucial factors that fuelled the development of guerrilla armies in the Pindus region were the aforementioned well-established feeling of independence from the state and its mechanisms, a tradition of rebellion connected to irredentist movements of the past, a long-standing tradition of independent groups that fought for 'national liberation' purposes, and the presence of some particularly important individuals. From this viewpoint one can discern the reemergence of warlords (*oplarhighoi*) or local leaders, some of whom had also been involved in the 1912–13 Balkan Wars. *Oplarhighoi* were people with great influence in their villages and even in neighbouring communities, who established armed groups by making use of kinship ties and local networks. The word *oplarhighoi* on the one hand evokes the nineteenth-century rebellions against the Ottomans, and on the other hand the Balkan Wars when semi-irregular forces had sided with the regular Greek army. The heads of those semi-irregular forces were called chieftains or captains (*kapetanioi*). In Epirus most of these warlords decided to support Zervas and EDES, mainly because EDES offered them the chance to act in a semi-autonomous way. Some of the most famous warlords were Spyros Karambinas, Alekos Papadopoulos, Stylianos Khoutas, Kostas Voidaros and the leaders of the Koliodimitraioi family.[20]

By contrast, the *kapetanioi* that sided with ELAS had to co-operate with military officers and political commissars in a system designed to promote not just combat effectiveness but also the movement's political goals. By June 1943 an ELAS GHQ had been established in the mountains. Its members at that time were Aris Veloukhiotis, the former venizelist Colonel Stephanos Sarafis and a prominent communist named Andreas Tzimas.

By 1943 EAM was extending its political power across Greece and thus seriously challenging the occupation forces. It was also behaving antagonistically towards the small nationalist resistance organizations that had emerged by that time. The political antagonism between EAM and its rivals was clear to every observer. EAM had managed, nevertheless, to lead great demonstrations in Athens, organize strikes and mobilize thousands of non-communists. Women and youth were particularly attracted to it.[21] A youth movement (EPON-Eniaia Panelladiki Organosi Neon) was created by EAM, attracting thousands of young men and women.[22] The wholehearted acceptance of women into left-wing organizations, with its explicit challenge to pre-war hierarchies of age and gender, provoked a fierce reaction from the conservative element of Greek society. EAM also enjoyed extensive approval among intellectuals and writers.

But relations between the British and EAM were a major problem. The British supported EAM strictly for military reasons, but they did not trust it. It was considered a serious threat to Greece's political future. Gradually, EAM leaders started demanding that King George not be allowed to return to Greece without a referendum. The Greek government-in-exile was powerless to mobilize action on the mainland, and the British were fully aware that no serious royalist resistance organization had been formed there. But Churchill, not wanting to abandon King George II, insisted on his return to Greece after the war. The British now decided to support Zervas and the smaller nationalist groups in order to strengthen the power of the anti-communist bloc.[23] Zervas in fact was forced to support the return of the king in order to maintain his organization. EAM leaders, increasingly uncertain about British intentions, briefly pondered an agreement with Tito and the Albanian guerrillas. Finally, they decided to accept British supervision of resistance.

In July 1943, supervised by British HQ Middle East, a joint general headquarters of the Greek guerrillas began to operate in Pertouli, a village in central Greece. The Headquarters (KGSA) was to become the coordinating core of guerrilla actions. Operation Animals was planned in order to convince the Germans that an Allied invasion on the Greek coast was imminent. Where possible, British liaison officers started co-operating with guerrillas on the ground.[24] In Crete, where EAM was less powerful, various semi-independent warlords, such as Manolis Bandouvas and Petrakogiorgis, had formed armed groups that fought the Germans, and British espionage networks were highly active.[25] Elsewhere, although EDES and EKKA-5/42 were co-operating with ELAS in KGSA, tensions were always present.

For the occupiers, however, the guerrillas constituted a mounting threat. Yet the Italians, who controlled most of the country until summer 1943, were more reluctant to fight them than were the Germans or Bulgarians. This unwillingness was partly because the Italians' defeat at the hands of the Greek army was deeply ingrained within them. Though they were no less arrogant towards the Greek people compared with the Germans and Bulgarians, they were considered more lenient. Though it was far from the case that they eschewed brutality altogether, something to which their widespread destruction of villages testifies,[26] they were generally more hesitant about executing civilians.[27]

Following the collapse of Mussolini's regime, the Italian forces in Greece found themselves facing huge dilemmas in an immensely difficult situation. Some units tried unsuccessfully to negotiate with the Germans, while others tried to approach the guerrillas. In one infamous instance the soldiers of the Acqui Division, stationed on the island of Cephalonia, were massacred by their former allies.[28] A few months later, many of these formerly *gloriosi* (glorious soldiers) of the fascist regime were wandering around Pindus with 'holes in their boots', in the words of a survivor.[29]

The German army's response to Greek guerrillas was undeniably harsher, infused by the spirit of modern total warfare and the German military's particularly marked contempt for guerrilla movements. After the Italian collapse, more than ten German army divisions and various subsidiary forces were dispatched to the Balkan peninsula with the aim not just of suppressing guerrilla movements but also of securing the region against potential Allied invasion. General Wilhelm Speidel, subordinate to Colonel General Alexander Löhr's Army Group E, took charge of all occupied Greece save the newly extended Bulgarian zone. The powers of the SS and Police were extended also, with the appointment of a Higher SS and Police Leader in September 1943.[30] The new German command structure faced a burgeoning resistance movement and a population that, groaning under ongoing Axis exploitation, shortages of food and materials and increasingly intolerable levels of inflation, continued to resent the Axis occupation bitterly.[31]

In order to confront the guerrillas effectively, the Germans deemed it necessary to implement the toughest measures against civilian populations suspected of supporting them. Prior to the appearance of Greek guerrillas in serious numbers, the Germans, indeed even Hitler himself, retained a strong degree of respect for a people that had spawned ancient Greek civilization and shown resilience and bravery in modern times. But the emergence of resistance led the Germans to think differently about Greeks. The new attitude is exemplified in a typical order by Löhr to local German commanders on 10 August 1943.[32] That said, a framework for markedly brutal anti-guerrilla conduct in the Balkans had already been set by the Wehrmacht in autumn 1941. In September 1941 the Armed Forces High Command had issued a decree that stipulated the execution of 100 hostages for every German soldier killed by guerrillas, and the following month the Wehrmacht had unleashed an especially ferocious reprisal campaign against the Serb national uprising.[33]

In order to control the Greek guerrillas, the German Armed Forces High Command ordered the 1st Mountain Division Edelweiss to Ioannina, capital of Epirus. The division, commanded by Lieutenant General Walter von Stettner, formed part of the newly created XXII Army Corps under General Hubert Lanz. The total number of German soldiers in the region exceeded 20,000 men.[34]

The Germans faced a situation in which death could come from lone snipers, guerrillas rarely wore insignia and avoided open battle involving hit and run tactics. Indeed, any civilian could be considered a suspect. In the words of General Lanz,

> During the entire period of the Occupation hardly a night and, from the summer of 1944, not a single day passed without a surprise attack, a mine explosion, or another act of sabotage occurring on one of the supply roads. Valuable material was consequently lost every time, frequently heavy casualties occurred, and only in a few cases did one succeed in locating and inflicting damage upon an enemy adept in clever operations.[35]

An example was the death of Colonel Josef Salminger on 30 September 1943, an event that prompted Lanz to order immensely harsh reprisals. The trap on the Ioannina–Arta road that led to Salminger's death had been constructed by two members of the Xirovouni Regiment of EDES, well known for their pre-war 'love of illegal practices'.[36] More generally, the Germans' brutal retaliatory measures included the burning of villages and the mass execution of civilians. In one particularly infamous episode, the peaceful village of Kommeno, south of Arta, suffered the execution of 317 of its inhabitants including women and children.[37] The massacre took place on 16 August 1943, carried out by members of the 98th Regiment of the 1st Mountain Division. The regiment, commanded by the same Colonel Salminger, whose days were numbered, was supposedly 'eliminating the guerrillas' who had previously made an appearance in the village. In fact, the village was not a guerrilla base, but rather had been forced to supply the *andartes* of both ELAS and EDES.[38]

* * *

The Germans' specific military aim in autumn 1943 was two-fold. They first sought to regain control of the main road between Epirus and Thessaly (Ioannina–Metsovo–Kalambaka), which ELAS had captured following Italy's capitulation. Secondly, they sought to put the resistance under heavy economic pressure by destroying its main bases of supply. The guerrillas were able to reorganize their forces with relative ease, but hundreds of villages, located mostly in the area of Pindus, were burned, executions were common practice and the economic damage was incalculable. Between July and October 1943 in Epirus alone, 210 villages were destroyed, 5,200 houses burned to the ground and 1,746 civilians executed. In Kalavryta in the Peloponnese, the 117th Infantry Division, commanded by General Karl le Suire, executed hundreds of civilians in reprisal for the killing of 78 of its soldiers by ELAS guerrillas.[39] Between March 1943 and October 1944, 21,255 Greeks had been killed by the occupying powers and a further 20,000 imprisoned.[40]

The German campaign also unleashed terrible Greek-on-Greek violence between ELAS and Greek anti-communist collaborators. Some anti-communists forces were provided by semi-independent warlords, mostly from Greek Macedonia. More extensively, the Germans utilized large numbers of Greeks in security battalions (*Tagmata Asfaleias*), founded by the government of Ioannis Rallis, who had replaced Konstantinos Logothetopoulos, Tsolakoglou's succesor, as prime minister in April 1943. The Germans found not just their fighting power useful, but more importantly their local knowledge. Few security battalionists were consciously pro-German; indeed, many convinced themselves that the British approved of their anti-communist actions. Many security battalionists were drawn from ethnic minorities, such as Turkish-speaking Greek Christians from Asia Minor; they hated the Macedonian Slavs who formed such a large mainstay of ELAS manpower. Others were bandits and other criminals motivated primarily by the opportunities for plunder that such work offered. In Macedonia, security battalionists were also recruited as a result of independent warlords approaching the Germans in order to maintain some sort of autonomy in the face of EAM's attempts to neutralize them. Religious, local and family ties played a major role in shaping the development of the security battalions. But what probably animated security battalionists above all, recruited from traditionally pro-royalist regions as so many of them were, was anti-communism. Whatever the motives of their personnel, the Germans frequently employed security battalions as an instrument of terror and to deter civilians from supporting ELAS.

Most of the civil strife that ravaged Greece in 1944 resulted not from the antagonism between ELAS and its rivals, but from that between ELAS and collaborationist forces.[41] By 1944 over 18,000 men were active in such forces.[42] The undoubted brutality of many collaborationist troops notwithstanding, however, there remains a difficult question for historians. It is not clear just how far the pressure that EAM put upon the population in many regions – their antagonism towards refugee Greek smallholders in western Macedonia, for instance, was severe – compelled many civilians to join the security battalions at a time when an eventual Allied victory looked increasingly likely.[43]

In October 1943, meanwhile, the political differences beween EAM/ELAS and EDES flared into open civil war. The surrender of the Italian Pinerolo Division to ELAS boosted the latter militarily and encouraged its leaders to believe that their forces could now destroy EDES. Meanwhile, Zervas thought the time right to break with the 'communists' of EAM and destroy its infrastructure. He had, after all, sided with his former royalist 'enemy' in March 1943 when, under a British initiative, he had sent two letters to King George informing him that he would not oppose his return to Greece if the British were to sanction it.

The battles were fought from October 1943 until February 1944 in the Tzoumerka region, the 'apple of discord' for both ELAS and EDES, and were for many years seen as the 'first round' of KKE's attempt to seize power. Tzoumerka had an enormous geo-strategic significance for both organizations. For ELAS, its capture would signify the 'unification' of the area with Thessaly and the establishment of an exceptionally robust bridgehead in the Epirus region. On the other hand, for EDES, which was deprived of 'mainland affiliations', abandoning Tzoumerka would automatically signify the organization's confinement to western Epirus – as indeed subsequently came to pass. The military situation at the local level seemed negative for ELAS, however. Despite its efforts to assemble an effective force of regional guerrillas, EDES' dominance was incontestable.

This was clear in the number of villagers who joined its forces.[44] The greatest significance of the clashes between ELAS and EDES was that they banished the very last chance of a solid, unified resistance, and catalysed mutual hatred among those sections of the civilian population that supported them. Moreover, the conflict brought dramatic consequences for the inhabitants of the regions held by the guerrillas.

The multiple pressures upon EDES led Zervas to strike a 'gentlemen's agreement' with the Germans, while at the same time he was being instructed by the British in Cairo to abstain from any kind of operation in order to avoid civilian casualties.[45] This move, according to Christopher Woodhouse, was similar to the *kapaki* – the practice of the *klefts* and *armatoloi* of the Ottoman era who negotiated with the Turks every time they faced difficulties, but were ready to confront them again when circumstances changed.[46] In the same way, the forces of EDES attacked the Germans once more in summer 1944, again provoking a fierce German reaction.

As a result of the conflict between EAM/ELAS and EDES, the region of Epirus became split into two distinct entities. On the one hand there was EAM's Free Greece (Elefhteri Ellada), which, following the Pláka agreement of 29 February 1944, included Zervas's former strongholds in the eastern part of the prefecture. On the other hand, there was EDES' Free Mountainous Greece (Elefhteri Oreini Ellada), the western region beyond the Árakhthos River. In the EDES-controlled region, guerrillas were reorganized by means of 'militarization' – namely, transforming the guerrilla groups into organized troops which gave the impression of a regular army. In the EAM-controlled region, local ELAS guerrillas were also reorganized, elections were held and a provisional government set up. While both sides spent most of the time until summer 1944 preparing for the aftermath of the impending German retreat, they also raced to take over the region's main urban centres.

The political situation was complicated further after George Papandreou formed a government-in-exile of 'national unity' in May 1944. Negotiations in Lebanon had paved the way for a political compromise with EAM. EAM's leaders were uncertain about the upcoming agreement, however. Among other things, they were now accused by their opponents of the destruction of 5/42 Regiment, of the execution of Colonel Psarros in Klima Doridas in April 1944, and of being implicated in a mutiny within the Greek army of the Middle East that had led to the resignation of the prime minister-in-exile, Emmanouil Tsouderos. Eventually, however, EAM decided to support a 'national unity' government under Papandreou. Papandreou, strongly supported by Churchill, was confident he would be able to tackle EAM with British help if necessary. The situation, then, was far from stabilized.

In summer 1944 major German offensives were launched all over Greece in order to suppress the guerrilla movement. Again, however, the operations failed in their ultimate goal despite the Germans' ferocious retaliatory measures.[47] By the end of October 1944 German forces had withdrawn from mainland Greece and the country was liberated. Athens was evacuated by the Germans on

12 October and thousands celebrated in the capital's streets. But the celebration would be short-lived. For one thing, though EAM/ELAS was controlling most of the country, with the exception of parts of Epirus and eastern Macedonia, battles were still being fought in most areas of the countryside between ELAS and the security battalions. ELAS exacted fierce vengeance upon collaborators during the closing months of 1944. In Euboia and western Macedonia in particular, the looting and terror that the security battalions had inflicted upon EAM/ELAS-supporting villages was answered with a brutal ELAS campaign against the families of collaborationist troops and also of gendarmes.[48]

Meanwhile, the Germans increased the likelihood of eventual civil war between EAM/ELAS and EDES by abandoning ammunition to both mutually antagonistic organizations. In the weeks up to December 1944, relations between EAM/ELAS and the non-communist element of the provisional government and its supporters deteriorated further. This set the scene for the final prominent episode in Greece during the Second World War, the Battle of Athens. Given that the battle had its origins in the years of occupation and resistance, it deserves some discussion here.

Immediately following the liberation, the British were too busy harrying the fleeing Germans to assist Papandreou extensively, and this temporarily increased his reliance upon EAM/ELAS. Meanwhile, EAM's high levels of support and the intimidatory tactics it readily utilized strengthened its authority in the areas it already controlled, and encouraged it to extend its control further. It now sought to punish not just collaborators, but also prominent supporters of the old Metaxas regime, and also imposed communist-style policies upon the areas it controlled. None of this reassured the rest of the provisional government that EAM intended to adhere to democratic principles in the future. A further flashpoint came with the return of the Greek Mountain Brigade from service in Italy, which EAM feared would form the nucleus of a new Greek army outwith its control, and which indeed some liberals and impartial observers feared might be used to try to install another royalist dictatorship. Yet when Papandreou agreed to disband the brigade, General Ronald Scobie, the abrasive commander of Allied forces in Greece, vetoed his decision for fear of weakening the forces that might halt a future communist takeover. This, and the fact that the British were allowing some former collaborators in their custody considerable freedom of movement, in turn alarmed EAM/ELAS. Relations deteriorated further as the British registered movements of ELAS troops in the direction of Athens.

In late November, talks in Athens to demobilize the *andartes* broke down. In the first days of December, EAM ministers resigned from the government, demonstrations broke out around the capital upon which the police opened fire and EAM supporters retaliated by blockading and attacking the city's police stations. It is unclear how far, if at all, each side was deliberately provoking a civil war type situation, but such was the position they were now in. EAM/ELAS does not appear to have wanted to launch a full-scale attack against the British; after all, its main forces were locked in combat in Epirus with EDES. But the British, despite being initially caught off balance by ELAS snipers, soon hit back in a counter-offensive supported by many conservative Greeks who saw in it an opportunity to finish off ELAS in the capital. The combination of air strikes and overwhelming manpower that the British employed led to many civilian as well as combatant deaths.[49]

The defeat in Athens meant that EAM was in no position to dictate terms to the British or to the new prime minister, Nikolaos Plastiras.[50] EAM/ELAS now lost its advantage in the rest of the country also. The British denied food to rebellious areas, and EAM was forced to increase taxation in the areas it controlled. This antagonized a population already increasingly Anglophile in its sympathies, grateful for its recent liberation and fearful that the strong preponderance of Macedonian Slavs in EAM/ELAS would lead it to concede territory to Greece's Slavic neighbours. Neither Stalin nor Tito, concerned not to antagonize the Western Allies unnecessarily, proffered practical help to EAM/ELAS. Moreover, when the British rounded up 15,000 leftist sympathizers, ELAS reacted by executing hundreds of members of 'reactionary families' and lost massive moral capital, domestically as well as internationally, in the process.[51]

EAM/ELAS now sought peace and demobilization in return for an amnesty and free elections – though it was careful to hide its better quality arms first for future use.[52] In February 1945 the Varkiza Agreement was signed in Athens, and the resistance armies were disbanded. General elections and a referendum on the fate of the monarchy were to be held. But the situation was still not stabilized. In 1946, full-scale civil war broke out between the communist and anti-communist camps. American intervention in 1947 was crucial, and led to the defeat of the communists in 1949. The origins of this war, like those of the Battle of Athens before it, were to be found in the period of occupation and resistance.

*   *   *

The historiography on the Greek resistance has addressed it mainly with regard to the struggle between EAM/ELAS and its rival resistance organizations, and how each sought to impose hegemony upon its opponents. EAM's policy towards its opponents was, and remains, particularly controversial in this regard. Particularly important questions relate to how far EAM was intending to impose a communist regime at the end of the war, the organization's social composition, how it radicalized much of the population and how far the full-scale civil war that broke out in 1946 was a genuine continuation of the struggle between the left-wing and anti-communist resistance movements during the years 1943–4. The debate over 'red' and 'white' terror – that is to say, communist and anti-communist violence – during the period has been particularly strong during the last fifteen years or so.[53] Other studies over the same period have addressed themes such as collaboration, the impact of local and family feuds upon the formation of the guerrilla armies, the social identity of the participants and the role of ethnic minorities in the resistance.[54] Young scholars are particularly active in furthering study, at a time of great political and economic crisis in Greece which many perceive as resembling earlier times of instability and turmoil.

Notes

1. G. Mavrogordatos, *Stillborn republic: social coalitions and party strategies in Greece 1922–1936* (Berkeley, Cal., 1983).
2. S. Sepheriades, 'Small Rural Ownership, Subsistence Agriculture, and Peasant Protest in Interwar Greece: The Agrarian Question Recast', *Journal of Modern Greek Studies*, 17 (1999).
3. Neni Panourgia, *Dangerous Citizens. The Greek Left and the terror of the state* (New York, 2009), pp. 39–48.
4. Hellenic Army General Staff, *An Abridged History of the Greek-Italian and Greek-German War* (Athens 1997).
5. A. Beevor, *Crete: The Battle and the Resistance* (London, 1991).
6. On German occupation arrangements see Hans Umbreit, 'Towards Continental Dominion', in Bernhard R. Kroener, Rolf-Dieter Muller, Hans Umbreit, Ewald Osers, John Brownjohn, Patricia Crampton, Louise Willmott, *Germany and the Second World War Vol. V: Organization and Mobilization of the German Sphere of Power. Pt 1: Wartime administration, economy, and manpower resources 1939–1941* (Oxford, 2000), pp. 9–404.
7. Violetta Hionidou, *Famine and Death in Occupied Greece, 1941–1944* (New York, 2006), pp. 32–48.
8. The numbers vary between 500,000 and 100,000. See E. Bournova-G.Progoulakis, 'Oi oikono-mikes sinthikes stin periodo tis Katohis' ('The economic conditions in the Occupation period'), in H. Fleischer (ed.), *Katohi-Antistasi 1941–1944 (Occupation-Resistance 1941–44)* (Athens, 2010), pp. 57–63.
9. The ultimate result was the death of 50,000 Greek Jews, most of them residents of the hitherto flourishing Jewish community of Thessaloniki. As the fate of the Greek Jews did not have a major impact upon the growth of the Greek resistance – though some escaping Jews did join the resistance – these tragic events are largely outside the scope of this chapter. The reader is directed to Mark Mazower, *Inside Hitler's Greece: The Experience of Occupation, 1941–44* (New Haven, Conn., 1992), pp. 235–61; *idem*, *Salonica – City of Ghosts: Christians, Muslims and Jews, 1430–1950* (London, 2005), pp. 421–42; Steven B. Bowman, *The Agony of Greek Jews, 1940–1945* (Palo Alto, Cal., 2009).
10. Tsolakoglou resigned from the government in 1942 and was replaced by Dr Konstantinos Logothetopoulos.
11. H. Vlavianos, 'The Greek Communist Party: in search of a Revolution', in Tony Judt (ed.), *Resistance and Revolution in Mediterranean Europe 1939–1948* (London, 1989), pp. 168–72.
12. A. Kitroeff, 'Greek peasantry from dictatorship to occupation', in Robin Higham and Thanos Veremis (eds), *Aspects of Greece 1936–40. The Metaxas Dictatorship* (Athens, 1993), pp. 63–84.
13. David H. Close, *The Origins of the Greek Civil War* (London, 1995), pp. 5, 51, 65, 75, 95.
14. A. Rossos, 'Incompatible Allies: Greek Communism and Macedonian Nationalism in the Civil War in Greece', *Journal of Modern History*, 69/3 (1997).
15. G. Margaritis, *Apo tin itta stin exegersi (Ellada anoixi 1941–fthinoporo 1942) (From Defeat to Revolt. Greece spring 1941–autumn 1942)* (Athens, 1993).
16. On EAM see in particular Mark Mazower, *Inside Hitler's Greece, passim*.
17. For accounts by these principal eyewitnesses, see E.C.W. Myers, *Greek Entanglement* (London, 1955); C.M. Woodhouse, *Apple of Discord: A Survey of Recent Greek Politics in their International Setting* (London, 1948).
18. R.V. Boeschoten, *From Armatolik to people's rule: Investigation into the collective memory of rural Greece 1750–1949* (Amsterdam, 1991).
19. See J. Handrinos, 'The Organisations of National Resistance' ('Oi organoseis tis Ethikis Antistasis. Katagrafi kai Analysi'), in H. Fleischer (ed.), *Katohi-Antistasi 1941–1944 (Occupation-Resistance 1941–44)* (Athens, 2010), pp. 77–108.
20. Vangelis Tzoukas, 'Oi oplarhigoi tou EDES stin Ipeiro. Topikotita kai politiki entaxi (The War-lords of EDES in Epirus. Locality and political integration)', PhD dissertation, Panteion University of Political and Social Sciences (Athens, 2003).
21. Tasoula Vervenioti, 'Left-wing Women between Politics and Family', in Mark Mazower (ed.), *After the War was Over. Reconstructing the Family, Nation and the State in Greece, 1943–1960* (Princeton, New Jer., 2000), pp. 105–21.

22. Odette Varon Vassard, *I enilikiosi mias genias. Neoi kai Nees stin Katohi kai tin Antistasi (The coming of age of a generation. Young men and women in Occupation and Resistance)* (Athens, 2009).

23. Procopis Papastratis, *British policy towards Greece during the Second World War 1941–44* (Cambridge, 1984).

24. Lars Baerentzen (ed.), *British Reports on Greece 1943–44 by J.M. Stevens, C.M. Woodhouse and D.J. Wallace* (Copenhagen, 1982).

25. Beevor, *Crete*, pp. 235–83.

26. Davide Rodogno, 'Italian Soldiers in the Balkans: The experience of the occupation', *Journal of Southern Europe and the Balkans*, 6/2 (2004).

27. Lidia Santarelli, 'Muted Violence: Italian war crimes in occupied Greece', *Journal of Modern Italian Studies*, 9/3 (2004).

28. Charles T. O'Reilly, *Forgotten Battles: Italy's War of Liberation 1943–45* (Lanham, Md., 2001), pp. 100–1.

29. R. Galiberti, *Trypia Arvyla* (Athens, 1999).

30. Hans Umbreit, 'German Rule in the Occupied Territories 1942–1945', in Bernhard R. Kroener, Rolf-Dieter Müller, Hans Umbreit, Derry Cook-Radmore, Ewald Osers, Barry Smerin and Barbara Wilson, *Germany and the Second World War Vol. 5: Organization and Mobilization of the German Sphere of Power. Pt 2: Wartime administration, economy, and manpower resources 1942–1944/5* (Oxford, 2003), pp. 5–291, here pp. 42–5.

31. *Ibid.*

32. A. Löhr in M. Zekedorf (ed.), *I Ellada kato apo ton agkiloto stavro – Dokoumenta apo ti germaniki Katohi (Greece under the Swastika. Documents from the German Occupation)* (Athens, 1991).

33. On the Germans' 1941 campaign in Yugoslavia see Walter Manoschek, *Serbien ist judenfrei: Militärische Besatzungspolitik und Judenvernichtung in Serbien 1941/42* (Munich, 1993); Klaus Schmider, *Partisanenkrieg in Jugoslawien 1941–1944* (Hamburg, 2002), pp. 54–103; Ben Shepherd, *Terror in the Balkans: German Armies and Partisan Warfare* (Cambridge, Mass., 2012), pp. 83–147.

34. H.F. Mayer, *Blutiges Edelweis Die 1. Gebirgs-Division im Zweiten WeltKrieg* (Berlin, 2007) (Greek trans., *Aimatovammeno Entelvais: H 1h Oreini Merarxia, to 22o Soma Stratou kai I egklimatiki drasi tous stn Ellada, 1943–1944* (Athens, 2009)).

35. (General) H. Lanz, *Partisan Warfare in the Balkans* (US Army, European Command, Historical Division, 1952), pp. 7–8.

36. Tzoukas, 'The Warlords of EDES', pp. 50–130.

37. M. Mazower, *Inside Hitler's Greece*, pp. 190–200. See also H.F. Mayer, *I Blutiges Edelweis Die 1. Gebirgs-Division im Zweiten Weltkrieg* (Berlin, 2007) (Greek trans., *Aimatovammeno Entelvais, H 1h Oreini Merarxia, to 22o Soma Stratou kai I egklimatiki drasi tous stn Ellada, 1943–1944*), Vol. 1, pp. 294–314.

38. Mazower, *Inside Hitler's Greece*, pp. 190–200.

39. Mayer, *Aimatovammeno Entelvais*, Vol. II, pp. 111–12; Mazower, *Inside Hitler's Greece*, p. 179.

40. Umbreit, 'German Rule in the Occupied Territories 1942–1945', p. 45.

41. Close, *The Origins of the Greek Civil War*, pp. 90–1, 115.

42. Ian F.W. Beckett, *Modern Insurgencies and Counter-Insurgencies: Guerrillas and their opponents since 1750* (New York, 2001), p. 67.

43. S. Kalyvas, 'Red Terror. Leftist Violence during the Occupation', in Mark Mazower (ed.), *After the War was Over*, pp. 142–83.

44. The local regiment of EDES was one of the best units of the Andartiko. By the summer of 1943 it numbered 1,370 guerrillas. See V. Tzoukas, 'Oi oplarhigoi tou EDES stin Ipeiro. Topikotita kai politiki entaxi ('The Warlords of EDES in Epirus. Locality and political integration)', PhD dissertation, Panteion University of Political and Social Sciences (Athens, 2003), p. 244.

45. J.L. Hondros, *Occupation and Resistance: The Greek Agony 1941–44* (New York, 1983).

46. C.M. Woodhouse, *The Struggle for Greece 1941–49* (New York, 1976), p. 91.

47. S. Dordanas, *To aima ton athoon. Antipoina ton germanikon arxon katoxis sti Makedonia, 1941–44 (Blood of the innocents. Reprisals of the German occupation forces in Macedonia, 1941–44)* (Athens, 2007).

48. Close, *The Origins of the Greek Civil War*, p. 115.

49. On the causes and course of the December 1944 fighting, see Mazower, *Inside Hitler's Greece*, pp. 368–72; Close, *The Origins of the Greek Civil War*, Ch. 5.
50. David Close and Thanos Veremis, 'The British Defeat of EAM, 1944–45', in David Close (ed.), *The Greek Civil War: Studies of Polarization* (London, 1993), pp. 97–128.
51. Mazower, *Inside Hitler's Greece*, pp. 370–2; Close, *The Origins of the Greek Civil War*, pp. 141–5.
52. Close, *The Origins of the Greek Civil War*, p. 144.
53. See for example Stathis Kalyvas, 'Red Terror. Leftist Violence during the Occupation'; *idem*, *The Logic of Violence in Civil War* (Cambridge, 2006); Giorgos Antoniou, 'The lost Atlantis of Objectivity: the revisionist struggles between the academic and public spheres', *History and Theory*, 46/4 (2007).
54. Mark Mazower, 'Historians at War: Greece, 1940–1950', *Historical Journal*, 38/2 (1995); Nikos Marantzidis and Giorgos Antoniou, 'The Axis Occupation and Civil War: Changing Trends in Greek Historiography, 1941–2002', *Journal of Peace Research*, 41 (2004).

Guide to Further Reading

Beevor, A., *Crete: The Battle and the Resistance* (London, 1991).
Close, David H., *The Origins of the Greek Civil War* (London, 1995).
Hionidou, Violetta, *Famine and Death in Occupied Greece, 1941–1944* (New York, 2006).
Hondros, J.L., *Occupation and Resistance: The Greek Agony 1941–44* (New York, 1983).
Marantzidis, Nikos and Giorgos Antoniou, 'The Axis Occupation and Civil War: Changing Trends in Greek Historiography, 1941–2002', in *Journal of Peace Research*, 41 (2004).
Mazower, Mark, *Inside Hitler's Greece: The Experience of Occupation, 1941–44* (New Haven, Conn., 1993).
Idem, 'Historians at War: Greece, 1940–1950', in *Historical Journal*, 38/2 (1995).
Myers, C.W., *Greek Entanglement* (London, 1955).
Rossos, A., 'Incompatible Allies: Greek Communism and Macedonian Nationalism in the Civil War in Greece', in *Journal of Modern History*, 69/3 (1997).
Vlavianos, H., 'The Greek Communist Party: in search of a Revolution', in Tony Judt (ed.), *Resistance and Revolution in Mediterranean Europe 1939–1948* (London, 1989).
Woodhouse, C.M., *Apple of Discord: A Survey of Recent Greek Politics in their International Setting* (London, 1948).
Idem, *The Struggle for Greece 1941–49* (New York, 1976).

Chapter 6

Italy

Massimo Storchi

The year 1943 was one of crisis in Italy's war effort. On the home front a series of strikes took place in the month of March in the major factories of Milan and Turin. More than 100,000 workers participated in these actions. They were the first major strikes of the Italian fascist era and the second in importance, after those in Amsterdam in 1941 protesting against the deportation of Jews, in fascist Europe. In addition, major bombardments had begun of the cities of southern Italy which affected, above all, Naples and Foggia. In the summer of 1943 the northern industrial centres of Milan, Turin and Genoa were bombed.

In terms of the front-line war effort in 1943, Italy was on the receiving end of a series of major setbacks, with the definitive defeat of the Italo-German troops in North Africa, followed by the landings of the Allied troops in Sicily which took place on 10 July. The defence of the island, which was carried out almost entirely by German troops, demonstrated, even more than the inefficiency and the lack of conviction of the fascist army, the passivity of the population before the defeat of its own army. The Allied troops, meanwhile, were welcomed by the Sicilians as 'liberators'.

The last phase of Mussolini's political crisis began on 16 July, when a group of fascist leaders, who were openly critical of his recent leadership, requested a meeting of the Fascist Grand Council, which had not met for four years. On 19 July the Duce met Hitler in Feltre. As usual, he was no match for the Axis leader and 'listened once again in silence to the bombastic monologue of Hitler'.[1] Rather than negotiating, as the Italian military command had requested, a withdrawal from the conflict, Mussolini accepted the Führer's offer to increase the number of German troops defending southern Italy. Meanwhile, Nazi Germany, which for several months had feared an Italian surrender, accelerated its plan – codenamed Operation Axis – for the military occupation of Italian territory.

On the same day as the meeting in Feltre, the first disastrous bombing of Rome took place. The residential areas of San Lorenzo, Tiburtino and Prenestino were devastated, with more than 1,500 civilian deaths.[2] The Pope, Pius XII, left the confines of the Vatican City to bring comfort to the victims, thereby breaking the self-imposed isolation of the papacy from Rome which had lasted for more than seventy years. With yet another demonstration of the impossibility of fighting effectively against the enemy, sections of the Court, of the military apparatus and of the Fascist Grand Council began to pressurize King Vittorio Emanuele III. They argued that the clear unpopularity of fascism and of

Mussolini risked bringing down the monarchy itself, and that the only course of action was to remove the Duce from his post.

In agreement with several fascist leaders, including Dino Grandi and Mussolini's son-in-law, Galeazzo Ciano, the monarchy, exploiting the divisions and the internal rivalries within the Fascist National Party, organized a show of strength which led to Mussolini losing a vote of confidence during the meeting of the Fascist Grand Council on 25 July 1943. The monarchy immediately exploited the internal crisis of fascism and the Duce was relieved of his powers. The nation was informed by radio at 10.45pm, and immediate demonstrations of unbridled joy were seen throughout the country. The fall of Mussolini was associated, by a large part of the population, with the end of a war that had been desired by and conducted by fascism. The following day the demonstrations continued despite the fact that the new President of the Council, the former head of the Army Pietro Badoglio, declared that the hostilities were to continue.

During the demonstrations the whole of Italy witnessed assaults on local Fascist Party headquarters and the destruction of the symbols of fascism and of portraits of Mussolini, but there were no acts of violence against the fascists. This was because the military remained strong in various parts of Italy and violently repressed the demonstrations. In the squares the populace sang the praises of both the king and the army and, with the anti-fascist prisoners now released from jail, the political opposition began to reorganize itself.

*   *   *

The 8 September 1943 represents a dramatic and fundamental date in the history of Italy. Even today the expression '8 September' has the significance of a dramatic event, of a moment of definitive but unforeseen crisis. On that day, in the late afternoon, the signing of the armistice between Italy and the Allies, which had taken place on 3 September, was made public. This is how Marshal Badoglio made the announcement on the radio:

> The Italian government, having recognized the impossibility of continuing in an uneven fight against the greater power of the adversary, and in the hope of saving further and graver disasters to the nation, has requested an armistice from General Eisenhower, the commander in chief of the Anglo-American forces. This request has been granted. As a consequence every act of hostility toward the Anglo-American forces by Italian forces must cease forthwith. Our forces must however react to any other attacks, from wherever they may come.

The enthusiasm of July gave way to a period of waiting and of concern. As each hour went by it became more and more obvious that a disaster had occurred: King Vittorio Emanuele III and his government had abandoned Rome and fled to Pescara (where he was unable to board an aircraft) and then to Brindisi, which had already been liberated by the Allies, but had left the armed forces behind without any precise orders. Badoglio's communiqué announcing the armistice

Italian front with fortified defensive lines, 1943–5.

had given the armed forces the ambiguous instruction, without further details, to respond generically to attacks 'from wherever they may come'. In the course of a few hours Italy found herself facing not only a reversal of alliances, but also an out-and-out collapse of the state which overwhelmed not only the armed forces, but also large sections of society. This situation was aggravated by the massive presence, from the summer of that year, of large numbers of German troops who were occupying the country according to the plans laid out in Operation 'Achse' (Axis).[3]

By now Italy was an exhausted country, its people dismayed, angry and de-motivated. These were the unequivocal signs of a defeat which had been developing over the last three years. The only way of saving the country from a catastrophe had been to withdraw from the conflict by signing an armistice with the Allies. The Nazis viewed this as an act of betrayal. Within a few weeks German troops had occupied the Italian peninsula, with the exception of those sections of territory that were already in Allied possession. By 19 September 82 generals, 13,000 officers and 400,000 Italian soldiers had been captured, of whom 180,000 had already been deported to Germany.[4]

The Italian soldiers who remained in Italy, who were by now well aware of the risks of ending up as German prisoners, sought in any way possible to evade capture. They received considerable assistance and solidarity in this respect from the Italian populace. This did not at that stage constitute a conscious form of resistance, but the help that was provided allowed many soldiers to overcome this most difficult of moments and to be able to wait and see, from their safe havens, how the situation would evolve.

The destiny of the Italian soldiers abroad (almost 1 million) was more dramatic. In Greece, Albania, Yugoslavia and France they were taken by surprise by the rapidity of events and, abandoned to their fate, most of them were captured by German troops and sent to labour camps in Germany. These soldiers, whose number exceeded 430,000, were not recognized as prisoners of war but were termed IMI (Italian military internees).[5]

*   *   *

Mussolini was arrested immediately after his meeting with the king on 25 July 1943, when he was advised that he had been removed from his post. He was kept prisoner in a variety of locations, but a German parachute unit managed, on 12 September, to free him from his last place of incarceration on the Gran Sasso mountain. From there he was transferred to Germany and, despite his precarious physical and psychological condition, was convinced by Hitler to resume command of Italy. A number of high-ranking Nazis, including Himmler and Goebbels, were, for a variety of reasons, against a return of Mussolini to power. In his speech of 10 September, which was dedicated to the situation in Italy, Hitler, having confirmed his high esteem for Mussolini, clarified the German attitude as follows: 'The measures established in order to protect German interests following Italy's decision to change sides are extremely harsh ... The previous example of the betrayal of Yugoslavia has been a salutary lesson for us'.[6]

The new embodiment of fascism was therefore born and planned in Germany and was completely subservient to the Third Reich. A clear manifestation of this was the regime's move from earlier discriminatory measures against Italian Jews to outright persecution in accordance with Nazi policy.[7] More generally, it was to provide Germany with an effective means of controlling men and resources.

1. An RAF Westland Lysander evacuating wounded Italian partisans. (*Imperial War Museum*)

2. *Maquisards* gathering supply canisters dropped by an Allied aircraft, 1944. (*Imperial War Museum*)

3. Officers of SOE and the French FTPF resistance group in Sussac, Limoges, August 1944. (*Imperial War Museum*)

4. Partisan sabotage in the Louvain region. (*Centre for Historical Research and Documentation on War and Contemporary Society, Brussels*)

5. *La Libre Belgique*, printed in a clandestine press in Liège in 1944. (*Centre for Historical Research and Documentation on War and Contemporary Society, Brussels*)

6. German troops enter Brno, Moravia, March 1939. (*Bundesarchiv, Bild 183-2004-0813-500, photo: Scherl agency*)

7. Corpses of two of Reinhard Heydrich's assassins in Prague, May 1942. (*Bundesarchiv, Bild 146-1972-039-14*)

8. General de Gaulle speaking on the BBC French Service. (*Public domain*)

9. A French resistance member setting an explosive charge on a railway line. (*Imperial War Museum*)

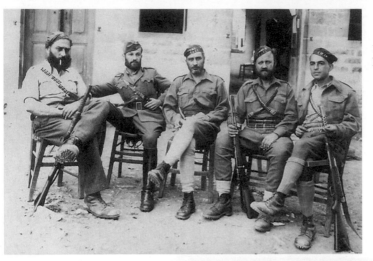

10. EDES guerrillas in Epirus. (*Private collection*)

11. General Napoleon Zervas, leader of EDES. (*Private collection*)

12. A body found in the river, Po di Ficarolo (Rovigo), April 1945. The British eyewitnesses noted that it was the body of a young girl tortured and killed by the Germans. (*Resistance Institute, Bologna*)

13. Italian partisans killed in reprisal. (*Reggio Emilia Resistance Institute*)

14. A variety of Dutch resistance newspapers. (*Instituut voor Oorlogs-, Holocaust- en Genocidestudies, Amsterdam*)

15. A Dutch resistance wireless operator. (*Instituut voor Oorlogs- en Genocidestudies, Amsterdam*)

16. Jubilant Polish Home Army members conversing after the outbreak of the Warsaw Uprising, August 1944. (*Imperial War Museum*)

17. The Warsaw Rising monument. (*Private collection*)

18. Jewish refugees are ferried out of Denmark aboard Danish fishing boats bound for Sweden. (*United States Holocaust Memorial Museum, Washington, DC*)

19. Squadron Leader J. Macadam meets three Norwegian resistance fighters in Oslo following the arrival of British forces in Norway. (*Imperial War Museum*)

20. Soviet partisans attack a village. (*Public domain*)

21. Two members of the Kovpak partisan group. (*Public domain*)

22. Soviet partisans young and old. (*Public domain*)

23. German troops search suspected Yugoslav Partisans. (*Bundesarchiv, Bild 101I-005-0012-18*)

24. Marshal Tito with cabinet ministers and staff in his mountain headquarters, May 1944. (*Taylor Library*)

German troops were not to be directly involved in administrative duties, as they were already heavily committed to defending the Allied advance in the south of Italy. On 18 September Mussolini spoke to Italians from Radio Munich proclaiming the birth of the Fascist Republican Party, whose secretary would be one of the hard men of the regime, Alessandro Pavolini, much favoured by the Nazi hierarchy.

Mussolini then announced the re-forming of the military corps of the militia which, a short time afterwards, became known as the National Republican Guard (GNR), under the command of Renato Ricci. At the end of September the government of the new fascist state was formed, of which Mussolini was president of the Council of Ministers and Head of State. On 1 December 1943 the new collaborationist state (which never had an official capital and whose various ministries were scattered around the Veneto and Lombardy, while Mussolini resided in the area of Salò on Lake Garda) took the name of the Italian Social Republic (RSI).

The Nazi occupation of Italy had as its principal aim the total exploitation of the human and material resources of the country. Italy, although heavily stretched by the war, could boast in the areas of the centre and the north of the country an economy that was still substantially productive, both in the industrial sector as well as in agriculture. Italy also had a large workforce at its disposal which represented an important resource for the economy of the Reich, by now in some difficulties. The attempt, which was immediately initiated under the leadership of the Nazi Labour Minister, Fritz Sauckel, to recruit 1.5 million workers for the Reich was, however, a complete failure. Only 75,000 co-opted workers were sent to Germany. The attempt, which was characterized by an indiscriminate manhunt, not only failed in its objectives but also alienated many of those who had been initially attracted by the cash incentives offered to enrol. Its immediate effects were to send many men to the nascent resistance movement. A rather better result was achieved by the Einsatzgruppe, part of Organization Todt (OT), which busied itself by employing local labour in Italy in order to build fortifications and to assist in the war effort. Even then, the numbers were insufficient for the requirements of the war.[8]

During the occupation, the German troops made frequent use of forced labour, often employing drastic methods. Deportations and forced recruitment took place, which were particularly frequent in the Apennine hills around Tuscany and Emilia between the months of August and October 1944. It is estimated that, by the beginning of 1945, at least 240,000 workers were engaged in fortification building at the front. However, it had not been possible to deport to Germany a huge number of workers, as many of these were already involved in armament production. Of the 45,000 civilian deportees, around 1,200 were workers who had been captured during the new wave of strikes in March 1944.[9]

* * *

In the days after 8 September not all the soldiers decided to flee. In the north and south of the country there were many episodes of spontaneous resistance. These were isolated and hopeless attacks which were immediately stamped out by the superior German forces. Important incidents took place in the centre and north of Italy. Such was the case with the desperate defence of Rome where, even though the Italian supreme command had, despite the numerical superiority of the forces it commanded, decided not to defend the capital against the Germans, soldiers and civilians fought together at Porta San Paolo. Elsewhere, in Matera on 21 September, the first open revolt against German occupation took place. This was a spontaneous revolt that was also encouraged by the proximity of the advancing Allied troops. What happened in September and throughout the rest of 1943 constituted, without exception, examples of spontaneous and non-organized resistance.

In this context, the acts of resistance carried out by Italian troops abroad were particularly important. In Greece the Acqui Division, which comprised around 11,500 men, was stationed on the island of Cephalonia in the Ionian Sea. At a meeting of these soldiers a decision was taken to resist the Nazi troops, although they were well aware that they would receive no reinforcements and that defeat was certain. After 12 days of fighting, in the course of which more than 1,250 soldiers and 65 officers lost their lives, General Gandin, the Italian commander, was forced to surrender. The German soldiers shot on the spot some 4,905 soldiers and officers who had lain down their weapons, while others were captured. The few men who escaped joined the Greek partisans.[10]

At the other garrisons in the Aegean, including the 7,600 men stationed on the island of Leros, Italian soldiers defended themselves until the inevitable surrender. There, from 12–16 November, they fought, along with 5,000 British troops against nearly 2,700 German attackers. In the area of Barletta, the Nazi parachutists took two days to gain control of the city. From these few and desperate episodes, clear signs emerged of opposition to the war and a hostility towards the fascist regime that had brought the country to its knees.

*   *   *

The 'four days of Naples' are perhaps the most important example of spontaneous resistance that took place after 8 September. The city had been badly affected by the Allied bombings. With the population on its knees, the forthcoming arrival of the Anglo-American troops led to a revolt against the German occupation, which had been characterized by lootings and other forms of excess. The spark for the uprising was the announcement of forced labour conscription for all men between 18 and 33 years of age. Hardly anyone had replied to the call-up when, on 28 September, the first attacks on German soldiers took place in the city centre. By the following day the insurgents numbered around 1,000, although they had no real political or military leadership. The Germans did not hesitate to bombard the city while, in the battles that ensued, both the elderly and the young were killed. After four days of clashes the German commanders had no option but to negotiate a truce with the insurgents, which allowed them to leave the city to the Allied troops. When the Allies arrived on 1 October they found Naples already liberated.[11]

The revolt in Naples, encouraged by the proximity of the Allied troops, resonated around occupied Italy, but the situation in the centre and north of the country did not permit similar uprisings: every attempt at resistance had to confront the harsh reaction of Nazi troops, ever ready to carry out immediate reprisal attacks.

The first groups of partisans found it very difficult to resist the troops of the Reich for any significant length of time. In Boves in Piedmont, where one of these first groups, which had been created by former soldiers of the Italian army, was active, the German troops carried out one of their first reprisals. On 19 September, following the capture of two German soldiers from the SS Leibstandarte Panzer Division 'Adolf Hitler', the commander negotiated with the local priest for the return of the soldiers in exchange for the safety of the village and its inhabitants. Notwithstanding the fact that the hostages were set free, the Germans killed 24 civilians, including the mayor and the priest himself, who were burned alive, and destroyed 350 houses. The village was subject to another attack a few months later, and a further fifty-nine civilians were killed.[12]

The first men who had sought refuge in the mountains, from Abruzzo in the centre of Italy to Piedmont in the north, did not have clear ideas about their future. Up until the middle of November the majority of these groups consisted of dispersed former soldiers, together with others who were avoiding the forced drafts into the ranks of the reconstituted fascist army. It was necessary to create militarily effective groups who could move from a strategy of survival and waiting to a strategy of military action. This change was by no means simple and required time: there were very few weapons available and at this early stage it was difficult to identify potential leaders. These came initially in the shape of dispersed officers and, in subsequent weeks, they were augmented by politically mature individuals. However, the relationship between these two leadership elements was not always straightforward. These first mountain bands, established in the autumn of 1943 and comprising around 3,800 men,[13] began actual fighting from the spring of 1944 onwards, having busied themselves in the initial phase, above all, in acts of sabotage and in the procurement of weapons. From the spring onwards armament difficulties were partly resolved as a result of Allied air drops.

In the initial phase of the resistance, the activities of the Cervi peasant family played a significant role. The Cervi band, made up of seven brothers, had already been involved in acts of armed resistance prior to 8 September. They were the first group to act in the mountains of Emilia. Of Catholic extraction, their anti-fascist commitment had brought them closer to communist ideology, with a particular fascination for the myth of the socialist paradise of the Soviet Union. They had gone up into the mountains immediately after the armistice, in order to organize an initial clandestine military structure. The Cervi were, however, forced to return to the low ground, when they realized that the minimum conditions required for action did not at that stage exist. They were captured at their house in Gattatico on 25 November together with their father and a number of Allied prisoners, to whom they had offered shelter. On 28 December 1943, as an act of reprisal for a partisan action, all seven were executed by fascists at the shooting range in Reggio Emilia. Their mother died, consumed with grief, a few days later. The father, who survived the massacre, wrote his memoirs (entitled *My Seven Sons*) after the war and they became an extraordinary international literary success.[14]

*   *   *

Some of the men who had looked for shelter in the mountains between September and November 1943 abandoned the struggle – either going into hiding or agreeing to enrol in the RSI. The reasons for their choice lay in the harshness of the forthcoming winter, or in the discouragement provided by the evident numerical disparities between the forces involved.

The partisan formations grew slowly, as a result of this inevitable process of selection. They were organized by the anti-fascist parties who deferred to the CLN (Committee of National Liberation),[15] which was divided into various provincial committees and co-ordinated, in occupied Italy, by the CLNAI (Committee of National Liberation for Upper Italy), whose headquarters were in Milan.[16] Although the political parties were, therefore, responsible for the organization of the various formations, it was the partisans themselves who frequently undertook their own education as soon as they entered the armed bands. Their youth, their lack of a prior political education (this was a generation that had been born and grown up under the fascist dictatorship), their desire to avoid the fascist drafts, coupled with their hopes for a better future, were all elements that influenced their choice in favour of one or other group, together with the differing distribution of the formations around the territory. For example, Garibaldi brigades prevailed in Emilia Romagna, Justice and Liberty brigades were well represented in Piedmont and Catholic formations featured in Lombardy and the Veneto.

From a quantitative point of view, the Justice and Liberty brigades, which were politically aligned to the Action Party, comprised around 20 per cent of the combatants, while the Garibaldi brigades, organized by the Communist Party, comprised around 50 per cent of the resistance front. There then followed, in numerical terms, the 'autonomous' formations, so-called because they were formally politically unaligned (subsequently many of them would, however, join the Liberal Party). From the spring of 1944 a number of Catholic formations began to emerge, who had a range of different denominations, such as 'green flames', 'Italian brigades' and 'People's brigades'. There was a smaller presence of 'Matteotti' (socialist) brigades and of 'Mazzini' (Republican) brigades. There were also a few active groups which did not recognize the CLN, such as the anarchist brigades (in Tuscany, Genoa, Turin and Milan), the Roman 'Red Flag' movement and other Marxist movements, which were to the left of the Communist Party.

The Italian resistance did not have a single charismatic leader. Three men headed the CVL (Volunteer Corps for Liberty – the military arm of the CLN) which was instituted in June 1944 in order to create a united command of all partisan formations.[17] They were the overall commander, Raffaele Cadorna, whom the Allies desired in this position because he was a career soldier, and two 'political' deputy commanders: Luigi Longo (a communist), the head of the Garibaldi brigades, and Ferruccio Parri (an Actionist), founder and leader of the Justice and Liberty brigades.

At all levels of command relationships were not always straightforward, whether as a result of the different ideological and tactical approaches, or as a result of the competition linked to the increase in numbers of the formations and the associated need for weapons. In the main, however, unity was maintained until the end of the conflict.

During the resistance, the different ranks found in the orthodox army (with the single exception of the autonomous brigades) carried no weight and all hierarchies were questioned. In the words of one historian, '[w]hile in the traditional type of army a certain lack of personality, a passive adherence to routine and to old-style hierarchies were indispensable virtues ... the partisan war required greater elasticity, independence and, above all, a profound ethical dimension'.[18] This led to the construction of a 'new style' army, a precursor of, it was hoped, a new society to be created once the war was over. The commander had to enjoy the personal trust of his men, a trust he had acquired through a continuous demonstration of abilities and courage in his conduct of guerrilla warfare. These were men who already had a high degree of autonomy, which they maintained even after the establishment of various zonal commands. They jealously guarded their own spaces, and did not always have good relations with the political leaders. In various circumstances the role of commander was bestowed following a vote of the members of the brigade, while frequently there were cases of commanders being refused by combatants who were unwilling to accept people who were forced upon them from above.

The figure of the commissar, who was already present in the first units of the Red Army, made a further appearance in the International Brigades in Spain. Many anti-fascist combatants had themselves fought in Spain, meaning that the commissar resurfaced in Italy as well. It is possible to detect the presence of a commissar from the earliest times, in the Garibaldi brigades as well as in the Justice and Liberty brigades, while the autonomous formations – which took their example from the organizational structures present in the regular army – were more hostile to this figure. The commissar was officially introduced by the high command in the summer of 1944.

Often shaped politically by previous experiences of clandestine activities, the commissar had a political and 'educational' role towards the partisans, hoping to motivate them to fight. The partisans wished to free themselves from their experience of fascist education, but lacked any kind of political culture. For this reason, the conversations and the meetings with the commissars offered the opportunity for an initial apprenticeship in politics.

The commissar also had operational roles: he was an individual in continuous contact with the upper echelons of anti-fascism and with the political party to which he adhered. To these organizations he sent periodic accounts of the military actions that had taken place, and reports on the men involved. His liaison role could lead to him being asked to choose new partisans, or even reorganize the formations which, as time passed, were aggregated into units of larger dimensions.

It was important for the partisan formations, which were continually moving around their localities, to have access to reliable information about the enemy and to keep in continuous contact with the other groups. This role was carried out by messengers, almost always women, at times very young women, who were the only people able to move around the territory controlled by the Nazi-fascists without running the risk of immediate arrest. The messengers carried out a fundamental role. In addition to their task of transmitting orders and information, they ended up transporting everything: food, clothes, weapons, propaganda materials. These were high-risk activities.

The resistance received fundamental support from women. The participation of women contributed to initiating the process of female emancipation. This was slow but irreversible, and was the prelude to a radical transformation in Italian society, which at the time was still organized along rigorously patriarchal lines. Within the partisan formations women discovered, one step at a time, that they were in charge of their own destiny, and began to think of themselves as being in a new dimension, in opposition to the lower and subordinate role of the woman as 'mother and exemplary wife', according to the fascist stereotype that had been constructed on a pre-existing masculinist foundation. In addition to the messengers, women made decisive contributions in terms of assistance, hospitality and looking after clandestine combatants. During the 1940–3 conflict, women had taken the place of men in factories and in the fields. With the partisan struggle, they began to live the life of the bands and to shoulder weapons, so much so that 2,275 women were shot or died in action during the course of the resistance. If the resistance can be considered the means by which an entire generation developed, it was all the more so for the presence of women. Living with the responsibilities and the risks of war made them more able to recognize their own rights and to exercise, in the new society that would be born after the war, an active role in public life which went beyond the traditional barriers created in the private sphere.[19]

The absence of support structures for the partisan formations was the fundamental reason why it was necessary to establish, as is the case for all forms of guerrilla warfare, direct relations with the civilian population. In the early stages, the partisan formations needed to find temporary refuges and, above all, deal with the lack of food which, in the short term, was one of the most pressing problems for these irregulars.

The relationship between the resistance and civilians was formed, above all, in the countryside and differed from zone to zone. The long-term history of those territories played an important role, as did the potential to build relations of mutual aid and assistance. It is important to recall that many partisan actions took place in mountainous areas, the Alps and the Apennines, areas that had been historically disadvantaged in terms of their economic and social profile. It was necessary to hone efficient guerrilla tactics without provoking reactions against the population. This was not always easy, however, and when it came to reprisals, the resistance forces were almost always routed, and the local population was left exposed to Nazi-fascist violence.

The relationship with the populations in other areas, such as in the Emilia Romagna valleys, was more straightforward. There, partisan actions were linked to the widespread hopes for social emancipation. Matters were more difficult, however, in the territories on the eastern frontier where, along with the desire for liberation, the national question co-existed with the expansionist desires of the Slovene and Croatian partisan formations, who were assisted by Yugoslavian troops.

* * *

The resistance movement had a history and characteristics that differed from area to area and from region to region. In various areas of the south, it is more accurate to speak of occasional movements of revolt rather than of an out-and-out resistance movement. The resistance was fairly weak in the centre of Italy; in particular, there was no final insurrection in the city of Rome, the only large Italian city not to encounter a revolt at the moment of liberation. It was only in Tuscany that a partisan movement developed along similar lines to that in the north. The insurrection in Florence, which lasted from 29 July to 1 September 1944, represented the first show of strength – with over 2,800 armed citizens – and of political organization by the CLN.[20]

The resistance movement in Emilia Romagna was in many ways unique when compared to other experiences of armed struggle. Here the movement had mass dimensions, allowing the partisan formations to carry out their activities not only in the mountains but also on the plains. In 1921 and 1922 this agricultural region had seen the development of the fascist movement, which had established itself by attacking the peasant classes and destroying union organizations and other democratic bodies such as the co-operatives. The region was characterized by a powerful link between the young partisans and the population to which, in the main, they belonged. In the context of a civil war, the struggle took on strong class aspects. This meant that the extent of popular involvement in the battles ensured that they were not just about driving out the fascists and the Germans. It was also about constructing new democratic structures capable of transforming the economic and political organization of local-level and national-level society once the war was over.

In the course of 1944, in various zones of the north, partisan formations were able, capitalizing on the weaknesses of the fascist troops and on the heavy commitments of the Germans at the front line, to temporarily liberate areas of territory. Thanks to the support of the population, it was possible to introduce the first forms of democratic organization in Italy twenty years after the beginning of the fascist dictatorship. Situations were different according to territory or to the time they were set up, and so it was not possible to create a coherent set of rules and statutes in these partisan republics. However, the reintroduction of free elections and the handing over of administrative control to elective personnel represented a significant move in the political education of important zones in occupied Italy. The first of these was the Republic of Montefiorino (Emilia: Modena and Reggio, 22 June–3 August);[21] there then followed, among others, the Republic of Val d'Ossola (Piedmont: Novara, 10 September–21 October), the Republic of Carnia (Friuli: Udine, 26 September–beginning of December) and the Republic of the city of Alba (Piedmont: Cuneo, 10 October–2 November).[22] From the military point of view, the partisan republics demonstrated the strength that the resistance movement had achieved. It had grown numerically in the late spring due to the arrival of large numbers of young men fleeing the fascist draft. Furthermore, the movement had been strengthened from the beginning by Allied weapons and equipment drops. The brief existence of the partisan republics highlighted a difference between partisan tactics based on guerrilla actions ('bite and flee') and the political necessity of maintaining a position for a certain length of time. The partisan republics were probably undervalued by the Allies, as they could have been employed subsequently as bridgeheads beyond the enemy lines, thereby shortening the length of the war on the Italian front.

Partisan attacks were always based on the principle of surprise and rapid escape. The decision to fight in this way was unavoidable, given the numerical superiority of the enemy and the huge disparities in available weapons, and was reinforced each time the partisan forces committed the error of fighting on open ground or attempting to defend their positions to the bitter end. Only in the last months of the war were there large-scale battles, which almost always ended with the victory of the resistance forces who were now fully armed and capable of responding effectively to the enemy.

The relationship between the partisan formations and the Anglo-American army, which from the summer of 1944 assisted the armed struggle with materiel and men, proved decisive. With the arrival of Allied liaison officers, the partisan formations were able to participate effectively in the Allied military effort on the Italian front, providing precious information on the movements and whereabouts of German troops, carrying out sabotage attacks behind enemy lines and attacking enemy positions.[23] This relationship became so close that, in the autumn of 1944 along the Gothic Line, several partisan formations crossed the lines in order to fight directly under Allied command.[24]

But for the partisans, guerrilla tactics were always at the centre of their activities: small formations moved rapidly around their area, exploiting their local knowledge and the logistical support of the local population, ready to attack the enemy, ideally at some distance from centres of population, and then withdraw immediately. The partisans, as voluntary soldiers, learned – frequently at extreme risk to themselves – guerrilla tactics in the course of various actions carried out against the enemy. This was a difficult and bloody apprenticeship; the majority of defeats were, in fact, a consequence of technical errors or an underestimation of the enemy, which was in turn always ready to punish severely any naive errors or slips. The number of partisans enrolling represented a problem for some months; the arrival of so many young men who were dodging the military drafts – in particular in spring and summer 1944 – created difficulties because of the lack of equipment, food and available weapons. In a matter of a few weeks the brigades grew to the extent that it became impossible to provide, in the short term, the necessary organizational framework. As a consequence, forces that were numerically strong, but militarily weak, were created. They were inevitably exposed to the risk of attack from Nazi-fascist troops.

The resistance not only developed in the mountains and on the plains, but also managed to organize itself in the cities. Given the proximity to German command structures and enemy repression, the resistance in the cities needed to manage itself in a different way. Large formations, of the type that existed in the mountains, could not function successfully. So small clandestine outfits (sometimes made up of only three or four individuals), known as the GAP were set up by the Italian Communist Party.[25] The first GAP action took place in Novara on 6 October 1943, when four soldiers of the RSI were killed, but the most spectacular action was the killing on 29 October of the commander of the militia in Turin. There was a continuous escalation of such activities: on 15 December the commander of the GNR in Reggio Emilia was killed; on 18 December the party secretary of Milan, Aldo Resega, fell in an ambush, and little more than a month later it was the turn of his counterpart in Bologna, Eugenio Facchini.[26]

In order to combat anti-fascist activities in both the cities and the mountains, the Nazi-fascist authorities issued increasingly draconian regulations. These ranged from curfew (the duration of which would be continuously increased) to a ban on the use of cars and even bicycles (a method of transport frequently used by the *gappisti* – members of GAP, groups of 'patriotic' or 'partisan' action) to the regulation, which was enforced in many areas, to affix on the door of each household a certificate detailing all occupants. This tactic was aimed at establishing the identity of all concerned during a search of the premises. Nonetheless, all of these directives proved insufficient to prevent a growth in partisan activities and the creation of a network of informers, made up of handsomely paid spies who were recruited from the population.

When in the summer of 1944 popular participation grew rapidly, it was decided to create a new type of formation: the SAP (squad of partisan action). These squads were largely made up of people who had supported GAP operations in the past, but had not gone underground. By maintaining the cover of their own jobs, they were able to participate, above all at night, in attacks and GAP actions.

* * *

The new embodiment of fascism represented by the RSI immediately appeared to the large majority of Italians like a ghost from the past. This was a regime that had brought Italy into the war and which now continued its alliance with the Germans despite the fact that defeat looked inevitable. Under the colours of Republican Fascism, a number of violent individuals who had been marginalized during the regime were able to make a comeback. They now found a space in which to carry out their private and/or political vendettas by joining with those young men and women who were born under fascism and grew up surrounded by fascist ideology, and were convinced of the necessity of restoring the honour of the nation after the betrayal of 8 September.[27] The declared aim of Republican Fascism was to seek immediate revenge on all of the traitors of 25 July and 8 September who, as far as the fascists were concerned, included not only out and out anti-fascists, but also all those who had been fascists up to 25 July, who had refused to join the last embodiment of Italian fascism.

In the context of this hunger for vendetta, there were no restraints on violence. The re-established military corps of Salò immediately initiated the hunt for the draft dodgers, and did not hesitate to imprison the relatives of the young men on the run. As they frequently avoided the direct control of the German commanders (and therefore created problems for the occupier who sought to balance coercion with co-existence), they embarked upon a spiral of violence that often exceeded the cruelty and harshness of the Nazis themselves. The repressive military structure of the RSI was from the very start a product of the rivalries between a number of strong personalities in the new regime. The GNR created by Renato Ricci was in direct conflict with the army, which had been reconstituted under the command of General Rodolfo Graziani, while Prince Junio Valerio Borghese organized his own personal force, the Decima Mas, which numbered almost 15,000 men and which placed itself under the orders of the German army.

The military corps of the RSI which, according to propaganda had been established to defend the territory from the Anglo-American invaders, was used almost exclusively by the Germans against the resistance forces; only a few outfits fought directly against the Allies. This situation led to an even further increase in the violence, which was also directed against the civilian population. In the summer of 1944 the progressive disintegration of the GNR, combined with the slowness with which the divisions of Rodolfo Graziani's army were taking shape, led the secretary of the Fascist Republican Party, Alessandro Pavolini, in direct conflict with Graziani, to pursue his project of militarizing the party by enrolling all its male members from the age of 18 to 60 into military service. By doing this Pavolini was going back to the origins of fascist squadrism. However, the project never reached fruition and of the estimated 487,000 members (an optimistic estimate) only 20,000 ended up enrolled, and of these only 4,000 formed combat units: the Black Brigades. These units were used exclusively in anti-partisan operations, distinguishing themselves for the ferocity of their actions: executions, the torture of prisoners and the sacking of villages were their bread and butter, so much so that their actions frequently led to protests even from German commanders.[28]

In addition to the various military corps of the RSI, a number of autonomous bands excelled in the use of torture, either acting on their own, or with the complicity of the fascist authorities themselves. One of the most ferocious individuals concerned was Pietro Koch,[29] who was protected by Buffarini Guidi, the Minister of the Interior. Within the framework of the internal struggle between fascist leaders, the minister of justice in Salò ordered Koch's band to cease activities, and very soon its members simply passed directly under the command of the police. The extent of the violence was further evidenced by the frequent display of the bodies of the executed partisans, left as a warning to the people – an atrocious public spectacle in the streets and squares of occupied Italy which would have as a dramatic epilogue the public execration of the bodies of Mussolini and his retinue in Milan on 29 April 1945.

The practice of leaving the dead in the squares began almost immediately after 8 September, and was a technique that the Germans had already used in other countries of occupied Europe. An order issued by Albert Kesselring, German commander-in-chief in Italy, on 12 August 1944 authorized its use in Italy too, with the most famous example being that of the thirty-one young men hanged and left to swing from the trees in Bassano del Grappa.[30] According to Santo Peli, 'the exposure of bodies, and the denial of burial for the combatants, and in general the display of inhuman violence became a standard method for maintaining the control of the territory'.[31] To quote from Kesselring's order entitled 'The New Rules of Partisan Warfare', 17 June 1944:

> The fight against the partisans must be carried out with all means at our disposal and at the utmost levels of severity. I will protect any commander who, in the choice and in the severity of the means adopted in the struggle against the partisans, goes beyond what is our normal moderation. In this case the old principle, by which an error in the choice of means used to reach an objective, is always better than inaction or negligence ... The partisans must be attacked and destroyed.[32]

The Nazi occupation of Italy trampled, as elsewhere, upon every international war convention. The massacre of civilians was an integral part of the strategy put in place to control Italian territory, combined with the systematic exploitation of men and resources carried out through the twenty months of the occupation. All of this, it goes without saying, took place with the full collaboration of the fascists of Salò. Although the levels of destruction never reached those of Eastern Europe, more than 10,000 Italian civilians were killed by Nazis and fascists, in the course of more than 180 massacres carried out throughout the entire peninsula.[33] The first massacre took place in Sicily on 18 August 1943, before the armistice itself, when the retreating German troops killed sixteen people in Castiglione di Sicilia (Catania). The last was in Bolzano on 3 May 1945, a day after the war in Italy officially ended, with fifteen victims.

The most tragic period was June to August of 1944, when German troops retreating through Tuscany carried out some of the most ferocious massacres: Niccioleta, 13 June 1944: 83 victims; Civitella Val di Chiana, 29 June: 150 victims; Bucine, 29 June: 60 victims; Meleto, 4 July 1944: 94 victims; S. Anna di Stazzema, 12 August 1944: 560 victims; Fucecchio, 23 August 1944: 178 victims.[34]

Some massacres were carried out as reprisals, as was the case at the Ardeatine caves in Rome (24 March 1944: 335 victims), which was a response to a partisan attack that had killed 33 German troops in the centre of the city.[35] But for the most part the massacres were indiscriminate attacks on the civilian population, including old people, women and children, and were part of a strategy aimed at keeping the area behind the lines safe and protecting channels of communication. The civilian populations were held to be jointly responsible for partisan actions, as Kesselring confirmed in his own statement in his defence in October 1946:

> Even if we consider the events according to a partial description, one realises that the inhabitants of that village were in some way implicated. The fact that 'peaceful citizens' were killed in their beds is entirely consonant with the fact that they were themselves implicated. What Italian would have gone peacefully to bed at 9.30 on a June morning, after all those hours of combat in a village near the front, as if nothing had happened. Knowing the Italians as I do, I can say that no one would have behaved in that way.[36]

This is what happened in Monte Sole (770 victims), where the Nazi-fascists did not restrict themselves to destroying the Stella Rossa partisan brigade, but vented their fury on the civilians whom they believed were accomplices of the partisans.[37] The war against the civilians was carried out in Italy, not just by specially trained units, like the SS, but also by other units of the Wehrmacht, in particular the army's Feldgendarmerie and the Hermann Göring Division. They were assisted by Italian units from the GNR, the Black Brigades, and the Decima Mas.

*   *   *

The German troops began their occupation of Italy when the outcome of the war was already decided. The German military strategy on the Italian front was aimed at slowing down as much as possible the inevitable Allied advance, which had in the first months after the landings in Sicily moved at a worrying speed: Sicily was occupied in only thirty-eight days and Naples, already liberated, welcomed the Anglo-Americans on 1 October. In order to halt the advance, fortified defensive lines were set up one after the other. The first of these was the Gustav Line (Minturno–Cassino–Roccaraso–Fossacesia), which defended the centre and south of Italy. This was followed by the Gothic Line, or 'green line', which ran through the north of Italy.

The Gothic Line ran from one side of the peninsula to the other, from Cinquale near Massa to Pesaro. During the great Allied offensive of the spring and summer of 1944, the fortification of the Gothic Line was accelerated in preparation for the imminent clash which took place at the beginning of that autumn. But the bad weather and the increasing lack of importance of the Italian front, in view of the Normandy landings as well as those in the south of France, meant that by the summer a large number of Allied troops had already been transferred to the north. For this reason, the Allies were forced to stop the advance at the Apennines, a few kilometres from Bologna, on 27 October 1944. With a radio message of 13 November 1944 the British general Harold Alexander, supreme commander of the Allied forces, announced to the Italian partisans that the final offensive would be delayed until the following spring. This was perhaps the most difficult moment for the Italian resistance, which had grown in numbers and in offensive capacity, but which was now obliged to engage in a further unforeseen struggle which would last the entire winter, and was particularly tough in the Apennines and in the plains. It was now necessary, in conditions that were ever more difficult, to formulate a new strategy that would guarantee the survival of the formations, but also ensure the maintenance of their offensive capacities.

In the last months of war the levels of violence reached their highest point, in a harsh struggle in which no quarter was given, and in which the fascist formations, by now aware of the imminent settling of accounts, distinguished themselves by their cruelty and excesses.[38] The anti-partisan operations in the mountains, and the executions on the low ground, above all along the main arteries of communication, continued without interruption right up to the final collapse. A few months before the final offensive the partisans in Bologna were able to pin down the Germans for an entire day in the course of house-to-house battles in the area of Porta Lame. This was a prelude to the final attack which, beginning in the first days of April, saw full collaboration between partisan formations and Allied troops, who managed rapidly to crush the last resistance of the Nazis and the fascists. The majority of the cities in the north were in fact liberated by partisans, starting with Bologna (21 April), Modena (22 April) and Reggio Emilia (24 April). The liberation of Genoa and Turin required fierce fighting. The situation was also difficult in the Veneto, with Venice being liberated on 28 April, while the Yugoslavian presence in Trieste held back the Italian partisan insurrection in that city. On 2 May 1945 the German troops in Italy surrendered, and the RSI ceased to exist: the accounts with Nazism were closed, but they were still open as far as fascism was concerned. During the days of liberation, and in the weeks to follow, there were numerous episodes of summary justice and vendetta towards those fascist collaborationists who had most tarnished themselves with crimes committed during the course of the twenty months of the occupation. The date of 25 April (the insurrection in Milan) became the National Festival of the Liberation.

When the RSI collapsed, Mussolini attempted to find a personal route to safety. By now abandoned by the Germans, and having proclaimed that he would attempt a final resistance, he accepted an offer of negotiation with the CLN. But faced with the request for unconditional surrender (which nevertheless guaranteed his safety), he tried a final escape disguised as a German soldier. Stopped, and then identified by partisans at Lake Como, he was arrested in Dongo, and shot at Giulino di Mezzegra on 28 April, on the orders of the CLN of upper Italy, together with his lover Claretta Petacci. Their bodies, together with those of the last fascist leaders, including Pavolini, were transferred to Milan where they were put on display in Piazzale Loreto, the same place where the Germans had carried out a massacre of partisans in July 1944.[39]

* * *

A communiqué from the Potsdam conference, 2 August 1945, detailed the country's position: 'Italy was the first of the Axis powers to break with Germany. She made a decisive contribution to Germany's defeat, and has now joined the

Allies in the war against Japan … Italy liberated itself from the Fascist regime and is making good progress towards the re-establishment of a government and democratic institutions.'[40] The dramatic display of the bodies of Mussolini and other leading fascists in Piazzale Loreto was the symbolic end of the struggle against fascism. From a military point of view the resistance had been able to grow and develop, through various phases during the last twenty months of the war, to the extent that it could carry out a full role, with the employment of guerrilla tactics, in assisting the decisive campaign of the Allied armies in Italy. With their support, in terms of arms, supplies and strategic direction, the partisan formations (who at the end of the struggle comprised more than 20,000 recognized combatants) managed to engage effectively the Nazi occupation army as well as the fascist collaborationist forces. They obliged the enemy military commanders to maintain at the rear of the front huge quantities of men and equipment in order to keep control of the territory, thereby taking them away from the front line, and inflicting considerable damage in terms of structures, armaments and loss of life. Certainly, the efficiency of the partisan movement was patchy and its success relied heavily on the level of co-operation of the local populations: where this was higher (as was the case in the plains of Emilia Romagna), it was possible to extend military activity to the level ground with continuous attacks on the German rear. The partisan formations in these areas reached a level of military efficiency that allowed them to be used. Such was the case with the attack on the HQ of the 51st German Motorized Corps at Botteghe di Albinea on 27 March 1945, in joint actions with soldiers of the British SAS, who had been parachuted into the zone for that purpose.

The human cost testifies to the widespread commitment over a period of twenty months of so many young Italians. But the resistance had not only a military value, but also a political one. As Alcide De Gasperi, the President of the Council of Ministers, noted at the peace conference in Paris, during a speech aimed at obtaining concessions for Italy:

> The losses in the resistance against the Germans, before and after the declaration of war, amounted to more than 100,000 men killed or lost in action. This figure does not include the military and civilian victims of the Nazis in the concentration camps, and the 50,000 patriots killed in the partisan struggle. This second war lasted for eighteen months, during which time the Germans retreated slowly northwards despoiling, devastating, and destroying what little the bombardments had spared.[41]

The resistance had demonstrated the existence of another Italy, much different from the nationalist and imperialist country that had brought war to so many nations, first in Africa, and then in Europe – an Italy that had been capable of fighting hard in order to construct a real democracy.

The partisans played a decisive role in putting Italy on a path towards democracy, which led to the foundation of the Republic in 1946. The formations of the CVL, which the Allies ordered to be rapidly demobilized, given the large communist presence within it, provided the political, administrative and trade-union personnel needed for the new Italy. After they had put their weapons down, the partisans returned to their jobs, but many became members of Parliament, mayors, administrators and entrepreneurs, and so contributed to Italian national life in the years to follow. Where the resistance did not develop, and had little influence (above all in the south), there was no such beneficial leadership renewal. The continuity between the fascist state and democratic Italy was more marked in these areas, and slowed down development and progress in large sections of the country.

The development of official and institutional memory of the resistance was by no means linear. The resistance never became simply part of Italian history, but would for decades be at the centre of conflict and political battles. In the 1950s the persecution of partisans during the Cold War placed it at the margins of public memory, while from the 1960s onwards the risks of a shift to the right in the Italian political set-up, and the progressive modernization of the economy and of society, led to a re-evaluation of the resistance experience. This extended to a re-assessment of the levels of popular support and the social dimensions of the movement.

The resistance provided a firm set of values, and a solid anti-fascist identity, which permitted Italians to associate clearly the historical rupture with the fascist experience. This awareness, however, did not go as far as fully recognizing the extent of fascist war crimes committed during and after the resistance. The formula '*italiani brava gente*' ('Italians are good people'), which was solidly grounded in popular consciousness, allowed many shameful episodes of the fascist past, such as the ferocious repressions in Libya, the use of poison gas in Ethiopia,[42] the embracing of Nazi-style anti-Semitism, and massacres carried out by fascist troops in Yugoslavia,[43] to be all but forgotten.

Without Allied help the resistance would not have won. Nevertheless, the partisans made a decisive contribution to the Italian campaign, with their numbers on average fluctuating between 110,000 and 130,000 individuals, numbers that rose to around 250,000 to 300,000 during the days of the insurrection. This contribution is mirrored in the authority that the resistance generation acquired as it became a ruling class, and successfully carried out the political and social reconstruction of democratic Italy. There were also other types of resistance, such as that practised by soldiers who refused to join the RSI and were instead deported to German labour camps; the network of protection and assistance provided by the Church and by its priests; and the widespread popular participation that made possible, even with acts of passive resistance, the partisan activities of the resistance forces.

In recent years, the discussions about Italian identity, ushered in by the end of the Cold War, have given new energy to the debate on the significance of the resistance and its place in collective memory.[44] It is in this context that the discussions around historical revisionism have occurred, as well as a new politics of memory, embodied in new monuments, museums, parks and other resistance-related sites. Furthermore, much attention has been given in recent years to issues of immigration and to the movement against racism – all areas of discussion in which the legacy of the partisans and of the resistance are clearly present.

Translated by Philip Cooke.

Notes

1. Gianluca Falanga, *L'avamposto di Mussolini del Reich di Hitler. La politica italiana a Berlino (1933–1945)* (Milan, 2011), p. 269.
2. U. Gentiloni Silveri and M. Carli, *Bombardare Roma. Gli alleati e la 'città aperta' (1940–1944)* (Bologna, 2007).
3. On these operations see L. Klinkhammer, *L'occupazione tedesca in Italia. 1943–1945* (Turin, 1993), pp. 24–48.
4. G. Hammermann, *Gli internati militari italiani in Germania* (Bologna, 1999).
5. G. Schreiber, *I militari italiani internati nei campi di concentramento del III Reich* (Rome, 1992); N. Labanca, 'Internamento militare Italiano', in *Dizionario della Resistenza*, ed. by Enzo Collotti, Renato Sandri and Frediano Sessi, Vol. 1: *Storia e geografia della Liberazione* (Turin, 2000) pp. 113–19.
6. Frederick William Deakin, *The brutal friendship. Mussolini, Hitler and the fall of Italian Fascism* (London, 1962) (Italian trans. *Storia della Repubblica di Salò* (Turin, 1963)), pp. 709–11.
7. For further details on the RSI's involvement in the Holocaust, see Deakin, *Storia della Repubblica di Salò*, pp. 832–5; L. Picciotto, *Il libro della memoria: gli ebrei deportati dall'Italia, 1943–1945* (Milan, 1991).
8. L. Klinkhammer, *L'occupazione tedesca in Italia*, pp. 131–74.
9. On the strikes see S. Peli, *Storia della Resistenza italiana* (Turin, 2006), pp. 62–7.
10. G. Rochat and M. Venturi (eds), *La Divisione Acqui a Cefalonia. Settembre 1943* (Milan, 1993).
11. On the specific situation in Naples and the insurrection there see Gabriella Gribaudi, *Guerra totale. Tra bombe alleate e violenze naziste. Napoli e il fronte meridionale 1940–1944* (Turin, 2005).
12. On the Boves massacre see T. Matta, 'Boves', in E. Collotti, R. Sandri, F. Sessi (eds), *Dizionario della Resistenza*, Vol. II: *Luoghi, formazioni, protagonisti* (Turin, 2001), pp. 370–2.
13. This statistic, which is difficult to verify, is proposed by G. Bocca, *Storia dell'Italia partigiana* (Milan, 1995), pp. 93–7.
14. The father, A. Cervi, who survived the massacre, wrote his memoirs (entitled *I miei sette figli*, ed. R. Nicolai (Turin, 2010; first edn 1955)) after the war and they became an extraordinary international literary phenomenon.
15. The CLN was set up on 9 September 1943 and comprised representatives of the Italian Communist Party (PCI), Christian Democracy (DC), the Action Party, the Socialist Party (PSIUP), the Liberal Party (PLI) and the Party for Labour Democracy.
16. On Alfredo Pizzoni, the president of the CLNAI during the final phase of the struggle, see T. Piffer, *Alfredo Pizzoni: il protagonista cancellato della guerra di Liberazione* (Milan, 2005).
17. On the activities of the CVL see G. Rochat (ed.), *Atti del Comando Generale del Corpo Volontari della libertà* (Milan, 1972).
18. Peli, *Storia della Resistenza italiana*, p. 6.
19. On women in the resistance see Peli, *Storia della Resistenza italiana*, pp. 182–7; M. Addis Saba, *Partigiane. Tutte le donne della Resistenza* (Milan, 1998).
20. G. Francovich, *La Resistenza a Firenze* (Florence, 1969).
21. E. Gorrieri, *La Repubblica di Montefiorino. Per una storia della Resistenza in Emilia* (Bologna, 1966).
22. For an effective literary account of the Republic of Alba see the title story in the collection by B. Fenoglio, *I 23 giorni della città di Alba* (Turin, 2006).
23. D. Ellwood, 'Gli alleati e la Resistenza', in *Dizionario della Resistenza*, Enzo Collotti, Renato Sandri and Frediano Sessi (eds), pp. 242–54.
24. C. Silingardi, *Una provincia partigiana. Guerra e Resistenza a Modena 1940–1945* (Milan, 1998), pp. 394–407.

25. M. Giovana, 'I Gruppi di azione Patriottica: caratteri e sviluppi di uno strumento di guerriglia urbana', in *La guerra partigiana in Italia e in Europa*, in *Annali della Fondazione Micheletti* (Brescia, 2001), p. 134 n. 8.

26. L. Bergonzini, *La svastica a Bologna: settembre 1943–aprile 1945* (Bologna, 1998), pp. 36–40.

27. On the rebuilding of the army, see G. Pansa, *Il gladio e l'alloro. L'esercito di Salò* (Milan, 1991). On the organization of the RSI, see L. Ganapini, *La repubblica delle camicie nere* (Milan, 1999).

28. D. Gagliani, *Brigate Nere. Mussolini e la militarizzazione del Partito Fascista Repubblicano* (Turin, 1999).

29. M. Griner, *La banda Koch: il reparto speciale di polizia, 1943–44* (Turin, 2000).

30. S. Peli, 'La morte profanata. Riflessioni sulla crudeltà e sulla morte durante la Resistenza', in S. Peli, *La Resistenza difficile* (Milan, 1999), pp. 121–36.

31. Peli, *Storia della Resistenza in Italia*, pp. 109–10.

32. Cited in L. Baldissara and P. Pezzino, *Il massacro. Guerra ai civili a Monte Sole* (Bologna, 2009), p. 305.

33. M. Franzinelli, *Le stragi nascoste: l'armadio della vergogna, impunità e rimozione dei crimini nazifascisti, 1943–2001* (Milan, 2002).

34. M. Battini and P. Pezzino, *Guerra ai civili. Occupazione tedesca e politica del massacro. Toscana 1944* (Venice, 1997).

35. A. Portelli, *L'ordine è già stato eseguito. Roma: le Fosse Ardeatine. La memoria* (Rome, 1999).

36. TNA 311/359, voluntary statement by prisoner of war LD1573, General Field Marshal Albert Kesselring about the atrocities which occurred in the operational area of the Army Group C during the struggle against Italian Partisans from 1943 to 1945, 17 October 1946.

37. L. Baldissara and P. Pezzino, *Il massacro*.

38. The theme of violence within the context of the civil war is discussed with great clarity in C. Pavone, *Una guerra civile. Saggio storico sulla moralità nella Resistenza* (Turin, 1991), pp. 413–514.

39. M. Dondi, 'Piazzale Loreto', in M. Isnenghi (ed.), *I luoghi della memoria. Simboli e miti dell'Italia unita* (Bari, 1996).

40. R.H. Rainero, *Il trattato di pace delle Nazioni Unite con l'Italia: Parigi, 10 febbraio 1947* (Bologna 1997), p. 99.

41. D. Preda, *Alcide De Gasperi federalista europeo* (Bologna, 2004), p. 241.

42. M. Dominioni, *Lo sfascio dell'Impero. Gli italiani in Etiopia 1936–1941* (Bari, 2008).

43. C. Di Sante (ed.), *Italiani senza onore. I crimini in Jugoslavia e i processi negati (1941–1951)* (Verona, 2005).

44. L. Paggi, *Il popolo dei morti. La Repubblica italiana nata dalla guerra (1940–1946)* (Bologna, 2009); G. Contini, *La memoria divisa* (Milan, 1997); M. Storchi, 'Post-war violence in Italy: a struggle for memory', *Modern Italy*, Vol. 12, no. 2 (June 2007), pp. 237–50.

Guide to Further Reading

Behan, Tom, *The Italian Resistance* (London, 2009).

Cooke, Philip, *The Legacy of the Italian Resistance* (New York, 2011).

Idem, *The Italian Resistance: an anthology* (Manchester, 1997).

De Hoog, Walter, *Tulipano: a story of wartime Italy 1944–1945* (North Charleston, South Car., 2012).

Hood, Stuart, *Carlino* (Manchester, 1985).

Lett, Gordon, *Rossano – A Valley in Flames. An Adventure of the Italian Resistance* (Kindle edition).

Morgan, Philip, *The Fall of Mussolini* (Oxford, 2007).

Pavone, Claudio, *A Civil War. A History of the Italian Resistance* (London, 2013).

Slaughter, Jane, *Women and the Italian Resistance* (Denver, Col., 1997).

Chapter 7

The Netherlands

Marjan Schwegman

When German troops invaded the Netherlands (see Chapter 2, p. 34 for map) on 10 May 1940, the country was unprepared for war. There had been no foreign occupation since the Napoleonic era and no involvement in a European war for more than a hundred years. Thanks to a policy of strict neutrality, the Netherlands had managed to stay out of the First World War. The Dutch government had hoped it could continue to pursue this policy, engendering a sense of immunity that soon turned out to be unfounded. The Dutch capitulation was signed on 15 May 1940, after only five days of combat and bombing, the destruction of the centre of Rotterdam being the most shocking incident. Less than two years later, at the beginning of 1942, the Empire of the Dutch East Indies was taken by the Japanese.

Queen Wilhelmina had been able to leave the country with the Dutch Cabinet on 13 May 1940. She settled in London, where a Dutch government-in-exile was formed. It maintained the Netherlands' formal existence as an independent state. It was therefore in a position to influence the Dutch under German occupation, with Wilhelmina as the unofficial leader of the government and the main source of inspiration for the resistance.[1] In her speeches for Radio Orange the queen did not shrink back from strong language: '*Wie op het juiste oogenblik handelt, slaat den Nazi op den kop*' ('He who acts at the right time, will hit the Nazi on his head').[2]

In the Netherlands, Hitler appointed a so-called Aufsichtsverwaltung (Supervisory Civil Administration) under the leadership of Arthur Seyss-Inquart, an Austrian who was given the title of Reichskommissar (High Commissioner). He was assisted by four Generalkommissare (General Commissioners) and fourteen Beauftragten (Commissioners) in the eleven provinces and the three largest cities Amsterdam, The Hague and Rotterdam. The Generalkommissare took charge of the Dutch ministries, which since the flight of the Dutch Cabinet to London had been run by the highest civil servants of the departments, the so-called Secretaries General. Although Seyss-Inquart issued decrees that had the force of law throughout the war, the Dutch civil administration was left intact, with Seyss-Inquart and most of his Generalkommissare limiting themselves to outlining policy and supervising the administration. The country was therefore controlled by only several hundred German civil servants.[3] The exception to this maintenance of the existing structures was the way the country was policed. SS-Brigadeführer Hanns Albin Rauter was appointed as Generalkommissar für das Sicherheitswesen as well as Höhere SS-und Polizeiführer (General Commissioner for Security and Higher

SS and Police Leader). In this capacity he controlled the German Security Police (SiPo), the Security Service, or Sicherheitsdienst (SD), and the Ordnungspolizei, the German civil order police, popularly called Grüne Polizei because of their green uniforms. The Dutch police was also subordinated to Rauter. During the occupation, the role played by the German police in maintaining law and order and in fighting the resistance grew increasingly important. In 1942 Rauter had about 23,000 men of the Ordnungspolizei and the Waffen-SS at his disposal. About a third and later a quarter of all German troops on Dutch territory, then, were tasked with subjugating the population and eliminating internal enemies of the Third Reich.[4]

The main goals of the German occupying power were to maximize the exploitation of the Dutch economy and manpower resources for the benefit of the German war economy, to realize the Nazification of the Netherlands through the conversion of the Dutch population to National Socialism and the organization of Dutch society along National Socialist lines, and last but not least to solve the 'Jewish question'.[5] The occupying power succeeded in realizing the first and the third goal that it had set itself, of which the success in exterminating the Dutch Jews is the most tragic demonstration: of the 140,000 so-called full Jews, as many as 100,000 did not survive the war.[6] However, the occupying authorities did not succeed in their bid to Nazify Dutch society. One could even say that these efforts provided the most important impulse for the growth of the Dutch resistance.

Right from the beginning, some people developed resistance activities on a very small scale. Producing primitive illegal news leaflets was one example. Until 1942, these activities posed no real danger to the German authorities. It was only from 1942 onwards, with the growing hope for (and, on the German side, fear of) an Allied invasion, that the resistance grew in numbers, along with a hardening in the German policy of repression. Still, according to the Dutch historian Louis de Jong, 'unwilling adjustment was the rule, intentional resistance the exception' throughout the occupation, as was indeed the case in other European countries.[7] De Jong calculates that, until September 1944 (when the Allied forces liberated the southern part of the Netherlands), 25,000 people were active in 'the' organized resistance. Out of a population of about 9 million, this is a very small number.[8]

There is more to say about numbers, however.[9] De Jong bases his calculation on a very limited definition of 'resistance', counting only those activities that developed in secret and that were carried out in a structured organization. He therefore implicitly excludes the big strikes of 1941, 1943 and 1944 (on which, see below). The same goes for all public expressions of patriotism, which the German authorities punished rather severely. Examples include the mass wearing of a carnation (the favourite flower of Prince Bernhard, husband of Queen Wilhelmina's daughter Juliana) on the occasion of Bernhard's birthday on 29 June 1940, or the hanging out of laundry in the colours of the Dutch flag. De Jong's calculation also excludes all those activities that were part of the ever-growing infrastructure that made resistance possible. According to estimates, this infrastructure comprised about 500,000 people who supported the resistance by small acts, like the baker giving more bread than allowed to a family that took care of people in hiding. Moreover, one could say that those individuals, mainly women, who took care of people hiding in their houses, resisted the policy of the occupying power even though they did not consider themselves as members of an illegal organization. Even the act of going into hiding may be considered an act of resistance, since those who did it thwarted the goals of the German authorities: Jews who evaded deportation, for instance, or students who opposed Nazification by not signing the required declaration of loyalty to the regime. The total number of people who went into hiding has been calculated as 350,000. If one includes all these categories in a definition of the Dutch resistance, the number of people involved would be much higher than 25,000. Still, on the whole, it is undoubtedly true that only a minority of the Dutch population was active in any form of resistance.[10]

Alongside familiar elements like the creation of an illegal press, the stirring up of strikes, the organization of escape routes, help for those evading forced labour and persecution, espionage, sabotage and paramilitary activities, the Dutch resistance had its own peculiar variations. Due to the country's geographical position and topography – there were no mountains and very few large continuous forest areas within the total of $33,000km^2$ – a partisan movement did not develop. Moreover, the Netherlands had no common frontier with a neutral country, while the North Sea was heavily guarded by the Germans. Escaping by land was complicated, because several countries had to be traversed. Escaping by sea was very dangerous also, indeed almost impossible. Only 200 people successfully crossed the North Sea in small boats, whereas in comparison 80,000 Norwegians managed to arrive in neutral Sweden.[11] In the densely populated Netherlands, the creation of secret airfields for the dropping of secret agents or supplies for resistance groups was almost impossible. Thus the Dutch resistance was largely cut off from outside help. More than elsewhere, people were forced to act alone, especially in the countryside. According to Henri Michel, this explains why the Dutch resistance was 'primarily a moral and intellectual resistance',[12] while organized military resistance was virtually non-existent.

The necessity of acting alone also accounts for one of the most fascinating aspects of the history of the Dutch resistance. Until the German occupation, Dutch society had been a segmented society. Calvinists, Roman Catholics, Social Democrats and Liberals were neatly separated from one another. These socio-political arrangements in the Netherlands are usually referred to as *verzuiling* (pillarization). Individuals were used to following the leaders of their *zuil* (pillar) in all matters, and were inexperienced in making their own decisions. With the German authorities' elimination of most pre-war social, political and religious bodies, the deep segregation of Dutch culture was ended, at least institutionally. Of the various resistance groups and organizations that developed during the occupation, none was directly instigated by the pre-war leadership of political parties or social and religious movements. As a consequence, people had to rely on their own conscience instead of on the moral authority of traditional leadership. Whereas this may be seen as the biggest challenge for Dutch society during German occupation, this is especially true for the resistance, in which people had to decide matters of life and death.

* * *

The history of occupation and resistance in the Netherlands is distinguished by four phases. During the first phase, which lasted until the spring of 1941, the actions of the German occupiers, partly reflecting the Germans' on-going military success, were both confident and relatively mild. They hoped to convert the Dutch population to National Socialism by employing a moderate approach. Nevertheless, immediate measures were implemented to achieve the first of the objectives mentioned above, the restructuring of the Dutch economy to benefit the German war economy: a distribution system was introduced and the Dutch were called upon to volunteer for employment in Germany. The first anti-Jewish measures were also implemented.

During this period, the vast majority of the Dutch population tried their best to continue their life as it had been before. However, an examination of war diaries shows that outward passivity concealed a wounded national pride, as well as a dislike of National Socialism and anger at the curtailment of personal freedom.[13] Numerous attempts were made to escape to Britain: across the sea, or across land to Belgium, France, Switzerland and Spain, or via Sweden. It is therefore not surprising that the first forms of clandestine activities, such as the falsification of papers and the development of an international network of safe contacts, evolved from these escape attempts. The resistance was still unstructured and chaotic, and usually the work of independently operating individuals. Their general motivation was a dislike of National Socialism and of the regime's attempts to Nazify the Netherlands.

This aversion was expressed in a number of ways. For instance, there were all sorts of expressions of patriotism, both in the personal and in the public sphere. People vented their frustrations by writing anti-German poems for the feast of St Nicholas,[14] and by telling anti-German jokes. Anti-German slogans appeared in public spaces. The Germans did not take this undermining of their authority lightly. For instance, during the summer of 1940, the Landesgericht (a German justice of the peace court) in The Hague sentenced a nurse to three years in prison for chalking an anti-Hitler slogan on a tree in a park.[15]

There was a need, right from the beginning, for information and news untainted by German propaganda, and as a result people listened secretly to the BBC and to the special Dutch-language broadcasts of Radio Orange, transmitted under the aegis of the government-in-exile. The first clandestine newspapers also appeared: *De Waarheid*, *Vrij Nederland* and *Het Parool*.[16] The illegal media in turn created other forms of resistance: clandestine print shops were established, while other people secretly tried to gather news from reliable sources using primitive equipment.

A striking aspect of the early phase of organized resistance was the extensive involvement of Dutch military personnel in it. Many of the military who were demobilized after capitulation were deeply hurt by the defeat and frustrated by their enforced passivity. The first organized form of resistance, the Geuzenaktie, which started on 15 May 1940, was the work of servicemen: a handwritten pamphlet, referring to the legendary Geuzen ('the Beggars') who stood up against the Spanish during the Dutch Revolt of 1566 to 1579, incited the population to resist.[17] In addition, the much larger Orde Dienst (OD, Order Service) came into being; this was a military style organization in which many high-ranking servicemen took part.[18] Founded to prevent a revolution after the occupiers were defeated, this was a resistance group motivated by love for the House of Orange, hatred of National Socialism and distaste for the 'spirit of capitulation'. The latter was expressed, for example, by ex-Prime Minister Hendrik Colijn. Among other things, the OD committed sabotage, smuggled weapons, developed espionage activities and established illegal telephone connections. The fact that such military personnel, along with practically everyone else active in the resistance movement during this period (with the exception of the communists), lacked any kind of experience with regard to the development of clandestine activities and the associated need for absolute secrecy became apparent during the spring of 1941. It was at this point that the German authorities struck a huge blow against them and made a series of arrests among the Geuzen and the OD. These arrests resulted in a mass execution in the Sachsenhausen concentration camp in May 1941. Those who escaped arrest went underground.

Resistance against persecution of Jews only took place on a small scale: in October 1940, when all Dutch civil servants were forced to sign the so-called Aryan Declaration, only 2 per cent refused. However, when all Jewish employees were subsequently dismissed, six Protestant churches protested. There was particular unrest in university circles: a student strike was organized in Delft and on 26 November 1940 Professor Rudolph Cleveringa, in a now-famous speech, protested against the dismissal of his Jewish colleagues at Leiden University. These protests and the closing of two universities (Leiden and Delft) formed the basis for the subsequent participation of a relatively large number of students in resistance activities. The resistance of Erik Hazelhoff Roelfzema, known as the 'Soldier of Orange' since his memoirs published under that title were turned into a very popular film, had its origins here.[19]

The most noticeable forms of resistance against the first anti-Jewish measures took place in Amsterdam. Young Jewish men organized themselves into assault groups to counter the increasing anti-Jewish street violence by the Weer Afdeling (the WA, the militia of the Dutch National Socialist Movement, the NSB).[20] The strike that broke out on 25 February 1941 is well known.[21] Several individual communists played an important role in organizing the strike. Thousands of Amsterdam labourers responded to their strike call, and protested against the manner in which 400 Jewish boys and men had been transported to Mauthausen concentration camp after being publicly humiliated and abused in the centre of Amsterdam. The strike lasted two days and contributed to a hardening of the German regime: in March 1941 three of the strikers were executed along with fourteen arrested Geuzen, including their leader, Bernardus IJzerdraat. These were the first executions in the Netherlands. They mark the end of a period in which the regime tried to convert the Dutch population to the National Socialist ideal via a moderate approach. The executions also ushered in a new phase in the history of the Dutch resistance: a new generation of resistance fighters stepped forward, one with more experience than the first. The mass arrests that took place in the spring of 1941 also forced many more individuals to go underground. This development stimulated the foundation of new resistance activities on a larger scale than before.

*   *   *

At the same time, the occupation of the Netherlands entered its second stage, one that would last until spring 1943. The fact that the Soviet Union and the United States entered the fight increased hope for an Allied victory among the population, and diminished the confidence of the German occupier. This development was reinforced by the successes of the Allied forces in North Africa at the end of 1942, and by the German defeat at Stalingrad in early 1943. The regime in the Netherlands hardened: punishments for acts of resistance became more severe and the number of executions increased. In May 1942 it was decreed that mere *membership* of a resistance organization merited the death penalty. The distribution system was also expanded during this period, and regulations for the Arbeitseinsatz (labour deployment in Germany) were tightened. Moreover, mandatory identity cards were introduced, and in July 1942 the first deportations of Jews to Poland took place.

Playful, symbolic expressions of protest, such as Dutch citizens wearing carnations in a public display of affection for the House of Orange, were now a thing of the past. Anti-German sentiments most certainly increased, but were expressed only in the private sphere. Civil disobedience, such as listening to the BBC and Radio Orange, now took place on a large scale.

The most spectacular collective protest during this period was the wave of strikes that erupted in April and May 1943. The strikes were a reaction to the announcement that soldiers of the Dutch army, released from captivity and demobilized in June 1940, would be transported to Germany as prisoners of war and put to work there. Strikes took place in the industrial regions of Twente in the east of the country, in the mines in the south and at the Philips factories in Eindhoven. Even rural areas responded with strikes: in the north, for example, milk deliveries stopped. It was evident from the large number of participants in this wave of strikes (about 500,000) that this was a manifestation of pent-up anger that had been simmering for quite some time. The regime reacted with a heavy hand: a state of siege was declared, and during the first week of the strikes 175 individuals were summarily executed.[22]

Besides this public protest, the underground resistance also increased in size and activity during this period. A certain degree of professionalization took place as a result of the tragic experiences of the early stages of occupation. For example, cell systems and other measures were designed so that resistance fighters knew as little as possible about each other, thereby preventing strings of arrests.

Experiences with betrayal led to the establishment of an underground information system, which alerted resistance groups to possible infiltrators. This resulted in the first assassinations of these dangerous individuals and, of course, the inevitable moral dilemmas for those who planned and carried out these assassinations.

The illegal press expanded during this period and there was an increase in espionage and sabotage activities. Falsification of identity documents and other papers also took place on a much larger scale. However, the most important type of resistance was helping individuals go into hiding. It was during this period, in autumn 1942, that the Landelijke Organisatie voor Hulp aan Onderduikers (LO, national organization for assistance to people in hiding) was founded. It would later become the largest organization of its kind. This body illustrates the way in which separate, dispersed resistance activities were grouped into a larger, professionally structured unit during this period. The LO was founded by two individuals: Helena Kuipers-Rietberg, known in the resistance as '*Tante Riek*' ('Aunt Riek') and Frits Slomp, a Reformed Church minister, known as '*Frits de Zwerver*' ('Frits the Nomad'). Helena Kuipers lived in the east of the Netherlands, in Winterswijk, where a camp was located for the Dutch Arbeidsdienst (employment service), in which men who were mobilized for the Arbeitseinsatz were trained for labour in Eastern Europe. A number of these men tried to go into hiding in the region. Helena Kuipers and her husband helped by finding safe houses for them. Helena Kuipers was a deeply religious woman who was at the same time gentle, unrelenting and uncompromising. After the war, Slomp related in a television interview how Helena had convinced him to establish the LO. Up until that time, Slomp had been travelling through the region like a nomad, inciting people to resist. He was terrified of being picked up by the SD and for that reason did not travel by train, but got around by bike. One day, when he was in Winterswijk, he met Helena. According to Slomp the conversation that ensued went as follows:

> 'Say Frits, we should found an organization so that we can find places for these people who want to hide. Now I was thinking that you should be the one to do it; that you should travel around the country to get people interested in the idea.' And I said: 'I don't have the nerve for that. The places where I go, I meet people and I go there by bicycle, but I don't dare to travel by train.' She looked at me and said something I shall never forget. 'Listen old man, would it be so terrible if you were to die while thousands of boys would be saved?' And that was that.[23]

Thus, the LO arrived on the scene and soon developed into a national organization with local branches, in which representatives exchanged addresses of safe houses. Helena was the leader of the LO, but in August 1944 she was arrested. By way of the German concentration camp in the Dutch town of Vught, she arrived in Ravensbrück in September 1944, where she succumbed to typhoid late that year. She managed to throw a note from the train that was to transport her to Ravensbrück, and it was delivered safely to her husband and her children: 'Dear

Piet and children. We are on the train, waiting to be taken away. Where to? We don't know. May God protect you. Pray for each other. Your loving mother.'[24]

The LO also helped Jews, but finding safe houses for them was significantly more complicated than for non-Jews. Smaller resistance groups focused specifically on saving Jews, and primarily on saving Jewish children. It was easier to find places to stay for them than for adult Jews. A resistance network that smuggled children was created around the Jewish nursery school located opposite the Hollandsche Schouwburg, a theatre in Amsterdam from where the city's Jews were deported to the Westerbork transit camp. Babies were transported in backpacks, and larger children travelled on the backs of bicycles to safe houses in other parts of the country.

One of the factors that made it difficult to find safe houses for Jews and non-Jews was that it was often necessary to change addresses due to imminent danger. This caused major problems, especially before the autumn of 1942 (that is, when help for individuals in hiding increased). For instance, Pim Boellaard, a member of the OD who went into hiding in the autumn of 1941, was compelled to find his own safe houses. During the eight months in which Boellaard was in hiding, he used nine safe houses on a fairly regular basis, and occasionally slept at other addresses also. Because food aid had not yet been organized at that point, Boellaard often went hungry.[25] It was typical for a resistance fighter in hiding, like Boellaard, to remain active in the resistance. This was also true for others, like Gerrit Jan van der Veen.[26] He was at the head of an organization, the Persoons Bewijzen Centrale (PBC, Identity Cards Centre), which specialized in falsifying identification papers. As was the case quite frequently, one thing led to another, and Van der Veen gradually radicalized and started to carry out acts of sabotage. It became necessary to adopt a false identity and leave his wife and children. As a consequence he led a nerve-wracking nomadic existence.

For resistance fighters like Van der Veen, hiding was only one of many measures they had to take in order to lead an illegal existence. Adopting a false identity and breaking all contact with family, relatives and friends was a given. Other than an occasional note or a brief encounter, no contact with loved ones was possible. That this was one of the most difficult sacrifices is apparent from the ingenuity with which the aforementioned Pim Boellaard succeeded, despite everything, in meeting his wife and his son Willem. On 12 January 1942 he went on a skating trip with them: 'Always with 100 metres between us, yet together on deserted stretches. It's wonderful to be able to see each other this way', said Boellaard in his memoirs.[27]

*   *   *

The second phase in the history of Dutch resistance ended with the wave of strikes of April and May 1943. This led to a new influx of people going into hiding, because many demobilized servicemen wanted to avoid becoming prisoners of war again. As a result the third phase, which lasted from spring 1943 until September 1944, was characterized by ever-increasing disruption of Dutch society. Moreover, the German occupation regime radicalized in the spring of

1943 as a consequence of the defeat at Stalingrad and the Allied successes in the Mediterranean region. Acts of resistance were punished more severely and traitors, male and female, were increasingly employed in order to round up resistance groups. Recruitment for the Arbeitseinsatz was heavy-handed, to say the least. Students were obliged to sign a loyalty declaration, demobilized soldiers were taken away as prisoners of war, shortages became ever more severe and the deportation of Jews continued until September 1944, by which time they had virtually been eliminated from Dutch society.

The prospect of an imminent Allied victory and the hardening of the regime motivated many more people to join the resistance. The role of women became more important, because men increasingly ran the risk of being picked up for the Arbeitseinsatz if they showed themselves in the street. Sympathy for the resistance also increased, which among other things made it somewhat easier to find addresses for people in hiding. Resistance organizations became more specialized. Radicalization also took place and during this period all types of armed resistance became more significant. This was in response to specific measures by the occupier, who for instance tried to make it more difficult to go into hiding by decreeing that all individuals must collect their ration cards personally at the distribution office. As a result, resistance groups began raiding distribution offices to seize ration coupons for people in hiding. This type of activity was increasingly the work of special assault groups, nationally organized into the Landelijke Knokploegen (LKP, National Federation of Assault Groups), which worked closely with the LO. Between May 1943 and September 1944, 233 raids on distribution offices took place, of which about two-thirds were successful.[28]

Raids also took place on registry offices, in order to prevent the occupier from accessing the personal information of wanted individuals. A famous example of such a raid is the one on the Amsterdam Registry Office, which took place on 27 March 1943, under the leadership of Gerrit Jan Van der Veen. As more and more resistance fighters were imprisoned, raids on prisons also increased in order to free incarcerated comrades. Two of the best-known Dutch resistance fighters lost their lives in mid-1944 as a result of failed rescue attempts: the Calvinist farmer and Assault Group leader Johannes Post, and the aforementioned van der Veen. They were arrested and executed by firing squad.

In brief, radicalization took place in many different ways during this period. This is also apparent from the increasing number of assassinations committed by resistance members. Although much discussion took place in the clandestine media about the pros and cons of killing dangerous opponents, little if anything is known about discussions on this sensitive topic among resistance fighters themselves. Decisions to assassinate individuals were accompanied not only by moral objections against the killing of fellow human beings, but also by the question of whether the risk of retaliation and the consequent death of innocent civilians were worth the 'benefits' of an assassination. Statements from resistance fighters who survived the war indicate that assassinating someone was viewed as an extremely difficult assignment. The resistance fighters who participated were frequently shaken by their actions, even to the extent of becoming psychologically unbalanced. This caused them to take risks, leading to their arrest. For instance, Hannie Schaft, the legendary red-haired girl who had killed several Dutch Nazis and collaborators, knew very well that she was one of the most wanted resistance fighters. She nonetheless went out to transport illegal papers, which were discovered at a German checkpoint. There had been no need to take this risk, because other messengers had been available.[29]

The increase in the number of assassinations was the result of another characteristic phenomenon during this third phase: betrayal became an almost overwhelming factor in the history of the Dutch resistance. Using the help of traitors, who were sometimes recruited from among resistance fighters themselves, the Germans succeeded in infiltrating the very core of the resistance. One of the most tragic examples of this development is the so-called 'Englandspiel'.[30] Of the Dutchmen who succeeded in reaching Britain via the North Sea or over land, approximately 200 individuals returned to the Netherlands as secret agents. After the Germans had captured several of thest agents and got one of them to establish radio contact with Britain, German military intelligence (the Abwehr) tried to convince London that the network of secret agents in the Netherlands was functioning normally. All through the period March 1942 to November 1943, the British Special Operations Executive continued sending weapons, explosives and secret agents to the Netherlands. All were captured by the Germans. The Englandspiel cost the lives of 132 individuals and led to the arrest of many others. The result was that the Dutch resistance movement remained isolated. And yet, the Englandspiel did not provide the Germans with the information they were looking for: the time and place of the planned invasion of north-west Europe.

Another characteristic of this period was that people were looking ahead: the clandestine press published extensive discussions about the political, social and cultural transformation of Dutch society. Articles were written about the desirability of breaking down its segregated structure, and of the creation of a united progressive party, but also about the question of what the moral standards and values of a post-war society would be now that pre-war certainties had been shattered. These discussions included topics on public affairs, such as the question of what the principle of justice in the 'new' Netherlands would be, but also issues at the personal level, such as marital fidelity, euthanasia and others.

A strong plea was issued in the clandestine press, in the context of a longing for social renewal, for the amalgamation of resistance forces. This plea fell on deaf ears among many resistance groups. Not until the summer of 1944, when the Dutch government-in-exile emphasized the necessity of increased coordination, did a secret meeting in Amsterdam of representatives of twenty-two different resistance groups lead to the formation of a relatively small 'Contact Committee'. This committee was intended to provide some sort of coordination between the various resistance groups. It appears that the desire to unite forces originated mostly from the top of the resistance movement. Amalgamation was not a big step for these resistance leaders, because they had been involved in creating nationally organized resistance groups such as the LO, the LKP and the Raad van

Verzet (RVV, Council of Resistance). However, many groups remained independent, retaining a strong local character.

After the Allied invasion of Normandy, the Dutch government in London and the Allied forces urged the Dutch population not to revolt against the German occupier. This call was not addressed to resistance organizations, who had 'their own instructions and [knew] what to do', as Prime Minister P. Gerbrandy added in his pre-recorded radio speech. In anticipation of Operation Market Garden (the Allied air-ground offensive to gain control of the bridges crossing the branches of the River Rhine at Nijmegen and Arnhem) new instructions were issued in September 1944. These wide-reaching orders to protect vital parts of the infrastructure against German destruction demonstrate that the Allied authorities had no realistic idea of the capabilities of the resistance organizations.[31] Initially the Allied advance appeared to progress smoothly. Maastricht was liberated on 14 September and Allied airborne forces arrived at Arnhem on 17 September. However, the subsequent failure of Operation Market Garden halted the Allied advance and divided the Netherlands into two. The liberated south developed completely differently from the north and the west of the Netherlands, which were not liberated until the spring of 1945. With the liberation of the southern part of the country, occupation and resistance in the northern part entered its fourth and final stage.

*   *   *

The contrast between north and south was reinforced by the railway strike, which was called by the Dutch government-in-exile on 17 September in order to support the Allied advance. As a countermeasure against the strike the Germans prohibited the transportation of food and fuel by ship to the western part of the Netherlands, resulting in a winter that came to be characterized by hunger and hardship. An additional consequence of the failure of Operation Market Garden was that 30,000 railway strikers now had to go into hiding. This increased the demand for illegal assistance to them in the occupied part of the Netherlands.

Another crucial development during this last phase of the occupation was the amalgamation of (armed) resistance groups into the Nederlandsche Binnenlandsche Strijdkrachten (Dutch Forces of the Interior, abbreviated as BS). This occurred after the Allied forces and the Dutch government-in-exile had called for it on 5 September 1944. Only if the desired merger took place would the Allied forces look after the delivery of weapons and explosives. The LKP, the RVV and the OD amalgamated to form the BS, under the supreme command of Prince Bernhard. The task of the BS was to support the Allied invasion with focused resistance actions, and to maintain order in the period between the German capitulation and the return of the Dutch government and queen.

Initially, due to internal struggles and a shortage of weapons and explosives, the BS did not function smoothly. Once these issues were resolved, all kinds of sabotage acts took place, aimed at the destruction of the German transportation and communication infrastructure. Specialized resistance units were created, focused for example on the establishment of illegal telephone networks intended to facilitate contact with the liberated part of the Netherlands. Resistance fighters who broke through enemy lines operated as liaison officers. For instance, Jos Mulder-Gemmeke succeeded in October 1944 in crossing the bridge at Heusden under a barrage from German as well as Allied troops (among whom was a British soldier who would become her third husband in 1947). Stuffed into her shoulder pads were microfilms that she was transporting via Brussels to the Dutch secret service in London. She subsequently got herself parachuted back into occupied territory in March 1945, where she landed in a ditch. Having sustained serious back injuries, she was rescued by resistance fighters and spent the remainder of the occupation in bed.[32]

The increase in sabotage acts was accompanied by an increase in reprisals. One such reprisal was intended to avenge an act of resistance that killed one German officer and seriously wounded another. It took the form of a raid on the village of Putten on 1 October 1944. The Wehrmacht, which assumed an increasingly important role in the fight against the resistance alongside (and sometimes at odds with) the SiPo, burnt the village to the ground and deported 660 men and boys. Only 10 per cent of them survived the camps. A total of about 1,000 Dutch civilians were executed by the Germans during this period, including many resistance fighters. The occupiers had abandoned any semblance of justice after the Allied invasion, and resistance fighters were imprisoned or executed without any form of due process.[33]

In spite of the intensified repression, resistance groups in the occupied part of the Netherlands were quite active during this last phase of the occupation. Besides the aforementioned armed actions, the illegal press was there to maintain morale and satisfy the craving for news. Providing help to individuals in hiding continued, but this became more and more complicated because of the food shortages. Due to the elimination of normal means of transportation, the bicycle became increasingly important for the resistance, wooden tyres replacing rubber ones. Women occupied a more visible role in the resistance as the occupiers focused increasingly upon hunting down men for the Arbeitseinsatz. During a large raid in Rotterdam in November 1944, for example, 50,000 men were arrested and taken away. The role of female couriers became increasingly important: in prams and under corsets and bras they transported illegal leaflets, espionage material and weapons. Although the German authorities initially did not suspect these mostly young, innocent-looking women, they took more severe action against them during the final phase of occupation, indeed right up to the last day. For instance, in Amsterdam during the night of 4 and 5 May 1945, Annick van Hardeveld was shot dead from a car by the Grüne Polizei. She was on a bicycle, dressed in a Red Cross uniform, on her way to a resistance group to deliver a message. Because she had just heard the news about the approaching capitulation, she was wearing a Dutch flag over her uniform. It was a fatal mistake.[34]

The German capitulation on 5 May 1945 deprived the armed resistance of the opportunity to contribute to the liberation of the Netherlands. The resulting

frustration worsened when it became evident that the College van Vertrouwens-
mannen (College of Trustees), appointed by the Dutch government in London,
had been negotiating with the Germans about a relaxation of the repression and
about the possibility of food drops by the Allies. Nor did the resistance play any
role in the negotiations surrounding the German surrender.

The feeling of being ignored by the Dutch government-in-exile also led to
considerable irritation and frustration in the liberated parts of the Netherlands.
The government-in-exile (which did not return to the Netherlands until the
entire country had been liberated) delegated authority in the south of the
Netherlands to the Militair Gezag (MG, Military Authority). The MG had
extensive jurisdiction, including the right to arrest people suspected of having
collaborated with the Germans. This led to clashes between the MG, as the
representative of the legitimate government in London, and the resistance groups
who attempted to follow their own political agendas. However, resistance leaders
were gradually incorporated into the government apparatus; thus demobilization
of the resistance had already started before the eventual surrender of Germany.[35]

* * *

In assessing the general character and impact of the Dutch resistance we may
conclude that the occupation of the Netherlands ended with a sense of disappointment for many resistance fighters. Many of them had expected that the war
would lead to a radical political, social and cultural transformation of Dutch
society. Even though resistance fighters did not agree among themselves as to
what this transformation should actually look like, they had at least been
expecting to play an active role in the process. However, during the latter phase
of the occupation the foundation was laid for the restoration of former relations
and, thereby, the preservation of the segmented structure of Dutch society.
Following a brief period of hope for a 'breakthrough', the Netherlands returned
after 1946 to the old, familiar pre-war patterns. It was not until the 1960s that a
radical shift took place, one which, according to some historians, can be seen as a
delayed effect of changes that had occurred during the German occupation.[36]

Even when using a broad definition of resistance, it is evident that the resistance movement in the Netherlands had a limited reach. Not until spring 1943,
when the existence of people other than Jews was threatened (members of
the Dutch army, students, men between the ages of 18 and 50), did the resistance
movement expand. Large numbers of people went into hiding and had to be
helped. Assisting people in hiding (along with everything associated with it,
including armed activities) became one of the most important forms of resistance
in the Netherlands. However, the deportation of Jews was already in full swing
when such help began to be organized on a larger scale. Paramilitary resistance
did not play an important role in the Netherlands; nor did espionage. The
clandestine press, on the other hand, played a crucial part from the beginning in
boosting the morale of the Dutch population. The press also served as the
primary antidote for National Socialist propaganda.

None of this meant that the Dutch resistance was able to make a significant contribution to preventing the destruction of the Dutch Jews. Nevertheless, by their large-scale assistance to people who sought to avoid the Arbeitseinsatz, the resistance *was* able to do some harm to another important objective of the regime: the economic exploitation of the Netherlands for the benefit of the German war economy. At the same time, what is true for the Dutch resistance in general is valid here also: the effect was primarily moral, not material. This moral effect is most evident when considering the failure of Nazification. The resistance definitely contributed to this lack of success by promoting and channelling anti-German sentiments in numerous ways.

Every historian writing on the Dutch resistance needs first to consider the image of the resistance created in the early post-war years. The first historical work that was dedicated to the history of the German occupation, *Onderdrukking en Verzet* (Oppression and Resistance), laid the foundation for an image of Dutch resistance that endured until the mid-1960s.[37] This study was distributed in the Netherlands in instalments which eventually grew to four volumes in size. Each segment of the ideologically varied resistance movement was presented in terms of the role it had played in the Dutch struggle for national survival. The nation, it was claimed, had been united in its rejection of National Socialism, and the resistance movement had been the most radical expression of this general attitude. However, such radicalism posed a problem for anyone who was not an author of *Onderdrukking en Verzet*: the choice of an illegal existence had often been accompanied by all kinds of unconventional behaviour, behaviour that in the eyes of many had undermined the unity of the nation. Some even spoke of 'unpatriotic' behaviour that should not be held up as an example for others. For this reason, post-war representations of the Dutch population stressed the collective suffering and struggles of the nation. Special attention to the distress of specific groups, such as the resistance or the Jews, did not fit well with this story. Even in *Onderdrukking en Verzet*, the persecution of the Jews was described as a tragedy that did not belong to the history of the Netherlands.

In addition, and partly in opposition to the conception of the Netherlands during the German occupation that predominated until the mid-1960s, resistance groups wrote their own histories. These came in the form of memoirs, commemorative books, interviews, (auto)biographies and monographs. Since this is a form of 'partisan' historiography, the depictions are often biased and hagiographical. Moreover, the image is fragmented because, with the occasional exception (*Onderdrukking en Verzet*), each *zuil* recorded its own resistance history. The fragmented nature of these resistance histories is further reinforced by their local and regional character.

The image of the resistance in the Netherlands since 1945 has not only been determined by amateur and professional historians. There have been memorials, monuments and autobiographies – such as that of Eric Hazelhoff Roelfzema, the legendary Soldier of Orange.[38] Fiction, film and television documentaries demonstrate that the resistance remains a popular and important theme up to this day. It is striking that, although complexity was for a long time absent in the historiography, it was present very early on in fiction writing and in the films based on that writing. As early as the 1940s and 1950s, authors such as Simon Vestdijk and Willem Frederik Hermans published novels expressing doubts about the aura of sainthood that surrounded the resistance.[39] These novels undermined the black-and-white image of oppression and resistance that was prevalent during these decades. Perhaps new, more complex histories of the resistance will draw their inspiration from this early fiction.

Notes

1. For Wilhelmina's role during the war see Cees Fasseur, *Wilhelmina. Krijgshaftig in een vormeloze jas* (Amsterdam, 2001).
2. Radio speech of Queen Wilhelmina on the occasion of the German attack on the Soviet Union, broadcast by Radio Orange (24 June 1941); available at: http://hmi.ewi.utwente.nl/choral/radiooranje.html. In popular memory these words of the queen are remembered as: 'will hit the Kraut on his head' (in Dutch: '*slaat den Mof op den kop*').
3. For a description of the structure of the Aufsichtsverwaltung see Peter Romijn, *Burgemeesters in oorlogstijd. Besturen onder Duitse bezetting* (Amsterdam, 2006), pp. 130–59. The estimate of the number of officials in the German civil administration, which is not in his book, was kindly provided by the author.
4. No precise figures on the number of German military and police men are available. After June 1940 two divisions of the German army were stationed on Dutch territory. A third division was added in 1941 and a fourth one in 1942. In that year the forces of the German army numbered probably 50,000 to 60,000 in total, mainly deployed at the coast manning the defences against an Allied invasion. In addition, there were small units of the German navy and the Luftwaffe stationed in the Netherlands. De Jong estimates the number of security forces (Ordnungspolizei and Waffen-SS together) at 20,000 to 23,000. L. de Jong, *Het Koninkrijk der Nederlanden in de Tweede Wereldoorlog*, 14 vols (The Hague, 1969–88), Vol. 4-1 (1972), pp. 115–17.
5. Louis de Jong, *The Netherlands and Nazi Germany* (Cambridge, Mass., 1990), p. 33.
6. Bob Moore, *Victims and survivors. The Nazi persecution of the Jews in the Netherlands 1940–1945* (London, 1997).
7. Louis de Jong, preface to Werner Warmbrunn, *The Dutch under German Occupation* (Stanford, Cal./London, 1963), pp. v–x.
8. De Jong, *The Netherlands and Nazi Germany*, pp. 47–8.
9. For different calculations see Dick van Galen Last, 'The Netherlands', in Bob Moore (ed.), *Resistance in Western Europe* (Oxford, 2000), p. 214. All calculations of the numbers of resisters are quite general. On the basis of the available literature it is not possible to break down the various branches of the resistance movement in a reliable way.
10. In this contribution I limit myself to the resistance in the Dutch territory in Europe. For examples of resistance to the Japanese occupation of the Dutch East Indies see Madelon de Keizer and Marije Plomp (eds), *Een open zenuw. Hoe wij ons de Tweede Wereldoorlog herinneren* (Amsterdam, 2010).
11. Van Galen Last, 'The Netherlands', p. 190.
12. Henri Michel, *Les mouvements clandestins en Europe* (Paris, 1965), p. 63.
13. Bart van der Boom, *'We leven nog.' De stemming in bezet Nederland* (Amsterdam, 2003).
14. For these poems see Hinke Piersma, *Zou de goede Sint wel komen. Sinterklaasgedichten uit de Tweede Wereldoorlog* (Amsterdam, 2009).
15. *De Telegraaf* (19 August 1940).
16. For the underground press see Lydia Winkel and Hans de Vries (eds), *De ondergrondse pers 1940–1945* (Utrecht, 1989).
17. For the Geuzen, see Harry Paape, *De Geuzen* (Amsterdam, 1965).
18. For the OD see J.W.M. Schulten, *Geschiedenis van de Ordedienst. Mythe en werkelijkheid van een verzetsorganisatie* (The Hague, 1998).

19. E. Hazelhoff Roelfzema, *Soldaat van Oranje, '40–'45* (The Hague, 1971), English trans., *Soldier of Orange* (London, 1972); *Op jacht naar het leven. De autobiografie van de Soldaat van Oranje* (Utrecht, 2000), English trans., *In pursuit of life* (Stroud, 2003). Filmed as *Soldaat Van Oranje*, directed by Paul Verhoeven (released 22 September 1977), American version *Soldier of Orange* (released 16 August 1979).
20. Erik Schumacher and Josje Damsma, *Hier woont een NSB'er. Nationaalsocialisten in bezet Amsterdam* (Amsterdam, 2010).
21. For an assessment of the impact of this strike and the ways in which it has been remembered see Annet Mooij, *De strijd om de februaristaking* (Amsterdam, 2006).
22. Liesbeth van der Horst, *April–Mei '43. De stakingen als keerpunt* (Amsterdam, 1998).
23. Ad van Liempt, *Verzetshelden en moffenvrienden* (Amsterdam, 2011), p. 15.
24. *Ibid.*, p. 20.
25. For Boellaard see Jolande Withuis, *Weest manlijk, zijt sterk. Pim Boellaard (1903–2001). Het leven van een verzetsheld* (Amsterdam, 2008).
26. For Gerrit Jan van der Veen see Anita van Ommeren and Ageeth Scherphuis, *'Die man had moeten blijven leven.' Gerrit Jan van der Veen en het verzet* (Amsterdam, 1984).
27. Withuis, *Weest manlijk, zijt sterk*, p. 110.
28. Van Galen Last, 'The Netherlands', p. 201.
29. Ton Kors, *Hannie Schaft. Het levensverhaal van een vrouw in verzet tegen de nazi's* (Amsterdam, 1976).
30. M.R.D. Foot, L. Marks and L. Pot, 'The Englandspiel', in M.R.D. Foot (ed.), *Holland at war against Hitler: Anglo-Dutch relations 1940–1945* (London, 1990), pp. 120–56.
31. De Jong, *Het Koninkrijk*, Vol. 10a-1 (1980), pp. 8, 284–5.
32. Jaus Müller, 'Op de fiets door de frontlinie. Jos Mulder-Gemmeke (1922–2010), verzetsvrouw en drager Willems-Orde', *NRC-Handelsblad* (23 December 2010), available at http://archief.nrc.nl/.
33. Madelon de Keizer, *Putten. De razzia en de herinnering* (Amsterdam, 1998).
34. 'Annick van Hardeveld', available at: http://nl.wikipedia.org/wiki/Annick_van_Hardeveld.
35. Peter Romijn, 'The Synthesis of the Political Order and the Resistance Movement in the Netherlands in 1945', in Gill Bennett (ed.), *The End of War in Europe 1945* (London, 1996), pp. 139–47.
36. One of these historians is Hans Blom. See J.C.H. Blom, 'The Second World War and Dutch Society: continuity and change', in A.C. Duke and C.A. Tamse (eds), *Britain and The Netherlands*, Vol. V, *War and Society* (The Hague, 1977), pp. 228–48; J.C.H. Blom, *Crisis, Bezetting en Herstel. Tien Studies over Nederland, 1930–1950* (Gravenhage, 1989).
37. J.J. van Bolhuis, C.D.J. Brandt, H.M. van Randwijk, B.C. Slotemaker (eds), *Onderdrukking en Verzet*, 4 vols (Arnhem, 1949–55).
38. See n. 19 for bibliographical and filmographical details.
39. S. Vestdijk, *Pastorale 1943. Roman uit de tijd van de Duitsche overheersching* (Rotterdam, 1948), no English trans. available. Filmed as *Pastorale 43*, directed by Wim Verstappen (released 20 April 1978); Willem Frederik Hermans, *De donkere kamer van Damocles* (Amsterdam, 1958), English trans. *The Dark Room of Damocles* (London, 1962). Filmed as *Als Twee Duppels Water*, directed by Fons Rademakers (released 21 February 1963).

Guide to Further Reading

De Jong, Louis, 'The Dutch Resistance Movements and the Allies, 1940–1945', in *Proceedings of the Second International Conference on the History of Resistance Movements – Milan, 26–29 March 1961* (Oxford, 1964).
Van Galen Last, Dick, 'The Netherlands', in Bob Moore (ed.), *Resistance in Western Europe* (Oxford, 2000), pp. 189–222.

Chapter 8

Poland

Paul Latawski

The invasion of Poland in 1939 by Nazi Germany and the Soviet Union led to one of the most brutal occupations experienced on the European Continent during the Second World War. Winston Churchill, in a speech given in May 1941, stated that 'in severity and scale' the oppression employed in the Nazi occupation of Poland exceeded that of any occupied country in Europe.[1] The loss of statehood combined with the extreme violence of ideologically driven occupiers led to geopolitical reordering and mass murder on a very large scale. By war's end, the Polish state was territorially shifted westward and had suffered population losses of over 6 million, or 21 per cent of its pre-war population.[2] Polish resistance during the Second World War developed for both historic and contemporary reasons. Resistance to foreign occupation was deeply rooted in the nineteenth-century insurrections and conspiratorial movements, which were in turn a reaction to the partitions and loss of statehood at the end of the eighteenth century. More immediate factors stemmed from the nature of the occupation, which posed an unprecedented threat to statehood and the very existence of the nation itself.

If the threat to Poland was without precedent, then so too was the comprehensiveness of resistance to preserve and restore national life. In an age of total war, the Poles responded with a model of total resistance. Polish resistance to occupation in the Second World War integrated political, military and societal responses in such a comprehensive fashion that it has been described as forming an 'underground state'. At the core of the complex matrix of Polish resistance was the military effort of the Armia Krajowa (AK) or Home Army. Given the peripheral role of the Polish communist contribution to wartime resistance, the emphasis of this chapter will be on the broadly based, non-communist AK. Thus will the chapter examine the AK by focusing on its structure, development and eventual fate from the outbreak of the war in 1939 to its conclusion in 1945.

* * *

Germany invaded Poland on 1 September 1939 and defeated the Polish army in the course of six weeks' fighting. On 17 September, the Soviet Union joined Germany's aggression, leading to the two powers partitioning Poland. Until Germany invaded the Soviet Union in June 1941, Poland had two different occupation zones. Despite the ideological differences between the Nazi and Soviet regimes, in practical terms there was little to distinguish between Poland's two occupiers. Each regime sought to extinguish the Polish state, and eliminate or remove its population or keep it in servitude. Nazi racial ideology identified Poles as sub-humans (*Untermenschen*), while Soviet Marxist-Leninist ideology treated Poles as class enemies. German policy envisaged that the ultimate consequences for the Poles would be physical obliteration, removal or relegation to the status of a subject people who provided a pool of labour in the German-occupied portion of the country. The most chilling example of the realization of the most extreme aims of Nazi racialist ideology can be seen in the destruction of Poland's Jewish community in the Holocaust.[3]

The Soviet Union seized the ethnically mixed part of eastern Poland known as the Kresy, where the Poles formed local majorities only in some parts. The Soviet regime deliberately favoured the non-Polish Belorussian, Jewish and Ukrainian population of eastern Poland. All parts of the population were subjected to Sovietization, with political, social and economic life being changed to resemble that of the rest of the Soviet Union. The outbreak of the German-Soviet war in 1941 led to a Polish-Soviet rapprochement, with the Sikorski-Maisky Pact of July 1941 moderately ameliorating the condition of Poles on territory controlled by the Soviet Union. Nevertheless, the discovery in April 1943 of the mass graves of thousands of Polish officers executed by the Soviet authorities – the infamous Katyn Forest massacres – highlighted the fact that the German and Soviet occupations shared a common basis in murder and terror between 1939 and 1941.[4] The overall number of Polish officers shot by the Soviet authorities in the Katyn Forest, Starbelsk, Ostashkov and other locations in Belorussia and Ukraine was nearly 22,000.[5]

Redrawing boundaries and territorial reorganization followed the onset of the German and Soviet occupations of Poland in 1939. Prior to the outbreak of hostilities, Germany and the Soviet Union had reached a deal that partitioned the country along what became known as the Ribbentrop-Molotov Line. The boundary line between the two partitioning powers roughly approximated Poland's present eastern frontier. At the conclusion of military operations in October 1939, Germany initiated an annexation policy that incorporated sizeable chunks of Polish territory into the Reich. Large parts of western Poland in the north and south and even parts of central Poland contiguous to Germany were annexed. The administrative entities Reichsgau Dantzig-Westpreussen and Reichgau Warthcland incorporated nearly 92,000km^2 of Polish territory containing a population of 10.1 million, of which 8.9 million were Poles. Polish Upper Silesia in the south became part of the German Oberschlesien province. The remainder of German-occupied Poland became a colonial enclave containing 16 million Poles and covering a territory of 142,000km^2. Designated the General Government (Generalgouvernement) under the direction of Hans Frank, it was treated initially as a protectorate but with a long-term aim of full integration into Germany.[6]

While German policy did not incorporate all of the Polish territory acquired, the Soviet Union intended to absorb its territorial gains in their entirety. Pre-war

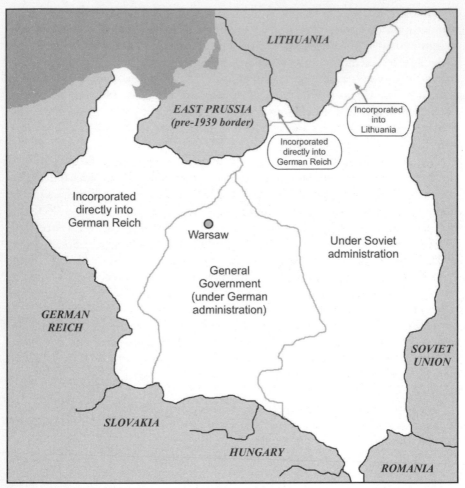

The partition of Poland, 1939.

Polish territory became part of the Belorussian and Ukrainian Soviet Socialist Republics following a rigged referendum the result of which was never in doubt. The Soviet Union gained from Poland territory amounting to 202,069km^2, with a population of over 13 million.[7] The German invasion of the Soviet Union in June 1941 placed all of pre-war Polish territory under German control. The boundaries of the General Government moved eastwards, but did not take in all of the Polish territory. The remainder of eastern Poland fell under other organizational entities, namely the Reichskommissariat Ostland and the Reichskommissariate Ukraine. Soviet control of eastern Poland was not re-established until the Red Army swept westwards in 1944.

All of these changes to boundaries and administrative arrangements were accompanied by mass deportations which had a dramatic impact on the Polish population. The Nazi regime expelled 923,000 Poles from Polish territory annexed to Germany, with most being dumped in the General Government.[8] Soviet deportations, however, exceeded those of Germany in the first two years of the war. More Polish citizens were removed to Central Asia and Siberia than those expelled by Germany prior to June 1940. In Soviet-controlled territory the impact on Poles, who formed between a quarter and a third of the population in eastern Poland, was more devastating. It comprehensively destroyed a pattern of settlement that had existed for centuries. The overall number of Polish citizens deported into the interior of the Soviet Union in this period can only be estimated. The most reliable sources suggest that 1.2 to 1.5 million were forcibly removed to the Soviet hinterland.[9] The tally of Polish population losses amounted to about 1 million Polish citizens who died as a result of Soviet 'liberation'. Many of the surviving deportees were never repatriated to Poland after the war.[10]

Terror against the Polish population began even before the conclusion of German military operations in Poland in 1939. From the entry of German forces into Poland, Operation Tannenberg targeted members of the Polish intelligentsia, politicians, military officers and clergy for elimination.[11] This decapitation, directed against Polish society by focusing on its elite, was underway before the establishment of an elaborate German security apparatus. Although the German occupation relied on the support of large numbers of German army and Luftwaffe formations based on Polish territory, the development of a sophisticated network of security services and police formations was central to control of the Polish population and the application of repressive action and terror. The German security apparatus comprised a complex web of agencies, among them the Ordnungspolizei or 'Orpo' (Public Order Police), which controlled a number of police formations including the Grenzschutz (Border Guard), Bahnschutz (Railway Police) and Werkschutz (Factory Police). In order to interface with the population, the lowest tiers of the pre-war Polish police continued to have a public-order role. In the eastern parts of Poland, locally recruited Ukrainian police served the Nazi regime.[12]

The Sicherheitspolizei or 'Sipo' (Security Police) was at the heart of the security apparatus. The Sipo's 4th Bureau, better known as the Gestapo, was particularly dangerous, as it was staffed by especially ruthless and ideologically driven functionaries. The Gestapo created networks of informers that numbered in the thousands across occupied Poland, for individuals in any society were vulnerable to compromise with skilled security forces unconstrained by legal or ethical codes. Individual Poles were subjected to curfew and other control measures. Many more infractions were now classified as capital crimes, and reprisals by summary execution became commonplace as a pacification measure.[13] The strength of the German occupation forces ranged between 50,000 and 80,000 in police formations during the course of the occupation, with the Wehrmacht presence fluctuating between 400,000 and 1 million.[14]

The Soviet security apparatus in the comparatively shorter period of occupation of eastern Poland between September 1939 and June 1941 showed itself to be more efficient than that of the Germans. The fact that the Polish community was a minority of the population there facilitated Soviet efforts to isolate it and, with mass deportations, remove it from occupied Polish territory. The NKVD (Narodnyy komissariat vnutrennikh del – the People's Commissariat for Internal Affairs) was the Soviet secret police organization in charge of repressive action. Clearly it had been gathering information on the population of eastern Poland years in advance of the occupation, and the NKVD's efficiency in gaining informers meant that Polish resistance organizations and activity were effectively suppressed.[15] Ironically, when Germany gained control of eastern Poland opportunities to build a Polish resistance network increased among the now greatly diminished Polish population. In economic terms, communization policy resulted in seizure of property, state ownership of enterprises and a general impoverishment of the population, as eastern Poland was subjected to a process intended to remake it into an image of the rest of the Soviet Union.

German occupation economic policy was one of naked exploitation of Polish territory. The occupation authorities expropriated natural resources, goods and businesses on a massive scale. This rapacious policy drained away economic capacity. By 1943, only 51,000 of the 195,000 commercial enterprises in existence in Poland before the war remained.[16] The German takeover of all financial institutions ensured that fiscal policy was conducted in such a way as to bring maximum economic advantage to Germany. The overall consequences of the economic policy of the German occupation were to impoverish the Polish population and push it to subsistence levels. The General Government was to become one large, if gradually diminishing, pool of unskilled labour.[17]

* * *

In political and military terms, the Polish underground state did not exist in isolation. It owed its allegiance to, and followed the direction of, the Polish government-in-exile that was resident in Paris and then later in London. The Polish government-in-exile, led by General Władysław Sikorski until his death in 1943, maintained continuity with the pre-war constitutional order but sought to build a more representative political participation than the pre-war government. This policy shaped both the political and military elements of the Polish underground state. The underground political institutions reflected this all-inclusive approach. Within occupied Poland, most of the pre-war political parties had representation on the Consultative Political Committee (Polityczny Komitet Porozumiewawczy – PKP), set up to provide a political unity and direction to underpin resistance activities. Only the extreme right and left (communists) of the political spectrum could not be accommodated in the unified underground structure.[18] The clandestine PKP functioned as the principal political body between 1940 and 1943, when it was then replaced by the Council of National Unity (Rada Jedności Narodowej – RJN).[19]

The political body of the underground state linked into the civil underground structures that gave substance to the concept of an underground state. The shadow structures of the state in occupied Poland were run by a clandestine organization called the Government Delegacy (Delegatura). The Delegatura included a full range of shadow departments numbering fifteen in total which had an important role in either planning for a transition once the occupation came to an end, or in supporting civil resistance against the occupation.[20] For example, the Department of Information and Press existed to create an underground press in order both to provide accurate information to the Polish population and to counter German propaganda. From the point of view of resistance, the former function had immediate importance. With German curtailment of Polish schooling beyond the elementary level, providing a Polish education system outside German control was the role of the Delegatura's Department for Education and Culture. The establishment of a clandestine school system meant that by 1944, more than 100,000 pupils studied in underground secondary schools.[21]

Providing guidance to the Polish population regarding behaviour during the occupation was the Directorate of Civil Resistance (Kierownictwo Walki Cywilnej – KWC), headed throughout the war by the politician Stefan Korbonski. At its most basic level, the KWC set out a 'Code of Rights and Obligations of a Pole' as guidance for individual behaviour in the face of the occupation. The Code emphasized the requirement for universal resistance to the occupation, and set boundaries as to what was permissible and what was not in relation to engagement with the occupying authorities. Detailed information was disseminated throughout Polish society and compliance was viewed as being grounded in Polish law, with an obligation to obey and comply with the Polish underground authorities.[22] The KWC had a justice and court system under its direction. In extreme cases of collaboration with the enemy, this led to underground court cases for treason and capital sentences being carried out by special units.[23]

The effectiveness of civil resistance in occupied Poland can be measured by the lack of organized collaboration with the occupation authorities. Although the Polish Communist Party's links to the Soviet Union might be considered the exception, collaboration was on an individual basis and not extensive. In the words of Stefan Korbonski, 'Poland produced no Quisling'.[24] Undoubtedly, the ideologically uncompromising policies of the occupying powers left little scope for finding partners among the Polish population, while the impressive wartime solidarity of Poles made civil resistance rather than collaboration the preferred response to occupation.[25]

The genesis of the military wing of the Polish underground state began even before the conclusion of hostilities in 1939 and evolved into its definitive structure by 1942. As in the case of underground political institutions, the Polish government-in-exile took a close interest in the organization of military resistance in Poland. A prominent officer in the interwar military establishment, General Kazimierz Sosnkowski, was made a distant commandant-in-chief of the underground military effort from Paris and later London. Sikorski worked through Sosnkowski to ensure that the military wing of the underground reflected his priorities. Exercising command over a clandestine military organization from a distant seat of government in London proved difficult. In practice, the underground military leadership in occupied Poland operated with great autonomy in the difficult conditions being experienced. On broad strategic issues, however, the Polish government-in-exile shaped the direction of military strategy.

The earliest attempt at creating a national organization to conduct resistance to occupation was the Service for Poland's Victory (Służba Zwycięstwu Polski, SZP). It proved ephemeral and after two months was replaced by the Union for Armed Struggle (Związek Walki Zbrojnej, ZWZ). The reasons for the creation of ZWZ were political, and marked the assertion of the Polish government-in-exile's policy toward resistance. The government-in-exile pursued a policy toward resistance that aimed to create a non-partisan military organization not tied to any political grouping, and operating within a framework that ensured a coherent strategy of resistance to German occupation. In February 1942, the ZWZ became the Armia Krajowa – AK, or Home Army. This event signified the consolidation of armed resistance groups representing various strands of political opinion into a unified structure. The only parts of the Polish political spectrum outside the AK represented the extreme right and left of politics. Although some resistance units of the political right joined the Armia Krajowa in 1943, others operated independently.[26] The Communist Party, with its tiny base of support, preferred to employ its clandestine units under direction from Moscow.[27] At its peak strength, the AK approached 400,000 members.[28] In terms of organized military resistance, the AK was unquestionably not only the most important resistance movement, but also the movement that was most representative of Polish politics and society. The Communist People's Army (Armia Ludowa, AL) never fielded more than 10,000, and its numerical weakness and the lack of popular support for the communists ultimately made them dependent upon Soviet support.[29]

*   *   *

The senior leadership of the military wing of the Polish underground state, the AK, was drawn from officers of the pre-war Polish army. Virtually all of the senior AK leadership had fought in 1939, and had at the end of the campaign entered into conspiratorial organizations with a view to developing national resistance. The involvement of the army in interwar Polish politics meant that these officers, to varying degrees, were prepared to act autonomously from political authority. Given this interwar legacy, the AK military leadership also needed to be acceptable to both the Polish government-in-exile in London and its local political appendage, the Delegatura, in occupied Poland. The military leadership that emerged, however, proved equal to the task of organizing resistance. Foremost among the senior military leadership was the Commander-in-Chief of the AK, Colonel Stefan Rowecki. Indeed, few officers could have been better suited to the task of leading military resistance.

Rowecki was appointed Commander-in-Chief of the ZWZ in June 1940. Aged 45 years, Rowecki's army career marked him out as an officer who merged the qualities of a military intellectual with those of a soldier who had operational military experience at the sharp end of his profession. His intellectual credentials were established by working in the Polish army's research and publishing institute during the 1920s, and by serving as editor and on editorial boards of most of the key military journals of the interwar period. As a prolific author of articles on a wide range of topics, his writing confirmed his place as a respected military intellectual. Some of his interwar research interests and writing clearly equipped him for his subsequent wartime role. In 1928, for example, Rowecki published a number of articles in the popular military journal *Przegląd Wojskowy* regarding military aspects of the civil war in Russia. One of these articles examined class war, civil war and partisan war in the light of the Soviet experience.[30] From the perspective of his future role as Commander-in-Chief of the AK, he published what was to be his most important book, *Walki Uliczne* (*Street Fighting*) in the same year. This publication was a comprehensive examination of urban warfare involving an insurgent enemy. The book included a study of communist doctrine for urban insurgency, along with case studies of attempted communist uprisings in Hamburg in 1923 and Tallinn in 1924.[31] This important title is little known outside Poland. It is nevertheless unique, insofar as it is one of the earliest studies of urban warfare involving irregular forces. This element of Rowecki's intellectual interests provided him with a thorough education in preparation for his wartime command of the AK.

At the outbreak of war in 1939, Rowecki was in command of the Warsaw Armoured-Motorized Brigade (Warszawska Brygada Pancerno-Motorowa), the second such formation in the late 1930s to join the Polish order of battle. This formation was in the process of training and equipping when war broke out in September 1939. In its incomplete state the brigade briefly experienced heavy fighting before quickly losing its operational effectiveness. Rowecki, with some other officers, returned to Warsaw after the disintegration of his command. There he embarked on a conspiratorial career that would eventually see him rise to the leadership of the AK. Known by a variety of pseudonyms including Grot, Rakoń, Grabica, Inżynier, Jan, Kalina and Tur, Rowecki more than any other figure shaped the development of the AK until his arrest by the Gestapo in June 1943.[32] Despite being the product of a politicized army, Rowecki ensured that a realistic military approach tied to the aims of his political masters guided the Armia Krajowa's strategy and operations.

Colonel Tadeusz Komorowski replaced Rowecki in July 1943 and remained the Commander-in-Chief of the AK until he became a German prisoner of war at the end of the Warsaw Rising in 1944. Komorowski, like Rowecki, was a professional soldier whose interwar military career was spent entirely within the cavalry. Apart from unit command appointments, he served as an instructor and later commandant of training establishments. In 1924, he represented Poland in equestrian events in the Paris Olympics. He began his underground role in 1939, and by 1941 was deputy commander of the ZWZ and in command of the Kraków district.[33] A less strong and less dynamic personality than Rowecki, he relied more on his deputies and was less politically astute than his predecessor.[34] Although he was a 'first-class gentleman' whose patriotism and courage were beyond question, he lacked Rowecki's intellectual vigour, clarity of thought and decisiveness.[35] His assumption of command of the AK came at a stage in the war that would prove especially critical and problematic to the future of Poland.

*   *   *

In the wake of the cataclysmic defeat in 1939, the emerging military structures of the Polish underground state and the Polish government-in-exile faced the major challenge of devising a strategy for resistance. The brutal policies of the occupying powers and the lack of capacity for Polish armed resistance proved significant limiting factors that necessitated careful planning, time and resilience if they were to be overcome. Jan Karski, a wartime courier between occupied Poland and Britain, described the work of Polish resistance as 'humdrum, secretive and dangerous'.[36] Between 1939 and 1943 the government-in-exile and the AK evolved a strategy that followed a measured and calculated policy of resistance which looked to the long-term liberation of Poland, and which offered the prospect of the greatest military impact combined with potentially the smallest cost to the civilian population. Komorowski reflected in his memoir that it was necessary to be 'morally convinced' that military gains justified the loss of civilian life.[37] On 15 November 1939, the government-in-exile issued its first guidelines for resistance. Its dominant themes were non-cooperation with the occupation authorities, and recognition that any armed action was likely to be weak and lead to heavy repression directed against the civilian population.[38] Under the conditions prevailing at that stage of the war, armed action could not deliver any clear and realistic political goals. According to the November 1939 Directive of the Polish government-in-exile, armed resistance could only lead to the 'extermination of Poles'.[39]

A month later, the government-in-exile issued a more comprehensive set of guidelines for the development of military resistance in occupied Poland. The new directive provided more detailed guidance and postulated armed resistance in two forms: 'combat-diversion action' and 'armed insurrection in the rear area of the occupying army'.[40] Because of the possible scale of German reprisals, 'combat-diversion action' was to be centrally managed and was to occur only under the direction of the government-in-exile and the AK military leadership.[41] The reason for setting up strong central command structures to direct 'combat-diversion action' was the need to balance military gains against cost to the civilian population. A further directive, issued on 16 January 1940, outlined five key tasks: systematic collection of intelligence, sabotage, reprisals, diversion and insurrection. Armed insurrection was a long-term aspiration intended to coincide with the return of regular Polish armed forces from abroad in the closing stages of the war.[42]

Rowecki's response was his own 'Organisational Directive No. 1', dated 7 February 1940 giving his intention 'to prepare in occupied territory a national insurrection [*powstanie narodowe*]'.[43] The planning for a national insurrection underwent a steady evolution between 1940 and 1942. By September 1942, the AK's definitive plan for a national insurrection emerged. Operational Report

No. 154 set out the criteria for launching a national insurrection: 1) the collapse of the German administration, party apparatus and population in occupied Poland, and 2) the voluntary or forced withdrawal of the German armed forces.[44] Rowecki's planning assumptions were that a catastrophic German defeat at the front, or the internal collapse of Germany, created favourable conditions for the launch of a national insurrection.[45] His thinking on a national insurrection was conditioned by his earlier experiences when he witnessed how rapidly 'demoralization' set in among a German army battalion that he and his soldiers had disarmed.[46] Moreover, the collapse of the Central Powers in 1918 and the earlier 1917 Bolshevik Revolution had created a political and military vacuum that had successfully been exploited in the cause of establishing the Polish state. Rowecki clearly believed that such a scenario could happen again.

During the formative period of the AK's strategic thinking between September 1939 and spring 1943, the long-term resistance strategy was set as a national insurrection in the closing stages of the war alongside controlled and selective armed action against the occupiers. The approach accepted that the war's duration was likely to be long. By a measured application of armed action the AK hoped to shield the civilian population from harsh reprisals. This is not to say that the AK was unwilling to engage in armed action against the occupation, but military gains had to justify fully the civilian cost of armed resistance. This brutal calculus was, in one way or another, the dilemma faced by every resistance organization in Europe throughout the Second World War.[47]

* * *

Preparation for a national insurrection created the means for conducting widespread diversionary action and of conducting partisan warfare in Poland's rural areas. The development of the AK's capacity for armed action was in keeping with early decisions to keep such military activity under strong central control. The earliest organization created for armed action was the Union for Retaliation (Związek Odwetu, ZO) in April 1940.[48] The ZO was employed to attack industry contributing to the German war effort, rail transport and petroleum products, and to take action against Gestapo agents or military units engaged in repression of the Polish population.[49] As a measure of its success, the ZO had by the second half of 1941 destroyed or damaged over 3,000 railway wagons.[50] Following Germany's invasion of the Soviet Union in June 1941, a second, separate organization was created, with the purpose of conducting diversionary operations to disrupt German lines of communications. Named Wachlarz, or the Fan operations, this small unit operated between the 1939 Polish-Soviet frontier and the line of the Dvina and Dnepr rivers.[51]

By 1943, diversionary activity had been consolidated into a new structure that subsumed both the ZO and Wachlarz organizations. With the new name of Diversionary Command (Kierownictwo Dywersji – Kedyw), all 'combat diversionary' operations were better integrated and made more effective. The mission of Kedyw remained largely unchanged from its predecessors. Kedyw also assumed the responsibility for establishing, training and controlling AK partisan units.[52] In the course of 1943 and 1944, AK partisan units increased in number and took advantage of the complex terrain and isolation afforded by Poland's tracts of forests and southern mountains.[53] Among the legendary AK partisan units was the one led by Jan Piwnik, who used the pseudonym of 'Ponury'. In the second half of 1943, Ponury's units operating in the Holy Cross Mountains (Góry Świętokrzyski) mounted audacious attacks on German targets. In July 1943, elements of his force ambushed a trainload of German troops on leave, killing about 200 soldiers including a general.[54] The organizational model adopted by the AK for armed action was built around strong central control. Moreover, the partisan units that were being developed served as a force-in-being which could be activated for a future national insurrection.[55]

Allied support for the AK originated largely from Britain. While SOE provided valuable help in supplying equipment, training and aircraft, the Polish government-in-exile exercised independent control of operations to Poland through the Sixth Bureau of the Polish General Staff in London.[56] The specially trained operatives dropped into Poland to work in the AK were an elite group known as the Cichociemny, or 'Silent and Unseen'. Between 1941 and 1944, 317 Cichociemny were delivered to occupied Poland.[57] The extent of outside aid to the AK from Britain was constrained by geographical factors and political calculation. The distance from airbases in Britain to Poland meant that few aircraft types could be employed and payloads were limited. Nevertheless, between February 1941 and July 1944 over 450 flights took place, delivering personnel and supplies to occupied Poland.[58]

*   *   *

The political and military thinking that underpinned AK plans for a national insurrection between 1939 and 1943 was based on the assumption that a German collapse would create the conditions for success. The Soviet Union was not really factored into the scheme, particularly during the period following June 1941 when its defeat and disintegration seemed a real possibility. By 1943, however, not only had the Soviet Union weathered its military crisis, but the Red Army's military successes had seen the military initiative on the Eastern Front shift away from Germany. The prospect of the Red Army 'liberating' Poland was now a growing certainty, and the consequences of these changing geopolitical circumstances were bound to impact upon AK plans. Indeed, given the earlier collaboration of the Soviet Union with Nazi Germany in the 1939 aggression against Poland, and the subsequent deportations, the entry of the Red Army onto Polish territory created geopolitical and military dilemmas that were virtually impossible to resolve.

Compounding the issues raised by Soviet military ascendancy in the East was a marked deterioration of Polish-Soviet relations in 1943. The discovery of the mass graves of Polish officers at Katyn in April and the Polish government-in-exile's call for a Red Cross investigation led to a break in Polish-Soviet relations that same month. The Soviet position was that this was a German crime, but circumstances and later evidence pointed to Soviet responsibility. Immediately following the severing of relations, the Soviet Union launched a Polish communist political organization called the Union of Polish Patriots (Związek Patriotów Polskich, ZPP) as the effective basis of a future rival Polish government. It also created, as the ZPP's military wing, a formation named Kościuszko Division. At this critical juncture, the Polish cause also suffered some catastrophic losses of key leaders. On 30 June, the Gestapo arrested Rowecki, the Commander-in-Chief of the AK; on 4 July General Władysław Sikorski, the respected leader of the Polish government-in-exile, died in an air crash at Gibraltar. The new leader of the government-in-exile, Stanisław Mikołajczyk of the Peasant Party, faced huge challenges in restoring Polish-Soviet relations and maintaining political unity among figures in his government. As the war entered its fifth year and the Red Army advanced westward, the need to find political and military solutions for the government-in-exile and the AK grew more acute.[59]

* * *

From mid-1943 to spring 1944, the Polish government-in-exile and the AK debated over how to respond to the prospect of Poland being liberated by the Soviet Union. It was clear that the earlier plans for a national insurrection based on German collapse were no longer relevant, or at least were in need of adaptation to the new circumstances. At their most stark, the debates between London and Warsaw centred on whether the AK should look to the long term and prepare to resist an eventual Soviet occupation, or materially assist the Red Army's advance through armed action. The views of the AK leadership prevailed and the policy adopted was for AK units to launch supporting attacks in the German rear areas in support of Soviet offensive operations. By aiding the Red Army, the AK aimed to demonstrate Poland's commitment as an ally and assert Polish political and military autonomy. Preparations for a national insurrection provided the basis for the rolling mobilization of AK units as the Red Army advanced. These AK operations had the code name of 'Tempest' ('Burza'). The major cities in Poland were excluded from Tempest plans, and arrangements for a general national insurrection remained extant should conditions permit.[60]

In January 1944, the Red Army crossed the pre-war eastern Polish frontier. This event led to the first Tempest operations that brought AK units into contact with the Red Army. What emerged was a pattern that would be repeated as the Red Army advanced through Polish territory. Initial and often successful military cooperation would give way to AK units being disarmed, followed by arrest and deportation of individuals, particularly officers, or incorporation of AK soldiers into the Polish communist forces. In many cases the Soviet forces executed AK soldiers, particularly officers. Tempest in the Wilno district in eastern Poland is indicative of the situation. Over 5,000 AK soldiers were mobilized and succeeded in capturing the city. Fighting then broke out as the Red Army arrested the officers of the AK units and then endeavoured to suppress the Polish units. Arrests and deportations followed as AK soldiers were systematically hunted down.[61] Wilno might have been an extreme example because of the level of armed clashes that took place, but Soviet actions during the Tempest operations

Changes to the German occupation of Poland, post-June 1941.

indicated that the AK was to be treated less as an ally than as an enemy. The Soviet response to Tempest only heightened the dilemmas faced by the AK leadership.

*   *   *

The problems with Tempest operations provided the immediate prelude to what was to be the climactic event of Polish resistance in the Second World War – the Warsaw Rising. The idea of an insurrection can be seen as an extension of Tempest, but this time in an urban setting. The AK leadership thought it possible for a rising to wrest Warsaw from German control before the Red Army arrived. In doing so, the leadership believed that a successful insurgency would affirm the place of the government-in-exile as the legitimate government of Poland.[62]

Given Soviet attitudes, however, the realization of political aims was dependent on distant support from Britain and the United States and a sea change in Soviet policy. In military terms, the AK's weakness meant that surprise and a good measure of luck were necessary in order to seize control of Warsaw. In short, the decision to launch the rising was a political and military gamble.

The Warsaw Rising began in the late afternoon of 1 August 1944. At the onset of operations, AK units had strength of about 22,000 men and women, but only 10 to 12 per cent of the insurgents were armed.[63] Sources vary as to the exact number of weapons available to AK soldiers, but they may have numbered fewer than 5,000 pistols, rifles and assorted machine guns. The most numerous item was in fact the hand grenade; at the onset of the rising an estimated 50,000 were available.[64] Tactically, the hand grenade was potent in the hands of the relatively unskilled cadres of the AK, particularly in close-quarter fighting in the urban landscape. The lack of numbers of light or support weapons such as mortars, however, meant that the AK had great difficulty in generating offensive combat power. The sources of weapons for the AK were varied and inadequate; they included arms from the Polish army hidden in 1939 or weapons from clandestine production, Allied air drops and armaments purchased or stolen from German and Italian soldiers.[65] Given these limitations, the AK soldiers worked to exploit the characteristics of the cluttered and congested urban environment to their advantage.

The strength of the German forces in Warsaw at the start of the rising consisted of about 16,000 military or security force personnel. The breakdown of forces included 5,600 to 6,000 German army soldiers, 4,300 personnel in SS and police units, 3,000 Luftwaffe ground personnel at Warsaw's two large airfields and 3,000 other Luftwaffe personnel manning the anti-aircraft guns in the city.[66] At peak strength German forces numbered over 21,000, with the overall total of Germans who fought in Warsaw probably higher given the number of units ordered into the battle.[67] German command structures were initially fragmented between the various military and civilian elements of the German occupation. Warsaw lay within the operational area of the German Ninth Army, but other formations and security elements operated in the city. The anti-aircraft (Flak) units were the responsibility of the Oberkommando der Luftwaffe (OKL), while the local security forces remained under the command of the occupation administration of the General Government. Four days after the start of the rising, with the arrival of reinforcements, German command and control arrangements were unified with the appointment of SS Obergruppenführer Erich von dem Bach-Zelewski to lead the suppression of the Rising.[68]

The Warsaw urban battle space presented challenges to both the German security forces and the Polish insurgents. Warsaw was a major transportation hub with railway lines and roads criss-crossing the city and the Vistula River. On the eastern bank of the Vistula was the district of Praga, but the majority of the city's population resided on the western bank. The western half of the city contained the Old Town and central areas in which the narrower streets and urban congestion tended to militate against German advantages in weapons and training.

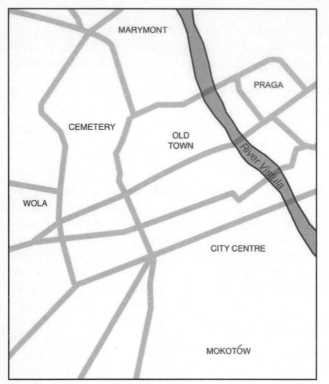

Districts of Warsaw and
transportation corridors.

More problematic for the Polish insurgents was control of the open areas in the city. The wider spaces of transportation corridors tended to favour the German forces, as their superior firepower made it easy for them to dominate these areas. The initial objectives of the insurgents included gaining as much control of the city as possible, and seizing airfields, radio stations and key transport infrastructure such as the rail and road bridges across the Vistula. As one would expect given their importance to the wider German military effort, many of these objectives were fortified and well defended by German security forces.[69]

In the first three days of the rising, the AK units held the initiative and managed to gain control of large swathes of the city. Running from the north, the AK held a large irregularly shaped island of territory. Its northern edge included the Old Town and the site of the former Jewish ghetto, which had been razed to the ground following the Germans' brutal suppression of the 1943 ghetto uprising. The western edge included the district of Wola and most of the large city cemeteries. The southern boundary included the central areas and Mokotów, with some isolated districts further south. Given the weakness in firepower, the perimeter of the main area held was large and included less built-up areas of the city, particularly in the west. Once the AK ceased offensive operations, with the help of the civilian population, an elaborate network of barricades was constructed across streets, turning many Warsaw districts into fortified zones.[70]

Likewise, buildings were fortified and lower-floor doors and windows blocked. Despite the preponderance of firepower, the AK compelled the German forces to fight house-by-house in order to regain control of many parts of the city. The skilful use of obstructions by a Polish insurgent force demonstrated how lethal an urban area was for a conventional army to fight in.

German counterattacks took place between 5 and 7 August. The aims of the counterattack had both a military and ideological dimension. In military terms, the German counterattacks were to move west to east and punch through corridors to the bridges over the Vistula. Warsaw being an important transportation hub, with the AK controlling areas astride east–west communications to the front-line German formations facing the Red Army, opening them up was an important military objective.[71] In ideological terms, the Nazi leadership saw an opportunity to eliminate Warsaw as a centre of national resistance. The orders of the assaulting units reflected this policy: no prisoners would be taken, the civilian population in the path of the attack was to be massacred and the city systematically destroyed.[72] When the counterattacks sliced through Wola, 'special' SS units, such as the Dirlewanger Regiment consisting of German criminals of various types, and the RONA Brigade commanded by Bronislaw Kaminski, massacred their way forward. As a result of the counterattacks, the military aim of control of most east–west arterial routes was achieved; in realizing the ideological objectives between 30,000 and 40,000 civilians were killed.[73]

As a result of German counterattacks, the areas held by the AK shrank and were broken into a number of smaller islands including the Old Town, central Warsaw, Mokotów and a few smaller locations in the south. The mass murder of civilians by German forces had some significant consequences. The Warsaw civilian population fled into AK-held parts of Warsaw for protection and the resolve of the AK to continue the fight to the end was strengthened. Following the initial German counterattacks the struggle for the Old Town became a major focus in the battle. Symbolically, both sides saw it as vital ground. The geography of the Old Town, with its narrow streets and substantial buildings, favoured the defender. However, the Old Town also housed large numbers of displaced civilians, who took advantage of the vital shelter offered by the multiple cellars in many buildings, and was subjected to constant artillery and aerial bombardment. For the cut-off Old Town, the sewers proved a vital route for communications and limited reinforcements. Nevertheless, it was only a matter of time before German forces prevailed; by the beginning of September they had captured the Old Town.[74] Other parts of the city continued to resist until the AK formally capitulated on 2 October. Against the odds, the rising had lasted sixty-three days.

The military failure of the Warsaw Rising can be seen as an inevitable consequence of the weakness of an insurgent force pitted against well-equipped regular German forces. The one variable that could have altered the AK's prospects was outside military aid from Poland's allies. The Warsaw Rising began as Soviet forces approached the city from the east. Indeed, Moscow initially exhorted the Poles to rise against the occupation, but then offered little practical support until late in the rising. Soviet inactivity undoubtedly contributed to the failure of the Warsaw Rising.[75] Support from Poland's Western Allies faced enormous difficulties in distance from Allied airbases. Nevertheless, Allied air crews did attempt supply flights and consequently suffered serious losses. Political pressure from Britain and the United States eventually forced Soviet agreement for shuttle flights of American bombers flying on to bases on Soviet territory. All of these efforts came late in the rising and did not improve the AK's military prospects.[76]

The obstacles to aiding the Warsaw Rising, however, were less military than political. By this stage of the war, the future of Poland was being guided by the interests of the major Allied powers – Britain, the Soviet Union and the United States. By the summer of 1944, the reality was that Poland's 'liberation' was to be the doing of the Red Army. This meant that the Soviet Union was in a position to dictate the post-war political settlement of the Polish question. Ultimately, the hierarchy of American and British interests focused not on Polish aims, but on co-operation with the Soviet Union in the common war effort against Germany and finding an agreeable post-war settlement. The Polish government-in-exile in London, and by extension the AK, was in too weak a position to shape the country's political future. Indeed, the government-in-exile was under intense pressure from Winston Churchill to reach a political deal with Stalin, make major territorial concessions to the Soviet Union and accept a provisional government that included Polish communists.[77] Although Churchill was more willing than Roosevelt to pressure Stalin to aid the AK in Warsaw, the efforts of the Western Allies ultimately displayed a lack of political will to support legitimate Polish political aims for the territorial integrity and democratic self-determination of post-war Poland.[78] As Timothy Snyder has observed, 'no sovereign Poland would become communist'.[79] The Polish question in 1944, like the Warsaw Rising itself, was determined by great power politics that offered little room for Polish aspirations.

The losses experienced during the sixty-three days of fighting for the city were massive. Civilian casualties numbered between 200,000 and 250,000; 700,000 civilians were evacuated from the city. AK losses numbered over 15,000 dead and missing and 25,000 wounded. About 15,000 became prisoners by the time of capitulation. German losses consisted of 26,000 casualties; 10,000 killed, 7,000 missing and 9,000 wounded. As the result of German policy, large parts of central Warsaw suffered systematic destruction that demolished over 10,000 buildings.[80] When the Red Army eventually 'liberated' Warsaw in January 1945, Soviet soldiers found a depopulated wasteland with the central areas of the city a sea of rubble.

*   *   *

The Warsaw Rising was a blow from which the AK never recovered. Formally disbanded in January 1945, its remnants transformed into anti-communist resistance groups that were soon overwhelmed by communist oppression. The communist takeover of Poland and the tragic failure of the Warsaw Rising have, however, tended to obscure the AK's impressive legacy from the wider perspective of European resistance in the Second World War. The development of the Polish underground state and the AK represents a major achievement in the face of brutal German (and Soviet) occupation. The comprehensiveness of resistance in Polish society, the absence of collaboration beyond the individual level and the sophistication of its resistance structures all make it, arguably, an apogee of wartime resistance in Europe. The fact that the AK efforts were not crowned with ultimate success enjoyed by resistance groups in other European states does not alter its importance in the story of resistance in Europe during the Second World War.

The historical memory of the story of the AK throughout the period of communist rule in Poland was largely preserved thanks to the Polish émigré communities in the West. These Polish émigré communities were an important source of memoirs and historiography regarding Polish wartime resistance. One of the most important archives of Polish wartime resistance resides in London – the Polish Underground Movement Study Trust (Studium Polski Podziemnej), established in 1947.[81] Although the historical memory of the AK did not entirely disappear in communist Poland, official efforts consistently sought to ignore or downplay its significance to the history of Poland.[82] With the collapse of communism in 1989, consideration of the legacy of the AK was freed from political constraints. The proliferation of monuments commemorating the AK, scores of historical works filling shelves in bookshops and the opening of a museum devoted to the history of the Warsaw Rising are all evidence of a renewed interest in this important episode in Poland's history.[83] The fact that the Polish Army's special forces today wear the shoulder flash Cichociemny ('Silent and Unseen') indicates how much of Poland's legacy of wartime resistance has been reclaimed from the deliberate downplaying of the communist period to assume a prominent place in Polish military tradition.[84]

Notes

1. Speech by Winston Churchill 'The Day Will Dawn', in *The Times*, 5 May 1941, p. 5.
2. T. Piotrowski, *Poland's Holocaust: Ethnic Strife, Collaboration with Occupying Forces and Genocide in the Second Republic, 1918–1947* (Jefferson, North Car., 1998), p. 304.
3. L.S. Dawidowicz, *The War Against the Jews 1933–1945* (New York, 1975).
4. J.T. Gross, *Polish Society under German Occupation: The Generalgouvernement 1939–1944* (Princeton, New Jer., 1979); *idem, Revolution from Abroad: The Soviet Conquest of Poland's Western Ukraine and Western Belorussia* (Princeton, New Jer., 1988); R.C. Lukas, *Forgotton Holocaust: The Poles under German Occupation 1939–1944* (Lexington, Ken., 1986); Piotrowski, *Poland's Holocaust.*
5. Anna M. Cienciala, Natalia S. Lebedeva and Wojciech Materski (eds), *Katyn: A Crime Without Punishment* (New Haven, Conn., 2007), p. 332.
6. R.C. Lukas, *Forgotten Holocaust*, pp. 6–7.
7. Piotrowski, *Poland's Holocaust*, p. 9.
8. *Ibid.*, p. 22.
9. Gross, *Revolution from Abroad*, p. 194.
10. Piotrowski, *Poland's Holocaust*, p. 20.
11. A.B. Rossino, *Hitler Strikes Poland: Blitzkrieg, Ideology, and Atrocity* (Lawrence, Kan., 2003), pp. 14–15.

12. S. Korbonski, *The Polish Underground State: A Guide to the Underground, 1939–1945* (New York, 1978), pp. 10–11; idem, *Polskie Siły Zbrojne w drugiej wojnie światowej Tom III Armia Krajowa* (London, 1950), pp. 426–8 (hereafter referred to as PSZIII).

13. Korbonski, *The Polish Underground State*, pp. 9–11.

14. Lukas, *Forgotten Holocaust*, p. 34.

15. Gross, *Revolution from Abroad*, pp. 147–8.

16. Lukas, *Forgotten Holocaust*, p. 29.

17. *Ibid.*, pp. 27–32.

18. Korbonski, *The Polish Underground State*, pp. 104–5, 111.

19. Norman Davies, *God's Playground: A History of Poland*, Vol. II *1795–present* (Oxford, 1981), p. 466.

20. Włodzimierz Borodziej, *The Warsaw Uprising of 1944* (Madison, Wis., 2001), p. 21.

21. Korbonski, *The Polish Underground State*, pp. 47, 50.

22. *Ibid.*, pp. 71–2.

23. See Paweł Maria Lisiewicz, *W Imieniu Polski Podziemnej: Z Dziejów Wojskowego Sądownictwa Specjalnego Armii Krajowej* (Warsaw, 1988).

24. Stefan Korbonski, *Fighting Warsaw* (New York, 1968), p. 31.

25. Korbonski, *The Polish Underground State*, p. 143.

26. *Ibid.*, p. 106.

27. *Ibid.*, pp. 22–33, 58–9.

28. PSZIII, p. 124.

29. Davies, *God's Playground*, Vol. II, p. 466.

30. A.K. Kunert and T. Szarota, *Generał Stefan Rowecki 'Grot' w relacjach i w pamięci zbiorowej* (Warsaw, 2003), pp. 11–21.

31. S. Rowecki, *Walki uliczne* (Warsaw, 1928).

32. Kunert and Szarota, *Generał Stefan Rowecki 'Grot' w relacjach i w pamięci zbiorowej*, pp. 11–21.

33. Andrzej Krzysztof Kunert (ed.), *Generał Tadeusz Bór-Komorowski w relacjach i dokumentach* (Warsaw, 2000), pp. 14–15. See also T. Bor-Komorowski, *The Secret Army* (London, 1951).

34. Comments by Sawicki and Bokszczanin in Kunert (ed.), *Generał Tadeusz Bór-Komorowski w relacjach i dokumentach*, pp. 106–8. See also Borodziej, *The Warsaw Uprising of 1944*, p. 44.

35. Quoted from Mitkiewicz in Kunert (ed.), *Generał Tadeusz Bór-Komorowski w relacjach i dokumentach*, p. 106.

36. Jan Karski, *Story of a Secret State* (Boston, 1944), p. 389.

37. Bor-Komorowski, *The Secret Army*, p. 137.

38. Directive Council of Ministers, 15 November 1939 in *Armia Krajowa w Dokumentach 1939–1945 Tom I Wrzesień 1939–Czerwiec 1941* (London, 1970), p. 6 (hereafter referred to as AKDI).

39. Piotrowski, *Poland's Holocaust*, p. 23.

40. Sosnkowski to Rowecki, Instruction no. 1, 4 December 1939 in AKDI, p. 11.

41. *Ibid.*

42. Sosnkowski to Rowecki, Instruction no. 2, 16 January 1940 in *ibid.*, p. 11.

43. Rowecki, Organisational Directive no. 1, 7 Feb. 1940 in *ibid.*, p. 145.

44. Operational Report no. 154, 8 September 1942, *Armia Krajowa w Dokumentach 1939–1945 Tom II Czerwiec 1941–Kwiecień 1943* (London, 1973), pp. 328–9 (hereafter referred to as AKDII).

45. *Ibid.*, p. 329.

46. Kunert and Szarota, *Generał Stefan Rowecki 'Grot' w relacjach i w pamięci zbiorowej*, p. 61.

47. See Paul Latawski, 'The *Armia Krajowa* and Polish Partisan Warfare, 1939–43', in Ben Shepherd and Juliette Pattinson (eds), *War in a Twilight World: Partisan and Anti-Partisan Warfare in Eastern Europe, 1939–45* (London, 2010), pp. 137–55.

48. PSZII, pp. 439–40.

49. Rowecki, Report no. 61a, 27 March 1941 in AKDI, p. 480.

50. PSZIII, p. 447.

51. Grzegorz Korczyński, *Polskie Oddziały Specjalne w II Wojnie Światowej* (Warsaw, 2006), p. 118.

52. PSZIII, p. 462.

53. M. Jasiak, 'Działanie partyzanckie na terenach górskich Polski południowo-wschodniej 1942–1945 Cz. I', in *Wojskowy Przegląd Historyczny*, XL (1995), pp. 57–8.

54. Józef Garliński, *Poland, SOE and the Allies* (London, 1969), pp. 125–30.
55. PSZIII, pp. 521–2.
56. Garliński, *Poland, SOE and the Allies*, p. 28.
57. Korczyński, *Polskie Oddziały Specjalne w II Wojnie Światowej*, p. 60.
58. Garliński, *Poland, SOE and the Allies*, pp. 235–6.
59. See George Kacewicz, *Great Britain, the Soviet Union and the Polish Government in Exile (1939–1945)* (The Hague, 1979); Edward J. Rozek, *Allied Wartime Diplomacy: A Pattern in Poland* (New York, 1958).
60. Krzysztof Komorowski (ed.), *Operacja 'Burza' i Powstania Warszawskie 1944* (Warsaw, 2002); Korbonski, *The Polish Underground State*, pp. 155–67.
61. Korbonski, *The Polish Underground State*, pp. 157–8.
62. Jan M. Ciechanowski, *The Warsaw Rising of 1944* (Cambridge, 1974), p. 243.
63. Krzystof Komorowski, 'Powstanie Warszawski', in Krzystof Komorowski (ed.), *Armia Krajowa: Szkice z dziejów Sił Zbrojnych Polskiego Państwa Podziemnego* (Warsaw, 2001), p. 305.
64. PSZIII, p. 680.
65. Korbonski, *The Polish Underground State*, pp. 63–5.
66. Tadeusz Sawicki, *Rozkaz: zdławić powstanie: Siły III Rzeszy w walce z Powstaniem Warszawskim 1944* (Warsaw, 2001), pp. 8–9.
67. J.K. Zawodny, *Nothing but Honour: The Story of the Warsaw Uprising, 1944* (London, 1978), p. 211.
68. Borodziej, *The Warsaw Uprising of 1944*, p. 79.
69. For an analysis of the Warsaw terrain see Krzystof Komorowski, *Bitwa o Warszawę: Militarne aspekty Powstania Warszawskiego* (Warsaw, 2004), pp. 89–97.
70. See Romuald Śreniawa-Szypiowski, *Barykady Powstania Warszawskiego 1944* (Warsaw, 1993).
71. Sawicki, *Rozkaz: zdławić powstanie*, pp. 31–51.
72. Borodziej, *The Warsaw Uprising of 1944*, pp. 79–80.
73. Joanna K.M. Hanson, *The Civilian Population and the Warsaw Uprising of 1944* (Cambridge, 1982), pp. 89–90.
74. Korbonski, *The Polish Underground State*, p. 185.
75. *Ibid.*, pp. 187–92.
76. Neil Orpen, *Airlift to Warsaw: The Rising of 1944* (London, 1984), pp. 155–63.
77. Kacewicz, *Great Britain, the Soviet Union and the Polish Government in Exile*, pp. 183–99; Rozek, *Allied Wartime Diplomacy*, pp. 229–64.
78. Piotr S. Wandycz, *The United States and Poland* (Cambridge, 1980), pp. 289–90.
79. Timothy Snyder, *Bloodlands: Europe Between Hitler and Stalin* (London, 2010), p. 210.
80. Hanson, *The Civilian Population and the Warsaw Uprising of 1944*, p. 202; Tadeusz Sawicki, 'Stragedia, działania wojenne, straty', in Stanisław Lewandowski and Bernd Martin (eds), *Powstania Warszawskie 1944* (Warsaw, 1999), p. 116; Zawodny, *Nothing but Honour*, pp. 210–11.
81. 'Historia, cele i zadania …', *The Polish Underground Movement Study Trust (Studium Polski Podziemnej)*, available at http://spp-pumst.org/index.php/spp/spp-londyn-historia-cele-zadania, accessed 1 August 2012.
82. Borodziej, *The Warsaw Uprising 1944*, pp. 142–6.
83. Museum Powstania Warszawskiego, available at http://www.1944.pl/.
84. Bogusław Politowski, 'Rażenie Gromem', in *Polska Zbrojna*, no. 4, (22 Stycznia 2012), p. 45.

Guide to Further Reading

Borodziej, Włodzimierz, *The Warsaw Uprising of 1944* (Madison, Wis., 2001).
Gross, J.T., *Polish Society under German Occupation: The Generalgouvernement 1939–1944* (Princeton, New Jer., 1979).
Idem, *Revolution from Abroad: The Soviet Conquest of Poland's Western Ukraine and Western Belorussia* (Princeton, New Jer., 1988).
Hanson, Joanna K.M., *The Civilian Population and the Warsaw Uprising of 1944* (Cambridge, 1982).
Korbonski, S., *The Polish Underground State: A Guide to the Underground, 1939–1945* (New York, 1978).

Latawski, Paul, 'The *Armia Krajowa* and Polish Partisan Warfare, 1939–43', in Ben Shepherd and Juliette Pattinson (eds), *War in a Twilight World: Partisan and Anti-Partisan Warfare in Eastern Europe, 1939–45* (London, 2010), pp. 137–55.

Lukas, R.C., *Forgotton Holocaust: The Poles under German Occupation 1939–1944* (Lexington, Ken., 1986).

Piotrowski, T., *Poland's Holocaust: Ethnic Strife, Collaboration with Occupying Forces and Genocide in the Second Republic, 1918–1947* (Jefferson, North Car., 1998).

Rossino, A.B., *Hitler Strikes Poland: Blitzkrieg, Ideology, and Atrocity* (Lawrence, Kan., 2003).

Chapter 9

Scandinavia

Chris Mann

On 9 April 1940 Germany invaded the two Scandinavian countries of Denmark and Norway. The survival of the Danish government after the country's rapid defeat produced a situation unique in Nazi-occupied Europe. However, despite the comparative mildness of the conditions in Denmark, the trepidations of occupation eventually led to the growth of a Danish resistance movement. In Norway the country's armed forces, with British and French assistance, managed to fight on for two months before defeat. Nonetheless, King Haakon VII and his government decided to continue the struggle from exile, providing a focus for those who wanted to resist back in Norway. Despite this both resistance movements were fairly passive due to a number of local and political factors. Neither group could seriously challenge the German hold on their country; liberation would only come with total German defeat. However, the actions of those brave individuals that did resist had important political and moral consequences in the war's aftermath.

* * *

By the early twentieth century both Denmark and Norway were moderately prosperous, stable, democratic, constitutional monarchies. They were on the periphery of Europe, literally in terms of their geography and metaphorically in terms of their involvement in great power politics. Norway had not been involved in war since the Napoleonic era, although there had been some tension in 1905 when the country gained independence from Sweden. Denmark had fought a brief if costly war in 1864 against Prussia, losing Schleswig-Holstein to her neighbour. Both countries had relied on a policy of neutrality in international affairs thereafter and this had served them well through the First World War. Despite the increasing belligerence of Germany in the late 1930s, neither country looked seriously to their defences. The Norwegians put their faith in the Royal Navy and the Danes, probably rightly, concluded that there was little that they could do if Germany did decide to invade. Both restated their neutrality and hoped that the gathering storm in Europe would break elsewhere.

Unfortunately it did not, as Scandinavia briefly became centre of attention in the unusual strategic situation of the early months of the Second World War. When war broke out, Grand Admiral Erich Raeder, the German Navy's Commander-in-Chief, recommended that it would greatly benefit German strategy to seize bases on the Norwegian coast. He therefore engineered a meeting between Vidkun Quisling, leader of Norway's small extreme right-wing party, the Nasjonal Samling (NS – National Unity), and Adolf Hitler on 14 December 1939. When Quisling outlined his fear of a British violation of Norwegian neutrality, Hitler claimed that he would intervene in good time although he preferred a neutral Norway for the time being.[1] However, Anglo-French interest in intervening in Scandinavia under the pretext of aiding Finland against the Soviet Union and the seizure by the Royal Navy of the German supply ship *Altmark* in Norwegian waters on 14 February 1940 changed Hitler's rather benevolent attitude.[2] Furious, he appointed General Nikolaus von Falkenhorst commander of the operation to invade, code named Weserübung. The seizure of Denmark was necessary to secure the supply route into Norway and provide forward air bases for the Luftwaffe operating to the north.

On 9 April Weserübung began. In Denmark, German troops quickly overwhelmed Danish border defences and overran Jutland. Copenhagen was captured in an audacious seaborne assault. After about six hours' fighting the Danish government ordered resistance to cease.[3] Similarly in Norway the Germans achieved a remarkable measure of surprise and what limited resistance the Germans met was improvised and inadequate, if somewhat more prolonged.[4] There was, however, the occasional Norwegian success. The sinking of the German cruiser *Blücher* in Oslofjord, which had on board the German command staff, allowed the Norwegian king, Haakon VII, and his government to escape from Oslo.

The British had pledged Norway armed assistance on 9 April. British, French and later Polish troops were landed in north and central Norway. However, in the face of German air superiority and tactical dominance on the ground the British evacuated central Norway on 1–2 May. In the north, however, the situation was somewhat different. The British had achieved complete naval dominance, being largely out of reach of German air power, and established forces ashore around the German-occupied port of Narvik. The opening of the German offensive against France and Belgium on 10 May, however, forced the Allies to reassess their commitment to Norway. On 25 May, as the situation in France worsened, the British decided to evacuate northern Norway as quickly as possible. Nonetheless, on 28 May French, Norwegian and Polish troops captured the port of Narvik to cover the safe withdrawal of Allied forces and, to deny future iron-ore exports to Germany, damaged the port facilities. The British and French withdrew eleven days later on 8 June and King Haakon and his government left Tromsø, bound for exile in Britain. The following day the Norwegian commander Major General Otto Ruge surrendered to General Eduard Dietl, commander of German forces in the Narvik area.[5]

*   *   *

The key motivation for the German invasion of Norway was the establishment of naval and air bases from which to attack Britain's maritime communications and loosen the Royal Navy's hold on the North Sea. The development of these facilities and the future exploitation of Norway's natural resources required calm.

Occupied Scandinavia, 1940–5.

General von Falkenhorst, now German military commander in Norway, had no wish to waste resources and manpower in 'anti-partisan'-style operations. The Germans therefore hoped to establish a reasonably stable, even consensual occupation regime. On 24 April 1940 Hitler sent Josef Terboven, long-serving Nazi Party official and Gauleiter of Essen, to act as Reichskommisar and establish an occupation government. Initially Terboven hoped to achieve this legally and in June persuaded the Norwegian parliament, the Storting, to write to the king, in exile in Britain, urging him to abdicate. Haakon refused, stating that his government had received its mandate to continue the struggle in Norway's last free parliament on 9 April 1940. The government-in-exile then issued an aide-memoire stating that '[i]t is the intention of the Norwegian government to continue the fight outside Norway in collaboration with our allies insofar as our means permit until final victory'.[6] This resolute stance did much to establish the king and government's legitimacy in the eyes of the Norwegian population. Yet on 10 September the Storting voted 75 to 55 to remove Haakon. Despite this staggering act of collaboration, Terboven and the members of the Storting failed to come to an agreement. The major sticking point was the scale of NS participation in the new government.

Terboven, therefore, was forced to turn to the man he thought of as 'stupid to the *n*th degree', Vidkun Quisling, when he came to set up a commissarial government.[7] The NS was clearly the Germans' natural ally and contained the only people available to staff Terboven's new regime. Quisling himself chose, at least initially, to remain outside the government. He did, however, continue as the Party's leader, or *Fører*. He eventually accepted the post of Minister-President in February 1942 when Terboven – in theory at least – handed control to the NS. Quisling put considerable effort into expanding his party and the nazification of Norwegian society. He claimed to Terboven that 'in hardly any other country is it as easy to bring about national revolution from above as it is in Norway'. This was because, in his opinion, the Norwegians were a law-abiding and stable people who if 'given a well-reasoned argument for change ... will soon accept it'.[8] Yet the task proved more difficult than he anticipated.

In Denmark, given the circumstances and speed of the German takeover, the situation was somewhat different. The terms of the surrender allowed the Danish government under Thorvald Stauning to stay in power with control over domestic policy. The judiciary, police and even a reduced miltary remained in Danish hands. In contrast to other occupied territories, the king, Christian X, stayed on the throne. However, press and radio censorship was imposed, political demonstrations were banned and relations with the Allied powers severed. There were fears that the small Danish Nazi Party, Dansmarks Nationalsocialistike Arbejderparti (DNSAP – Danish National Socialist Workers' Party) under Dr Fritz Clausen, might attempt to seize power. However, there was little need for the Germans to push the issue as they were receiving almost full cooperation from the Danish government.

Indeed, the Germans were almost equally concerned not to exacerbate tensions. After all, a calm Denmark meant smaller numbers of occupation troops and facilitated the steady exploitation of Denmark's economic resources. The country's agricultural sector was particularly valuable. Cecil von Renthe-Fink, the German plenipotentiary to Denmark, reckoned that:

> It is of the utmost importance for the maintenance of calm and order that economic life should be kept going and this will help to safeguard the security of the occupying forces and our military interests in the country. The best thing to do would be to keep the economy going by smooth, friendly cooperation with the Danish government and Danish industrialists. If we took over the administration directly, [it] would produce considerable points of friction.[9]

Yet the Germans repeatedly interfered in Danish politics and broke many of the guarantees made in April 1940. The Danes were forced to remove troublesome members of the government and were urged to support the German war effort more actively. When Germany invaded the Soviet Union in June 1941, the government was forced to ban the Communist Party. In November of that year, Denmark joined the Anti-Comintern Pact and accepted a recruitment drive for the Danish Free Corps, a volunteer corps established by the Danish Nazis, to serve on the Eastern Front. Nevertheless, Denmark was only obliged to act against Communists within the country's own borders; Denmark was not to be drawn into the Nazi-Soviet war. A number of other German demands were successfully rebuffed. The Danish government refused to enter a currency and customs union with Germany and managed to avoid starting negotiations over the return of South Jutland to the Reich. Nor did it implement discriminatory policies against its country's small Jewish population.

The bulk of the Danish population seem to have approved of this approach. Indeed, the government was very strongly endorsed by the Danish population when the new German plenipotentiary, Dr Werner Best, allowed elections to take place in March 1943. The turnout was a record 89.5 per cent, of whom 94 per cent voted for one of the four main coalition government parties.[10] Best took this as a vindication of his 'policy of understanding' with the Danes. In a report of April 1943 he claimed that the flow of goods from Denmark to Germany was high and increasing and that the country remained stable. Law and order were upheld without a major commitment of German troops.[11] However, the March election marked the high water mark of the Danes' policy of co-operation with their occupiers. Best was very quickly faced with a situation of increased Danish discontent given the exigencies of occupation and the growing likelihood of German defeat.

*   *   *

The surrender of Ruge's forces in northern Norway ended for most Norwegians any immediate thoughts of active resistance to German occupation. Indeed, Ruge exhorted his surrendering troops to 'wait, trust and be prepared'.[12] While they did so the Norwegian population could undertake a number of small spontaneous acts of defiance, such as cold-shouldering Germans and NS men, or wearing discrete symbols of resistance such as the paperclip. The first underground newspapers appeared in the summer of 1940. However, the main clashes occurred in response to the efforts of Quisling to change the nature of Norwegian society. In November 1940 the Supreme Court, the only major constitutional institution still functioning, resigned over the NS Minister of Justice Sverre Riisnæs' undermining of the principle of judicial independence. It thus aligned itself at a stroke with the burgeoning resistance movement. This moment marked the point for many when accommodation with the occupation regime became impossible. Indeed, the Chief Justice, Paal Berg, became the leader of the civilian resistance movement.[13]

Despite this, there remained a belief that the occupiers and the new regime would listen to reason. In the first half of 1941 a series of initiatives by the NS to bring professional and trade associations under the party's control led to a number of clashes. The Medical Association and the various Oslo hospital boards protested at the appointment of under-qualified members of the NS to senior positions.[14] The placing of all organized sport under NS control led to a wholesale boycott of organized competition. On 3 April 1941 the various civil service associations wrote a letter of complaint to Terboven in response to the attempt to enforce political conformity within their ranks. This was followed on 15 May by another protest letter from forty-three national organizations denouncing the Germans' and Quisling's policies as 'openly contrary to international law, Norwegian law and the Norwegian sense of justice in general ... which materially violate the protection of personal safety afforded by our laws.'[15] Terboven's response was to have three signatories arrested and summon the rest to the parliament. There he harangued them about their place in the new order and the consequences of future disobedience. He had another five arrested, a number of the associations dissolved and in others the leadership dismissed and replaced by NS supporters. Terboven had made his unequivocal support for Quisling and the NS clear. If the resignation of the Supreme Court ended the possibility of accommodation with the new regime, this incident is identified, in Norwegian historiography at least, as a moment when the civilian resistance went underground.[16] A result of this clash was that many of the key business and professional leaders including Paal Berg; Einar Gerhardsen, acting leader of the Labour Party in Norway; Gunnar Jahn, director of the Central Statistics Office; and Didrik Arup Seip, rector of the University of Oslo, together formed the Kresten (the Circle) on 20 June 1941. This was to act as the link between the government in London and the civilian leadership in Norway. Directly related to the Kresten, and containing many of the same members, was the Korordinasjonskomiteen (KK – Coordination Committee), which provided the executive leadership for the civilian resistance movement.[17]

Most trade and professional associations, which had been driven underground, were represented in the Kresten and the KK. Some new organizations were also established. One of the largest and most important examples of this was B-org (Bedriftsorganisasjonen – the Industrial Organization), created in May 1943. Its main purpose was a 'quiet sabotage' campaign against industries producing goods for Germany. As liberation neared B-org's role shifted, a little ironically, to industrial protection in anticipation of the Germans implementing a scorched earth policy. Set up at the same time was J-Org (Jernbaneorganisasjonen – the Railway Organization), which attempted to trace railway movements of German troop transport and commit the occasional act of sabotage. This became something more of a priority after the Normandy landings and during the Ardennes Offensive in mid- to late 1944, as the Germans tried to transfer troops from Norway to more vital fronts.[18]

The fact remains, however, that civilian resistance was largely reactive. The most obvious and famous examples of 'civil resistance' were in response to NS initiatives which gave the population something specific against which to resist. The NS attempted to inculcate the party's values in Norway's youth through the primary and secondary school curricula by making teachers 'work positively and actively to promote ... pupils' understanding of the new regime's ideology'.[19] Although the teachers' union managed to rebuff this initial attempt, Quisling made a far more concerted effort some eighteen months later, establishing a new compulsory teachers' union and introducing a NS national youth service very clearly based on the Hitler Youth. Much of the teaching profession signed a letter of complaint on 14 February, coupled with a mass resignation from the Teachers' Corporation. The regime's response was to arrest 1,000 teachers, about 1 in 10 of the profession, and 500 were transported to a concentration camp in northern Norway. Although the teachers eventually returned to work, the publicity the case received made it clear they were acting under duress.[20] The plans for the Youth League were quietly scrapped. A confrontation with the Norwegian Church went no better for Quisling. Of the 858 incumbent clergy, 797 resigned. All the bishops and another 55 priests were immediately interned, and a further 127 priests were dismissed from their parishes and 92 imprisoned. The churches emptied and there was no way the NS could adequately replace virtually the entire priesthood. Thus the government was forced to repeal the indictment, the priests returned to work and the churches filled again.[21]

1942 was a key year for the civilian resistance, as Quisling failed in his plan to nazify Norwegian society. Yet Quisling's great hope remained the securing of a peace treaty with Germany and then allying Norway to the Reich. He believed that making a military contribution in the struggle against Bolshevism would improve his case and he proposed introducing conscription for service on the Eastern Front. By January 1944 he and his justice minister Riisnæs had settled on the number of 75,000 men, using the mechanism of enlistment into the Norwegian Labour Service. The resistance issued a proclamation to boycott the call-up. Thousands of young men fled to the forests or into Sweden. The regime decided that the best way to enforce the scheme was to withhold ration cards from those who did not register. In August 1944 the resistance hijacked a lorry full of 150,000 of the cards.[22] The scheme, like so many others, was quietly dropped.

Although the actions of the Danish government in the early years of occupation were supported by the bulk of the population, there was something of a rediscovery of Danish national symbols and identity after the invasion. King Christian and the royal family provided a focal point for the population. The first major outburst of civil resistance occurred in the wake of the invasion of the Soviet Union and the Danish signing of the Anti-Comintern Pact. This was marked by a number of Communist-organized demonstrations in Copenhagen. An illegal press started up, the first paper to appear being the Communist *Land og Folk*. However, the sense that the war was turning against the Germans led to growing discontent with the policy of accommodation, despite the election results of March 1943. This dissatisfaction was encouraged by the BBC, SOE and the illegal press. Towards the end of August 1943 a wave of strikes and demonstrations swept through the major provincial towns. There were confrontations with German troops who fired on the strikers, causing hundreds of casualties. Under considerable pressure from Berlin, Werner Best demanded that the government bring the situation under control. He issued an ultimatum that prohibited public gatherings and strikes, established a curfew and introduced the death penalty. Rather than enact these measures, the government resigned. On 29 August the Germans seized full control of the country, arresting prominent figures and attacking the Danish military, although casualties were few.

The Germans instituted martial law and dissolved parliament. In the aftermath the country was administered by the civil service under Niels Svenningsen. Much of the population now accepted that collaboration was unacceptable. A unified resistance leadership emerged. The Frihedsradet (Freedom Council) was formed in September 1943, dominated by the four major resistance groups, the communists, Dansk Samling, a right-wing nationalist group, Frit Danmark, a mainstream bi-partisan group, and the Social Democratic Ringen. During the winter of 1944 the Frihedsradet was recognized by all groups as the leadership of the resistance and similarly acknowledged by London, Washington and Moscow. Despite the disparate groups involved, the Frihedsradet and resistance seem to have been remarkably united. Their crowning achievement was probably their response to the German intention to round up the country's Jews. With the help of a considerable section of the population, the Frihedsradet managed to organize the escape of 5,500 Jews to Sweden over the single night of 1 October 1943. Only 472 were caught and deported, of whom 52 died.[23] In terms of civil disobedience there was another major wave of strikes and demonstrations, starting in Copenhagen in June–July 1944. Again there were many casualties, but the strikes spread throughout the country that summer. As a result the Germans disbanded the Danish police force and deported 2,000 policemen to Germany.

*   *   *

After the shock of defeat there had to be a period of rebuilding and reflection before any military confrontation could even be considered. Weapons were hidden away. Likeminded individuals met occasionally, often under the guise of sports clubs. In Norway the embryonic policy of Milorg (Militærorganisjonen – Military Organization) was 'lie low, go slow' with the intention of building up a secret army ready for the day of liberation.[24] It also hoped to avoid the attentions of the German security forces and not provoke reprisals against the civilian population. Yet a secret army would require weapons, and training and the source of this equipment and expertise would need to come from outside. A Scandinavian section of SOE was established under Charles Hambro; it recruited among Norwegians in Britain, many of whom had fled from Norway across the North Sea, into its Norwegian Independent Company 1, later known as the Linge Company after its founder Captain Martin Linge. SOE sent its first radio operator into Norway in January 1941 and tentative links were established with the burgeoning Norwegian resistance movement. Yet there was something of a disparity in policy as SOE wanted to cause the Germans trouble while Milorg wanted quietly to build up its strength.

In March 1941 Norwegian members of Company Linge took part in a large-scale raid by British forces on the Lofoton Islands. The Norwegian foreign minister, Trygve Lie, claimed he and the Norwegian government-in-exile were 'unacquainted with the preparations for the raid'.[25] They were angered by the use of Norwegian troops without their permission, and their fury increased when news of people deported and property burned as reprisals taken by the Germans against the local population filtered back to London. This did not stop the British using the Linge men that December in two simultaneous raids against Vågsøy on the Norwegian west coast and, again, on the Lofotons. This time the raids threatened to provoke a full-blown crisis, with Lie claiming that 'the Norwegian government was one step away from publically taking a stand against the British action'. This was coupled with a crisis of confidence within the Linge Company as the men were caught between their own government and the British military. On top of all this, Martin Linge had been killed at Vågsøy. In the words of Lieutenant Colonel John Skinner Wilson, head of the newly formed Norwegian Section, 'the Linge Company was full of dissatisfaction and its founder and leader was not there to put matters right as he had been previously'.[26]

The compromise worked out between Charles Hambro, Deputy Director of SOE and Oscar Torp, the Norwegian Defence Minister, would have a profound influence on the way Milorg was run and its relationship with the British. Hambro was well aware that SOE could not operate in Norway without Norwegian support, and the Norwegians required British facilities, equipment and expertise. He proposed to Torp that they set up an Anglo-Norwegian Collaboration Committee (ANCC) and promised that SOE 'will not initiate any expedition to or against Norway without the knowledge and the consent of the committee who will, of course, be at liberty to report directly to you'.[27] In return Torp visited the Company to steady their morale. At a stroke both the Norwegian resistance and the government-in-exile were brought to the centre of SOE policy-making towards Norway. The ANCC had three Norwegian members from the Norwegian High Command's Department IV (Forsvarets Overkommando – FO IV). FO IV was responsible for Milorg and relations with SOE. As a result of discussions between Milorg and the government-in-exile in November 1941, Milorg was integrated into the Norwegian armed forces, accepting the authority of King Haakon and his government.

Actual practical cooperation on the ground between SOE and Milorg took rather longer to establish. As Lieutenant Colonel Wilson noted, many British officers still considered 'that all SOE organization should be independent of Milorg'.[28] The British were particularly wary of what they considered to be the amateurs of Milorg and their rather slack attitude to security. As one British memo put it, 'of all the races on the earth there surely is none so indiscrete as the Norwegians'.[29] Indeed, while 1942 might have been a key year for the civilian resistance, it was much less successful for its armed counterpart. There followed a series of disastrous operations and confrontations with the German security forces. In April 1942 two SOE agents in the west-coast village of Televåg ended up in a shoot-out with the Germans. In the resulting reprisals the town was destroyed, its population deported and eighteen hostages shot. A number of SOE and Milorg agents were captured in the Oslofjord area in the early summer, paralysing the resistance in that region. In the north in September and October, a joint SOE-British commando raid on Glomford power station and an SOE attack on the mines at Fosdalen led to the imposition of a state of emergency in the Trøndelag area and twenty-nine executions.[30]

In September Wilson finally addressed the issue of coordination, stating that 'in future the duty of SOE, so far as internal organisation in Norway is concerned, is to do its best to meet the request of the Norwegian High Command and SNM [Secret National Movement – Milorg] for assistance in the provision of trained personnel, arms and transport'.[31] SOE, the FO IV and the Central Leadership of Milorg in Oslo under Jens Christian Hauge agreed that planning, training and the provision of equipment should be undertaken by SOE. Milorg would provide the manpower for the underground army.[32] This did not stop SOE undertaking sabotage activities. The standard procedure was to land a team of Linge men who would then launch an attack, often supported by the local Milorg. They attacked the iron-pyrite mines at Orkla near Trondheim in February and October 1943 and the Stord mines near Bergen and the Arendal silicon carbide factory in November 1943. But the most famous example was Operation Gunnerside against the Norsk Hydro Heavy Water Plant at Vemork near Rjukan in Telemark province. Heavy water can be used as a moderator in an atomic pile and the intelligence that the Germans had increased production indicated that they were working on an atomic bomb. A commando team from the Linge Company led by Joachim Rønneberg attacked and destroyed the plant in February 1943. Although there is some debate as to the truly vital nature of the raid, the judgement of SOE's official historian M.R.D. Foot is worth quoting: 'If SOE had never done anything else, Gunnerside would have given it claim enough on the gratitude of humanity.'[33]

*   *   *

As the invasion of north-west Europe neared, the Supreme Headquarters Allied Expeditionary Force (SHAEF), which would direct the forthcoming campaign, ordered that, as no Allied military offensive would take place in Norway, 'no steps must be taken to encourage overt action, since no outside support can be forthcoming'.[34] However, many members of Milorg chaffed at this enforced inactivity, particularly in the wake of the momentous events in France. In October 1944 SHAEF relented and issued the following order:

> While there is no change in our policy with regard to the resistance in Norway, your advice that some action should be taken in Norway, to maintain the morale of the indigenous resistance movement, is accepted. It is therefore agreed that, as it is now known that the enemy is withdrawing some of his forces from Norway, Special Forces HQ may arrange for a

limited number of attacks to be carried out … on the main Norwegian railway routes. You are requested to ensure that these attacks are kept to the minimum which you consider necessary to maintain Norwegian morale.[35]

In fact, this railway traffic became a priority target in December, as the German Ardennes Offensive opened with SHAEF ordering the 'maximum rail and road sabotage'.[36] Over 1,000 Milorg men, trained and equipped by SOE targeted the Norwegian railway system, destroying ten bridges and, according to Wilson, delaying German railway traffic by about a month.[37] Further confusion was created by Gunnar Sønsterby of the famous Oslo Gang, who blew up the building in Oslo housing the German railway administration staff. Recent research has cast some doubts on Wilson's claims, however, as German documents indicate that eleven divisions were withdrawn from Norway between D-Day and the end of the war.[38] However, Milorg's primary role in the last months of the war was to prepare to protect Norwegian infrastructure after a German surrender. There were estimated to be over 350,000 undefeated Germans in Norway (there turned out to be more than 400,000). The British were well aware that the 30,000 troops available for the liberation 'were not enough to deal with any concerted resistance'.[39] Thus the 40,000 trained and armed members of Milorg were vital during the days following the German surrender. Displaying great restraint Milorg took control of key sites, maintained order and ensured the smooth arrival of Allied troops. As Wilson wrote, '[i]t is not too much to say that the self-control and discipline displayed by the Home Forces was its most remarkable feature'.[40]

* * *

Danish military resistance was also slow to develop, understandably so given the circumstances of the first two years of the occupation. SOE formed a Danish section in October 1940 and made contact with intelligence officers from Danish General Staff. The first two SOE agents were dropped into Denmark in December 1941. Carl Bruhn, leader of the mission, was killed when his parachute did not open. It was a loss that the Danish Section head, Ronald Turnbull, reckoned set back SOE operations by a year and a half.[41] In addition the Danish army was not enthusiastic about any sabotage campaign that might undermine the government's position. The Danish officers were more interested in developing a secret army, similar to that in Norway, to act in concert with a British invasion or for use in the event of a German collapse. The crisis of the summer of 1943 and the resignation of the government made the whole issue much more straightforward and SOE suddenly found its task a great deal easier. The communist resistance was the best organized but other groups were very quickly established over the autumn. The number of sabotage attacks increased, aided by the provision of plastic explosive by the British. The dissolution of the army and resultant army command's decision to take direction from the Frihedsradet, one of whose members was from SOE, allowed large numbers of soldiers to take an active role in the resistance, where their military expertise was gratefully received.

There was never going to be a partisan-style war in Denmark; its geography precluded it. Thus the main military activity was sabotage, and the two most active groups were BOPA (Borgerlige Partisaner – rather oddly the 'Bourgeois Partisans', given that they were communists) and 'Holger Danske' (a legendary Danish hero) of Dansk Samling. BOPA carried out the first railway sabotage and undertook about 80 to 90 per cent of the industrial sabotage in Copenhagen. The 6 June 1944 BOPA attack on the Globus factory in Copenhagen, which made parts for the V2 rocket, comprised a full-scale commando raid involving 100 men and a protracted exchange of fire.[42] Overall, there were an estimated 2,680 sabotage actions by a core of about 1,000 or so activists. Their effect is difficult to quantify; it ought particularly to be noted that Denmark's main contribution to the German war effort was agricultural and that that sector was never targeted.[43] A similar campaign to Norway's was launched against the railway system in Jutland in an effort to disrupt German troop movements during the Ardennes Offensive. Again some doubt has also been cast on the effectiveness of this campaign but SHAEF reckoned that:

> In Holland and Denmark the steady interference with railways caused strain and embarrassment to the enemy over a considerable period. The striking reductions in flow of troops and stores from Norway early in 1945 undoubtedly had an adverse effect on the reinforcement and reforming of units which the enemy had to undertake for the battles both east and west of the Rhine.[44]

The final major contribution made by the Danish military resistance was to the liberation. By the end of the war its membership had reached about 50,000. There had been fears that the Germans might institute some sort of scorched earth policy or make a final stand on Danish territory. As it was, the liberation was undertaken smoothly by the British Second Army as part of the general German surrender. There was no need for the secret army to rise and there was a simple transition to civilian rule. On 5 May 1945, members of the armed resistance were able to step into the open and undertake actions to preserve some semblance of calm and order in the febrile atmosphere of liberation by protecting vital infrastructure, aiding in the disarmament of German forces and preventing any last minute acts of sabotage.

As Danish historian Knud Jespersen put it, in Denmark, rather than setting the country 'ablaze', SOE 'ended up as something like a fireguard' ensuring the 'flames of war and resistance' were quickly and effectively extinguished after German defeat.[45]

*   *   *

The German invasion of Norway and Denmark brought five years of occupation by a ruthless totalitarian power, introducing the two countries' population to the concepts of arrest and imprisonment without trial, concentration camps, torture, deportation and execution. However, the extent of Nazi terror in Scandinavia should not be overstated. The Danes and Norwegians sat high in the

Nazis' racial hierarchy. As 'non-German Germanics', they were never subjected to the extremes of Nazi rule that many others under German occupation suffered, although both countries' Jewish minorities were targeted.[46] Considering the rapid and overwhelming defeat of both Norway and Denmark, the growth of the resistance movements was slow, at least in the early days of occupation. Both countries seemed to have a remarkable faith in the legal process and the Germans' willingness to be reasonable.

For Denmark the survival of self-government in the aftermath of defeat made making a number of distasteful compromises with the Germans worthwhile. Although a democratic Denmark's indefinite survival in the Greater Reich was unlikely, short-term German policy was remarkably restrained and rational.[47] The population endured the lightest of any of Germany's occupation regimes. The Danish economy profited well from the arrangement. Given these circumstances, and perhaps the lack of a viable alternate policy or even centre of loyalty – the king and government were still in Denmark – the bulk of the population accepted this situation, as the results of the March 1943 election showed. In Norway, the parliament proved willing to negotiate with Terboven in the aftermath of defeat. Norwegian civilian groups such as the Supreme Court, the teachers, the clergy or the trade unions showed a remarkable faith in the power of the protest letter until finally disabused by Terboven. Thus Norwegians rejected cooperation and suffered considerably harsher treatment. Yet the issue was more straightforward; Quisling's government was clearly a puppet regime only kept in power by the Germans, and the Norwegians had a focus for continued resistance in the king and his legitimate government-in-exile in Britain.

This chapter perhaps provides an impression of remarkable unity among the populations of both countries, but particularly that of Norway, in the face of German occupation. This requires some qualification. Both Norway and Denmark were homogeneous, tolerant, democratic societies, which had been at peace for some time. The assault that Quisling in particular made on Norwegian society was met with considerable resolution. Almost all Quisling's initiatives ended in failure. Yet resisting Quisling was rather different to confronting Terboven and the Germans. Indeed, members of the NS seem to have recognized this towards the end. Finn Støren, a foreign policy adviser, told Quisling in March 1945 that 'I have a feeling that the German authorities are deliberately making fools of you, Mr Minister-President, and of the *Nasjonal Samling* ... Under a pretence of friendship and cooperation, they manage to make our administration share their guilt as plunderers and oppressors.'[48] Terboven was willing to let Quisling act as a 'lightning rod', and would cheerfully allow him to fail if it did not affect German interests. He wanted stability. There was after all a massive German military presence in Norway. The Wehrmacht did not want to be worrying about its lines of communication and rear areas. In effect, this allowed the civilian resistance to direct its efforts against Quisling at a cost that was lower than it would have been had it been focused on the Germans.[49] Danish civil society did not face the same ideological challenge as that posed by Quisling to his compatriots. By the time the government resigned in August 1943, the Germans were more concerned with maintaining stability than implementing a new order. And although the strikes of 1943 and 1944 were a cause for concern, the German grip on power was never really threatened.

Nor did either of the armed military resistance groups in Norway or Denmark ever seriously threaten German control. Indeed, both were fairly passive – and in Denmark virtually non-existent until the autumn of 1943 – as their main purpose was to exist as an army-in-being ready for the liberation. Both movements maintained good relations with Britain and SOE, even though in Norway they took a while to come to an effective working arrangement. In Norway's case, it is also worth noting the high number of occupiers, an estimated one German to every ten Norwegians, so seriously confronting the Wehrmacht was never really an option. There was no open rebellion as in Yugoslavia or Poland, or even a Vercors moment, despite the ruggedness of much of Norway's terrain.[50] The sabotage actions in both countries were of modest military effect, the heavy water action and arguably the railway offensive aside. However, both campaigns were psychologically important for national self-image and pride. Indeed, the symbolic value for the Danes was particularly crucial. The high-profile acts of resistance undertaken in the last two years of the war against the Germans demonstrated that Denmark was now firmly in the Allied camp, with all that would entail in the post-war world.[51]

The role played by the resistance during the Second World War has remained very much part of both Denmark and Norway's national consciousness. Broadly speaking, both countries' populations maintain a belief in what has been termed the 'grand narrative' of stoic resistance in the face of Nazi tyranny. There are excellent museums in Oslo, the Norges Hjemmefrontmuseum (The Norwegian Resistance Museum), and the Friheddmusett (Liberty or Resistance Museum) in Copenhagen, which present a largely traditional view of the occupation. However, there has been some challenge to this view by academic writers over the years. Largely the debate has been concerned with the nuances of collaboration and patriotism or the effectiveness of military resistance. Hans Fredrik Dahl, a senior academic at the University of Oslo, caused some furore in the mid-1990s by implying that the German occupation of Norway was more benign than was commonly assumed. He was strongly challenged by the bulk of Norwegian academic historians.[52] In general, however, areas of controversy have been about quite specific issues such as the often overlooked contribution of the communists, complicity or otherwise in the Holocaust, extra-judicial killings by the resistance and the treatment of women and their offspring as a result of relationships with German soldiers.[53]

Furthermore, the experience of the Second World War also shaped Scandinavian politics. Prominent members of the resistance dominated post-war society and politics in Norway. Most obviously, the trauma of 9 April 1940 led to a rejection of neutrality and the enthusiastic embrace of collective security in both countries in the form of NATO membership. Rather more controversially, the Danish Prime Minister Ander Fogh Ramussen used the debate about Danish behaviour in the Second World War to justify Danish involvement in the conflicts in Iraq and Afghanistan. In a speech in 2003 Ramussen was the first major politician to publically criticize the capitulation of 9 April and the subsequent cooperation policy. In future, he maintained, Denmark should make an active contribution to defending freedom and human rights abroad.[54] While most Danish historians disagreed with the lack of nuance in his interpretation, it illustrates the resonance that the war and resistance still have in Scandinavia.

Notes

1. Reflections of the C-in-C Navy on the Outbreak of War, 3 September 1939; Report of the Commander-in-Chief Navy to the Führer, 10 October 1939; Report of the C-in-C Navy to the Führer, 8 December 1939; Minutes of a Conference with Herr Hauglin and Herr Quisling on 11 December 1939; Report of the C-in-C Navy, 12 December 1939, in *The Führer Conferences on Naval Affairs, 1939–45* (Annapolis, Md., 1990), pp. 37–8, 47, 63–7. Regarding the 14 December meeting, see Hans Fredrik Dahl, *Quisling: A Study in Treachery* (Cambridge, 1999), pp. 154–8.

2. TMI (International Military Tribunal, Nuremberg), Tome XV, Deposition de l'amiral Raeder, 17 May 1946 cited in François Kersaudy, *Norway 1940* (London, 1990), p. 44. For the importance of Swedish iron ore see Thomas Munch-Petersen, *The Strategy of Phoney War* (Stockholm, 1981).

3. Earl Ziemke, *The German Northern Theatre of Operations, 1940–1945* (Washington DC, 1959), pp. 59–62.

4. Johannes Andenæs, Olav Riste and Magne Skodvin, *Norway and the Second World War* (Oslo, 1966), p. 49.

5. Kersaudy, *Norway 1940*, pp. 209–26; Donald Macintyre, *Narvik* (London, 1959), pp. 196–9.

6. The National Archives (TNA, formerly the Public Record Office, Kew), FO 371/24838, Aide-Memoire from the Norwegian Ministry of Defence, 10 July 1940.

7. Joseph Terboven, cited in Dahl, *Quisling*, p. 188.

8. Quisling to Terboven, cited in Dahl, *Quisling*, p. 244.

9. Renthe-Fink's political situation report of 15 April 1940, cited by Philip Giltner, *'In the Friendliest Manner': German-Danish Economic Cooperation during the Nazi Occupation of 1940–1945* (New York, 1998), p. 31.

10. Claus Bjørn, 'Denmark', in I.C.B. Dear and M.R.D. Foot (eds), *The Oxford Companion to the Second World War* (Oxford, 1995), p. 294.

11. Best's report of April 1943 cited in Richard Petrow, *The Bitter Years* (London, 1975), p. 184.

12. Otto Ruge, cited in Tore Gjelsvik, *Norwegian Resistance* (London, 1979), p. 72.

13. Gjelsvik, *Norwegian Resistance*, pp. 26–7; Olav Riste and Berit Nøkleby, *Norway 1940–1945: The Resistance Movement* (Oslo, 1970); p. 20; Ole Kristen Grimnes, *Hjemmefrontensledelse* (Oslo, 1977), p. 46.

14. Maynard Cohen, *A Stand against Tyranny: Norway's Physicians and the Nazis* (Detroit, Mich., 1997), pp. 117–18.

15. Protest letter of 15 May 1941, cited in Riste and Nøkleby, *Norway 1940–1945*, pp. 27–8.

16. Gjelsvik, *Norwegian Resistance*, p. 39, Riste and Nøkleby, *Norway 1940–1945*, p. 28; Andenæs, Riste and Skodvin, *Norway and the Second World War*, p. 70. See also Arnfinn Moland, 'Norway', in Bob Moore (ed.), *Resistance in Western Europe* (Oxford, 2000), p. 231.

17. Hans Fredrik Dahl, Guri Hjeltnes, Berit Nøkleby, Nils Johan Ringsal and Øystein Sørensen (eds), *Norsk Krigleksikon, 1940–1945* (Oslo, 1995), pp. 226–7.

18. Ivar Kragland and Arnfinn Moland, *Norge I Krig*, Vol. 6, *Hjemmefront* (Olso, 1987), p. 202.

19. Riste and Nøkleby, *Norway 1940–1945*, p. 24.

20. Gjelsvik, *Norwegian Resistance*, pp. 58–65. See also Dahl, *Quisling*, pp. 256–60.

21. Moland, 'Norway', p. 227; Dahl, *Quisling*, p. 260.

22. Alf Sanengen, 'Kampen mot A T og Arbeidsmobiliseringen', in Sverre Steen (ed.), *Norges Krig, 1940–1945*, Vol. III (Oslo, 1950), pp. 344–6.

23. Bjorn, 'Denmark', p.294; Hans Kirchoff, 'Denmark', in Bob Moore (ed.), *Resistance in Western Europe* (Oxford, 2000), p.107.

24. Arnfinn Moland, 'Milorg and SOE', in Patrick Salmon (ed.), *Britain and Norway in the Second World War* (London, 1995), p.141.

25. Trygve Lie, *Kampen for Norges Frihet 1940–1945* (Oslo, 1958), p.220. It is worth noting, however, that this claim is contradicted by British contemporary sources. See TNA, DEFE 2/141, *Tip and Run Raids on the Lofoton Islands*, 2 January 1941.

26. *Norges Hjemmefrontmuseum*, Olso (NHM), Colonel J.S. Wilson, 'SOE Norwegian Section History, 1940–45' (unpublished, 1945), p.17. Hereafter Wilson Report.

27. TNA, HS 2/127, Hambro to Torp, 25 November 1941 and Hambro to Torp, 12 January 1942.

28. NHM, Wilson Report, p.174.

29. TNA, HS 2/224, Operation Claymore, 3 February 1941.

30. Haakon Holmboe, 'De Som Ble Tatt', p.473 and Helge Sivertsen, 'Hjemmstykenne', pp.666–8 in Steen (ed.), *Norges Krig*, Vol. III, see also Olav Riste, *London-Regeringa*, Vol. I (Oslo, 1973, 2nd edn, 1995), p.218.

31. NHM, SOE Boks 5 – 10/3/20. Directives on Policy in Norway, 'SOE Long Term Policy in Norway', 21 September 1941.

32. Arnfinn Moland, 'Milorg and SOE', p.146.

33. M.R.D. Foot, *SOE: The Special Operations Executive 1940–45* (London, 1984), p.211. For an alternative view see Adrian Weale, *Secret Warfare* (London, 1997), p.79.

34. NHM, SOE Boks 5 – 10/3/20 Directives on Policy in Norway, *Draft Directive from SHAEF: Resistance – Norway*, 29 August 1944.

35. NHM, SHAEF to SFHQ, 26 October 1944 in the Wilson Report, Appendix G – Action against German Controlled Norwegian State railways.

36. NHM, SOE Boks 5 – 10/3/20 Directives on Policy in Norway, *SHAEF Directive for Norwegian Resistance*, 7 December 1944.

37. NHM, Wilson Report, p.143.

38. See Moland, 'Milorg and SOE', p.149.

39. TNA, WO 106/1985, GON 111/1, Lieutenant Colonel Garner Smith to Lieutenant Colonel Stockdale, 26 May 1945.

40. NHM, Wilson Report, p.164.

41. Knud Jespersen, *No Small Achievement, SOE and the Danish Resistance 1940–1945* (Odense, 2002), p.84.

42. See John Oram Thomas, *The Giant Killers: The Danish Resistance Movement, 1940–45* (London, 1975), pp.178–81.

43. Kirchoff, 'Denmark', p.109.

44. SHAEF Report of 18 July 1945 cited by Jespersen, *No Small Achievement*, p.512.

45. Knud Jespersen, 'SOE and Denmark', in Mark Seaman (ed.), *Special Operations Executive: A New Instrument of War* (Oxford, 2006), p.199.

46. See H.D. Loock, 'Weserübung – a Step towards the Greater Germanic Reich', *Scandinavian Journal of History*, 2/1-2 (1977), p.88.

47. Giltner, *'In the Friendliest Manner'*, p.170.

48. Finn Støren cited by Andenæs, Riste and Skodvin, *Norway and the Second World War*, p.81.

49. Ole Kristian Grimnes, 'Occupation and Collective Memory in Norway', in Stig Ekman and Nils Edling (eds), *War Experience, Self-Image and National Identity: The Second World War as Myth and History* (Stockholm, 1997), p.137.

50. See chapters on France, Poland and Yugoslavia in this volume.

51. See Jespersen, 'SOE and Denmark', p.200.

52. In May 1995 Dahl wrote a series of articles expressing a degree of support for David Irving in the newspaper *Dagbladet*, which also addressed the nature of the Nazi occupation regime in Norway. See Moland, 'Norway', p.245; Synne Corell, 'The Solidity of the Narrative: The Occupation in Norwegian History Culture', in Henrik Stenius, Mirja Österberg and Johan Östling (eds), *Nordic Narratives of the Second World War* (Lund, 2011).

53. See Moland, 'Norway', pp. 244–5 and the relevant essays in Stig Ekman and Nils Edling (eds), *War Experience, Self-Image and National Identity. The Second World War as Myth and History* (Stockholm, 1997) and Stenius, Österberg and Östling (eds), *Nordic Narratives of the Second World War*.
54. See Uffe Østergård, "Swords, Shields or Collborators': Danish historians and the debate over the German Occupation of Denmark', in Stenius, Österberg and Östling (eds), *Nordic Narratives of the Second World War*, pp. 40–6.

Guide to Further Reading

Baden-Powell, Dorothy, *Operation Jupiter: SOE's Secret War in Norway* (London, 1982).
Gjelsvik, Tore, *Norwegian Resistance* (London, 1979).
Hæstrup, Jørgen, *Secret Alliance*, 3 vols (Odense, 1976–7).
Herrington, Ian, *The Special Operations Executive in Norway, 1940–1945*, PhD thesis (De Montfort University, Leicester, 2004).
Jespersen, Knud, *No Small Achievement: SOE and the Danish Resistance 1940–1945* (Odense, 2002).
Idem, 'SOE and Denmark', in Mark Seaman (ed.), *Special Operations Executive: A New Kind of War* (Oxford, 2006).
Kirchoff, Hans, 'Denmark', in Bob Moore (ed.), *Resistance in Western Europe* (Oxford, 2000).
Kraglund, Ivar, 'SOE and Milorg: Thieves on the Same Market', in Mark Seaman (ed.), *Special Operations Executive: A New Kind of War* (Oxford, 2006).
Lampe, David, *Hitler's Savage Canary*, 2nd edn (London, 2010).
Moland, Arnfinn, 'Milorg and SOE', in Patrick Salmon (ed.), *Britain and Norway in the Second World War* (London, 1995).
Idem, 'Norway', in Bob Moore (ed.), *Resistance in Western Europe* (Oxford, 2000).
Oram Thomas, John, *The Giant Killers* (London, 1975).
Petrow, Richard, *The Bitter Years* (London, 1975).
Riste, Olav and Nøkleby, Berit, *Norway 1940–1945: The Resistance Movement* (Oslo, 1970).

Films

The Heroes of Telemark, directed by Anthony Mann (1965).
Flame and Citron, directed by Espen Sandberg (2008).
Max Manus: Man of War, directed by Ole Christian Madsen (2009).

Chapter 10

The Soviet Union

Alexander Statiev

When the Germans invaded Russia in June 1941, many Soviet people perceived guerrilla warfare as a natural option. This was partly because a large and patriotic part of the population viewed resistance as a duty, and partly because the policies of the invaders and of the Soviet regime limited other alternatives. The rich guerrilla heritage in Russian culture suggested that armed resistance was possible, and sponsorship of guerrilla struggle by the Soviet government provided a practical opportunity to resist.

Russia had accumulated extensive experience in guerrilla warfare by the time of the German invasion. Colonel Denis Davydov, arguably the first modern strategist of guerrilla warfare, pioneered it in Russia in 1812. He deployed several Cossack regiments in the rear of the Napoleonic Grande Armée, seeking to intercept its supply lines. Napoleon ended the Russian campaign in failure mainly because of logistical problems, but guerrilla actions aggravated these problems and thus helped turn the retreat of the Grande Armée into a rout. Davydov, author of a best-selling memoir,[1] argued that guerrilla warfare in Russian conditions promised an attractive cost/benefit ratio. His ideas were coupled later with the captivating 'cudgel of people's war' metaphor coined by Leo Tolstoy,[2] who justified use of all possible means, including guerrilla warfare, to crush the Napoleonic invaders. The idea that guerrilla actions were a natural component of war became ingrained in Russian historical memory.

The 'cudgel of people's war' rose again in the wake of the Bolshevik Revolution. Partisan actions gave substantial help to the Red Army, often in crucial circumstances when the fate of the Bolshevik government was hanging by a thread. Siberian partisans attacked the long, vulnerable communication lines of the Whites led by Admiral Aleksandr Kolchak and thus contributed to his defeat. Ukrainian partisans led by the anarchist Nestor Makhno cut the supplies of General Denikin's White Volunteer Army when it was advancing on Moscow, thus helping the Bolsheviks to eliminate the greatest menace their regime ever faced. However, these Siberian and Ukrainian partisans allied with the Reds only as long as their primary enemy – the Whites – threatened their regions. They embraced the Decree on Land passed by the Bolshevik government and the system of local self-administration it established, but not the Bolshevik dictatorship. The Bolsheviks could not control even Red partisans, let alone other leftists. Partisans often ignored Bolshevik orders; their units had poor discipline and frequently engaged in plunder and pogroms, thus discrediting the Bolshevik government they claimed to support. As soon as the White menace vanished, many partisans rebelled against the ill-conceived Bolshevik policy of mandatory food procurement, believed to be a shortcut to the communist paradise. This forced the Reds to engage in exhausting counter-insurgency campaigns against their former allies. The Reds eventually defeated all of them, but only after they themselves had abandoned War Communism and adopted the New Economic Policy, a partial restoration of the market economy.

The partisan experience during the civil war left an ambiguous legacy among the Soviet leaders. They expected the next major war to be a conflict between the Soviet Union and several Western states, in which large parts of the country would be temporarily occupied by the enemy. They understood that guerrilla actions promised enormous benefits, not least because large parts of the country were ideal guerrilla terrain. Much of Russia, Belarus and northern Ukraine were covered with forests and swamps; the road network was poor and the invading armies would be confined to a few long roads surrounded by dense vegetation, which would give guerrillas an opportunity to fight on their own terms. The nation-in-arms concept, adopted by the Bolsheviks, presumed that the people would resist the invader. It was for this reason that the Bolshevik government organized a guerrilla infrastructure during the interwar period. The People's Commissariat of Internal Affairs (NKVD) maintained a pool of guerrilla experts; it trained demolition specialists and established partisan bases with weapon depots in the frontier regions. In Belarus alone the NKVD raised 6 partisan units, numbering between 300 and 500 men each and established weapon depots with mines, explosives and 50,000 rifles. Partisan heroes of the civil war, such as Nikolai Shchors, Sergei Lazo and Anatolii Zhelezniakov, acquired an iconic status in Soviet popular culture, and numerous novels, poems and songs glorified their endeavours. Thus was created the romantic image of the Red guerrilla.[3]

However, some top Soviet leaders, including Joseph Stalin, did not favour guerrilla warfare because they knew how difficult it was to harness armed resistance and direct it towards desired goals. They remembered the humiliating retreat from War Communism to the New Economic Policy forced on the Bolsheviks by rebels, many of whom had fought earlier as Red partisans. Such leaders perceived guerrilla warfare not as a weapon of choice but as a last resort. As Kenneth Slepyan puts it, '[a] truly popular and spontaneous partisan movement, embodying powerful, uncontrolled, and uncontrollable forces, contradicted the very core of Stalinist values emphasising order, control, obedience, discipline and hierarchy'.[4]

Since anti-White resistance during the civil war was mostly spontaneous, was not coordinated with the Red Army and involved mostly non-Bolshevik leftists, this experience did not facilitate a development of guerrilla strategic thought. Although Soviet soldiers and the population at large were aware that armed resistance could be an option in case of invasion, the Soviet General Staff had no doctrine of guerrilla warfare; it did not identify strategic goals and primary targets of potential armed resistance, nor did it study guerrilla tactics. It remained

Area occupied by Germany by June 1943. Main regions of partisan operations: Belarus, northern Ukraine and western and north-western Russia.

unclear who would command partisan units, supply them and coordinate their actions with the regular army.

This ambivalent attitude towards guerrilla warfare ended in the mid-1930s. The impressive growth of the Soviet military potential as an outcome of the first two five-year plans in 1928–37 led to an overoptimistic military doctrine presuming that, in a future war, the Red Army would rout the enemy during a brief offensive campaign outside Soviet territory. Adopted on the eve of the Great Purge of 1936–8, the doctrine signalled the end of Soviet preparations for guerrilla warfare. The notion that partisan actions might be useful became a heresy. Timofei Strokach, a future commander of Ukrainian partisans, recalled: 'If someone dared to say, even on 20 June 1941, that in case of attack by the fascist army our people in Ukraine, Belarus, Lithuania or Smolensk province might need to resort to guerrilla actions, this person would have been perceived as a panic-monger' and suffer the consequences. The NKVD dismantled the guerrilla infrastructure created in the interwar period, and executed major proponents of guerrilla warfare: Vasilii Blukher, Ieronim Uborevich, Iona Iakir, Vitalii Primakov and Jan Berzin.[5]

*   *   *

However, as soon as Stalin recovered from the breakdown he suffered during the first days of the German invasion, he called upon people of the occupied regions to resist the Nazis. The social environment in which partisans were to operate varied by region and depended on the local impacts of the Soviet interwar policies and the amount of strain these policies had caused, the regional variations of Nazi policies, and the strength of local nationalism. The urban population in the pre-1939 lands was generally loyal, and often fiercely patriotic, but partisans were to operate in the countryside and it was the sentiments of peasants that mattered. Many peasants remembered the shock of collectivization, the famine inflicted by the Bolsheviks in 1932–3, and the Great Purge, but their reservations should not be overstated. Charismatic Stalinism had a great ability to convert people to its cause despite the privations it inflicted; most peasants in the pre-1939 lands, especially the younger generation, perceived the Soviet regime as legitimate.

However, the solid majority of the rural population initially adopted a wait-and-see approach towards the German administration. Older peasants remembered the German army as the most decent among those armies that had rolled across their lands during the civil war, and expected nothing dramatic from the occupation; others hoped that the Germans might abolish the odious collective farms, and the hasty retreat of the Red Army undermined the morale of loyalists. Most peasants within the pre-1939 borders viewed partisans as a friendly force but did not join them. Such an attitude allowed partisans to operate in these regions, but their numbers remained low.

In contrast, the social climate in the borderlands annexed by the Soviet Union in 1939–40 precluded the possibility of resistance. During their brief presence there, the Bolsheviks had created many more enemies than friends. Borderland residents were horrified by mass deportations and other repressions, and the conflict of values promoted by communists with their own. Most of them hoped that the German invasion would bring change for the better.

The Soviet leaders ignored these variations in the social environment, and also the countless technical problems involved in armed resistance. Their first directives addressing guerrilla warfare demonstrated their gross incompetence in this matter. Stalin's secret order of 29 June 1941, the first that referred to guerrilla warfare, allotted to it one brief paragraph consisting of nothing more than generalities, such as an instruction to resist the invaders 'everywhere', and also encouragement of such senseless actions as blowing up highways. It did not say who was supposed to organize and lead the resistance, with what means and with what strategic priorities in mind. In the first public appeal to the nation on 3 July, Stalin merely repeated this paragraph and added another gem: he called on partisans to burn forests. As Il'ia Starinov, a commando colonel with an impressive record of covert operations, wrote later, '[f]rom a professional point of view, this was madness … If someone else but Stalin had said that partisans were to burn forests, this person would have been accused of treason.'[6] On 10 July, the State Defence Committee, the top Soviet wartime administrative agency, duly turned this bizarre idea into an operational order. On 21 July Colonel Rogatin, Head of Security in the rear of South-Western Front, instructed partisans to 'burn forests adjacent to the enemy's communication lines'. Few forests existed in the South-Western Front's area of operations; the enforcement of this monumental folly was to deprive partisans of the only cover they had.[7]

On 18 July 1941, when the Baltic region, Belarus, western Ukraine and most of Moldova had already been lost to the enemy, the Central Committee of the Communist Party finally issued the first document devoted entirely to guerrilla war. It ordered the regional party committees to set up underground resistance networks in the regions threatened by the enemy. These were to consist of communists and other loyalists, former guerrillas of the civil war and NKVD officers. Partisan organizational teams were to be sent to the regions that had already been occupied by the enemy. This directive was still quite vague: it did not specify exactly how resistance networks were to operate, who would supply partisans with weapons and train them, and what would be the command-and-control structure and strategic objectives of the resistance.[8] No top Soviet military or party agency issued directives on partisan warfare during the following ten months. This minimal effort to direct armed resistance shows that at that point the General Headquarters of the Red Army (Stavka) perceived it as an unimportant component of the war.

The resistance that emerged as the outcome of these vague instructions suffered from grave weaknesses. These flaws stemmed from inept leadership at all levels, the absence of strategy, daunting logistical problems and a lack of training. The partisan command-and-control system remained decentralized during the first year of war. Although it was the party that was to direct the guerrilla war, the resistance in practice was run by various agencies, such as regional party committees, People's Commissariat of Defence, the headquarters of the various fronts and armies, the Political Directorate of the Red Army and the Fourth

NKVD Directorate. All these agencies acted in an uncoordinated fashion.[9] In October 1941, the Political Directorate of the North-Western Front summarized the problems of armed resistance:

> The absence of a single centre directing the partisan movement inevitably causes numerous flaws ... Nobody supplies the partisan movement with radios ... nobody analyzes the experience of partisan struggle, nor do the fronts exchange positive experiences, and, until the present, we have received no instructions from the centre on the organization of the partisan movement ... The absence of centralized command also affects the selection of regional commanders. As a rule, these are people picked in an arbitrary fashion, ignorant in military and political matters ... The leading cadres receive no partisan [tactical] training; the system of supply and armament of the partisan movement is not developed. All these problems must be urgently solved.[10]

It took the Stavka seven months to come to the same conclusion. This sluggish reaction stemmed perhaps from the Stavka's indecision regarding two different concepts of guerrilla war. Although the party leaders maintained initially that partisans should be recruited only from staunch loyalists, most of them soon recognized that resistance should rest on the broadest possible social base. Yet the NKVD, headed by Lavrentii Beria, believed that such resistance would be ineffective, wasteful and difficult to control. Beria suggested commando-style operations conducted by teams of professionals, and insisted that the NKVD direct partisan warfare.[11] However, this approach ignored the political component of resistance, an element that was important on the Eastern Front. Incoherent leadership and strategic uncertainty undermined the operational efficiency of guerrilla war.

Contrary to the assumptions of the Communist Party, regional party leaders played only a minor role in fostering resistance because many of them had been mobilized into the Red Army and others had violated their orders by fleeing with the approach of the Germans. Four of the five commissars of the Crimean partisan districts failed to report for duty. Only four of forty-eight senior commanders serving in the eleven largest Ukrainian partisan formations were former party bureaucrats, whereas seven were NKVD officers and sixteen Red Army and frontier guard officers. Only two of the fifteen commanders of partisan units operating in Pinsk province, Belarus, were party functionaries.[12] Most party leaders were inept guerrillas. They had lost the initiative, dynamism and fervour they had shown during the revolution and instead become inert bureaucrats. They were reluctant to exchange comfortable city offices for a miserable existence in damp and mosquito-infested forest dugouts, and their superiors did not expect them to do so. Instead, the secretaries of district and town party committees were to remain in clandestine city apartments and coordinate the actions of the urban underground with the partisans.[13] Local people knew them, and with the arrival of the Germans these bureaucrats found themselves confined to their undercover quarters and cut off from the partisans. The actions of the urban underground were few, ineffective and sometimes counterproductive; the explosions of mined buildings in the historical centre of Kiev which it launched on 24 September 1941 outraged most of the city's residents. It also destroyed the apartment of the top underground leader, Ivan Kudria, burying all the fake identification cards, weapons, ciphers and clandestine addresses he had.[14] German counterintelligence quickly eradicated the urban underground cells, thus rendering leaderless the partisan units subordinated to those cells. Most of these units disintegrated.[15]

Since Stalin demanded that resistance be organized 'everywhere', the Stavka repeatedly attempted to launch guerrilla war in regions that offered partisans no cover: in the Ukrainian, Stalingrad and Don steppes, the thin Moldovan forests and the Dnepr and Kuban flood-lands.[16] The Germans destroyed all these units within days. Partisans cornered by the Romanian army in Odessa's catacombs were an exception; they remained there from October 1941 to February 1942. Blocked in the catacombs and having exhausted their food supplies, they conserved the bodies of their dead comrades in barrels and then ate them.[17] These futile attempts to organize resistance in the areas without cover continued until the end of the German occupation.[18]

The personal aptitude and devotion of regional bureaucrats were often the decisive factors in the success or failure of resistance. Aleksei Fedorov and Nikolai Popudrenko, the first and third party secretaries in Chernigov province, turned out to be talented and charismatic leaders. They established over 200 well-hidden weapon depots before the arrival of the Germans and then personally led partisans. Sidor Kovpak, Chair of the Executive Committee in Putivl, Sumy province, became the most famous partisan commander. He prepared 132 depots containing a wide variety of supplies, including rubber pipes for breathing under water.[19] Chernigov and Sumy provinces became the centres of partisan activities in eastern Ukraine. However, such leaders were a small minority. According to Starinov, 'no Red Army commander would have entrusted even a platoon' to Petr Kalinin, the Secretary of the Central Committee of the Belarusian Communist Party, appointed as head of the partisans in his republic. Colonel Mikhail Lobov, commander-in-chief of the Crimean partisans after July 1942, called his predecessor, Aleksei Mokrousov, 'a man who has lost his marbles, a drunkard unable to act as a leader in modern warfare', whereas Bortnikov, commander of the Fourth Partisan District in the Crimea was 'an absolutely stupid, ignorant and sick man'.[20]

Party bosses had plenty of time to organize resistance in the Crimea but they bungled the job. They brought gramophones to entertain themselves in the mountains but forgot maps, and they set the food and weapon depots in broad daylight and near the roads, so that the cargo could be brought directly by trucks. The depots did not contain a variety of supplies but identical items because it was easier to fill them this way. The Germans easily discovered most depots and when the partisans rushed to the surviving stores, they found themselves in possession of only basic items like sugar or salt. Some party leaders could not find their depots because they had been drunk when they had organized them. The gravest mistake made by the Crimean bureaucrats was the decision to limit partisan recruitment only to party activists, most of whom lived in cities and were of Slavic origin, and to ignore the rural Tatars, even though it was Tatars who populated the Crimean Mountains. This policy had fatal consequences. After the partisans lost their food depots, they had to confiscate food from Tatar peasants. The ruthless food procurements provoked an ethnic conflict with the Tatars. It was not the Germans but this conflict and the starvation it entailed that virtually eliminated the Crimean partisans: about 20 per cent of the partisans in three partisan districts starved to death, and of those who survived, many did so by consuming the bodies of their dead comrades. The morale of partisans plummeted and one-third of them deserted. The partisan activity in the Crimea virtually ceased in 1942 with only 150 fighters remaining operational.[21]

When the Central Committee ordered regional party agencies to raise partisan units, it did not say who would supply partisans. Few units had explosives; those who did have them often had no detonators. In the absence of explosives, the Political Directorate of the Red Army issued a manual in which it called on partisans to derail approaching trains by the force of four men pulling a rope tied to a rail after the bolts fixing the rails had been removed.[22] Pressed by their superiors to raise numerous partisan units and having no weapons to arm them, regional bureaucrats issued a series of pathetic directives encouraging partisans to kill the enemy 'with any means: axes, scythes, crow-bars, pitchforks, and knifes ... Strangle, cut down, burn and poison the fascist vermin.' The secretary of the Snezhino district party committee in Ukrainian Stalino province told peasants: 'Arm yourselves with axes. An axe is a terrifying weapon!'[23] No bureaucrat attempted to give an example of how to terrify Germans with an axe; instead they fled with the Red Army. Most of their axe-armed recruits went home.

The Germans meanwhile could rarely afford to use front-line formations in counterinsurgency. Most often they employed a variety of second-rate German units, minor Axis formations and collaborator auxiliary police. The latter made up a large proportion of counterinsurgents. Accordingly, prevention of collaboration was the primary political mission of partisans. Stalin's order of 29 June 1941 called on partisans 'to create unbearable conditions for the enemy and all his collaborators', and subsequently this task was present in every major instruction issued by the top partisan commanders. Ivan Syromolotnyi, representative of the Ukrainian Central Committee, expressed a common partisan sentiment in his report to the Ukrainian Partisan Headquarters: 'Had we fought only Germans, we would not have been upset but we also have to fight these assholes – police and Cossacks, fuck them! These whores cannot fight well and die like flies but they harass us.'[24] Carried away by this sentiment, partisans initially executed any military collaborators they captured and also representatives of the German administration picked from locals, sometimes along with their entire families.[25] The Stavka left the definition of collaboration to the discretion of partisans, and since no uniform policy existed, some units set the threshold for their qualification of collaboration too low and preventatively killed those who, in their opinion, were likely to collaborate even if they did not: village elders appointed by the Germans against their will, priests, prosperous peasants and members of diaspora groups who shared ethnicity with the enemy, such as Finns. The sweeping repressions conducted by partisans within the ideological framework of the Great Purge undermined their support. This terror effectively precluded the functioning of the German administration in many occupied regions; it also provoked a brutal civil war with revenge killings of civilians on both sides, and some villages requested protection from the Germans.[26]

The Soviet leaders did not understand the simple fact that guerrilla 'fish' could not survive without 'water' – people supporting the guerrillas' agenda. The Stavka had no time to establish a resistance infrastructure in the borderlands annexed in 1939–40 but attempted to create it with hasty and costly improvisations. It persistently sent teams of partisans into the borderlands. These teams were intended to serve as the nuclei of local resistance, but they perished within days because the attitude to the Soviet regime in the borderlands was overwhelmingly negative. By October 1941, 37 teams with a total of 770 men were parachuted into western Ukraine; most of them vanished without trace. Of twenty-five teams of partisan organizers sent to Lithuania in 1941–2, only three survived until 1943; all eleven teams sent to Latvia in 1942 perished, as did all forty-eight partisan organizers sent to Estonia.[27] The party bosses who dispatched hundreds of agents with suicidal missions to the borderlands acted in the tradition of Stalinist bureaucracy: display of zeal was more important than results, especially if the latter could be glossed over by over optimistic reports. Regional party leaders boasted of the number of partisans they had recruited but the NKVD were sceptical of their combat capacity since many partisan units were 'raised in haste, literally within several hours, from persons who do not know each other and cannot handle weapons'; they 'receive [only] brief instructions; as a result they have no clear idea what to do and how to do it'.[28] Many units had no maps or compasses, and even when they had them, they were a mystery to most partisans. In the 1930s, the NKVD trained a partisan unit for between three and six months;[29] in 1941–2 most partisans did not receive even basic training. Although the NKVD opened several partisan schools, these were small and few in number and open only to the partisan elite. Demolition experts graduated after five days of study at most. The training of radio operators was limited to several weeks, and their cipher training to several days. Before being sent to the enemy rear, these specialists had 'no more than two days' to learn parachute jumping, according to the instruction given by the top partisan commanders.[30] Such training could not produce tangible results: partisan casualties were considerably higher than those of their enemies; some units dispersed after their first clash with the Germans; radio operators could not handle radios or decipher messages; demolition men wasted scarce explosives; and many specialists died during parachute jumps.

Most partisan bands reportedly organized by party leaders never materialized, or they disintegrated with the approach of the Germans. The Moldovan Communist Party claimed to have raised 147 partisan units and sabotage groups with a total strength of 1,479 men in 1941, but by the spring of 1942 no partisans were operating in Moldova. In May 1942, the Stavka found only 37 units with 1,918 fighters of the 1,874 units with 30,083 fighters claimed to have been raised by Ukrainian Communists; perhaps all other reported partisans existed only on paper. Partisan commanders admitted in late 1942 that they had no knowledge of partisans operating in the Baltic provinces.[31] The whole territory of Ukraine, except for a small north-eastern enclave, was partisan-free. The partisans retained their strongholds in eastern Belarusian and Russian forests but their total number was small.

The resistance reached its nadir in early 1942. Its actions were few, un-coordinated, and ineffective in the absence of clear strategic objectives, and partisans focused on their own survival rather than attacks against the Germans. Most units dispersed by the winter of 1941–2, because of incompetent leadership, supply problems, low morale caused by the grave situation on the fronts, the wait-and-see attitude of the rural population and the inability of urban recruits to adapt to outdoor life. This miserable outcome of resistance efforts stemmed primarily from the ill-conceived interwar party policies, but the follies of partisan leaders at all levels also were responsible for an enormous waste of loyalists who strove to resist the invaders.

* * *

Yet a 'great turn' in partisan fortunes did occur in 1942. Beginning with this year, the numbers of partisans and their efficiency steadily grew. It happened because German repression forced the apathetic peasants into resistance, the Stavka refined the partisan command structure, the composition of partisan units devel-oped (luckily) not how the communist bureaucrats had intended, and the turning tide of war prompted numerous opportunists to join the partisans.

The German administration failed to preserve the tolerance it initially enjoyed. Operating within the framework of Nazi racial theories, it intended to Germanize a small part of the Soviet population, enslave a larger part and kill the rest or deport them to Siberia. Contrary to peasants' hopes, the Germans preserved collective farms. They also established a mandatory two-year labour duty in Germany, and burned down entire villages if men and women failed to report. In total, according to German sources, 2,792,669 Soviet labourers were shipped to Germany, where they lived in miserable conditions.[32]

The Nazis conducted counterinsurgency with the view that *Lebensraum* had to be cleared from the *Untermenschen* for the *Herrenvolk*, whatever the attitude of the people towards the communists or the invaders. The chief Nazi leaders encouraged indiscriminate repression in partisan-infested regions. An instruction signed by Field Marshal Wilhelm Keitel cited Hitler's order, according to which German soldiers had 'the right and the duty to use, in this fight, any means, even against women and children, provided they are conducive to success. Scruples, of any sort whatsoever, are a crime against the German people … No German participating in actions against bands or their associates is to be held responsible for acts of violence.'[33] Belarus suffered more than any other Soviet region during

the German occupation: it lost over 2 million dead, or a quarter of its population.[34] Indiscriminate repression in the Slavic regions forced people to defend
their lives, thus fuelling rather than undermining the resistance.

Soviet war propaganda accelerated this process. The dissemination of propaganda was among the major partisan activities. The Political Directorate of the
Red Army delivered millions of copies of leaflets and Soviet newspapers to
partisans.[35] These newspapers and leaflets, published in the local languages and
distributed among civilians, skilfully exploited their wounded nationalism and
called on the people to avenge the privations inflicted by the Nazis. Since many
peasants were still religious, the Soviet government dropped its militant atheism
and played the religious card to fuel resistance. Sergii, Patriarch of the Russian
Orthodox Church, appealed to people living in the occupied lands: 'All of you
should give full support to the partisans, and if you cannot directly fight in their
ranks, help them by all means.'[36] Partisans delivered the *Journal of the Moscow
Patriarchate* with patriotic appeals across the front and even sometimes prayed
with villagers.[37] The reversal of the policy towards religion suggested, wrongly,
that the Soviet regime was moving toward general liberalization, and rumours
circulated that the collective farms might be abolished after victory. The propaganda began rallying people, even those who disliked Stalinism, when they
realized what the goals of the Nazis were, and especially when the front began
moving westward.

By the spring of 1942, the Stavka finally accepted the idea that had been
expressed by various partisan commanders as early as the autumn of 1941: the
resistance would be most effective if it pursued strategic priorities identified by a
single centre. On 30 May 1942, the Stavka established the Central Partisan Headquarters in the Soviet rear, and also regional partisan headquarters subordinated
to the Central Headquarters. These command centres were to develop strategy
and direct partisans towards strategic objectives, coordinate the operations of
partisan units and their joint actions with the regular army, supervise partisan
logistics and monitor partisan discipline.[38] Stalin appointed Panteleimon
Ponomarenko, First Secretary of the Belarusian Communist Party, as head of
the Central Partisan Headquarters. This was a fortunate choice. Belarus was the
region with the highest proportion of partisans. Although Ponomarenko
remained in the safety of the Soviet rear throughout the war, he was a talented
planner. In September 1941, he sent Stalin a memorandum that was intellectually
superior to any order on partisan warfare ever issued by Stalin. Ponomarenko
identified enemy communications as the major target of guerrilla warfare. He did
not refer to Denis Davydov, who had come to this conclusion 130 years earlier, or
to partisans of the civil war who had acted in the spirit of Davydov, but presented
this idea as his own revelation. Eight months later, in May 1942, Stalin finally
endorsed the attacks on enemy communications as the major military goal of
guerrilla warfare and this remained the partisan priority until the end of the
occupation.

By September 1942, Stalin had made up his mind on the concept of partisan
war. In the desperate days when the Germans reached Stalingrad, he concluded

that 'rout of the German armies can only be attained by simultaneous actions of the Red Army and powerful and relentless blows delivered by partisan units in the enemy rear'. Drawing a symbolic analogy with 1812, he stated that resistance should involve 'the broadest social strata' and turn into an 'all-out people's war' against the invader, thus discarding Beria's concept of stealthy but narrow missions performed by professional commandos.[39] The centralized leadership, the clarification of the strategic priorities and the adoption of an 'all-out people's war' as official doctrine considerably increased the effectiveness of partisan actions and also facilitated recruitment to partisan units.

The party directives presumed that partisan recruits would come from three sources. Most of them would be local activists organized by regional party leaders; others would be members of a militia raised originally to combat German agents in the Soviet rear. With the approach of the Germans, the regional party leaders transformed about one-third of this militia into partisan units. Finally, NKVD commandos parachuted into the enemy rear with narrow military missions were to be the third and smallest component of the partisans.

However, during the first two years of the war on the Eastern Front, the largest component of partisan units came from a source unanticipated by the Soviet leaders. These were Soviet regulars from the armies surrounded and dispersed by the Germans. These soldiers had better discipline, morale, training and weapons than partisans raised by the party. In the summer of 1942, former regulars made up about 30 per cent of the partisans in Leningrad, Mogilev and Vitebsk provinces, between 40 and 50 per cent in Kalinin, Smolensk and Orel provinces and 60 per cent in Ukrainian partisan units.[40] These soldiers enhanced the combat capacity of the resistance.

Battle attrition, desertion of the urban residents unable to withstand the privations of outdoor life and an influx of peasant volunteers and draftees changed the initial composition of the partisan units. The proportion of peasants in them gradually increased and eventually made up between 40 and 60 per cent of all partisans who were not cut-off regulars, whereas the proportion of party members declined: it ranged from between 6 and 13 per cent of the total during the entire wartime period.[41] The 'cudgel of war' handled by Soviet activists turned into a 'cudgel of people's war'.

The Soviet victories on the fronts triggered mass defection of collaborators. This became possible after the Stavka revised its policy towards collaborators, having realized that most of them had collaborated because they had sought to escape starvation in POW camps. The partisans found that all collaborators 'can be divided in two groups: the first one, insignificant [in numbers] but most committed, are traitors who volunteered to serve the Germans because they hated the Soviet system. The second group – the vast majority – are people serving the Germans because of fear, loss of faith in the Red Army's victory and the desire to avoid deportation to Germany.' Most of them 'wait for a convenient moment to join the partisans or cross the front.'[42] Beginning with November 1942, Ponomarenko demanded that partisans 'convert all those who, having been deceived or misled or forced by starvation or terror, serve the Germans'; every defecting collaborator had to be given a chance 'to atone for his guilt by fighting for the liberation of the Motherland'.[43] During the last six months of 1943, over 10,000 collaborators switched sides, and they became a sizeable component of partisan units. Former collaborators made up 6.5 per cent of the eleven largest Ukrainian partisan formations. In October 1943, the frequent desertion of collaborators prompted Hitler to order their transfer to Western Europe.[44] Partisan documents show that former collaborators usually fought well as they were seeking to be pardoned; some even earned decorations. The instruction of the Central Partisan Headquarters stated that former collaborators who had fought as partisans had to be passed to 'special agencies', which decided their plight on an individual basis.[45] Most of them were pardoned but some were sentenced to several years in labour camps. In any case, by offering collaborators an opportunity 'to atone for their guilt' the partisans attained their major political goal: they frustrated the belated German attempts to raise anti-communist armies from Soviet citizens.

Partisans called themselves 'people's avengers'. They may have deserved this title at least in the Slavic lands but they were not people's defenders. Despite permanent abuse and random violence civilians experienced from the Nazis and their collaborators, the lives of those who were not marked for wholesale extermination, as were Jews and Sinti and Roma, was still safer in the partisan-free regions than in those penetrated by partisans but still controlled by the Germans. The emergence of partisans in a certain area meant trouble for most residents: indiscriminate German reprisals, partisan procurements in addition to the German requisitions, pressure to buy government bonds, conscription into partisan units and the presence of rowdy outsiders who often engaged in drunken brawls. If partisans faced a German punitive expedition, they usually retreated, leaving the civilians to their fate. A typical report of a Soviet official compared conditions in eastern Belarus, where resistance was strongest, and western Belarus where it was much weaker: in the east, Germans 'exterminated people quite brutally *because large partisan formations operated there*'; villages and towns 'were, as a rule, burned down and robbed by the Germans. In most villages Germans took away not only cattle and grain but also personal possessions and house utensils. Thousands of civilians perished ... almost no able-bodied men, youths or even children remain.' In contrast, in the western part of the republic, 'almost all villages and homesteads survived; people lived as they had done earlier, including a considerable number of men of military age ... Almost all cattle survived.'[46]

The Stavka knew that civilians paid an enormous price for partisan actions but ignored their plight. It followed a simple logic: the goal – victory – justified any means; those who lived in the occupied regions and did not resist had at best no value for the Soviet war effort and at worst worked for the Germans. As Stalin explained, '[a]ll [residents of occupied regions] should rise [against Germans] whether they want to fight or not ... Those who do not want to fight should be treated as deserters.'[47] This logic freed partisan commanders from a grave moral dilemma, in contrast to Western European resistance leaders who weighed the military and political benefits gained through guerrilla war versus the price civilians had to pay for its waging. Some scholars allege that partisans sought to provoke German repression and thus force people to resist. However, they provide no solid evidence for this claim; even if some field commanders did so, it was certainly not the policy of the partisan headquarters.[48] Rather, the Soviet state regarded the privations inflicted by German counterinsurgency as regrettable but inevitable in the battle against Nazism. The official policy towards civilians in the occupied lands changed in early 1943, when the Central Partisan Headquarters ordered partisans to protect civilians as much as possible. As an outcome of this order, large camps emerged in the forests harbouring Jewish and other refugees and escapees from labour draft and military conscriptions, even if they were useless for resistance.[49] Yet the protection of civilians remained a low partisan priority, and the brutal Nazi reaction to resistance made it safer to join the partisans than to face a punitive expedition. In this way, many people indifferent to communist ideology found themselves among the partisans.

In October 1942, the Stavka eliminated the institution of commissars in the Red Army as a superfluous element of command structure but preserved it in partisan units. In theory the commissar, usually a former Communist Party functionary, reported to the partisan unit commander, but in practice he often had as much power as the commander. Commissars were supposed to inspire partisans by being model fighters, but most of them were not: Iakov Mel'nik, a Ukrainian commander, invariably referred to his commissars as selfish drunkards and cowards.[50] However, given the important political mission of guerrilla warfare, the preservation of the commissar institution in partisan units was probably justified. Commissars had to ensure commanders followed the party line; they monitored units' morale, spread propaganda among the local population and recruited fighters. They also supervised the NKVD Special Sections running intelligence and counterintelligence services. This was an important job: the existence of a partisan unit depended on the efficiency of these services. The Germans acknowledged that partisan intelligence was far superior to their own, which allowed the partisans, in general, to escape punitive expeditions. Commissars and Special Sections established an informer network in every partisan unit and thus promptly received information on subversion or discipline violations. In October 1942, every partisan unit in the Karel-Finn Republic had one or two chief NKVD agents and between ten and twenty-one informers.[51] Partisan counterintelligence claimed to have apprehended hundreds of German agents during the war. While it is open to speculation as to whether most of these suspects had indeed worked for the Germans or were innocent victims of a witch-hunt, it is clear that the attempts of German intelligence to penetrate partisan units were, generally, futile. The Communist Party had learned a lesson from the civil war: it closely monitored partisans and preventatively eradicated suspected treason. After 1941, no incidents of mass defection by entire partisan units occurred, because the party maintained a firm political grip on partisans throughout the war.

However, it was less strict when it received reports on random partisan violence against civilians. Such incidents were frequent and they severely damaged the reputation of partisans and the Soviet authority they claimed to represent. Partisans lived off the land and requisition frequently turned into plunder, which, along with the crimes committed under the influence of alcohol, was the most typical breach of discipline. Rape and murder also occurred, but rarely in comparison with plunder and drunken brawls. Discipline varied greatly from unit to unit, depending on the personalities of commanders and commissars. Some commanders punished even petty theft with death; others turned a blind eye to such and other 'minor' offences, and some units turned into criminal bands that robbed peasants indiscriminately and sometimes killed them. The Central Partisan Headquarters demanded that any 'anti-Bolshevik attitude to the population must entail most severe penalties', and it did attempt to enforce this policy.[52] When Nikhifor Koliada, a prominent partisan commander in the Briansk region, was implicated in the plunder of civilians, he was arrested and brought across the front to face a court-martial.[53] Several other important commanders who allowed random violence shared his plight. If the Central Partisan Headquarters found that a guerrilla unit engaged in banditry, it ordered other units present in the same region to destroy the bandits. However, it had few means of controlling partisans in remote regions inaccessible to its inspectors, and some of these units committed crimes with impunity. Ukrainian and Polish nationalist guerrillas operating on the Eastern Front were, in general, more effective in curbing unauthorized violence against civilians belonging to their ethnic groups. However, the sanctioned violence of nationalists against other ethnic groups, let alone the random and sanctioned violence of the Nazis and their collaborators, far exceeded that of Red partisans, so that most people in the pre-1939 regions and many in the Slavic-populated borderlands viewed the Reds as a relatively benign force.

The persistent encouragement of guerrilla war by the Soviet state, the brutal German counterinsurgency and the victories of the Red Army led to a surge of armed resistance. Wounded patriotism fuelled by Soviet propaganda, the desire to extract revenge or escape the German labour drafts and sheer opportunism prompted an increasing number of people to join the partisans. Meanwhile, partisan leaders refined their strategy. In order radically to improve the command and control of guerrilla warfare, the Central Partisan Headquarters made a painstaking effort to equip its units with portable radios. By July 1942, 69 radios delivered to partisans secured close control over 200 units, and between 120 and 150 radios were on their way. The Stavka realized by the summer of 1942 that a resistance armed only with weapons captured from the enemy could not be effective, and brought crucial supplies to partisans via airlifts and by ground transportation through the gaps in the front. By June 1943, Ukrainian and Belarusian partisans were receiving seven or eight cargo flights daily. The deliveries of weapons considerably increased partisans' firepower. Ukrainian partisans acquired via airlifts 20 cannon, 272 trench mortars, 492 anti-tank rifles, 1,255 machine guns, 12,622 sub-machine guns, 3,507 rifles, 34,562 mines, 14.6 tons of explosives and an enormous quantity of ammunition.[54] Soon partisans were so well-armed that they outgunned counterinsurgents from collaborator and minor Axis formations. Better weapons and improved combat skills usually allowed the partisans to defeat such opponents. As SS officers noted, partisan bands attacked 'Hungarian units of any strength, and, up to the present, almost all such encounters ended with victories for the bands.'[55] Aircraft also brought inspectors from the Central Partisan Headquarters, who monitored fighters' morale and discipline, solved conflicts between partisan commanders, and ensured that their units followed the policies developed by the centre. Aeroplanes delivered various specialists, such as demolition experts, NKVD commandos, radio operators, Special Section officers and medics and returned back with wounded fighters. The data on five partisan units operating in western Ukraine show that between 24 and 43 per cent of the wounded were evacuated by aircraft, which perhaps included most of those who had received heavy injuries that could not be treated effectively in partisan camps.[56] The belief that those wounded could be evacuated boosted partisan morale.

The permanent radio contact with the Central Partisan Headquarters, coupled with a steady stream of crucial supplies via airlift, significantly improved the coordination between partisan units and opened new strategic opportunities. In the late summer of 1942, the Stavka recalled prominent partisan commanders to Moscow for the joint development of strategy. On 4 September 1942, Stalin met with them. The outcome of this meeting was the decision to launch deep raids by several partisan brigades into the western provinces of pre-1939 Ukraine and Belarus and thus transplant the guerrilla war to regions where it did not exist.[57] The brigades moved in a coordinated fashion by cumbersome routes, forcing the German security units to spread themselves thinly over large areas and thus preventing them from concentrating enough forces to block partisan penetrations. The raids were a stunning success: they served as a catalyst, igniting guerrilla war throughout all pre-1939 forest regions. Ponomarenko reported: 'Raiding units are quickly reinforced, and in most cases the enlistment of volunteers is limited by the lack of weapons. Partisan commanders are enlisting only those who bring their own weapons.'[58] Within a month of beginning their raids on 26 October 1942, the brigades commanded by Sidor Kovpak and Aleksandr Saburov had grown by 70 per cent. When the first 5 brigades crossed the Dnepr, they had between them 5,248 partisans. They suffered heavy casualties, yet by July 1943 these brigades had grown into 11 partisan formations with a total of 16,440 partisans.[59]

* * *

In 1942, partisans began joint actions with the Red Army. On 27 June, Ponomarenko instructed regional partisan headquarters to organize sections coordinating partisan operations with the military councils of the armies across the front. The first joint operations occurred in September 1942, when partisans attacked the communications of the German armies facing two Soviet offensives: one intended to break the blockade of Leningrad and the other was to surround Army Group Centre. Although the offensives failed, the partisans did fulfil their missions. After that, cooperation between regular and guerrilla forces became routine.[60]

The large volume of intelligence Stavka began receiving from partisans helped it to shape its operational plans. On the eve of the Battle of Kursk in the summer of 1943, partisans pinpointed eleven new German formations arriving at this sector of the front, which confirmed Stavka's suspicion that the Wehrmacht was preparing a major offensive.[61] The Stavka instructed the partisans to cut the German supply lines. Ponomarenko initiated Operation Rail War, a major attack on German communications between August and September 1943. It was followed by Operation Concert, launched between September and November 1943 during the battle for eastern Ukraine. In both cases, partisans attacked railways in a coordinated fashion with swarms of small sabotage teams that blew up the railways in many places simultaneously. These operations attained a limited success because the Central Partisan Headquarters measured partisans' efficiency in the number of steel rails destroyed rather than the period of traffic disruption. This prompted partisans to attack easier targets, such as secondary railways or even unused rusty spare trucks in remote corners of stations because, unlike vital railways, these were unprotected.[62] The Rail War began after the climax of the Battle of Kursk had already passed. Nonetheless the numbers of rails reportedly destroyed in both operations – 214,705 and 148,557 correspondingly – even if these numbers were grossly inflated, were large enough to considerably slow down the German railway traffic and thus facilitate the defeat of the Wehrmacht during these two major battles. The Germans reported that 5,250 locomotives suffered serious damage from partisans throughout 1943,[63] which also severely undermined the Germans' ability to supply their armies. The Central Partisan Headquarters learned from their mistakes, and the next concerted partisan attack on railways during the spectacular Soviet breakthrough in Belarus in June 1944 was more successful. This time, the partisans interrupted railway traffic for several crucial days, and forced the Germans to withdraw a part of their stretched manpower from the fronts and engage it in the protection of railways.[64] This Soviet offensive ended with the destruction of Army Group Centre, and partisans made an important contribution to this victory.

The growth of partisan units remained steady after 1942. By mid-1943 it had turned into an avalanche. The number of Ukrainian partisans who had permanent contact with the Ukrainian Partisan Headquarters increased sevenfold from June 1942 to July 1943 (from 3,063 to 20,747) and thirteenfold to January 1944 (39,387). The Central Partisan Headquarters reported that by 1 July 1943 it had registered a total of 139,583 fighters. Of these, 57.8 per cent operated in Belarus, 24.6 per cent in Russia, 15.7 per cent in Ukraine and 2 per cent elsewhere. The partisans became so strong in some provinces that areas they controlled merged into so-called partisan regions: large territories with re-established Soviet authority. By 1944, Belarusian partisans held 60 per cent of the republic's territory.[65]

Being encouraged by the outcome of the deep raids into the western parts of the pre-1939 lands, the Central Partisan Headquarters attempted to transplant guerrilla warfare to the regions annexed by the Soviet Union in 1939–40. However, the success rate of deep raids depended primarily on the local social environment. In the borderlands, it was often prohibitive for pro-Soviet resistance. Caught in the fierce fight between two totalitarian states, borderland residents formed their attitudes towards partisans – the representatives of Soviet power – by comparing their experiences during the interwar years, the brief Soviet presence between 1939 and 1941 and under the current Axis administration. Most borderland people were indifferent or hostile to communist ideals and believed life had been better before the Soviet occupation of 1939–41. As for their attitude to the Axis occupation, it depended on the regional differences in Axis policies.

The deep raids succeeded, to a degree, in western Belarus. Since Nazi rule was harsher there than in other borderland regions, most west Belarusians tolerated partisans, but they felt no attachment to the Soviet state, and few were enthusiastic enough to join armed resistance. Those who did participate were motivated by personal revenge or the opportunity to evade German conscription. Only in early 1944, with the German pressure to enlist into the collaborator Belarusian Regional Defence force mounting and the Red Army approaching, did west Belarusians begin joining the partisans en masse.[66]

The partisans made their first shallow intrusions into western Ukraine from Belarus in the summer of 1942,[67] followed by a spectacular deep raid by Kovpak's partisan brigade that reached the Carpathians in July 1943. However, the partisans could not establish strongholds in western Ukraine outside its northern regions, firstly because the population was hostile and secondly because they had to fight not only Germans but also the Ukrainian Insurgent Army (Ukrains'ka Povstans'ka Armia, UPA). This guerrilla force was raised by the Organization of Ukrainian Nationalists (OUN), a fascist group that sought to establish an independent authoritarian and ethnically pure Ukrainian state. UPA had initially solid support among west Ukrainians, especially in Galicia. A partisan commander, Petr Vershigora, reported in March 1944: 'Soviet partisans feel themselves in Galicia … as if in Germany'. Grigorii Balitskii, a Ukrainian partisan commander, wrote in his diary: 'The Germans do not always go to the forest but this scum [UPA] is in the forest and in small homesteads; that is why nationalist bands are far more dangerous than German punitive units.'[68]

Jews who had escaped the Holocaust, and a large Polish minority, passionately hated UPA because it engaged in thorough ethnic cleansing, killing all the Jews it could find, about 50,000 Poles in Volhynia and between 20,000 and 30,000 Poles in Galicia.[69] While disliking the Soviet regime, most Poles viewed partisans as their only defender against UPA and many joined the partisans. The Soviets raised three Polish partisan brigades and a smaller unit, all commanded by Poles. The presence of common mortal enemies – Nazis and UPA – facilitated the cooperation between partisans and the Polish Home Army (Armija Krajowa, AK), a nationalist guerrilla force loyal to the Polish government-in-exile. The relations between partisans and AK were complicated but in 1943 and the first half of 1944 they more often cooperated than clashed.[70] Other ethnic minorities also flooded to the partisans, driven by UPA terror. OUN reported that there were 'Jews, Belarusians, Poles, Gypsies, Muscovites and other rabble' in partisan units. OUN was surprised to find that 'the pro-Bolshevik sentiment in [Ukrainian] villages has risen notably' and that 'the people became so hostile to the Germans that, had the [raiding Red] partisans returned, half [of the population] would have joined them'.[71] Many west Ukrainians did in fact join, driven by hatred of the Nazis, disgust at the sporadic UPA collaboration with the Nazis, and desire to avenge relatives killed by UPA. These dynamics of popular sentiment and skilful political manoeuvring among west Ukrainian ethnic minorities allowed the partisans to turn the tables and establish their control over large regions in Polissia, Volhynia and Transcarpathian Ukraine. Given the initial absence of guerrilla infrastructure, the reserved attitude of west Belarusians and the hostility of most west Ukrainians, the traditional anti-Russian and anti-communist sentiments of Poles, and the presence of strong nationalist opponents, the outcome of the partisan effort to extend guerrilla war to the Slavic borderlands can be judged a sound success. Partisan operations in western Belarus and western Ukraine did facilitate the Soviet war effort, and did help the Soviet regime to shape public opinion and prepare the ground for the restoration of Soviet rule.[72]

The Baltic lands remained partisan-free throughout most of the war. Nazi policy there was milder than in the Slavic regions. The Balts remembered the annexation of their states by the Soviet Union in 1940–1 and the wave of deportations and other repression it brought. Since life under German occupation was bearable, Balts resented the partisans who provoked German reprisals and robbed wealthier peasants. The Germans kept small forces in the Baltic region, and it was not them but the native security agencies that were the major partisan opponent there. These were enemies as bitter as the Nazis but popular among the locals, and they outnumbered the partisans considerably. By 1944, a mere 234 partisans fought in Estonia, 856 in Latvia and 1,633 in Lithuania. No local resident joined the partisans in Estonia before 1944, all being Red Army or NKVD personnel, and no popular resistance ever emerged in this region. Most partisans operating in Latvia were ethnic Slavs, and most of those came from the pre-1939 lands. Only after the Latvian self-administration began mobilizations to SS divisions in late 1943 did Latvian partisan units gain some strength, and their number grew to 1,500 men by August 1944.[73] As a whole, the actions of partisans in the Baltic region, unlike those in western Ukraine and western Belarus, had little military or political impact.

After the Red Army overran the regions of partisan operations, the Stavka disbanded most guerrilla units but retained several partisan brigades and engaged them in fighting against Ukrainian and Lithuanian nationalists: it found that partisans, familiar with the local environment, were a more effective counterinsurgency force than regular NKVD divisions raised from outsiders. In 1944, 1,205 partisans fought nationalists in western Belarus and 10,000 in western Ukraine.[74]

When the Red Army approached the Soviet borders in the summer of 1944, the Stavka ordered several partisan brigades to move to the neighbouring states. These brigades were to perform a mainly political mission: to prepare the ground for the establishment of pro-communist regimes in Eastern Europe. Yet the

Stavka again ignored the differences of the local social environments. Partisans easily established their strongholds in Slovakia and with more difficulty in Poland – countries that had suffered from German counterinsurgency in the wake of the anti-Nazi uprisings there. Partisan organization teams with a total of 249 men sent to Slovakia in the summer of 1944 grew by mid-September into several units with a total of 15,153 fighters, and they operated far away from the Soviet border in the Tatra Mountains. However, partisans had no success in Romania, where people were apathetic, and in Hungary where anti-communist sentiments were strong. Only one of the eight partisan organization teams sent to the Romanian Carpathians – a first-rate guerrilla terrain – survived. Of the 11 teams sent to Hungary, only 4 survived and only one of them with 21 men operated outside the Slavic regions annexed by Hungary from Czechoslovakia in 1939.[75] The goal of partisan operations in the neighbouring countries was to support local leftists and thus make people aware of communism as a political alternative to the governments that had let them down during the Second World War.

* * *

The first official history of the Great Patriotic War[76] shaped the resistance mythology in Soviet historiography: Soviet people, motivated by patriotism and led by audacious, wise and committed party leaders, rose up all over Soviet territory from the first days of the occupation; the resistance enjoyed universal popular support and inflicted devastating casualties on the enemy. Several collections of primary documents and numerous partisan memoirs, all of them thoroughly censored, backed this image of resistance.[77] However, uncensored versions of these and many other documents that became available after the collapse of communism conclusively disprove this myth. They also reveal dark sides of partisan war: its extreme brutality, privations inflicted by partisans on civilians within the framework of a scorched earth policy, gross mismanagement of resistance during the first year of war on the Eastern Front, sanctioned and random violence against civilians who did not collaborate with the enemy, coercive recruitment, frequent drunken brawls and deadly internal conflicts in partisan units, and popular hostility in some regions. However, few solid revisionist studies of resistance have emerged in the post-Soviet space.[78] This happened because most Russian and Belarusian historians ignored the influx of new information and stuck to the interpretations of the Soviet period,[79] whereas scholars in the Baltic States and Ukraine studied mainly nationalist agencies rather than the partisans. As a result of a meagre academic contribution to public discourse on resistance during the post-communist period, popular memory of partisan war changed little in Russia and Belarus, whereas in the Baltic States most people embraced a new national mythology that shifted the label 'freedom fighters' from partisans to those who collaborated with the Nazis against the partisans, such as the Latvian SS or Estonian Omakaitse militia. The diversity of opinion about resistance is greatest in Ukraine, but it remains to be seen whether this diversity will produce a lively scholarly debate.

What does the new archival data tell us about the Soviet effort to unleash armed resistance? Given the excellent guerrilla terrain in many Soviet regions, the rich guerrilla heritage, the fervent patriotism of many Soviet people and the irrational policies of the invader, the effort of the Communist Party to ignite and direct armed resistance in 1941 must be judged as inept. However, having initially squandered the great potential for partisan warfare, the Soviet communists did eventually organize the strongest resistance of the Second World War. They did it in the same manner in which they conducted all major political campaigns: with the belief that no price is too high to attain the desired goals. This approach resulted in an enormous loss of Soviet loyalists and apolitical civilians.

The influx of the new archival data does not lead to a definitive conclusion to the earlier debate on the cost/benefit ratio of the resistance,[80] first because the statistics presented by its opponents cannot be used for this purpose. Partisans inflated their success to a degree that makes most numbers in their reports useless for researchers. The Central Partisan Headquarters claimed to have killed 303,950 enemy soldiers and 9,291 policemen, and wounded 79,168 enemy soldiers between 17 April 1943 and 13 January 1944 alone, which is a blatant lie.[81] The Germans claimed to have killed about 300,000 resistance members in the rear area of Army Group Centre alone, but in fact 'these represented cumulative totals of Communist Party functionaries, gypsies, the insane, [and] asocials, but primarily Jews in addition to partisans'.[82] The huge disparity between numbers killed during counterinsurgency operations and weapons captured by the Germans show that a large majority of victims were civilians. Although partisan units reported their own casualties fairly accurately, the Central Partisan Headquarters did not record them; an overall set of statistics on partisan casualties does not therefore exist. In any case, many more Soviet people lost their lives in the process of sweeping Nazi pacification than the number of Axis soldiers and their collaborators whom the partisans killed. Nonetheless, the partisans played an important role in the defeat of the Wehrmacht on the Eastern Front.

The body count excludes many variables relevant to the cost/benefit ratio of guerrilla war. Partisans seriously impeded the delivery of supplies to the German army, sometimes during decisive battles. They sent a large volume of valuable intelligence to the Red Army, which helped it plan its strategy. They undermined the morale of the invaders by demonstrating to them that Soviet political will was unlimited. The partisans paralysed the German civilian administration by terrorizing the petty officials on whom this administration rested; they impeded the economic exploitation of the occupied lands and thus damaged the German military potential. Aleksandr Gogun, a major critic of the partisan movement, believes that the actions of partisans pursuing the destruction of economic assets available to Germany were 'as important as or, probably, even more important than the sabotage of communications',[83] whereas the political component of the partisan war was perhaps even more important than the military one. In the words of John Armstrong, in a totalitarian system, 'the habit of conformity ... rests upon belief in the omnipotence of the regime far more than upon overt use of violence. Along with the omnipotence, goes the myth of the omnipresence of the regime's instruments of control … [The Soviet] *authority never completely vanished from most of the German-occupied territory*. Partisans were, therefore, the "long arm" of the Soviet regime.'[84] They boosted the morale of Soviet loyalists even when the fortunes of the Red Army were at their nadir and they prompted those sitting on the fence to abstain from collaboration, thus dooming German attempts to organize a native anti-communist opposition. Partisans saved many lives by sheltering those chosen for extermination, like Jews and Sinti and Roma and other refugees fleeing from random Nazi violence and the labour draft to Germany. Partisans enlisted thousands of recruits into their units and in this way depleted the workforce available to the Germans. They killed many nationalist guerrillas, thus undermining their ability to resist the Soviet re-occupation and preparing the ground for the restoration of Soviet rule.

Having analyzed the outcome of partisan efforts to disrupt enemy communications, reduce the economic assets of the German administration, undermine morale of German soldiers, supply the Red Army with intelligence, maintain a grip on the population of the occupied lands and recruit it for the resistance, the Stavka ordered partisan units not to cross the front with the approach of the Red Army, but to stay in the enemy rear instead.[85] This shows that the Soviet leaders assessed the overall cost/benefit ratio of partisan warfare as definitely positive, especially because they were concerned mainly with benefits rather than costs. The paramount Stalinist stratagem valid during war and peace – the goal justifies the means – presumed that the stiff price civilians paid for the waging of guerrilla war was unimportant in the context of the bitter fight on the Eastern Front.

Notes

1. Denis Davydov, *In the Service of the Tsar against Napoleon* (London, 1999).
2. Leo Tolstoy, *War and Peace* (New York, 1976), pp. 1114 15.
3. I. Starinov, 'Oshibki partizanskoi voiny', in A. Taras (ed.), *Malaia voina* (Minsk, 2000), p. 168. Zhelezniakov was not a partisan but most Soviets believed he was after a popular song claimed so.
4. Kenneth Slepyan, *Stalin's Guerrillas* (Lawrence, Kan., 2006), p. 16.
5. V. Zolotarev (ed.), *Partizanskoe dvizhenie* (Moscow, 2001), p. 25.
6. V. Zolotarev (ed.), *Russkii arkhiv* (Moscow, 1999), 9:18–20; V. Iampol'skii (ed.), *Organy gosudarstvennoi bezopasnosti SSSR v Velikoi Otechestvennoi voine* (Moscow, 2000), Vol. 2, Book 1:164; Starinov, 'Oshibki,', p. 169.
7. Aleksandr Gogun and Anatolii Kentii (eds), *'Sozdavat' nevynosimye usloviia dlia vraga i vsekh ego posobnikov'* (Kiev, 2006), p. 80; 'GKO postanovliaet', *Voenno-istoricheskii zhurnal*, 3 (1992), 18.
8. Zolotarev (ed.), *Russkii arkhiv*, 9:18-20.
9. Zolotarev (ed.), *Partizanskoe dvizhenie*, p. 42.
10. Zolotarev (ed.), *Russkii arkhiv*, 9:101.
11. *Ibid.*, 9:95; Slepyan, *Stalin's Guerrillas*, p. 112.
12. Zolotarev (ed.), *Russkii arkhiv*, 9:19, 47, 67; A. Mal'gin, L. Kravtsova and L. Sergienko, *Partizanskoe dvizhenie v Krymu* (Simferopol, 2006), p. 83; Aleksandr Gogun, *Stalinskie kommandos: Ukrainskie partizanskie formirovaniia* (Moscow, 2008), pp. 269–75.
13. Iampol'skii, *Organy*, Vol. 2, Book 1:417; Zolotarev (ed.), *Russkii arkhiv*, 9:43, 44.
14. Aleksei Popov, *Diversanty Stalina* (Moscow, 2004), 400.
15. Gogun, *Stalinskie kommandos*, pp. 68–71.
16. Zolotarev (ed.), *Russkii arkhiv*, 9:32.
17. Gogun and Kentii, *'Sozdavat' nevynosimye usloviia'*, pp. 28–30.

18. Zolotarev (ed.), *Russkii arkhiv*, 9:243, 260; *Rossiiskii gosudarstvennyi arkhiv sotsial'no-politicheskoi istorii* (hereafter cited as RGASPI), f. 69, op. 1, d. 392, l. 11; Gogun, *Stalinskie kommandos*, p. 446.
19. A. Fedorov, *Podpol'nyi obkom deistvuet* (Kiev, 1986), p. 17; O.V. Bazhan, S.I. Vlasenko, A.V. Kentii, L.V. Legasova and V.S. Lozitskii (eds), *Partizanskaia voina na Ukraine* (Moscow, 2010), 26.
20. Starinov, 'Oshibki', p. 171; RGASPI, f. 69. op. 1, d. 618, l. 51; Mal'gin, Kravtsova and Sergienko, *Partizanskoe dvizhenie v Krymu*,100.
21. Alexander Statiev, 'The Nature of Anti-Soviet Armed Resistance, 1942–44: the North Caucasus, the Kalmyk Autonomous Republic, and Crimea', *Kritika* 6/2 (2005), 303–10; Mal'gin, Kravtsova and Sergienko, *Partizanskoe dvizhenie v Krymu*, pp. 70–2, 83, 84, 101, 106. In the Fourth and Fifth partisan districts, 120 partisans had been killed by March 1942, whereas 150 starved to death.
22. Anatolii Chaikovskii, 'Pomoshch' sovetskogo tyla v organizatsii partizanskoi bor'by' (PhD Dissertation, Moscow, 1991), p. 492; Zolotarev (ed.), *Russkii arkhiv*, 9:78; Bazhan *et al.*, *Partizanskaia voina na Ukraine*, p. 31.
23. Iampol'skii, *Organy*, Vol. 2, Book 1:139; Chaikovskii, 'Pomoshch' sovetskogo tyla', p. 132.
24. Zolotarev (ed.), *Russkii arkhiv*, 9:18; Gogun, *Stalinskie kommandos*, p. 199.
25. Bazhan *et al.*, *Partizanskaia voina na Ukraine*, pp. 155, 165.
26. RGASPI, f. 69, op. 1, d. 748, ll. 247, 251; Bazhan *et al.*, *Partizanskaia voina na Ukraine*, pp. 144, 145, 156, 157; Erich Haberer, 'German Gendarmes and Belorussian Partisans', in Ben Shepherd and Juliette Pattinson (eds), *War in a Twilight World: Partisan and Anti-partisan Warfare in Eastern Europe, 1939–45* (London, 2010), pp. 117, 119.
27. RGASPI, f. 17, op. 88, d. 481, ll. 184–6; f. 69, op. 1, d. 726, ll. 109, 122, 123, 141; G.A. Shubin, *Iz istorii vsenarodnoi bor'by protiv nemetsko-fashistskikh okkupantov v zapadnykh oblastiakh Belorussii* (Volgograd, 1972), p. 57.
28. Iampol'skii, *Organy*, Vol. 2, Book 1:416.
29. Starinov, 'Oshibki', p. 169.
30. V.A. Smolii and V.S. Lozyts'kyi (eds), *Ukraina partyzans'ka* (Kiev, 2001), p. 244; Zolotarev (ed.), *Russkii arkhiv*, 9:59, 138, 152. The author of this chapter asserts on the basis of personal experience that it takes considerably longer time to learn how to demolish various types of bridges effectively.
31. RGASPI, f. 625, op. 1, d. 12, ll. 277, 277v; Gogun, *Stalinskie kommandos*, pp. 65–6; RGASPI, f. 69, op. 1, d. 725, l. 14; Zolotarev (ed.), *Russkii arkhiv*, 9:194.
32. V.I. Dashichev (ed.), *'Sovershenno sekretno!'* (Moscow, 1967), p. 100; Alexander Dallin, *German Rule in Russia* (London, 1957), p. 452.
33. Matthew Cooper, *The Phantom War* (London, 1979), p. 81.
34. A.I. Barsukov, A.V. Basov, A.S. Orlov, A.A. Paderin, Iu.A. Poliakov, V.A. Pron'ko, O.A. Rzheshevskii and S.A. Tiushkevich (eds), *Velikaia Otechestvennaia voina* (Moscow, 1999), 4:267; A. Prokhorov (ed), *Rossiiskii entsiklopedicheskii slovar'* (Moscow, 2000), 1:144.
35. Zolotarev (ed.), *Russkii arkhiv*, 9:100.
36. RGASPI, f. 17, op. 125, d. 188, l. 17.
37. RGASPI, f. 625, op. 1, d. 7, l. 565.
38. Zolotarev (ed.), *Russkii arkhiv*, 9:114, 115.
39. *Ibid.*, 9:59, 60, 114, 132, 133.
40. Vitalii Perezhogin, 'Iz okruzheniia i plena – v partizany', *Otechestvennaia istoriia*, 3 (2000), 29.
41. Kenneth Slepyan, 'The People's Avengers', in David Stone (ed.), *The Soviet Union at War* (Barnsley, 2010), pp. 170–1.
42. Gogun, *Stalinskie kommandos*, p. 193; Popov, *Diversanty Stalina*, p. 391.
43. Zolotarev (ed.), *Russkii arkhiv*, 9:165, 298, 300.
44. A. Okorokov and S. Drobiazko (eds), *Materialy po istorii russkogo osvoboditel'nogo dvizheniia* (Moscow, 1998), p. 250; Gogun, *Stalinskie kommandos*, p. 269; Wilfried Strik-Strikfeldt, *Protiv Stalina i Gitlera* (Frankfurt/Main, 1975), pp. 281–2.
45. Gogun, *Stalinskie kommandos*, p. 201; Gogun and Kentii, *'Sozdavat' nevynosimye usloviia'*, p. 123; Zolotarev (ed.), *Russkii arkhiv*, 9:316.
46. RGASPI, f. 17, op. 122, d. 66, ll. 9, 13, 15. The emphasis is mine.
47. Gogun, *Stalinskie kommandos*, p. 263.

48. Zarubinsky, for instance, supports his allegation with reference to an SS report on the interrogation of a rank-and-file partisan, whereas Gogun also refers to German reports, the opinions of AK commanders, OUN reports and a publication of a collaborator newspaper – sources of dubious credibility at best. O. Zarubinsky, 'The "Red" partisan movement in Ukraine', *The Journal of Slavic Military Studies*, 9/2 (June 1996), 405; Gogun, *Stalinskie kommandos*, pp. 325–8.

49. Zolotarev (ed.), *Russkii arkhiv*, 9:327; Kenneth Slepyan, 'Partisans, Civilians and the Soviet State', in Ben Shepherd and Juliette Pattinson (eds), *War in a Twilight World*, pp. 36, 43.

50. Zolotarev (ed.), *Russkii arkhiv*, 9:263; Bazhan *et al.*, *Partizanskaia voina na Ukraine*, 76; Iakov Mel'nik, *554 dnia partizanskoi voiny* (Moscow: OAO Moskovskaia tipografiia No. 6, 2006), 16, 20, 26, 31, 92, 121, 130.

51. Zolotarev (ed.), *Russkii arkhiv*, 9:130; RGASPI, f. 69, op. 1, d. 725, l. 2.

52. Zolotarev (ed.), *Russkii arkhiv*, 9:275.

53. A. Kentii and V. Lozyts'kyi (eds), *Vid Polissia do Karpat* (Kiev, 2005), p. 200; Gogun and Kentii, 'Sozdavat' nevynosimye usloviia', pp. 141–79; RGASPI, f. 69, op. 1, d. 748, ll. 80–3, 104; Zolotarev (ed.), *Russkii arkhiv*, 9:151, 159, 275; RGASPI, f. 69, op. 1, d. 747, ll. 48, 49; RGASPI, f. 69, op. 1, d. 180, l. 60.

54. Smolii *et al.* (eds), *Ukraina partyzans'ka*, p. 237; Zolotarev (ed.), *Russkii arkhiv*, 9:117, 120, 371, 377.

55. Gogun, *Stalinskie kommandos*, p. 199.

56. Chaikovskii, 'Pomoshch' sovetskogo tyla', p. 975.

57. Smolii *et al.* (eds), *Ukraina partyzans'ka*, p. 273.

58. RGASPI, f. 69, op. 1, d. 584, l. 40.

59. Gogun, *Stalinskie kommandos*, p. 95; Smolii *et al.* (eds), *Ukraina partyzans'ka*, p. 274.

60. Zolotarev (ed.), *Russkii arkhiv*, 9:116, 137, 141, 174–7, 321–3.

61. *Ibid.*, 9:448.

62. Starinov, 'Oshibki', 173, 174; Zolotarev (ed.), *Russkii arkhiv*, 9:296, 301, 305, 373.

63. Zolotarev (ed.), *Russkii arkhiv*, 9:458, 459; Gogun, *Stalinskie kommandos*, p. 210.

64. John Armstrong (ed.), *Soviet Partisans in World War II* (Madison, Wis., 1964), p. 32.

65. Gogun, *Stalinskie kommandos*, p. 108; Smolii *et al.* (eds), *Ukraina partyzans'ka*, p. 235; Slepyan, 'The People's Avengers', p. 165.

66. Shubin, *Iz istorii vsenarodnoi bor'by*, pp. 267, 274, 281.

67. On partisan actions in the borderlands see Alexander Statiev, 'Was *Smuglianka* a Lunatic or a *Siguranta*'s Agent-Provocateur? Peculiarities of the Soviet Partisan Struggle in the Western Borderlands', *The Journal of Strategic Studies*, 31/5 (October 2008).

68. Gogun, *Stalinskie kommandos*, pp. 119, 140.

69. Timothy Snyder, 'The Causes of Ukrainian-Polish Ethnic Cleansing 1943', *Past and Present*, 179 (2003), 202; Anatolii Rusnachenko, *Narod zburenyi* (Kiev, 2002), p. 176.

70. Gogun, *Stalinskie kommandos*, pp. 145, 289. The cooperation between AK and the Red partisans ended with the beginning of the Warsaw Uprising. This strained relations between the Polish government-in-exile and the Soviet Union, and after that partisans participated in the Soviet crackdown on the AK.

71. P. Sokhan', P. Potichnyj, H. Boriak, Ia. Dashkevych, V. Lozyts'kyi, R. Pyrih, O. Pshennikov, M. Ripetckyj and Iu. Shapoval (eds), *Litopys UPA, Nova Seriia* (Kiev, 1995–2008), 2:303, 11:98; *Tsentral'nyi derzhavnyi arkhiv hromads'kykh ob'iednan' Ukraïny*, f. 1, op. 46, d. 833, l. 474.

72. Statiev, 'Was *Smuglianka* a Lunatic', 756, 761, 765.

73. Zolotarev (ed.), *Russkii arkhiv*, 9: 480, 485; A. Raškevics (eds), *Na pravyi boi, na smertnyi boi* (Riga, 1968); 2:354.

74. Zolotarev (ed.), *Russkii arkhiv*, 9:495; Volodymyr Serhiichuk (ed.), *Desiat' buremnykh lit* (Kiev, 1998), pp. 54–6, 105, 144.

75. Smolii *et al.* (eds), *Ukraina partyzans'ka*, pp. 298–9.

76. P. Pospelov, G. Deborin, G. Zastavenko, G. Lekomtsev, N. Semenov, F. Tamonov, P. Shuktomov and A. Ekshtein (eds), *Istoriia Velikoi Otechestvennoi voiny Sovetskogo Soiuza* (Moscow, 1961–5).

77. For example, Fedorov, *Podpol'nyi obkom deistvuet*; Petr Vershigora, *Reid na San i Vislu* (Moscow, 1960); V. Klokov, *Kovel'skii uzel* (Kiev, 1981); V. Shauro and R. Kriuchok (eds), *Vsenarodnoe partizanskoe dvizhenie v Belorussii* (Minsk, 1967); S. Vaupshasov, *Na trevozhnykh perekrestkakh* (Moscow, 1988).

78. In fact, only one sound book-length study has been published in the post-Soviet era (Gogun, *Stalinskie kommandos*), though several important articles that investigate certain aspects of partisan war have also emerged.

79. V. Perezhogin, *Soldaty partizanskogo fronta* (Moscow, 2001); Leonid Grenkevich, *The Soviet Partisan Movement* (London, 1999); Zolotarev, *Partizanskoe dvizhenie*; Popov, *Diversanty Stalina*.

80. Cooper, *The Phantom War*, pp. 145–7; Armstrong, *Soviet Partisans*, pp. 31–9; Alexander Hill, *The War Behind the Eastern Front* (London, 2005), pp. 170–7.

81. Zolotarev (ed.), *Russkii arkhiv*, 9:458, 459. German records of the casualties inflicted by partisans are scattered, unsystematic and incomplete. According to these records, partisans killed and wounded during the entire war between 54,000 and 57,000 German soldiers, soldiers from countries allied to Germany, armed collaborators and German members of civilian administration in the area of Army Group Centre alone, and until June 1944 alone. Such figures, in other words, exclude the enormous number of casualties this army group suffered during its destruction, in which partisans also participated. Timothy Mulligan, 'Reckoning the Cost of People's War', *Russian History*, 9/1 (1982), 45–7. In addition, partisans also killed an unknown but much smaller number of Russian civilians whom they identified as collaborators.

82. Ben Shepherd, *War in the Wild East* (Cambridge, Mass., 2004), p. 84; Mulligan, 'Reckoning the Cost', 31.

83. Gogun, *Stalinskie kommandos*, p. 192.

84. Armstrong, *Soviet Partisans*, pp. 39–40.

85. Zolotarev (ed.), *Russkii arkhiv*, 9:164.

Guide to Further Reading

Armstrong, John (ed.), *Soviet Partisans in World War II* (Madison, Wis., 1964).

Cooper, Matthew, *The Phantom War* (London, 1979).

Fyodorov, A., *The Underground Committee Carries On* (Moscow, 1952).

Hill, Alexander, *The War behind the Eastern Front* (London, 2005).

Kagan, Jack and Cohen, *Surviving the Holocaust with the Russian Jewish Partisans* (London, 1998).

Levine, Allan, *Fugitives of the Forest* (Toronto, 1998).

Mulligan, Timothy, 'Reckoning the Cost of People's War', *Russian History*, 9/1 (1982).

Obryn'ba, Nikolai, *Red Partisan: The Memoir of a Soviet Resistance Fighter on the Eastern Front* (Washington DC, 2007).

Pell, Joseph and Rosenbaum, Fred, *Taking Risks* (Berkeley, Cal., 2004).

Schulte, Theo, *The German Army and Nazi Policies in Occupied Russia* (New York, 1989).

Shepherd, Ben, *War in the Wild East* (Cambridge, Mass., 2004).

Shepherd, Ben and Pattinson, Juliette (eds), *War in a Twilight World* (New York, 2010), section on the Soviet Union.

Slepyan, Kenneth, 'The Soviet Partisan Movement and the Holocaust', *Holocaust and Genocide Studies*, 14/1 (Spring 2000).

Idem, *Stalin's Guerrillas* (Lawrence, Kan., 2006).

Statiev, Alexander, 'Was *Smuglianka* a lunatic or a *Siguranţa*'s agent-provocateur? Peculiarities of the Soviet partisan struggle in the western borderlands', *The Journal of Strategic Studies*, 31/5 (October 2008).

Zarubinsky, O., 'The "Red" partisan movement in Ukraine', *The Journal of Slavic Military Studies*, 9/2 (June 1996).

Films

Trial of the Road (*Proverka na dorogakh*), directed by Aleksei German (1971).

Come and See (*Idi i smotri*), directed by Elem Klimov (1985).

Okkupatsiia. Misterii, directed by Andrei Kudinenko (2003).

Chapter 11

Yugoslavia

Vjeran Pavlaković

Interwar Yugoslavia, cobbled together in the immediate aftermath of the First World War, disintegrated rapidly after putting up token resistance against invading Axis forces in spring 1941. The Yugoslav state had inherited the legacies of two empires (Austro-Hungarian and Ottoman), three major religions (Roman Catholicism, Eastern Orthodoxy and Islam) and numerous ethno-national identities (Serbs, Croats, Slovenes, Bosniaks, Macedonians, Albanians, Germans, Italians and others), leading to two decades of crisis and instability that were only exacerbated by a royal dictatorship declared by King Alexander Karadjordjević in 1929. Considering that both democratic and authoritarian systems had failed to resolve Yugoslavia's seemingly insurmountable political and socio-economic problems, it is not surprising that a significant number of the country's citizens initially welcomed the new territorial configurations offered by Hitler's new order. However, the traditional South Slavic hatred of foreign occupation and the brutality of the domestic collaborationist regimes produced one of the most successful resistance movements in occupied Europe, the communist-led Partisans, who largely liberated their country without direct intervention from other Allied armies.

The war in Yugoslavia was far from a simple story of resistance and collaboration, fascism and anti-fascism; it was a tragic interethnic civil war, with horrific crimes committed against civilian populations and a spiralling level of violent reprisals and vengeance that continued long after the Second World War officially ended. The rebuilt Yugoslav state that emerged from the ashes of the war, the Socialist Federated Republic of Yugoslavia (SFRY), was founded upon the Partisan victory, infused with the selective memory and myths of the resistance struggle against fascism, and held together by the charismatic leadership of the Partisans' supreme commander, Josip Broz Tito. As Yugoslavia and its socialist self-management model disintegrated in a new wave of interethnic violence and war in the 1990s, the Partisan myths unraveled as independent states emerged that systematically revised the narratives of the Second World War in order to give the new ruling elites political legitimacy. Although varying in degrees from country to country, many former collaborators, war criminals and collaborationist movements have been rehabilitated since 1990, while the anti-fascist movement has been demonized and the values of anti-fascism seriously undermined by the rise of extreme nationalism.

*   *   *

The seeds of interwar Yugoslavia's destruction were sown almost immediately after the new state was declared on 1 December 1918, as rival conceptions of how the country should be organized characterized the political debates right up to the moment Axis forces invaded on 6 April 1941. The northern and western parts of the country (modern-day Slovenia, Croatia, Bosnia-Herzegovina and the Vojvodina region of Serbia) had been under Austro-Hungarian rule, and the intellectuals and elites supporting the Yugoslav idea had envisioned a federal system of equals. Serbia's leaders, however, viewed the Yugoslav project quite differently, especially since Serbia had been on the side of the victorious Allies and had paid a heavy price during the First World War. The Serbs had secured their independence from the Ottoman Empire and subsequently expanded their territory throughout the nineteenth and early twentieth centuries, eventually incorporating what is today Macedonia and Kosovo into the Kingdom of Serbia after the Balkan Wars of 1912–13. Tiny Montenegro, which had also won its independence from the Ottomans by 1878, was annexed along with the former Habsburg lands during Yugoslavia's unification after the end of the First World War. The Serbian elite's conception of the new Yugoslav state, initially named the Kingdom of Serbs, Croats and Slovenes (changed in 1929 to the Kingdom of Yugoslavia), was a centralized and unitary political system under the firm control of Belgrade and the Serbian monarch, King Alexander Karadjordjević.[1] The divisions over the two rival state-building concepts, federalism versus unitarism, paralysed successive governments during the initial parliamentary period (1918–29) and poisoned relations between Serbs and Croats, the two largest ethnic groups in Yugoslavia.[2] This unresolved 'national question' sabotaged all attempts at building a sustainable unified South Slavic state in the twentieth century.

The assassination of the Croatian Peasant Party leader Stjepan Radić, along with several other deputies in the National Assembly in Belgrade in 1928, prompted King Alexander to declare a royal dictatorship the following year in an attempt to restore order in the country. The political repression and continued rejection of Croatian demands only increased hatred of the regime and disappointment in the Yugoslav experiment. Moreover, efforts at imposing a Yugoslav identity on the various ethnic groups only provoked more resistance at the attempted cultural domination. The failure of political leaders to resolve Yugoslavia's 'national question' contributed to the growth of radical movements on both the extreme left and right. The Communist Party of Yugoslavia (KPJ) was formed in 1919, and was quickly banned but survived underground. By the late 1930s it was being slowly reorganized under the leadership of a new general secretary, Josip Broz Tito. The Ustaša (the Croatian word for 'insurgent') movement, formed in exile by Ante Pavelić in 1929, used terrorist methods in their fight for an independent Croatia and turned to Nazi Germany and Fascist Italy for support and ideological inspiration. In 1934, the Ustaše were complicit in King Alexander's assassination in Marseille, and their members in exile were subsequently interned by Mussolini after international pressure. During the regency of Prince Paul (King Alexander's son was not yet of age) and his prime minister

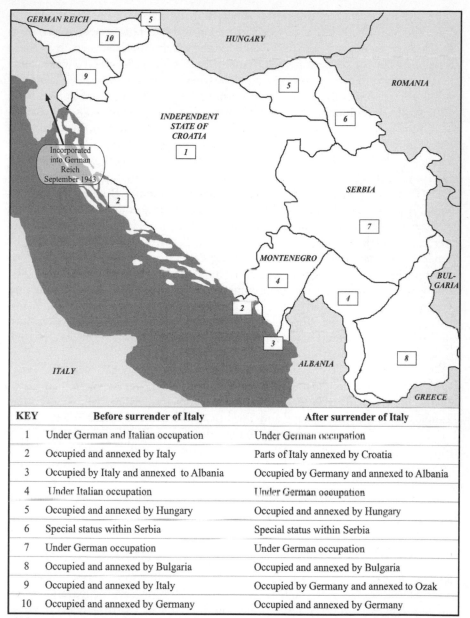

KEY	Before surrender of Italy	After surrender of Italy
1	Under German and Italian occupation	Under German occupation
2	Occupied and annexed by Italy	Parts of Italy annexed by Croatia
3	Occupied by Italy and annexed to Albania	Occupied by Germany and annexed to Albania
4	Under Italian occupation	Under German occupation
5	Occupied and annexed by Hungary	Occupied and annexed by Hungary
6	Special status within Serbia	Special status within Serbia
7	Under German occupation	Under German occupation
8	Occupied and annexed by Bulgaria	Occupied and annexed by Bulgaria
9	Occupied and annexed by Italy	Occupied by Germany and annexed to Ozak
10	Occupied and annexed by Germany	Occupied and annexed by Germany

Administrative boundaries of Axis-occupied Yugoslavia, 1941–5.

Milan Stojadinović, the repression against political opponents of the regime lessened, but a comprehensive political solution seemed out of reach.[3] The increasingly unstable situation in Europe, notably the internationalization of the Spanish Civil War of 1936–9, fed the ranks of both anti-fascists and those who desired an Axis invasion to end Belgrade's rule.

On 26 August 1939, only a few days before the outbreak of the Second World War, Croat and Serb leaders agreed to a compromise. This was the Cvetković-Maček Agreement, or Sporazum, named after Stojadinović's successor, Dragiša Cvetković, and the leader of the Croatian Peasant Party, Vladko Maček, which created an autonomous Croatian unit (Banovina Hrvatska) within the Kingdom of Yugoslavia. But festering national tensions remained; the more radical wing of the Croatian national movement felt that only full independence would satisfy the Croatian need for self-determination, while Serbs demanded their own federal unit and began to mobilize in the Serb-majority regions of Croatia. The internal weaknesses of the state were more than evident to the regent and his government, so when German pressure to join the Axis was applied in the spring of 1941, the Yugoslavs could not remain neutral for long. Prince Paul and his ministers signed the document that bound Yugoslavia to the Tripartite Pact on 25 March 1941, despite domestic disapproval of the Nazi regime.[4] Two days later, a bloodless coup was carried out by pro-British Yugoslav officers, led by General Dušan Simović, who declared King Peter II to be of age. The coup was accompanied by massive street protests in Belgrade that were later interpreted by communist historians as the beginning of the revolution. Although the new government quickly issued statements that all foreign treaties, including Yugoslavia's adherence to the Tripartite Pact, would be respected, Hitler was furious and immediately ordered plans for the invasion of Yugoslavia (Directive No. 25) to be put into motion.

On 6 April 1941, Germany's Operation Punishment began with the bombardment of Belgrade and a multi-pronged invasion of Yugoslavia that consisted mostly of German troops invading from Bulgaria, Romania, Austria and Hungary. The German Second and Twelfth Armies – 24 divisions, together with 1,500 aircraft – were joined by 23 Italian divisions with 670 aircraft attacking from the Italian frontier and Albania, and 5 Hungarian divisions.[5] Yugoslavia's army of thirty divisions, thinly spread out in an attempt to guard all of the frontiers, weakened by the defection of several Croatian units and generally caught unprepared for the invasion, fared poorly against the technically superior Germans. After resisting only twelve days, the Yugoslav Supreme Command capitulated on 17 April. The king and most of the government had already fled into exile. As Jozo Tomasevich noted in his comprehensive study of the partition and occupation of Yugoslavia during the Second World War, neither Germany nor Italy had wanted to break up Yugoslavia or create puppet states, since their interests were to have a compliant ally on the southern flank that would supply the Axis war machine.[6] However, once the invasion had shattered royal Yugoslavia, its neighbours quickly moved in to carve up the territory, either directly annexing or occupying regions that were deemed historically theirs or economically exploitable.[7]

The nature of the foreign occupation had a significant impact on the subsequent development of the resistance movement. For example, Croats in Dalmatia filled the ranks of the Partisans as a result of Italian repression on the coast and occupied islands, while the Albanians of Kosovo welcomed the annexation of their territory to Albania and the end of Serb domination. Nevertheless, the strategies of the Partisans and the unity of the KPJ's leadership around Tito ensured that the Partisan movement spread to all corners of occupied Yugoslavia by the end of the war.

Hungary annexed the Medjimurje and Baranja regions (today part of Croatia), and most of Vojvodina. Bulgaria absorbed a large portion of Macedonia and parts of south-eastern Serbia, while Italian-administered Albania was given most of Kosovo and the western parts of Macedonia. Slovenia was divided between Germany (the northern half including Maribor) and Italy (the southern half around Ljubljana), so the Partisan struggle there was a true liberation war that sought to preserve Slovenian identity in the face of forced Germanization and Italianization. Italy annexed parts of the Dalmatian coast, the area around Kotor Bay and most of the Croatian islands that were not already under Italian control after the First World War. She also stationed occupation forces in Montenegro and the Dalmatian hinterland, areas that were not directly annexed.[8] The Germans occupied Serbia and, after initially collaborating with Milan Aćimović, installed a quisling regime under the command of General Milan Nedić. Although Nedić was completely subservient to the Germans and had little influence over any government policy, he was able to mobilize military units such as the Serbian Volunteer Detachment (which eventually numbered about 12,000 men and was commanded by Dimitrije Ljotić of the fascist Zbor movement), the Serbian State Guard (24,000 men at its peak) and the Četniks of Kosta Milanović Pećanac (a varying force of 3,000–6,000 troops), which were all involved in various war crimes and atrocities.[9]

Hitler's decision to allow Pavelić's Ustaše, many of whom were interned in Italy, to establish the Independent State of Croatia (NDH – Nezavisna Država Hrvatska) on 10 April had the most far-reaching consequences for the development of a resistance movement and for German ability to convince the local population to accept the Nazi new order. Initially the Germans had approached Maček, the Croatian politician with the most legitimacy, to lead an Axis-aligned Croatia, but Maček's pacifism and belief in peasant democracy caused him to reject the offer. Pavelić was thus an unsavoury second choice, and the Ustaša's bloodthirsty reign of terror directed at Serbs, Jews, Roma and all political opponents of the regime resulted in the NDH becoming a hotbed of resistance to the occupiers and domestic collaborators. In fact, most Partisan military actions during the war took place on the territory of the NDH. Pavelić had been forced to relinquish much of the coast to the Italians in the Rome Agreements of 18 May, but had been allowed to annex Bosnia-Herzegovina, which included a large number of Orthodox Serbs. The regime coddled the Catholic Church as well as the Islamic leaders in Zagreb and Sarajevo, but sought to destroy the Serbian Orthodox Church and expel, convert or murder the Serbs who found themselves within the borders of the NDH. As Stevan K. Pavlowitch notes in his overview of the Second World War in Yugoslavia, 'the NDH was hardly independent; it was not a real state, but its leadership was determined it should be purely Croat'.[10]

Out of the NDH's population of just over 6 million, Croats numbered about 3.3 million, while the Serbs made up almost 30 per cent of the total inhabitants, or 1.9 million, who provided a large recruiting base for resistance to the regime.[11]

Shortly after the NDH was proclaimed, the regime enacted a number of racial laws against Serbs, Jews and Roma, followed by both systematic arrests of non-Croats and mass killings of Serbs by so-called 'wild' Ustaše.[12] The NDH soon established a system of concentration camps, the most notorious of which was Jasenovac on the banks of the Sava River.[13] The Germans and Italians divided the NDH into their respective zones of influence with often diametrically opposed interests. Despite its clear links with both fascism and Nazism, and evidence that it certainly lacked most characteristics of a truly independent state, Croatian nationalists in the 1990s sought to rehabilitate the NDH by recasting the Ustaše as anti-communists and Croatian patriots rather than war criminals and fascist collaborators. The brutal methods of the Ustaša dictatorship (all political parties were banned, and Pavelić declared himself *Poglavnik*, or Leader) swelled the ranks of the Partisan movement with Serbs trying to save their lives and Croats horrified at the reign of terror unleashed by the war.

Since the main theatre of Axis operations moved east after Yugoslavia's defeat, the Germans sought to minimize the number of troops they had to station in the region, and therefore relied on various collaborationist forces drawn from the local populations. In Slovenia the anti-communist forces were led by members of the pre-war Slovenian Peoples' Party and organized into units commonly known as the White Guard (Bela garda), though after August 1942 the Italian military command ordered all forces fighting the Partisans to join the Anti-Communist Volunteer Militia (MVAC – Milizia volontaria anticomunista). In Serbia, the Nedić regime had mobilized several of its own units as mentioned above, and cooperated with the nominally anti-fascist Četnik forces that spent the vast majority of time fighting their common enemy, the Partisans. The NDH's regular army, the Home Guard (Domobrani), was supplemented by the Ustaša military units, which were the most notorious enforcers of the regime and responsible for numerous atrocities against civilians and perceived enemies of the state. The German minority in the NDH, the Volksdeutsche, were given special treatment in the state apparatus and formed their own military units, such as the SS Prinz Eugen Division. Četnik forces in the NDH, especially in Dalmatia and the Lika region, openly collaborated with the Italian troops from the very beginning of the war, as was the case in occupied Montenegro. In Kosovo and the Albanian areas of Macedonia, Albanians carried out reprisals against the Serb population, many of whom had come as colonists during the interwar period, resulting in the mass expulsion of tens of thousands of civilians.[14] The Balli Kombëtar, an Albanian nationalist movement that initially resisted the Italian occupation, collaborated with the Germans and contributed to the formation of the SS Skanderbeg Division in 1944 in order to fight the Partisans, who were perceived to be restoring Serb dominance over the region. By the end of 1941, Axis forces in Yugoslavia numbered approximately 510,000 soldiers

(120,000 Germans, 280,000 Italians, 70,000 Bulgarians and 40,000 Hungarians), supported by 150,000 soldiers in collaborationist units.[15] Except for the final year of the war, the Axis forces had considerably greater numerical superiority than the resistance movement. The movement nevertheless steadily grew in strength, skill and equipment despite the concerted effort to crush it.

* * *

On the one hand, the considerable weaknesses of the interwar Yugoslav state and the divisions caused by the 'national question' allowed the various occupying forces to draw from a willing pool of collaborators who supported the new order in the Balkans. On the other hand, the peoples of Yugoslavia, and in particular the Serbs and Montenegrins, had a long history of fighting against foreign occupiers. Due to the rapid invasion of Yugoslavia and subsequent operations in Greece and the Soviet Union, many Yugoslav army officers and soldiers were not captured after Yugoslavia's defeat.[16] One group of those officers, led by Dragoljub 'Draža' Mihailović, began to gather in the village of Ravna Gora in central Serbia. Mihailović, who remained loyal to the king and government-in-exile located in London, organized his Četnik movement with the goal of rising against the occupiers when the expected Allied victory would be close at hand. He reached out to other Četnik groups in Serbia and the NDH and was quickly appointed Defence Minister by the exiled government. On 15 November 1941, the BBC announced that Mihailović was leading 'the first resistance in occupied Europe'.[17] While legends of his resistance movement spread in the West, his actual strategy was one of passivity and waiting for the Allied invasion. Horrific reprisals for attacks against German soldiers, such as the massacre of about 5,000 people in the Serbian towns of Kragujevac and Kraljevo in October, convinced Mihailović that direct attacks would threaten the biological survival of the Serbian people, especially considering the enormity of the crimes being committed against Serbs in the neighbouring NDH.[18]

Although Mihailović's Četniks were politically on the side of the Allies, hoped for an eventual Allied victory and rescued several hundred downed Allied pilots who had parachuted over Serbia, they increasingly compromised themselves over the course of the war by not attacking the occupying forces and in many cases directly collaborating with them in operations against the Partisans. According to Tomasevich, the Četniks engaged in only a few sporadic clashes with the Germans or Ustaša forces in the summer of 1941, which cannot be considered the beginning of true resistance. It was only in September that some Četnik units began fighting the occupying troops, alone or in conjunction with the Partisans, although this cooperation, as will be seen below, ended quickly.[19] It should be emphasized at this point that, unlike the Ustaše or Partisans, the various Četniks units were never firmly under one central command, even though ultimately Mihailović did have the authority of the government-in-exile behind him and was certainly aware of the activities of most Četnik formations operating in the region.

The Četniks had historically served as irregular troops alongside Serbian armies, and were ideal guerrilla fighters thanks to the support of the local population in Serbia's rural interior.[20] However, they represented a return to the old system – a centralized state dominated by the Serbian dynasty and the Serbian Orthodox Church. In fact, during the course of the war plans for a 'Greater Serbia' were circulated in which the other peoples of Yugoslavia would have even less territory than they had been allocated during the first Yugoslav experiment from 1918–41. Moreover, Četniks in the Bosnia-Herzegovinian part of the NDH and the Serb-populated Dalmatian hinterland began a campaign of mass murder and terror against Muslim and Croat populations in revenge for Ustaša crimes. The spiral of violence, vengeance and reprisal killings turned the NDH into a multi-sided battlefield and a bloody civil war within a war of occupiers and resistance. The Italian commanders in the NDH realized the advantage of working with the Četnik units that sprang up to resist Ustaša attacks, and by the late summer of 1941 there was open collaboration between Četnik leaders such as Momčilo Djuić from Knin and the Italian Second Army.[21] The legacy of Četnik crimes and open collaboration with fascist forces for most of the war make the legal rehabilitation of the Četnik movement in Serbia since 2010 deeply problematic, to say the least. This rehabilitation is related to attempts by Yugoslav successor states to come to terms with the past, and is even more difficult to accept when one considers that paramilitary groups adopting Četnik symbols and ideology committed atrocities against Croats and Bosnian Muslims in the wars of the 1990s.

Whereas the Četnik resistance against the Axis occupation has been exposed in the historiography as having been minimal at best, and mostly a product of wartime (and post-war Serbian émigré) propaganda, the communist-led Partisan movement either initiated, or more often co-opted, spontaneous mass uprisings throughout occupied Yugoslavia. The Partisans developed into a formidable army that was able to consolidate power in the closing phases of the war. Having been decimated by aborted revolutionary uprisings in the 1920s and police repression in the 1930s, the Communist Party of Yugoslavia (KPJ) could claim about 6,600 Party members and another 18,000 members in the Young Communist League of Yugoslavia (SKOJ – Savez komunističke omladine Jugoslavije) before the Axis invasion.[22] The Party itself was nearly disbanded and much of the leadership disappeared during Stalin's purges in the Soviet Union, but the emergence of a new general secretary, Josip Broz Tito, led to the KPJ's reorganization in the years immediately before the war. Tito came from a small village in Croatia near the Slovenian border, had fought in the Austro-Hungarian army on the Eastern Front and had become an efficient Comintern agent after many years spent in the Soviet Union and working within Yugoslavia. Although he was effectively running the KPJ from 1937 onward, when his predecessor Milan Gorkić was removed due to a debacle concerning the transportation of Yugoslav volunteers to the Spanish Civil War, Tito officially became General Secretary in 1939. He eliminated factionalism in the party and gathered a cadre of dedicated communist activists who were fiercely loyal to him and who would prove pivotal in transforming the underground organization into a successful guerrilla army.

Although, following the signing of the Ribbentrop-Molotov Agreement, the KPJ heeded Moscow's orders regarding its position towards Nazi Germany, Yugoslav Communists had from the outbreak of war in 1939 been instructing their cadres to gain military training and stockpile weapons. On 10 April 1941, the same day the Ustaše announced the founding of the NDH, the Central Committee met in Zagreb and established a Military Committee with Tito as its head. That said, there were no calls for resistance against the Axis invaders. This lack of immediate action was subsequently used to question the KPJ's 'true' anti-fascism, especially in Croatia, since the first organized Communist resistance took place only after Hitler's invasion of the Soviet Union in June.[23] However, it should be noted that the KPJ was still developing its military strategy in this early phase and lacked the manpower to mount any effective actions in the chaotic weeks following the attacks that destroyed royal Yugoslavia.[24] Tito and the Central Committee soon moved to Belgrade, concluding that it would be easier to lead operations from Serbia rather than under heavy Ustaša surveillance in Zagreb.

The German attack against the Soviet Union on 22 June allowed the KPJ to abandon its passive position. News of the invasion served as the spark for the formation of the first Partisan unit in Croatia, in a forest near the industrial town of Sisak.[25] Led by Vladimir Janjić-Capo and Marijan Cvetković, this unit sabotaged the important railway nearby. This constituted the first act of armed anti-fascist resistance in Croatia.[26] The initial group of about fifteen Partisans quickly grew to seventy-seven members, mostly Croats, and throughout 1941 they operated out of the Brezovica forest, where they are commemorated to this day. On 27 June the Military Committee was transformed into the General Staff of the People's Liberation Partisan Detachments of Yugoslavia (Glavni štab narod-nooslobodilačkih partizanskih odreda Jugoslavije),[27] and several days later, on 4 July, the Central Committee of the KPJ issued a call for a general uprising throughout occupied Yugoslavia.[28]

Although the KPJ's cadres sprang into action and began sabotage operations and sporadic attacks against the occupiers, the events that followed departed radically from the revolutionary script imagined by the Communists and subsequently rewritten in post-war historiography. Namely, the KPJ had envisioned a mostly urban guerrilla movement that would capture the cities in anticipation of a rapid victory by the Soviet Union. The expected arrival of the Red Army never materialized, as the summer of 1941 only yielded news of crushing defeats at the hands of the Wehrmacht. But massive uprisings did take place throughout occupied Yugoslavia, particularly in the Serb-populated regions of Croatia and western Bosnia-Herzegovina. Although Ustaše apologists argue that the repressive measures were justified because Serbs were rebelling against the state, there is evidence that mass atrocities against Serb civilians in Glina, Veljun, Gudovac and other places in the regions of Lika, Kordun, and Banija took place in the spring of 1941, before any organized uprisings led by Communists or Četniks had taken place.[29] The uprisings took the form of classic peasant rebellions that lacked an ideological foundation. Although the KPJ later attributed these uprisings to local Communist organizations, research in the last twenty years has confirmed that they were fuelled by villagers trying to survive the onslaught of either the Axis occupiers or, more often, domestic collaborators.

The uprising in Croatia and Bosnia-Herzegovina on 27 July is illustrative of the complexity and fluid nature of the insurgents in the early phases of resistance. Serb villagers in Srb and in Drvar organized a massive uprising, nominally under the command of a local KPJ cell, attacking all symbols of the NDH regime and ambushing Ustaša and Domobrani forces sent to restore order.[30] In reality, the Communists were few in number, while a significant number of the rebels fell under the influence of Četniks led by local pre-war politicians who promoted a Greater Serbian agenda and who had been spreading anti-Croat propaganda since the Cvetković-Maček Agreement of 1939. Horrific reprisal attacks by the Serb rebels against the few Croat and Muslim settlements in the region accompanied the uprising, and included the brutal murders of Catholic pilgrims and clergy as well as the destruction of the towns of Boričevac and Kulen Vakuf in August and September. As noted by Marko Attila Hoare in his account of the 27 July uprising, 'although the communists at its head spoke with the rhetoric of internationalism, many of the rebel leaders and troops it encompassed were Serb-nationalist in orientation'.[31] In fact, the insurgents took advantage of the weak Communist influence to come to a ceasefire agreement with Italian commanders shortly after the uprising (in the village of Otrić on 11 August 1941), and for the rest of the war the Partisans fought desperately to wrest the local population from the control of the Četnik forces. In other parts of Bosnia-Herzegovina and Serbia, Serb rebel groups often fluctuated between fighting for the Četniks or for the Partisans, switching sides at various times in the war more often for opportunistic rather than ideological reasons.[32]

Each republic in the SFRY celebrated the beginning of their armed uprising as one of the most important holidays and symbols of Brotherhood and Unity. The chronology of uprisings began with 7 July (Serbia), 13 July (Montenegro), 22 July (Slovenia), 27 July (Croatia and Bosnia-Herzegovina) and ended with 11 October (Macedonia). As demonstrated with the case of Croatia and Bosnia-Herzegovina, not all of the uprisings can be attributed exclusively to the KPJ, but the Communists were effective in quickly shifting their tactics and appropriating the often spontaneous peasant rebellions for their own goal of communist revolution. At this early stage Yugoslav veterans from the Spanish Civil War played an important role in organizing the peasants hiding in the woods into legitimate fighting units. Nearly 1,700 Yugoslavs had fought with the Republic's International Brigades in Spain, where they had suffered heavy casualties but gained valuable military experience.[33] Although guerrilla warfare was not widely practised in the Spanish conflict, many veterans, known as Španci, had received training as officers, commanded considerable moral authority as revolutionaries and had forged an unbreakable discipline and loyalty to the party while surviving in French internment camps after the Republic's fall in 1939. Tito ordered an operation to smuggle the imprisoned Španci back into Yugoslavia, and then dispersed them throughout the country to take command of the nascent Partisan units. These veterans were dispatched in particular to regions where interethnic violence had destroyed relations between Serbs, Croats and Muslims.[34] For example, Marko Orešković, a Croat veteran of the Spanish Civil War, was sent to the Lika and Bosanska Krajina regions to convince the Serb rebels not to allow the Ustaša atrocities to provoke them into collective revenge against the Croat population, but instead to develop the Partisans as a multinational resistance movement.

The core of the Partisan military forces consisted of detachments (*odredi*), which were tied to a region and often carried the names of the local areas where they were formed. They usually numbered about 100 soldiers, but could have as many as 1,000 fighters, divided into smaller units of 20 to 50 Partisans.[35] Although some units initially carried the name guerrillas (*gerilci*), the name was quickly changed to Partisans (*partizani*). Tito's orders issued on 10 August 1941 were specific as to how the Partisans must represent themselves to the outside world: 'Partisan detachments are named "national-liberation" because they do not belong to any political party or group, not even the Communist Party, regardless of the fact that Communists are fighting in the front lines.'[36] Even though the Partisans sought to create a broad People's Liberation Front movement that included anti-fascists from across the political spectrum, and furthermore incorporated (and amnestied) individuals who defected from collaborationist units such as the Četniks and Domobrani, the KPJ had absolute control over all Partisan armed forces from the beginning. When joining a Partisan detachment, new recruits had to take the following oath:

> We, the people's Partisans of Yugoslavia, armed ourselves to fight mercilessly against the bloodthirsty enemies who conquered our country and now exterminate our peoples. In the name of freedom and justice, we swear to fight with discipline, persistently and fearlessly without sparing our blood or our lives, until we completely destroy the fascist conquerors and all of the domestic traitors.[37]

The detachments were the easiest way to mobilize fighters in the early days of the war, but eventually the Partisans created larger units as well as command structures modelled on regular armies in order to wage the 'people's uprising' called for by the KPJ more effectively.

In mid-September 1941, Tito and the General Staff moved out of Belgrade and into western Serbia, where the Partisan movement was gaining strength. On 26 September, Tito held a meeting in the village of Stolice near Krupanj. He renamed the central command the supreme staff and assigned general staffs for each future republic, which would coordinate military operations based on regional conditions. The red star with a hammer and sickle was adopted as part of the uniform, along with the tri-horned hat (as used in the Spanish Civil War) and orders that national symbols (for example, the Croatian or Serbian tricolour flag) would be used by units mobilized in each republic. As described in an SFRY-era volume on the Partisan movement,

> detachments usually controlled two or three districts. Their organizational structure was composed of battalions, sometimes companies but seldom of only platoons. Political commissars were introduced in all units, and they were equally responsible, along with the commanders, for directing and controlling the units as well as for politically educating the soldiers. Military units also featured cells of the Party organization ... which were of great help to the leaders of the unit, particularly in the execution of combat missions, strengthening discipline, and in political work with the population.[38]

It was increasingly clear that Tito's Partisans were seeking to do more than expel the occupiers and restore the old regime; they wanted power and to carry out a communist revolution, which would quickly lead to open conflict with the other potential resistance movement, the Četniks.

As the mass uprisings and reprisal killings spread throughout the territory of the NDH in the summer and early autumn of 1941, the situation in Montenegro and Serbia developed quite differently. In the rugged mountains of Montenegro, an insurgency against the Italian occupiers yielded wide swathes of liberated territory. The Communist leadership in Montenegro, including one of Tito's closest associates, Milovan Djilas, tried immediately to implement a full-scale revolution and the accompanying Red Terror against suspected 'kulaks' and other class enemies.[39] The premature revolution divided Montenegrin society, which was still based on clan loyalties and tight-knit communities. Nationalists loyal to the pre-1918 royal family clashed with the overzealous Communists, and a vigorous offensive by the Italians – accompanied by Muslim, Albanian and eventually Četnik auxiliaries – in the winter of 1941 restored some semblance of control over the region. Djilas was reprimanded for his 'leftist errors' and the Partisans drew the lesson that, at this stage of the war, it was important to maintain support from across the political spectrum under the umbrella of the People's Liberation Front – even as the foundations for a future communist state were being built in the People's Liberation Committees established in all liberated territories.

In Serbia, the war against the occupiers also rapidly transformed into a civil war that is still referred to as the 'fratricidal war' (*bratoubilački rat*). Tito had been aware of the existence of Mihailović's Četniks and arranged a meeting with the Četnik leader on 19 September, even before the meeting in Stolice, to negotiate some kind of joint strategy against the Axis forces. Both Tito and Mihailović had an interest in unifying their movements – the Partisans wanted to create a resistance movement that was as broad as possible, and the government in exile had ordered Mihailović to work with anyone fighting the Axis – but neither leader could allow themselves to give up command. Despite generally agreeing to cooperate in resisting the Germans, no official strategy was developed since ultimately 'the different concepts of resistance were irreconcilable'.[40]

While the Partisans captured the town of Užice with its important armaments factory on 24 September, the Četniks increasingly began to weigh up options other than resistance. According to Tomasevich, the Četniks of Draža Mihailović were in fact drawn into the uprising only because they could not stand by and permit the leadership of the mobilized Serbian population to fall completely into the hands of the Communists; they did not want the administration in liberated parts of the country to become exclusively Communist controlled, and they were afraid of Communist terror in liberated areas and wanted to prevent it. But Mihailović never became fully committed to the uprising nor, as we shall see, did he stay with it for long.[41]

Tito and Mihailović met unsuccessfully for a second time on 27 October between Ravna Gora and Užice, but differences of opinion and disagreements had already led to clashes between Partisan and Četnik forces. In early November this escalated into open warfare when the Četniks tried to overrun Užice.

The Partisan-Četnik negotiations and subsequent conflict were soon to be overshadowed by a German offensive that had begun in late September against 'communist bandits' in Serbia, which in communist historiography came to be known as the First Enemy Offensive (out of a total of seven 'Enemy Offensives' during the war). Mihailović, concluding that Tito was a Soviet agent and that the Partisans represented the greatest threat to the post-war political situation, met with German representatives in the village of Divci on 11 November to try and come to some kind of arrangement that would spare the Četniks from retaliatory German attacks.[42] Although the Germans rejected any kind of working relationship with the Četniks – they had in fact demanded Mihailović's surrender – from this moment onward the Četniks turned away almost entirely from any kind of resistance and focused their manpower against their main enemies, the Partisans. On 29 November, the Partisan defence of Užice collapsed and Tito and the supreme staff fled into the Sandžak region between Serbia and Montenegro. The Četnik forces that had not been directly collaborating with the Nedić regime were also routed, and Mihailović was forced into hiding in Montenegro while most of his troops dispersed. Former Partisan commander Vladimir Velebit, reflecting on the initial insurgency in Serbia, characterized it as a typical 'peasant uprising' that 'flares up quickly but is equally rapidly extinguished. It grows effectively when the going is good and when there are successes, but as soon as the uprising experiences its first defeats the mood wears thin and desertions soon follow.'[43] While Serbia had been the heart of the resistance movement in the summer of 1941, from the end of 1941 until the autumn of 1944 the main theatre of resistance operations shifted to the west as the Partisan movement gained strength and survived a series of relentless attacks.

The experiences of the fledgling Partisan forces in 1941 convinced Tito that a new kind of unit needed developing if the resistance movement wanted effectively to counter the numerical and technical advantages of the Axis forces and domestic collaborators. On 21 December in Rudo, near the border of Serbia and Bosnia-Herzegovina, Tito organized the First Proletarian Brigade, commanded by Spanish Civil War veteran Koča Popović. It served as a mobile shock unit not tied to a specific area like the other Partisan detachments.[44] By the end of 1941, the Partisans could field about 80,000 individual fighters organized into 51 detachments, 29 independent battalions, 1 brigade, and a number of platoons, against enemy forces estimated to be 8 times more numerous.[45]

A debate that inevitably permeates any historical discussion in the former Yugoslavia is the question of the ethnic component of the resistance movement. During the SFRY, and especially in the decade leading up to the bloody wars of socialist Yugoslavia's dissolution, nationalist Serb circles perpetuated the myth that Serbs made up the overwhelming majority of victims and resistance fighters during the Second World War. This myth is still part of the political discourse in the region.[46] It is true that during the first year of the uprising, the majority of Partisans were Serbs, especially in Croatia where the Serb population was faced with extermination at the hands of the state; by the end of 1941 Serbs constituted 77 per cent of the Partisan units in Croatia.[47] However, the extinguishing of the uprising in Serbia after 1941 and the steady increase in the number of Croats joining the Partisans means that, overall, Croats contributed to about 22 per cent of the operative strength during the course of the war, even though they comprised 16 per cent of the total population of Yugoslavia.[48] The key to the Partisans' eventual success was their commitment to being a multiethnic resistance movement in the midst of a brutal internecine struggle.

*   *   *

After the initial mass uprisings of the summer of 1941 and the subsequent defeats in Serbia and Montenegro in the autumn, Tito and his Partisans had to find a way to protect the constantly moving supreme staff from relentless Axis attacks, as well as establish the foundation of revolutionary governments in the territories that had been liberated. The collapse of the Užice Republic and the supreme staff's retreat into Bosnia-Herzegovina made it clear that larger and more manoeuvrable Partisan units were necessary, so in addition to the First Proletarian Brigade, 5 more brigades of 850–1,200 fighters were organized in the first six months of 1942 (3 Montenegrin, 1 Bosnian-Herzegovinian and 1 Serbian). As the fighting shifted to the western regions of Yugoslavia, the numbers of units in those republics increased dramatically. By December 1942, there were 18 Croatian, 10 Bosnian-Herzegovinian, 4 Slovenian and 3 Montenegrin brigades and 1 Serbian brigade operating throughout Yugoslavia.[49] In addition to the brigades, Partisan forces included 36 detachments and 45 independent battalions. In total, the Partisans could count an estimated 150,000 soldiers arrayed against approximately 930,000 Axis troops and domestic collaborators by the end of 1942.[50]

The Partisans had been able to increase their numbers steadily despite the difficult conditions, heavy losses and continued numerical superiority of their enemies because of their willingness to provoke enemy retaliation. While the Četniks had opted for either passivity or open collaboration, partly to spare the civilian population from reprisal killings, the Partisans realized that attacks against civilians provided them with a constant supply of new recruits of survivors who had fled into the forests and hills. A SFRY-era military encyclopedia explains that by

> choosing a strategy of Partisan warfare, the military-political leadership of the insurgency (the Central Committee of the KPJ and the Supreme Staff) were aware that the Partisan war must be, first of all, an offensive, active form of warfare, that strategic initiative cannot be lost, and that the Partisans must always have the freedom to choose the field of battle.[51]

The rugged mountains of Bosnia-Herzegovina, Montenegro and parts of Croatia were ideal for guerrilla warfare, and pockets of liberated territories sprang up throughout Yugoslavia. In the cities, Communist cells that had suffered heavy losses in the first months of the Axis takeover (especially in Croatia) recovered and carried out important spying missions, sabotaged German and Italian transportation and communication networks, published propaganda material and recruited young people to join the resistance movement gaining strength in the countryside.

Equipment and weapons were constantly lacking in the first years of the resistance. The insurgents in 1941 had fought with farming tools and crude firearms, and the loss of the Užice armament factory meant that the Partisans often relied on captured weapons prior to receiving steadier supplies from the Allies. Photos of the early detachments show Partisans wielding a motley collection of weapons and a patchwork of uniforms and gear, often taken from dead or captured enemy soldiers. In the NDH, the Domobrani units (the regular army) were known to surrender on multiple occasions and hand over their weapons and equipment to the Partisans, unlike the more fanatical and disciplined Ustaša militia.[52]

In early 1942, Tito renamed the command structure the supreme staff of the People's Liberation Partisan and Volunteer Army of Yugoslavia (Vrhovni štab Narodnooslobodilačke partizanske i dobrovoljačke vojske Jugoslavije), and ordered the establishment of military organs of government behind the front lines. These special units were charged with 'housing and supplying units, mobilizing local populations, commanding military workshops and storage facilities, organizing medical units and Partisan field hospitals, regulating the transport of troops and materials, ensuring peace and order in the liberated territories, protecting the political organs of the revolutionary government, organizing the intelligence services, and waging a war against spies and collaborators'.[53] The latter activities increased as the war gradually turned in favour of the Partisans and they liberated more territory. As will be discussed below, it was the revolutionary struggle for power and the harsh war unleashed against real or perceived class enemies that transformed the heroic anti-fascist struggle into a brutal post-war Stalinist-style dictatorship.

In addition to the successful use of guerrilla tactics, the Partisans offered a political programme that offered the promise of a new Yugoslav society infused with the utopian visions of communist ideology. In contrast, the Četnik movement fought for a return to the pre-war political system, only this time more centralized than before. It also fought, according to documents and publications issued during the war years, for the goal of, essentially, creating an ethnically homogeneous Greater Serbia. This limited support for the Četniks among non-Serbs.[54] The Ustaše were equally exclusive in their nationalist objectives; the NDH was envisaged as a state cleansed of Serbs, Jews, Roma and Croats who did not support the regime, the latter group growing larger as the true nature of Pavelić's dictatorship became apparent. The KPJ, meanwhile, offered the only true multinational option in the maelstrom of interethnic violence. The Partisan struggle had three characteristics that were present throughout the war, and at times one factor had precedence over the other:

- A national liberation war in the sense of anti-fascist resistance to defeat the occupiers and their domestic allies;
- A national liberation war in the sense of resolving Yugoslavia's 'national question';
- And, a socialist revolutionary war intended to overthrow the pre-war system.

One of the greatest appeals of the KPJ's platform was its promise of a federal Yugoslav state and equality among the nations, including those national groups who had not been among the titular nations in the Kingdom of Serbs, Croats and Slovenes – Macedonians, Montenegrins, Muslims and Albanians. Although the Comintern policy on Yugoslavia since the 1920s had shifted away from advocating the break-up of the country, the national question was identified as a central issue that could be used to win support. In 1937, the Communist Parties of Croatia (KPH – Komunistička partija Hrvatske) and Slovenia (KPS – Komunistička partija Slovenije) were established as proof that the KPJ was just as committed to opposing Greater Serbian chauvinism as it was to opposing capitalist exploitation.[55]

The establishment of main staffs in each future republic and the use of national flags, symbols and heroes in Partisan units also indicated that the leadership of the KPJ was conscious of the importance of the 'national question' both to the anti-fascist struggle and to the post-war state it intended to create. In the first years of the war, the main staffs operated with considerable independence and often with national goals in mind, especially when the supreme staff was unable to exert true control over the entire Yugoslav territory. Despite the formal federal structure, ultimate power was always centralized in the hands of Tito and the Central Committee of the KPJ.[56] For example, when Tito deemed that the Croatian Partisan leadership was acting too independently, he replaced the commander of the Croatian main staff, Ivan Rukavina, in July 1943, and its political commissar, Vladimir Bakarić, in November of the same year.[57]

The revolutionary aspects of the People's Liberation Movement were often minimized, either to appeal to a broader spectrum of possible supporters in Yugoslavia or because of pressure from the Allies, but from early on it was evident that the resistance movement promised a profound social transformation. A traditional patriarchal system was the norm in most parts of Yugoslavia, which was an overwhelmingly rural country when the war began. The KPJ, however, sought to include women in the political arena, and in 1942 established the Women's Anti-fascist Front (AFŽ – Antifašistički front žena) which promised their social emancipation. About 100,000 women were active in the People's Liberation Struggle, of whom 25,000 lost their lives, 90 were awarded the honour of People's Hero and about 2,000 were officers by the end of the war.[58] In the new nationalist discourse in the 1990s in Croatia and other former Yugoslav republics, women were expected to return to their traditional gender roles as mothers and homemakers, while female Partisans were demonized as hysterical murderers poisoned by communism.[59]

As the Partisans expanded their resistance operations (as well as continuing battles against the Četniks, their primary domestic enemy), reorganized their forces and recruited volunteers from all ethnic groups, the Germans realized that neither domestic collaborators nor Italian occupation troops could stabilize the region enough to protect German economic and communication interests in Yugoslavia. The lower-quality troops used only for occupation and pacification were bolstered by reinforcements intent on carrying out offensive operations, while the German command negotiated with the Ustaša regime regarding relations between the NDH armed forces and the Wehrmacht. The 7th SS Volunteer Mountain Division Prinz Eugen became active, after initial low numbers of volunteers, in March 1942, and was used extensively in anti-Partisan operations.

In January 1942, German units backed by Italians and Ustaše attacked the Partisans in eastern Bosnia-Herzegovina (known as the Second Enemy Offensive), forcing the supreme staff to retreat south and establish its headquarters in the town of Foča.[60] On 1 March 1942 Tito formed the Second Proletarian Brigade, immediately prior to another enemy offensive (the Third, which lasted from March until June) which pressured Partisan forces in eastern Bosnia, the Sandžak and northern Montenegro. Again, Ustaša forces (including the infamous Black Legion), Domobrani, Italian troops and Četniks assisted the Germans in an attempt to encircle and destroy the main body of the Partisan forces.[61] Although they suffered heavy losses, the Partisans were once more able to escape annihilation. Later in the summer of 1942, another large offensive surrounded Partisan forces and civilians near the Kozara Mountain in northern Bosnia-Herzegovina, resulting in 12,000 insurgent and civilian casualties and thousands of prisoners, many of whom were sent to the Jasenovac concentration camp or executed soon after being captured.[62] While these battles were, strictly speaking, defeats for the Partisan forces, the fact that the main fighting force and the supreme staff evaded destruction meant they were victories in the long term, as the resilient movement could recruit from an increasingly broad base of supporters. Moreover, Axis operations had pushed the supreme staff and the main Partisan shock troops into western Bosnia-Herzegovina, where they were able to link up with Croatian Partisans. The results of the year's operations convinced the German command in Zagreb to obtain full control over Croatian military forces and military operations in the German zone of the NDH, eroding even more of the little 'independence' the Ustaša state supposedly had.

The struggle for control in Yugoslavia was not only being waged on the ground, but also lay in winning support from the Western Allies. As mentioned previously, Mihailović was considered by the Yugoslav government-in-exile to be leading the resistance movement, a myth that was perpetuated by the Western media.[63] British agents had been sent to both the Četniks and the Partisans in 1941 in order to help coordinate their attacks against the Germans. As relations deteriorated and the situation grew increasingly chaotic, Britain's Special Operations Executive decided to continue supplying Mihailović, who was in contact with them through a radio transmitter, even though it was becoming evident that the Četniks were not engaged in resistance activities at all.[64] In early 1942, the Partisans were still wary of the British, and they still believed that Soviet supplies and help were going to arrive at any moment; in reality, the Soviets did not send a mission to the Partisans until 23 February 1944.[65] In the summer of 1942 the Partisans publicly labelled Mihailović a traitor, which added to British doubts about the level of Četnik actions against the occupiers.

In an attempt to gain legitimacy, Tito and the Partisan command organized the first meeting of the Anti-fascist Council of the People's Liberation of Yugoslavia (AVNOJ – Antifašističko vijeće narodnog oslobodjenja Jugoslavije) in the town of Bihać in north-western Bosnia-Herzegovina on 26–7 November 1942. The main force of the Partisans had completed a 'long march' through Bosnia-Herzegovina and had been able to gain many new fighters, but the AVNOJ session created an umbrella organization for all of the liberation councils administering occupied territory. The slogan 'Death to fascism – freedom to the people' was officially adopted, and delegates (including non-Communists) from across Yugoslavia laid out an initial framework, albeit hazy, for the future political structure of the country. In November, Tito had also ordered the creation of larger tactical and operational units, namely divisions (numbering between 2,500 and 4,000 soldiers) and corps (consisting of 2 to 4 divisions and auxiliary units).[66] This reorganization enabled the main staffs to issue commands at the corps level without having to contact individual units, thus simplifying the command structure.

While the main theatre of operations in 1942 was centred on the territories encompassed by the NDH, parts of Montenegro and the Sandžak, the Partisan movement simultaneously developed elsewhere. In Slovenia, the Partisans were able to create a truly broad Liberation Front (Osvobodilna fronta) including several pre-war organizations, because German and Italian annexation of Slovenia and the accompanying legal system threatened the very existence of the Slovenes as a nation. Slovene Partisans maintained communications with the supreme staff and other units, but for the most part the course of events unfolded separately from other regions. In contrast to Slovenia, large-scale Partisan operations developed slowly in Macedonia and Kosovo, especially since in the latter province many Albanians perceived Italian rule as liberation from Serbian oppression.[67] Macedonia, which featured favourable terrain for guerrilla-style warfare and an unresolved national question, remained out of KPJ hands until 1943, because the Bulgarian authorities had effectively infiltrated the Communist organization in the area. It was the organizational skills of Montenegrin Communist Svetozar Vukmanović-Tempo and the changing situation later in the war that allowed the Partisan struggle to develop more broadly in Macedonia.[68]

The year 1943 represented a big turning point in the war, not only because of the survival of the Partisan forces after two major offensives but also because the Allies finally switched their support to Tito's troops, setting the course for the eventual victory of the Communist-led People's Liberation Movement. Between January and April 1943, the Axis forces carried out Operation Weiss (the Fourth Enemy Offensive in the Yugoslav historiography) in three phases, mobilizing six German, three Italian and two Domobrani divisions, as well as several Ustaša and Četnik units, in order to try and crush the main Partisan forces in Bosnia-Herzegovina.[69] The conduct of both the Partisans and their opponents in these operations was exceptionally brutal. In addition to massacres of civilian populations on all sides, Axis forces rarely took Partisan prisoners and Tito's troops often liquidated all captured Germans, Italians, Ustaše and Četniks.[70] The fighting culminated in the Battle of the Neretva in March, when Partisans initially blew up all the bridges spanning the Neretva River gorge. They then crossed over the twisted ruins of a bridge at Jablanica to reach the eastern bank in a desperate gamble to save the supreme staff and thousands of wounded and weakened comrades suffering from a typhus epidemic. Upon crossing the river, the Partisans surprised a large concentration of Četniks and delivered such an overwhelming blow against them that the Četnik movement never recovered as an effective fighting force.[71] The Partisans had again suffered heavy losses (some 12,000 troops), but were able to break through into Montenegro and severely cripple their main competitor for post-war control.

In March, the Partisans sent a high-level delegation including Vladimir Velebit, Milovan Djilas and Koča Popović to negotiate with the Germans, primarily in the cause of prisoner exchanges and an attempt to get the Germans to apply the international laws of war to captured Partisan troops rather than to execute them on the spot. The Partisans argued that the Četniks were their primary enemy and hoped that the Germans would halt their offensive.[72] These controversial negotiations were revealed in the 1970s, and some revisionist historians have depicted this as proof that the Partisans collaborated just as much as other groups during the war. However, the German high command rejected any kind of compromise with Tito's 'bandits', other than agreeing to certain prisoner exchanges. Furthermore, while Pavlowitch argues there was a 'de facto ceasefire that lasted for more than six weeks', in an interview Velebit dismisses any notion that these were true negotiations but, rather, meetings with individual commanders concerning prisoner exchanges.[73]

Shortly after escaping the trap at the Neretva River, the main force of Partisans and the supreme staff were encircled in south-eastern Bosnia-Herzegovina during the Fifth Enemy Offensive (Operation Schwarz) from May to June 1943. Cornered in the canyons and gorges of the Sutjeska River, the Partisans broke out and saved the supreme staff but had to leave behind several thousand wounded soldiers, who were killed by Axis troops. It is estimated that around 7,500

Partisans lost their lives, including a high percentage of recently recruited Croats from Dalmatia, nearly a third of the forces engaged in the battle.[74] The epic struggle and the tenacity of the Partisans in continuing to fight against all odds was witnessed by William Deakin, part of a high-level British mission to the Partisan supreme staff, who had been parachuted into Montenegro in early May. His reports were pivotal in convincing SOE and British commanders that it was the Partisans, not the Četniks, who deserved Allied support. This was confirmed by a newly arrived American liaison officer, Captain Melvin O. Benson, in July. While increasingly more Allied liaison officers were smuggled into Yugoslavia to serve with the Partisan forces, notably Sir Fitzroy Maclean who arrived in September 1943, Mihailović was being gradually cast off by the Allies. It was clear that he was not even capable of carrying out sabotage missions, let alone engaging Axis troops; the British pulled out their liaison officers stationed with Mihailović in early 1944.

Italy's capitulation on 8 September 1943 flooded Partisan units with captured armaments and resulted in mass Partisan recruitment of Croats, especially from the Dalmatian coast and the Croatian islands formerly under Italian control. An insurgency exploded in the Istrian peninsula, a region with a mixed Italian, Croat and Slovene population that had been annexed by Italy after the First World War. The Slavic population had been persecuted under the fascist regime, and the liberation movement there was an expression of a broad revolt against Italian rule that cut across ideological lines (for example, many Catholic priests supported the Partisan movement). However, newly arrived German troops quickly reversed the Partisan gains in this region and recovered the territory abandoned by their erstwhile allies (known as the Sixth Enemy Offensive carried out in the winter of 1943–4). Yet even though the Germans made sure they held on to the major cities and kept their transportation lines open, and their Ustaša allies were determined to fight to the end, the tide had clearly turned in Yugoslavia as in other theatres of operation.

By the end of 1943, the Partisan movement fielded approximately 300,000 fighters, double the number of the year before, while Axis forces and domestic collaborators stayed steady at about 920,000 troops.[75] Despite the heavy losses in the onslaught of 2 major enemy offensives, Partisan forces were organized into 9 corps, 28 divisions, 103 brigades and 105 detachments. The spontaneous rebel groups that had emerged in the summer of 1941 had developed into an experienced fighting force that had introduced officer ranks and a strict code of military discipline. Special Partisan units were established for national minorities such as Albanians, Germans, Italians, Hungarians and other foreigners, many recruited from captured enemy forces. On 23 January 1943, the Partisans established the First Naval Detachment, and following the capitulation of Italy they created the Navy of the People's Liberation Army of Yugoslavia. The first base for the fledgling Partisan air force was created on 14 October of the same year. After the Tehran Conference in November 1943, the Partisans were recognized as the legitimate resistance movement by the Allies, and the amount of supplies increased.[76] Although Tito welcomed the support of the Allies, he also feared a potential Allied invasion of the Adriatic coast and would have more than likely have resisted such an operation, given that it would have threatened his long-term plans of taking power in post-war Yugoslavia.

Politically, the Partisans organized a second session of AVNOJ, this time in the town of Jajce. Although not all of the delegates could make it because of the wartime conditions, meaning those from Croatia and Bosnia-Herzegovina were proportionately more represented, the meeting on 29 November 1943 was considered to be the founding act of socialist Yugoslavia (it was celebrated as Republic Day (*Dan republike*) in the SFRY). The key decisions reached at Jajce included the restructuring of the country into six federal units, the appointment of a temporary government, the promotion of Tito to the rank of marshal and the political office of prime minister and the denying of the right of return of the Serbian monarch, King Peter II. The sessions of the national anti-fascist councils (such as the first session of National Anti-fascist Council of the People's Liberation of Bosnia-Herzegovina (ZAVNOBiH) on 25 November 1943 and the third session of the National Aanti-fascist Council of the People's Liberation of Croatia (ZAVNOH) on 8–9 May 1944) became the bearers of statehood for the republics that would join the Yugoslav federation. All the other republics eventually established their own anti-fascist councils which, along with the main staffs, were critical in defining the federal structure of socialist Yugoslavia and its claim of having solved the 'national question'. The republican borders discussed at AVNOJ and subsequently confirmed in the years after the war formed the basis of the state borders after the western republics declared independence in 1991.

As the Partisans survived various enemy offensives, transformed their guerrilla fighters into a formidable force and replaced the old government in exile with a new political power, the individual making the key decisions was Tito. Already during the war a personality cult was developing around him, which only intensified in the post-war years. Numerous books have been written about Tito as a military commander, world statesman and symbol of Yugoslav unity. In recent years, however, several new books published in the region seek to paint a picture of a dictator who opportunistically betrayed his comrades in Moscow in order to grab power.[77] Yet despite his later faults and willingness to crush opposition to one-party rule by the KPJ, his military skills and effective use of guerrilla tactics undeniably place Tito among the top resistance leaders during the Second World War.

In 1944, the Partisans were able greatly to increase the size of the liberated territories under their control, where they developed the socio-political model that would be implemented once the war ended. However, the Germans and their regional allies continued to hold all the major urban centres, and effectively kept open the transportation routes that would allow them to withdraw their troops from the Balkans as it became increasingly evident that they were losing the war. Nevertheless, the Partisans threatened German plans enough to spur the Germans into organizing another military operation, this time specifically targeting Tito and the Partisan leadership. In May 1944, the Germans carried out Operation Rösselsprung (Knight's Leap), also known as the Seventh Enemy

Offensive, which involved a surprise assault by German airborne units para-chuting into the town of Drvar. The sacrifice of several hundred Partisan youths who counterattacked the German troops and supporting Axis ground forces converging on Drvar gave Tito and his staff enough time to escape from his hidden cave headquarters and eventually be transported by Allied aircraft to the Dalmatian island of Vis.[78] The failure of the German operation – the 500th SS Parachute Battalion suffered massive casualties during the attack – and Tito's reestablishment of his headquarters under Allied protection left no doubt that the Partisans were the only legitimate resistance movement in Yugoslavia. Tito ordered the creation of several Yugoslav People's Defence Corps (Korpus narodne obrane Jugoslavije), whose units were entrusted with 'defending the People's Liberation Struggle, protecting the achievements of the revolution, and fighting the remaining counterrevolution'.[79] In August 1944, the Yugoslav government-in-exile abolished the position Mihailović held and began nego-tiating with Tito about the post-war political model. The Americans, however, continued to maintain contact with Mihailović because numerous Allied airmen who had been shot down over Yugoslavia were located on Četnik territory. In 2005, American president George W. Bush posthumously awarded the Legion of Merit to Mihailović for rescuing over 500 Allied airmen, sparking controversy in the region, since the rehabilitation in Serbia of the Četnik movement white-washed their war crimes and atrocities against civilians during the war.

By autumn 1944, the Red Army was pushing through Romania and Bulgaria and was poised on the Yugoslav frontier. In early September, Tito secretly flew to Moscow where he met with Stalin and negotiated Soviet support in taking Belgrade. Unlike the Red Army's occupation of other Eastern European countries, Tito received a pledge from Stalin that Soviet forces would enter Yugoslav territory only with the goal of liberating the Serbian capital city, and then immediately continue north towards Germany. The battle for Belgrade lasted from mid-September until the city was overrun by Soviet, Yugoslav and Bulgarian forces on 20 October. The Partisans had been weak in Serbia since 1941, but the liberation of Belgrade was followed by the massive mobilization of Serbs as well as a settling of accounts with collaborators and other class enemies, both real and alleged. An American liaison officer, Franklin Lindsay, noted how the Partisans were increasingly open about their post-war intentions: 'After the German retreat from Belgrade in October 1944 the consolidation of the Partisan revolution entered its final phase. It had been well-planned, its groundwork skillfully laid … now it was being carried to completion with thoroughness, efficiency, and ruthlessness.'[80] Tito and the supreme staff relocated to Belgrade, which was again established as the capital of the reorganized Yugoslav state. By the end of 1944, Partisan forces numbered approximately 600,000 individuals, organized into 17 corps, 57 divisions, 228 brigades and 80 detachments.[81]

*   *   *

During the final months of the war in 1945, the former guerrilla forces completed their transformation into a regular army. The People's Liberation Partisan Army was renamed the Yugoslav Army (Jugoslavenska armija), and on 1 January 1945 three army groups were created (First, Second and Third Armies), followed by the Fourth Army on 2 March 1945. The four armies were each led by a Spanish Civil War veteran, and were tasked with the final liberation of the country. The Partisans' first major test in conventional warfare occurred during spring 1945 when they assaulted German and NDH defensive lines west of Belgrade in what was known as the Syrmian Front (Sremski front). Tito's forces suffered heavy casualties in the frontal assaults, which subsequently led some Serbian nationalists to accuse the Partisans of sacrificing newly recruited Serbs (many of whom had formerly been Četniks) in unnecessarily bloody attacks. The front was broken on 12 April, allowing the Partisan forces from Serbia to push westward and join up with the other armies in pursuing the remaining Axis troops through Zagreb and into Slovenia.

Tito's goals were not merely to restore the old borders of the Kingdom of Yugoslavia, but also to annex territories that either Austria or Italy had gained after the First World War peace treaties. While Partisan troops secured Rijeka and the Istrian peninsula and eventually incorporated them into the SFRY, the Yugoslav army's occupation of Trieste was ultimately unsuccessful and led to a series of crises with the Western Allies until the border was finally demarcated in 1954. Tito also supported Enver Hoxha's communist forces in Albania, which the former intended should be incorporated in a future Balkan communist federation, as well as the communists in Greece. Both of these interventions created tensions with the West and with Stalin, who was angered at Tito's ambitions. By the end of the war, Tito's forces numbered almost 800,000 troops, along with a loyal political and military cadre that had emerged from the difficult years in the forests and mountains of Yugoslavia.

More important than expanding Yugoslavia's borders was dealing with the domestic opponents who opted to resist the Communists until the bitter end. The NDH's political leadership, military units and accompanying civilians fled the Partisan advance through Slovenia towards Austria in early May 1945, where they hoped to surrender to the British and escape communist retribution. Battles raged between the First, Second and Third Partisan armies and the retreating NDH forces, which mixed with retreating units of German, Slovenian, Serbian, Montenegrin and other pro-Axis troops. Even though Germany capitulated on 8 May, these forces fought until 15 May, when the main body of NDH soldiers and officers tried unsuccessfully to surrender to the British at the Austrian town of Bleiburg. Instead, the British insisted they surrender to the Partisans, as per agreements between the Allied leadership, and sent NDH soldiers who had previously surrendered back into Yugoslavia. This marked the beginning of the Križni put (Way of the Cross), the death marches into camps across Yugoslavia and mass liquidations without proper trial of tens of thousands of prisoners.

Estimates of the number of people killed in the battles leading up to the surrender at Bleiburg or liquidated in the death marches afterwards vary greatly and have been subject to considerable exaggeration. But recent estimates suggest 45,000 to 55,000 Croats out of an approximate total of 80,000 victims across all ethnic groups.[82] The vast majority of deaths took place in locations throughout Slovenia (some 200 mass graves), Croatia (700 mass graves), Bosnia (90 mass graves) and elsewhere across Yugoslavia as a result of the forced marches and the brutal conditions in internment camps. From 1990, Croats began attending the annual commemoration at Bleiburg. This had long been considered a taboo in socialist Yugoslavia, and was used as proof that Croatia was a victim in any Yugoslav state and thus needed independence.

More problematic in the process of coming to terms with the past is the fact that the Bleiburg narrative depicts only Croats as victims of the victorious Partisans. However, the majority of post-war liquidations were not carried out because of ethnic hatred (although revenge against the Ustaše and other collaborators certainly played a role), but because of the KPJ's strategic goals of taking power and eliminating class enemies. For example, tens of thousands of Serbs, including former Četniks and members of the Nedić regime, were killed in Serbia after the Partisans liberated Serbia in 1944; these victims of Communist repression simply never made it to Bleiburg with the other collaborators.[83] The fragmentation of the historiography of the Second World War in the former Yugoslavia resulted in the 'nationalization' of the historical narratives. For example, viewing the Četnik movement as having operated only within Serbia, or viewing events such as Bleiburg only through the lens of Croat victims outside of the broader Yugoslav context, have enabled nationalist politicians to manipulate traumas from the Second World War.

* * *

Alongside the Soviet Partisans, Yugoslavia's resistance movement was the largest and most successful guerrilla force in occupied Europe during the Second World War. Moreover, the Communist-led Partisans liberated the majority of their country without direct help from the Allies, apart from the brief intervention of the Red Army in October 1944 during the battle for Belgrade. The lack of Soviet troops meant Yugoslavia was a special case in communist Eastern Europe, enabling the victorious Tito not only to consolidate power over the entire country in the aftermath of the war, but also to stand up to Stalin after 1948 and forge Yugoslavia's unique path towards communism. In later years Yugoslav historiography minimized Allied material support, from both the West and the Soviets, and exaggerated the accomplishments of the resistance movement as the regime increasingly relied on the narratives of the Second World War for legitimacy. The bloody struggle against domestic enemies and the internecine atrocities against civilians were deemphasized in favour of a narrative that concentrated on the heroic victory over foreign occupiers.

The Partisans were more successful than their domestic opponents because they offered a multiethnic future state (unlike the genocidal Ustaše) and a new socio-political model (in contrast to the Četniks, who envisioned a return to a discredited monarchist and centralized Yugoslavia). The promise of a federal Yugoslavia that resolved the 'national question' and the use of national symbols in the various Partisan units proved decisive in the struggle for power. The Partisans had clear goals throughout the chaos of the civil war: taking power and carrying out a communist revolution. The disintegration of the old order – the former regime was in exile, various intellectual and economic elites were killed by the occupiers and collaborators, and the socio-political system was radically transformed under the new conditions of Axis domination – created a vacuum that enabled the communists to secure political control once the war ended.

Although the first Yugoslav state (1918–41) had been a failure that had alienated many non-Serbs, the peoples of the region chafed at foreign rule and the Partisans were able to mobilize the population effectively with their slogans of national liberation. Even the Croats, who along with the Albanians were the most bitter about the Yugoslav experience, realized that the NDH was a fascist state that murdered its own population and allowed the Italians to annex most of the coast, which resulted in the large number of Croats who eventually joined the Partisan movement. However, the promises of democracy and a federal system of equal republics were not kept by the victorious Communists, who implemented a brutal Stalinist dictatorship and carried out forcible collectivization in the first few years after the war.

The Partisan movement was glorified domestically and abroad, and provided a much needed morale boost during the war and political legitimacy afterwards. Yet historians have questioned the actual effectiveness of the Partisans in the overall course of the war. Walter Laqueur argues that in the early phases of the war, when attacks against Hitler's war machine were most needed, the Partisans were at their weakest and unable to influence the major operations taking place. They fought mostly against second-rate occupying troops and domestic collaborators. After Italy's capitulation, Partisan strength grew significantly, but it was the catastrophic defeats Hitler suffered on the Eastern Front that sealed the fate of the Nazi imperial project. Reflecting on all guerrilla activity during the Second World War, Laqueur concludes that 'the probable truth is that the political impact of partisan activity was far greater than its military contribution'.[84] This was certainly the case in Yugoslavia, where the anti-fascist struggle immediately shifted into the consolidation of political control and the destruction of any remaining elements of the pre-war system after the defeat of Nazi Germany.

Unlike most other Eastern European Soviet satellites, where resistance had less impact and where communism was associated directly with Soviet occupation, the SFRY was able to build legitimacy upon the domestic resistance movement. Tito, Brotherhood and Unity, and the Yugoslav People's Army were the pillars of the post-1945 Yugoslav state. On the one hand, the regime's construction of cultural memory was almost exclusively focused upon the Partisan legacy and the heroic myths of resistance. Films, commemorative events, symbols and the transformed public space emphasized the People's Liberation Struggle throughout Yugoslavia, but were always subjected to the Party's monopoly over the official historical narratives of the war. On the other hand, memories of those who fought on the 'wrong side' and an open dialogue about the past were forbidden. These taboo themes exploded into the political arena in the late 1980s and early

1990s when communism, and shortly afterwards the Yugoslav state, disintegrated. The new pluralism did not always contribute to the establishment of liberal democracy in the former Yugoslavia. In fact, former fascist collaborators were rehabilitated as victims of Communist terror and all anti-fascists were condemned as bloodthirsty Stalinists. This was compounded by the fragmentation of the historiography along new national and ethnic lines. The traumatic emotions of the wars in the 1990s continue to affect how the recent past is interpreted in the former Yugoslavia, and the ideological battles of the Second World War still permeate contemporary politics. A younger generation of scholars has nevertheless begun to emerge that is willing to research the complexities of Yugoslavia's resistance movement and reach out beyond the parochial nationalist narratives that have characterized the field in the last two decades.

Notes

1. King Peter I Karadjordjević (1844–1921), known as 'the Liberator', oversaw Yugoslavia's unification, while his son, Aleksandar Karadjordjević, served as regent until 1921. The act of unification on 1 December 1918 was the elderly king's last public appearance.
2. Ivo Banac, *The National Question in Yugoslavia: Origins, History, Politics* (Ithaca, New York, 1984).
3. J.B. Hoptner, *Yugoslavia in Crisis, 1934–1941* (New York, 1962); Dejan Djokić, *Elusive Compromise: A History of Interwar Yugoslavia* (New York, 2007).
4. Stevan K. Pavlowitch, *Hitler's New Disorder: The Second World War in Yugoslavia* (London, 2008), pp. 10–13.
5. Jozo Tomasevich, *The Chetniks* (Stanford, Cal., 1975), pp. 65–7.
6. Jozo Tomasevich, *War and Revolution in Yugoslavia, 1941–1945: Occupation and Collaboration* (Stanford, Cal., 2001), p. 47.
7. For a detailed description of the Axis partition of Yugoslavia, the structure of the occupational regimes and the various collaborationist movements, see *ibid.*, pp. 47–379.
8. For a detailed study on the Italian 'happy occupation', see Eric Gobetti, *L'occupazione allegra: Gli italiani in Jugoslavia* (Rome, 2007). For relations between the NDH and Italy, see Nada Kisić Kolanović, *NDH i Italija: političke veze i diplomatski odnosi* (Zagreb, 2001).
9. Pavlowitch, *Hitler's New Disorder*, pp. 58–9.
10. *Ibid.*, p. 31.
11. Marko Attila Hoare, *Genocide and Resistance in Hitler's Bosnia: The Partisans and the Chetniks, 1941–1943* (Oxford, 2006), p. 19.
12. For example, the 'Decree regarding racial affiliation and the decree regarding the protection of Aryan blood and the honor of the Croatian people' was passed on 30 April 1941, less than three weeks after the NDH was established. *Hrvatski narod* (Zagreb), 1 May 1941, p. 1. For more details on the NDH, see Fikreta Jelić-Butić, *Ustaše i Nezavisna Država Hrvatska* (Zagreb, 1978); Sabrina P. Ramet (ed.), *The Independent State of Croatia, 1941–45* (London, 2007).
13. Several recent books on the history of Jasenovac include Nataša Mataušić, *Jasenovac 1941–1945* (Zagreb, 2003); Tea Benčić Rimay (ed.), *Jasenovac Memorial Site* (Jasenovac, 2006); Mišo Deverić and Ivan Fumić, *Hrvatska u logorima, 1941–1945* (Zagreb, 2008).
14. Pavlowitch, *Hitler's New Disorder*, p. 81.
15. Petar V. Brajović-Djuro, *Yugoslavia in the Second World War* (Belgrade, 1977), p. 222. The figures given for both Axis troops and Partisan forces come from official Yugoslav government sources, which were in all likelihood inflated to emphasize the contribution of the Partisans to the defeat of fascism.
16. About half of the Yugoslav army, 344,162 officers and troops, were captured, but most of the Croats and Macedonians were quickly released, leaving about 200,000 prisoners (largely Serbs) in German camps. Some 300,000 other soldiers escaped capture after the short war. Matteo J. Milazzo, *The Chetnik Movement and Yugoslav Resistance* (Baltimore, Md., 1975), p. 5.

17. Pavlowitch, *Hitler's New Disorder*, p. 64. The Western media perpetuated the myth that Mihailović's Četniks were actively engaged in fighting the Germans at a time when there were few positive things to report in the struggle against Hitler. Walter J. Roberts, *Tito, Mihailović and the Allies, 1941–1945* (Durham, 1987), p. 39.

18. The German High Command ordered that for every killed German soldier 100 people were to be executed, and for each wounded German 50 hostages were to be put to death. Tomasevich, *War and Revolution*, p. 69.

19. Tomasevich, *The Chetniks*, pp. 132–5.

20. For an overview of Četniks before 1941, see Tomasevich, *The Chetniks*, pp. 115–22.

21. Milazzo, *The Chetnik Movement*, pp. 50–60.

22. Ivan Jelić, *Jugoslavenska socijalistička revolucija, 1941–1945* (Zagreb, 1979), p. 83.

23. The attempt to discredit Croatia's anti-fascist movement by revisionist historians since the 1990s was closely associated with the rehabilitation of the Ustaše and the deterioration of Serb-Croat relations during the Croatian War of Independence (1991–5). The Croatian right-wing continues to demonize the entire anti-fascist resistance and not just the communist totalitarian system established after 1945, and even recent media articles question the motives of the KPJ's calls for an uprising against the occupiers, seeking to portray Croatian anti-fascists as being merely Soviet stooges. For example, see the text on the Croatian Cultural Council's portal on 13 July 2011 titled 'The meaning of 22 June or the directives of the Comintern and Party discipline', at www.hkv.hr/izdvojeno/vai-prilozi/s-/umanovi-vladimir/8726-znaaj-22-lipnja-ili-o-kominterninim-direktivama-i-partijskoj-disciplini.html.

24. Vladimir Velebit, a high-ranking Croatian Partisan, noted that the conditions for an effective uprising were present only after the elite German units that had occupied Yugoslavia left for the Eastern Front. Mira Šuvar (ed.), *Vladimir Velebit: svjedok historije* (Zagreb, 2001), p. 261.

25. Nikola Anić, *Narodnooslobodilačka vojska Hrvatske, 1941–1945* (Zagreb, 2005), pp. 20–1.

26. Ivo Goldstein, *Hrvatska 1918–2008* (Zagreb, 2008), p. 279. Speakers at the 22 June commemoration have often stated that this was the first anti-fascist unit in occupied Europe, but Nikola Anić rejects this myth and notes that anti-fascists had already been operating in Poland, Norway and France following their defeat by Germany. Anić, *Narodnooslobodilačka vojska*, p. 34.

27. Various authors have translated *narodnooslobodilački pokret* either as National Liberation Movement or the People's Liberation Movement, since the word *narod* can have both meanings. For the purpose of this chapter, I have chosen to use the People's Liberation Movement version.

28. In socialist Yugoslavia, 4 July was celebrated as Fighter's Day (*Dan boraca*). 'Jugoslovenska narodna armija', in *Vojna enciklopedija*, Vol. 4 (Belgrade, 1972), p. 136.

29. Ivo Goldstein, *Hrvatska 1918–2008* (Zagreb, 2008), pp. 263–7.

30. Danilo Damjanović Danić, *Ustanak naroda Hrvatske 1941. u Srbu i okolini* (Zagreb, 1972).

31. Hoare, *Genocide and Resistance*, p. 134.

32. According to Tomasevich, during 1941 the Četniks' 'most effective anti-Partisan technique in this time before all-out conflict was that of subverting Partisan detachments from within', *The Chetniks*, p. 161.

33. Almost 800 Yugoslavs died fighting in the Spanish Civil War. Of the 350 veterans who made it back to Yugoslavia, about 250 fought as Partisans, and 59 were awarded the highest medal, People's Hero, for their contribution in the People's Liberation Struggle. See Vjeran Pavlaković, 'Matija Gubec Goes to Spain: Symbols and Ideology in Croatia, 1936–1939,' *The Journal of Slavic Military Studies*, 17:4 (December 2004).

34. Orders given by Tito, dated 4 September 1941, in Pero Damjanović (ed.), *Josip Broz Tito Sabrana djela*, Vol. 7 (Belgrade, 1983), p. 112. For the problems of including more Croats in the Partisan ranks, see the orders given to the Partisan high command in 'Bilten Vrhovnog štaba NOPOJ', Nos 7–8 (1 October 1941), reprinted in *ibid.*, pp. 136–8.

35. Anić, *Narodnooslobodilačka vojska*, p. 28.

36. Brajović-Djuro, *Yugoslavia in the Second World War*, p. 63.

37. Anić, *Narodnooslobodilačka vojska*, p. 28.

38. Brajović-Djuro, *Yugoslavia in the Second World War*, p. 49.

39. Pavlowitch, *Hitler's New Disorder*, pp. 74–80. Djilas provides considerably more detail in his dramatic narrative of the Partisan struggle in his memoirs. Milovan Djilas, *Wartime*, trans. Michael B. Petrovich (New York, 1977).

40. Roberts, *Tito, Mihailović and the Allies*, p. 31.

41. Tomasevich, *The Chetniks*, p. 140.

42. *Ibid.*, pp. 149–51.

43. Šuvar, *Vladimir Velebit*, p. 258.

44. Branko Dubravica, *Vojska antifašističke Hrvatske* (Zagreb, 1996), p. 9. The Soviets expressed anger at Tito's decision, since it was deemed that relations with the Allies would be jeopardized if the Partisans were seen to have an overtly communist character. Roberts, *Tito, Mihailović and the Allies*, p. 58.

45. 'Jugoslavenska narodna armija', in *Enciklopedija Jugoslavije*, Vol. 6 (Zagreb, 1990), p. 145.

46. The President of the Republika Srpska in Bosnia-Herzegovina refused to celebrate 25 November (commemorating the formation of Bosnia-Herzegovina's anti-fascist council and basis for republican status in the SFRY), arguing that the Bosniaks were abusing this holiday since it was the Serbs who gave the greatest contribution to the anti-fascist struggle. *Politika* (Belgrade), 22 November 2011, online at www.politika.rs.

47. Ivo and Slavko Goldstein, 'Srbi i Hrvati u narodnooslobodilačkoj borbi u Hrvatskoj', in *Dijalog povjesničara – istoričara*, Vol. 7 (2002), p. 263, online version at http://www.cpi.hr/download/links/hr/7243.pdf. Serbs in Croatia, representing between 4–5 per cent of the total population of Yugoslavia, contributed about 10 per cent of the total number of Partisans throughout the course of the war. *Ibid.*, p. 265.

48. Dubravica, *Vojska antifašističke Hrvatske*, p. 3.

49. *Ibid.*, pp. 18–19. The first Croatian brigade with a majority of Croats (78.8 per cent), the First Dalmatian Proletarian Brigade, was formed in early September 1942. *Ibid.*, pp. 14–15.

50. 'Jugoslavenska narodna armija', in *Enciklopedija Jugoslavije*, p. 146; Jelić, *Jugoslavenska socijalistička revolucija*, p. 99.

51. 'Jugoslovenska narodna armija', *Vojna enciklopedija*, p. 137.

52. Tomasevich, *War and Revolution in Yugoslavia*, pp. 424–34. Tomasevich quotes nationalist politician Stjepan Buć, who called for the dissolution of the Domobrani armed forces because 'today it is a center [*sic*] for the dissemination of troop demoralization, which arms the Partisans and kills the confidence of the people in its defensive activity'. *Ibid.*, p. 431.

53. 'Jugoslavenska narodna armija', *Enciklopedija Jugoslavije*, p. 146.

54. For details on Četnik objectives and goals, see Tomasevich, *The Chetniks*, pp. 166–78.

55. The other republican and autonomous province Communist Parties were established during the war: Serbia in 1941; Bosnia-Herzegovina, Macedonia, Montenegro and Vojvodina in 1943; and Kosovo in 1944.

56. For details on the national question during the Second World War, in particular related to Croatia, see Jill Irvine, *The Croat Question: Partisan Politics and the Formation of the Yugoslav Socialist State* (Boulder, Col., 1993).

57. Dino Mujadžević, *Bakarić: politička biografija* (Zagreb, 2011), pp. 73–7.

58. Jelić, *Jugoslavenska socijalistička revolucija*, p. 93.

59. Renata Jambrešić-Kirin, *Dom i svijet: o ženskoj kulturi pamćenja* (Zagreb, 2008).

60. Brajović-Djuro, *Yugoslavia in the Second World War*, p. 77. The main force of the First Proletarian Brigade had to retreat over the mountains in freezing temperatures and lost 172 men (along with numerous amputations) in a heroic episode immortalized as the March over Mount Igman.

61. It was during this period that the NDH authorities and the Četniks in Bosnia-Herzegovina negotiated their first agreements to work together against the Partisans. Tomasevich, *The Chetniks*, pp. 227–31. See also Nikica Barić, 'Relations between the Chetniks and the Authorities of the Independent State of Croatia, 1942–1945', in Sabrina P. Ramet and Ola Listhaug (eds), *Serbia and the Serbs in World War Two* (London, 2011), pp. 182–5.

62. Pavlowitch, *Hitler's New Disorder*, pp. 121–2.

63. On 25 May 1942, *Time Magazine* ran a cover featuring Mihailović as leading the resistance movement in Yugoslavia with over 150,000 guerrilla fighters. Twentieth Century Fox released a propa-

ganda film in early 1943 titled *Chetniks! The Fighting Guerrillas*, which was pulled from circulation once the facts of Četnik collaboration and atrocities became apparent.

64. For a detailed account of Tito and Mihailović's relationship with the Allies and memoirs of some of the Allied officers involved in supporting the Partisans, see Roberts, *Tito, Mihailović, and the Allies*; F.W.D. Deakin, *The Embattled Mountain* (New York, 1971); Franklin Lindsay, *Beacons in the Night: With the OSS and Tito's Partisans in Wartime Yugoslavia* (Stanford, Cal., 1993); Fitzroy Maclean, *Eastern Approaches* (London, 1949). A more critical analysis of the divisions within Britain's Special Operations Executive can be found in Heather Williams, *Parachutes, Patriots and Partisans: The Special Operations Executive and Yugoslavia, 1941–1945* (London, 2003).

65. Roberts, *Tito, Mihailović, and the Allies*, p. 203.

66. 'Jugoslavenska narodna armija', *Enciklopedija Jugoslavije*, p. 146; Dubravica, *Vojska antifašističke Hrvatske*, pp. 35, 40.

67. After the invasion of Yugoslavia, nationalist Kosovar Albanians took revenge on the Serb colonists who had been settled there during the interwar period, resulting in thousands of deaths and a wave of refugees who fled to Serbia proper. Tim Judah, *Kosovo: War and Revenge* (New Haven, Conn., 2000), pp. 28–30.

68. Pavlowitch, *Hitler's New Disorder*, pp. 208–9.

69. Brajović-Djuro, *Yugoslavia in the Second World War*, pp. 109–11.

70. For example, Djilas offhandedly remarks how the Partisans killed an entire Italian battalion after the fall of the town of Prozor in February 1943, when they 'vented their bitterness' and 'shared with our officers a malicious joy' that Italian commanders would see the corpses of their soldiers floating down the Neretva River. Djilas, *Wartime*, p. 220.

71. Tomasevich, *The Chetniks*, pp. 231–51. The events of this battle are dramatically portrayed in the Oscar-nominated film *The Battle of the Neretva* (1969), which was the most expensive Partisan film ever made.

72. Tomasevich, *The Chetniks*, pp. 244–6.

73. Pavlowitch, *Hitler's New Disorder*, p. 160; Vladimir Velebit, *Tajne i zamke Drugog svjetskog rata* (Zagreb, 2002), pp. 281–91.

74. Tomasevich, *The Chetniks*, pp. 254–5; Brajović-Djuro, *Yugoslavia in the Second World War*, pp. 115–18. Another expensive Partisan film depicted the events in this operation, *The Battle of Sutjeska* (1973), which featured Richard Burton as Tito, who was wounded during the fighting.

75. Jelić, *Jugoslavenska socialistička revolucija*, p. 99

76. According to Yugoslav sources, Anglo-American military aid between October 1943 and May 1945 included 388 artillery pieces, 2,660 mortars, 107 tanks, 13,447 machine guns and 137,000 rifles. Soviet aid, which began in 1944, consisted of 895 artillery pieces, 65 tanks, 3,364 mortars, 68,000 machine guns and 96,000 rifles. 'Jugoslovenska narodna armija', *Vojna enciklopedija*, p. 138.

77. Milovan Djilas, *Tito: The Story from the Inside*, trans. Vasilije Kojić and Richard Hayes (New York, 1980); Phyllis Auty, *Tito: A Biography* (New York, 1970); Richard West, *Tito and the Rise and Fall of Yugoslavia* (New York, 1994); Pero Simić, *Tito: Fenomen stoljeća* (Zagreb, 2009); Todor Kuljić, *Tito: sociološkoistorijsko studija* (Zrenjanin, 2004).

78. The day of the attack, 25 May, was commemorated in the SFRY as the Day of Youth (*Dan mladosti*) as well as Tito's birthday, and became a central political ritual that reinforced Tito's cult of personality.

79. 'Jugoslavenska narodna armija', *Enciklopedija Jugoslavije*, p. 147.

80. Lindsay, *Beacons in the Night*, p. 253.

81. 'Jugoslavenska narodna armija', *Enciklopedija Jugoslavije*, p. 147.

82. Martina Grahek Ravančić, *Bleiburg i križni put 1945* (Zagreb, 2009); *Pogled (Novi list)*, 23 June 2007, p. 12.

83. Research by Serbian historian Srdjan Cvetković has led him to conclude that no fewer than 60,000 people were victims of communist terror in Serbia, and approximately 150,000 victims for all of Yugoslavia. Srdjan Cvetković, *Izmedju srpa i čekica: represija u Srbiji 1944–1953* (Belgrade, 2006), p. 140.

84. Walter Laqueur, *Guerrilla Warfare: A Historical and Critical Study* (New Brunswick, New Jer., 1998), p. 205.

Guide to Further Reading

Auty, Phyllis, *Tito: A Biography* (New York, 1970).

Brajović-Djuro, Petar V., *Yugoslavia in the Second World War* (Belgrade, 1977).

Deakin, F.W.D., *The Embattled Mountain* (New York, 1971).

Djilas, Milovan, *Tito: The Story from the Inside*, trans. Vasilije Kojić and Richard Hayes (New York, 1980).

Idem, Wartime, trans. Michael B. Petrovich (New York, 1977).

Djokić, Dejan, *Elusive Compromise: A History of Interwar Yugoslavia* (New York, 2007).

Hoare, Marko Attila, *Genocide and Resistance in Hitler's Bosnia: The Partisans and the Chetniks, 1941–1943* (Oxford, 2006).

Irvine, Jill, *The Croat Question: Partisan Politics and the Formation of the Yugoslav Socialist State* (Boulder, Col., 1993).

Lindsay, Franklin, *Beacons in the Night: With the OSS and Tito's Partisans in Wartime Yugoslavia* (Stanford, Cal., 1993).

Milazzo, Matteo J., *The Chetnik Movement and the Yugoslav Resistance* (Baltimore, Md., 1975).

Pavlowitch, Stevan K., *Hitler's New Disorder: The Second World War in Yugoslavia* (London, 2008).

Ramet, Sabrina P. (ed.), *The Independent State of Croatia, 1941–45* (London, 2007).

Ramet, Sabrina P. and Listhaug, Ola (eds), *Serbia and the Serbs in World War Two* (London, 2011).

Roberts, Walter R., *Tito, Mihailović and the Allies, 1941–1945* (Durham, 1987).

Tomasevich, Jozo, *The Chetniks* (Stanford, Cal., 1975).

Idem, War and Revolution in Yugoslavia, 1941–1945: Occupation and Collaboration (Stanford, Cal., 2001).

West, Richard, *Tito and the Rise and Fall of Yugoslavia* (New York, 1994).

Williams, Heather, *Parachutes, Patriots and Partisans: The Special Operations Executive and Yugoslavia, 1941–1945* (London, 2003).

Films

Battle of the Neretva, directed by Veljko Bulajić (1969).

Battle of the Sutjeska, directed by Stipe Delić (1973).

Underground, directed by Emir Kusturica (1995).

Duga mračna noć (*Long Dark Night*), directed by Antun Vrdoljak (2004).

Cinema Komunista, directed by Mila Turajlić, (2010).

Index